THE GUN DIGEST BOOK OF

GUNSMITHING TOOLS
...and Their Uses

by **JOHN E. TRAISTER**

DBI BOOKS, INC., NORTHFIELD, ILL.

STAFF
EDITOR
Robert S.L. Anderson
PRODUCTION MANAGER
Pamela J. Johnson
COVER PHOTOGRAPHY
John Hanusin
PUBLISHER
Sheldon L. Factor

About Our Cover

Pictured on our cover are but a few of the many, many gunsmithing tools made and/or distributed by Brownells, Inc. The Montezuma, Iowa, firm has long been the best (and often the only) source of tools, equipment and supplies for the amateur and professional gunsmith. Brownells lists over 14,000 items in a catalog that should be called the "wish book" for craftsmen; it's used by gunsmiths, stock makers, knife makers, jewelry makers and hobbyists of all sorts.

Copyright © MCMLXXX by DBI Books, Inc., #1 Northfield Plaza, Northfield, Ill 60093, a subsidiary of Technical Publishing, a company of the Dun and Bradstreet Corporation. Printed in the United States of America. All rights reserved. No part of this book may be reproduced, stored in a retrieval system or transmitted in any form or by any means, electronic, mechanical, photocopying, recording or otherwise, without prior written permission of the publisher.

The views and opinions of the author expressed herein are not necessarily those of the publisher, and no responsibility for such views will be assumed.

ISBN 0-910676-08-9   Library of Congress Catalog Card #80-67743

CONTENTS

CHAPTER 1: Tools to Get You Started 4

CHAPTER 2: A Place to Work 21

CHAPTER 3: A Workbench for Everyone 29

CHAPTER 4: Portable Electric Drills 38

CHAPTER 5: The Third Hand 47

CHAPTER 6: Rx for Long Gun Life 58

CHAPTER 7: Files and Their Kin 66

CHAPTER 8: Woodworking Tools 78

CHAPTER 9: Bluing Equipment 94

CHAPTER 10: The Multi-Purpose Moto-Tool 113

CHAPTER 11: Soldering and Welding 122

CHAPTER 12: Mini-Lathes for Gun Work 130

CHAPTER 13: The Drill Press 140

CHAPTER 14: The Bench Grinder 149

CHAPTER 15: Lathes for Metal Work 158

CHAPTER 16: Milling Machines 169

CHAPTER 17: Miscellaneous Gunsmithing Tools 180

CHAPTER 18: Plating Firearms 193

CHAPTER 19: Gunsmithing: Continuing Education 202

CHAPTER 20: Introduction to Pro Gunsmithing 212

CHAPTER 21: Gun Parts 218

CHAPTER 22: Gunning Calculations 224

CHAPTER 23: Gunsmith's Library 229

CHAPTER 24: Glossary of Firearms Terms 232

CHAPTER 25: Directory of Trade Sources 241

Appendix 249

1
TOOLS TO GET YOU STARTED

HIGH-QUALITY work in any trade or profession can be accomplished only with high-quality tools and a proper knowledge of their use. The gunsmithing profession is no exception. Therefore, the main objective of this chapter is to introduce the basic gunsmithing tools that are required for high-quality work. Further objectives include the proper use of these tools and how to select the best ones available for gun repair and maintenance in general.

The basic gunsmithing tools described in the paragraphs to follow are found on the workbench of practically all professional gunsmiths. This tool list below covers the minimum essential tools needed to do good work on the usual kind of firearm in need of repair. They are the "rock" on which to build or expand your professional assortment of fine tools and instruments. They should be the best quality that you can afford.

Gunsmith screwdrivers
Pin punch set
Pliers
Hammers
Knife
Spring vise
Bench vise
Sight base file
Pillar file
Scribe hook
Brushes
Wood rasp
India stones
Allen wrench set

Gunsmith Screwdrivers

The selection of gunsmith screwdrivers should be given careful consideration since a marred or otherwise damaged screwhead is a sure indication that an amateur has tackled the job. The efficient holding power of a screwdriver depends upon the

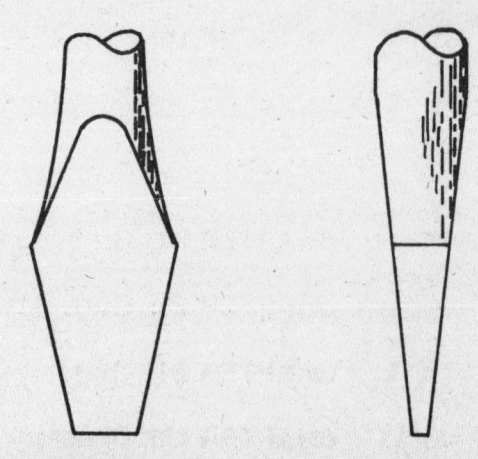

This common double-wedge type screwdriver (front and side view) is not the best choice for gun work.

quality of steel in its blade, the design of the blade, and the external force that may be applied to the screwhead. The blade should also be fitted to the width of the slot for best results.

For instance, if a common double-wedge type screwdriver were used in a deep screw slot, the blade would transmit its torque to the top of the screw slot. With such a small slot area coming in contact with the blade, there is a good chance that the screw will be scored or worse yet, cause one section of the screwhead to break off. Wedge-shape tips also tend to back the driver out of the screw slot—again causing damage to the screwhead.

A screwdriver tip, ground to properly fill a screw slot, is ideal for gun repair work since the torque is applied at the bottom of the slot where the screw is the strongest; also, that blade will fill the slot completely (and should be the same width as the shank).

A set of 8 Grace gunsmith screwdrivers is shown in the photo below. They are made from

IMPROPER FIT

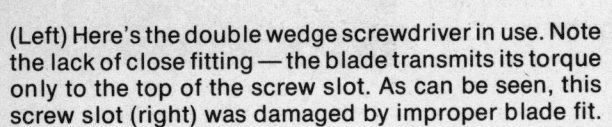

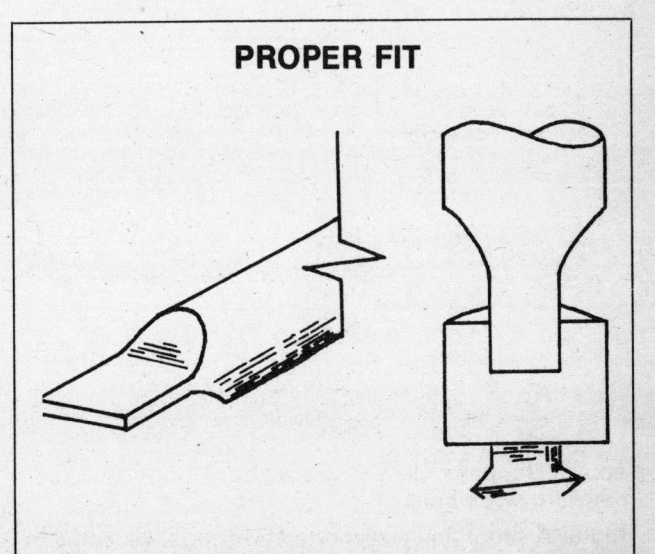

(Left) Here's the double wedge screwdriver in use. Note the lack of close fitting — the blade transmits its torque only to the top of the screw slot. As can be seen, this screw slot (right) was damaged by improper blade fit.

PROPER FIT

(Left) This particular blade is ideal for gun work. It has been cut to conform perfectly to a screw of specific dimensions. (Right) Notice that this screwdriver blade fits the screw slot perfectly.

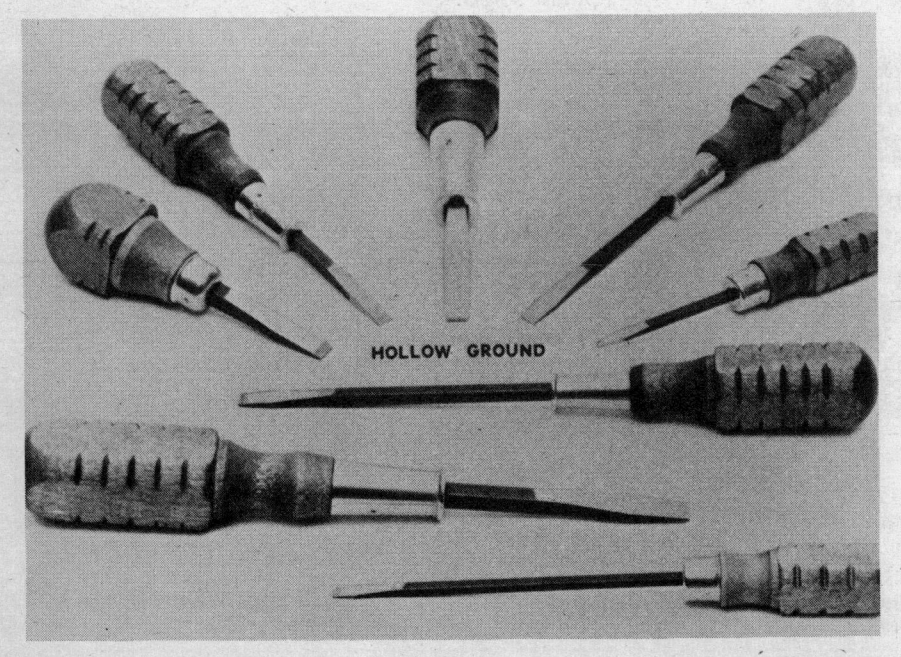

HOLLOW GROUND

A set of Grace Metal Products screwdrivers has long been a favorite with knowledgeable gunsmiths.

standard taper bit screwdrivers with the tip of each bit ground parallel for a short distance back to give a better fit to gun screwheads. They have a high-quality feel and will handle 95% of your needs around the gunshop. If you select this set, you will also need a stock bolt screwdriver with a ½" blade, about 15" long. A set of jeweler's screwdrivers will also come in handy.

Another good set of screwdrivers is made by Chapman Manufacturing Company. This set contains one screwdriver handle, an extension, 12 slotted head adapters, 2 phillips head adapters, a midget ratchet and 1 Allen hex-type adapter. This kit will handle nearly all of your gun repair needs, but you'll still need a long-shank bolt screwdriver as described previously.

The adapters for the Chapman screwdriver handle are relatively inexpensive and should be reshaped (if necessary) to conform to a specialized job such as an extra thin screw slot. When grinding adapters, however, be careful not to let the temperature get too hot (above 400°F) or they will lose their hardness.

Reshape the adapter so that it fits the screw slot exactly. Then inspect each adapter under a magnifying glass before use. Also carefully dress off

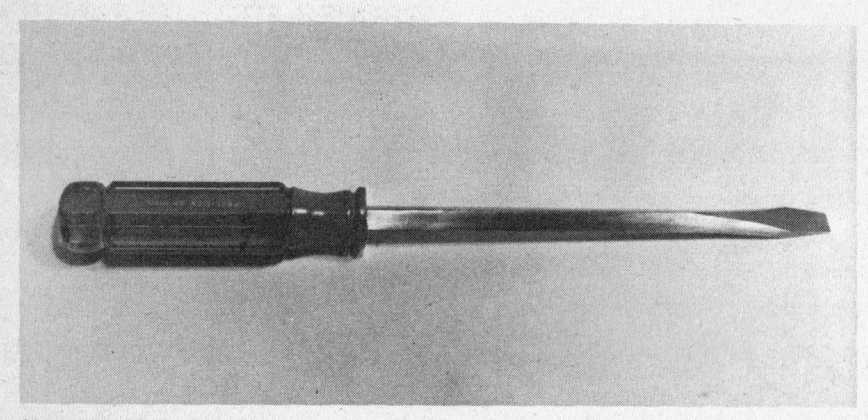

(Above) This particular screwdriver has a long shank and ½" blade. It's ideal for removing stock bolts.

(Right) A set of fine jeweler's screwdrivers will come in handy for the many small screws you will encounter during normal gunsmithing chores.

(Left) The Chapman screwdriver set is another popular item. It comes with 15 different tips, a screwdriver handle, ratchet and extension — all packed in a form-fitting box.

(Right) Depending upon your strength, you may find the use of the Chapman ratchet handy when it comes to cinching down larger screws such as the tang screw on the Winchester Model 94. The best method of tightening down these sorts of screws may amount to using the regular screwdriver handle for preliminary tightening followed by the ratchet for final torquing.

any burrs which may be present before attempting to remove any screw. Use great care at all times as one slip can damage the finish on an expensive firearm.

Strength of the individual adapter relates closely to its size, diameter, width of blade, thickness and the like. In general, the smaller the adapter, the weaker it is, and therefore, the less torque that can be applied. The chart below shows the realistic torque for Chapman slotted gun screw adapters.

Even with a fine set of gunsmith screwdrivers, you must understand that there are some screws which cannot be removed with a screwdriver. All screws are not made, fitted or installed in the exact same manner. Neither are all screws manufactured with a proper "thread-to-thread" tolerance. Few of them are ever visually inspected before use and, therefore, they can carry a burr or chip which may jam them in position. Some screws—especially those used to secure gun sights—have a holding compound applied to them so they will not back out under recoil. It also makes them difficult, or impossible, to remove with a screwdriver.

Tapping the screwdriver in the screw slot will sometimes help to loosen the screw. This tends to drive the screw forward in the thread slot affording

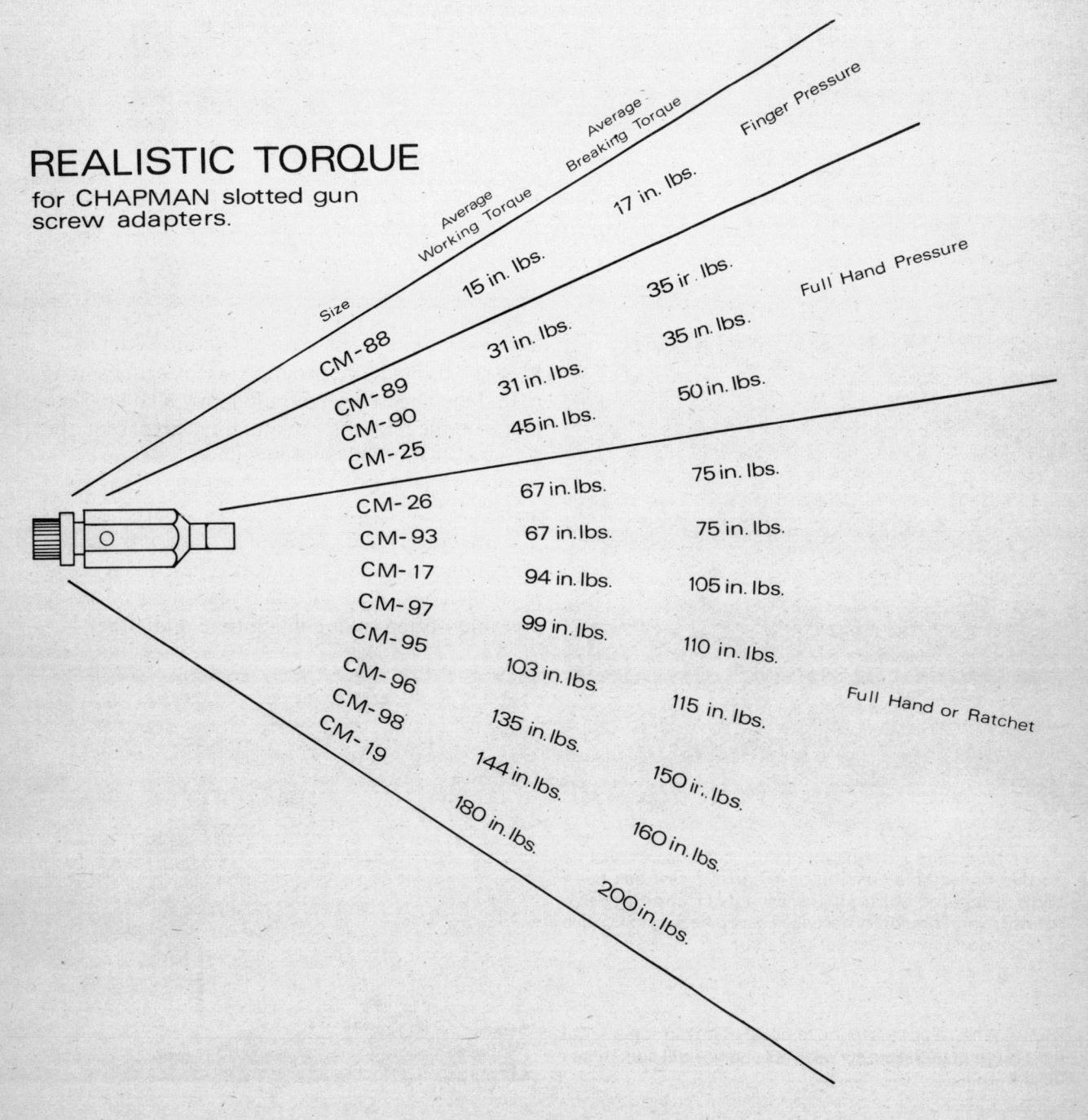

REALISTIC TORQUE
for CHAPMAN slotted gun screw adapters.

Size	Average Working Torque	Average Breaking Torque	
CM-88	15 in. lbs.	17 in. lbs.	Finger Pressure
CM-89	31 in. lbs.	35 in. lbs.	
CM-90	31 in. lbs.	35 in. lbs.	Full Hand Pressure
CM-25	45 in. lbs.	50 in. lbs.	
CM-26	67 in. lbs.	75 in. lbs.	
CM-93	67 in. lbs.	75 in. lbs.	
CM-17	94 in. lbs.	105 in. lbs.	
CM-97	99 in. lbs.	110 in. lbs.	
CM-95	103 in. lbs.	115 in. lbs.	Full Hand or Ratchet
CM-96	135 in. lbs.	150 in. lbs.	
CM-98	144 in. lbs.	160 in. lbs.	
CM-19	180 in. lbs.	200 in. lbs.	

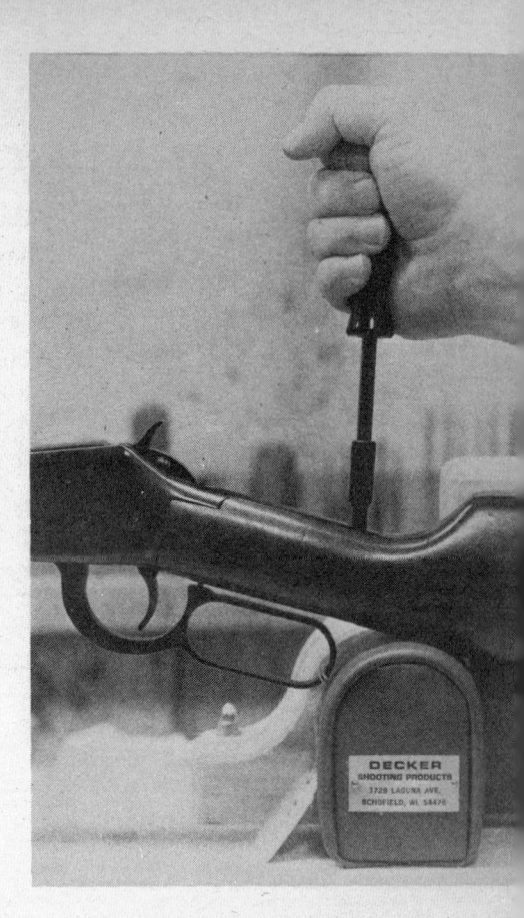

(Left) "Torque" doesn't necessarily mean brute force. In many cases, the right amount of torque can be applied with the fingers alone. (Right) Here's an example of a fair amount of torque being used to secure the tang screw to a Winchester Model 94.

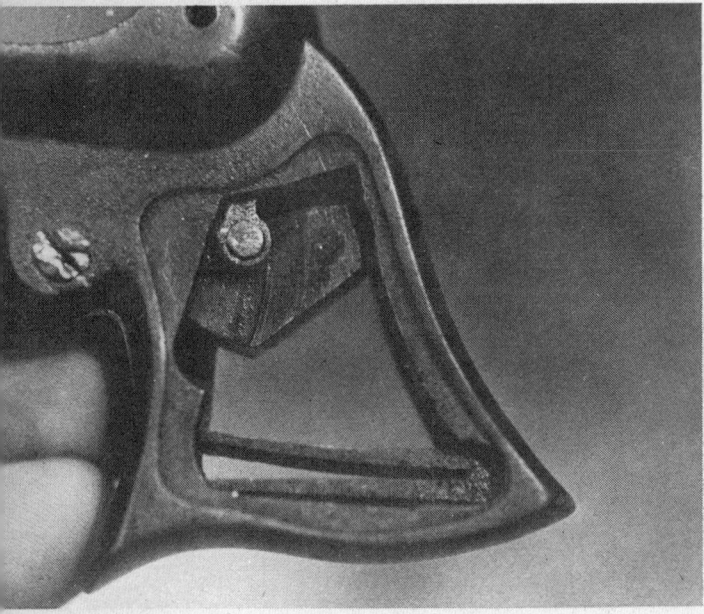

movement—in most cases. Liquid Wrench or WD-40 (commercial products used for loosening rusted metal screws and bolts) may also be tried. Heat applied to the surrounding area (not the screw itself) should be tried only as a last resort as intense heat will draw the hardness from most metals.

Remember, once a screw is broken, it is too late for common sense or judgment. The broken screw must then be drilled out and replaced the best way possible—often taking much time and effort.

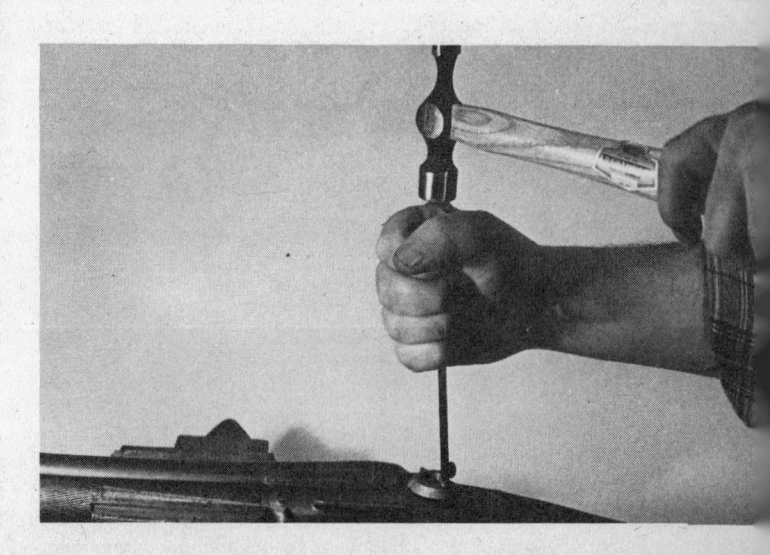

Here's an example of how-not-to-do-it. The screw visible on this collectable Remington 4-barrel pistol has been badly buggered through the use of an improper-size screwdriver. This sort of damaged screw head is indicative of work done by the rankest amateur.

(Right) When it comes to the removal of frozen screws, the light tapping of the screw itself (as shown) will sometimes do the trick.

Pin Punch Set

A set of punches is required for removing the assembly pins used in most firearms. A Grace pin punch set will handle 90% of your shop needs. Each punch is made to fit a certain pin in a gun action and the kit consists of 5 pin punches, 1 starter punch and 1 center punch.

Brownell's offers a special gunsmith's replaceable punch set that allows the tips to be replaced should they bend or break. The handles are made of steel with a removable knurled-chuck to hold the pins. The pins may be ground down to the exact length required for each job—giving the user a set of custom punches with a minimum investment.

There are four types of pins used in firearm assembly: the common steel pin, serrated pins, roll or spring pins and flared-tip pins. Before attempting to remove any pin, examine it carefully to determine just what type it is. Then use the appropriate punch to remove it. The object is to remove the pin without damaging it, the surrounding finish, or internal parts.

You must first position the gun so the pin will

For any firearm disassembly/assembly chore a quality set of drift punches is indispensable. Sets like the one shown below and to the right are available from any of the gunsmithing supply houses.

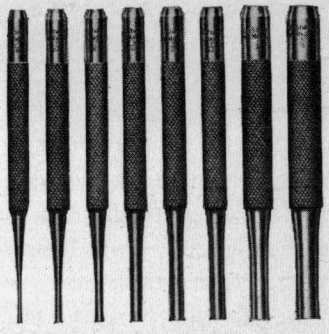

THE FOUR TYPES OF PIN PUNCHES

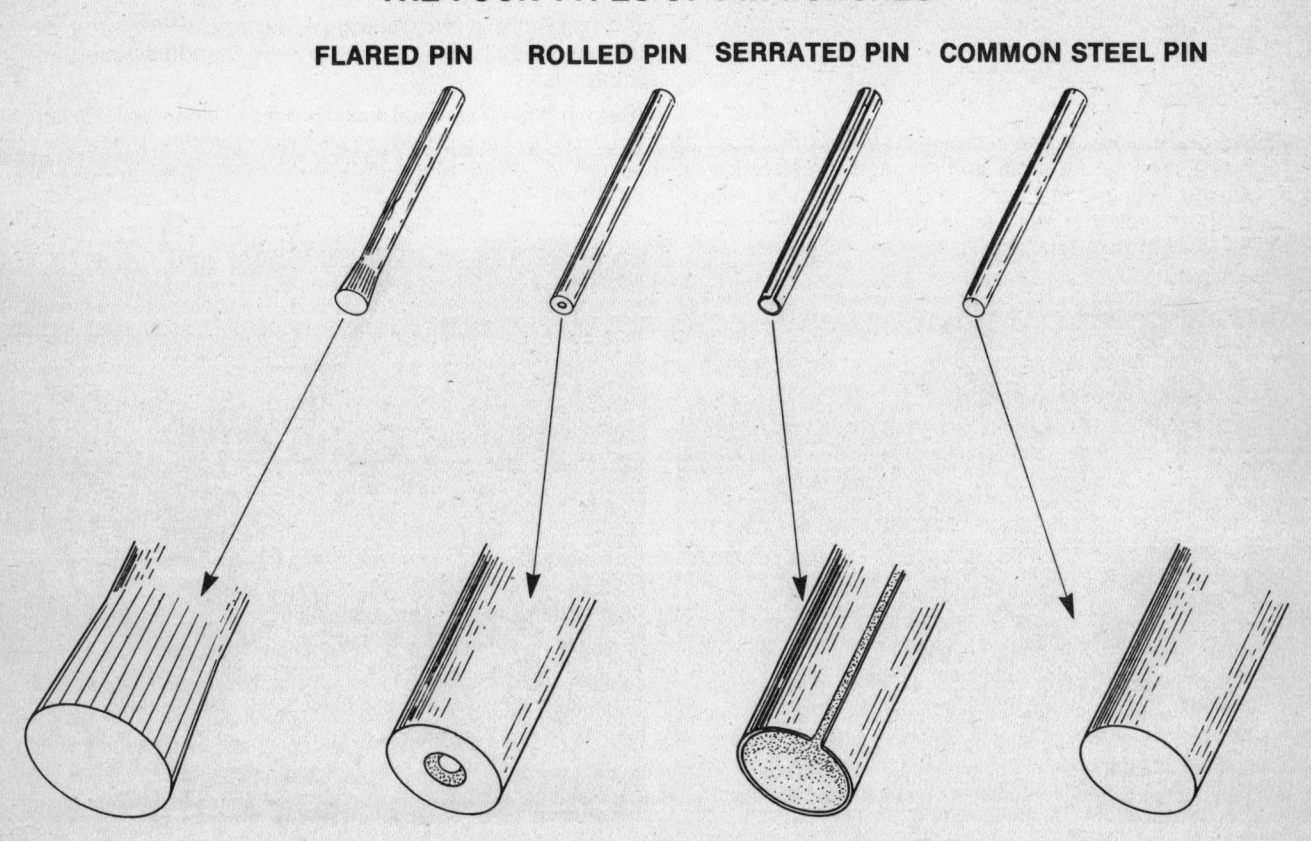

FLARED PIN **ROLLED PIN** **SERRATED PIN** **COMMON STEEL PIN**

have clearance to be driven out. A padded vise works most of the time, but sometimes this is going to a lot of trouble just to remove one pin. I use a piece of a shotgun stock that was sawed off prior to installing a recoil pad—it keeps the gun high enough off the bench for driving out pins. A starter punch is used to get the pin started. This is the short, tapered, flat nose punch found in most gunsmith pin punch sets. I hold the punch squarely on the pin and then give it a short, medium-heavy tap. If it resists, I give it a harder blow. Once the pin moves, a pin punch just a bit smaller than the pin is used to drive it the rest of the way out.

If you suspect that the pin is serrated, you obviously must hit the pin on the opposite end from the tiny serrations to avoid damaging the pin or the gun parts. A close examination will reveal which is the serrated end; use a magnifying glass if necessary.

The increasing use of roll or spring pins in modern firearms makes it necessary to use special roll pin punches for removal. They permit the removal and re-use of the same pin without glaring damage to the pins. A kit of punches in sizes from $1/16''$ to $3/16''$ will take care of most of your needs in the gunshop.

Select the proper size punch for the pin and then insert the pilot into the hollow pin until the driving

(Above and below) When removing pins, work on a flat surface and be sure the pin won't meet any resistance on its way out. To avoid resistance, the author used a piece of cut-off buttstock that has a stock-bolt hole in it — the pin will slide right through.

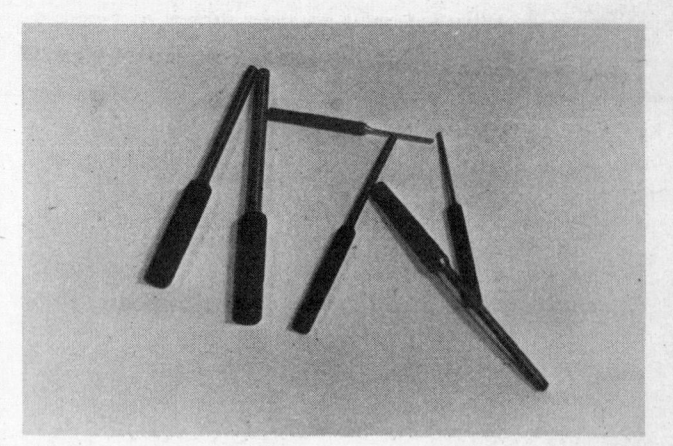

(Above) Roll-pin punches come (by necessity) in a number of sizes and shapes. It pays to have a good selection on hand.

(Below) If a screw head has been worn to the point where you can't get any purchase with a screwdriver blade, a pin punch will often do the trick when accompanied by some light tapping with a hammer.

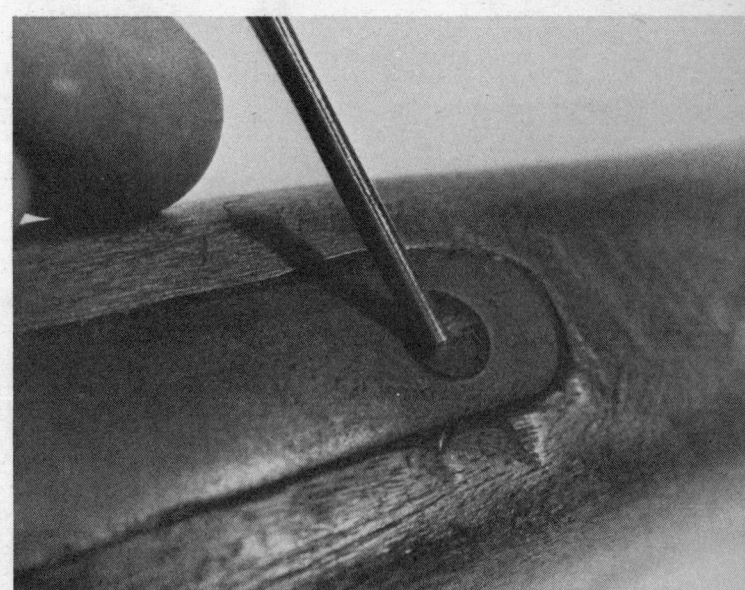

shoulders rest on the end of the pin. Then drive out the pin as discussed previously. Be sure to clean and oil the pin before replacing it.

Besides removing gun pins and using center punches for drilling, punches in general have many other uses around the gunshop. For example, a stuck screw can sometimes be loosened by tapping it with a pin punch to get it moving. Secure the firearm in a padded vise, then place the tip of the punch inside the outer edge of the screw slot and tap it with a hammer. This will usually start the screw turning when other methods have failed.

A center punch can also be used to raise metal in the bottom of dovetail slots when they are too loose to hold the sights properly. Merely rest the barrel on a solid object that won't mar the finish, and then give several hits with the center punch (a dozen or so should do it). Try the dovetail sight and, if it's still not tight enough, raise more metal with the center punch. A ballpeen hammer may also be used to *lightly* peen the shoulders of the slot downward to hold the sight tighter.

While we're on the subject of dovetail sights, you'll need some special punches for removing and installing dovetail sights. Conventional pin punches will mar its finish every time.

A nylon drift punch is very handy for installing and removing dovetail sights. The perfect size is a 4" long piece of nylon 5/16" in diameter. This will take care of the majority of front-sight removals. Sometimes, however, you will encounter an extremely tight dovetail sight and the nylon drift punch is going to bend. In these cases, you'll need a rectangular bronze punch as it provides a far superior surface than round punches with which only a small portion of the punch contacts the piece—often resulting in upsetting and deformation. By contrast, on many parts, such as sights, the square-end punch gives almost 100% contact—reducing tool and part damage. A good size is ¼"x¼" square. Most come in 12" lengths and can be cut into several punches.

Of course you can make your own custom punches to fit any size hole from discarded twist drills and other hardened pieces of cylindrical stock. If you need larger punches, try searching around old car junk yards. Besides being able to purchase all the old automobile valve stems you need to grind into drift pin punches, you'll find many other useful scraps that can be made into other gunsmithing tools . . . and usually at next to nothing in cost.

A center punch can be used to raise metal in the bottom of dovetail slots when they are too loose to hold the sights properly.

A rectangular bronze punch gives a far superior surface than round punches when it comes to removing dovetail sight bases.

For finding material to make your own parts, try searching around junk yards—you'll be amazed at the number of useful items to be found.

Pliers

Perhaps no other tool on the workbench is required to do more jobs than the various pairs of pliers that should be in any gunshop. The assortment shown is the one I use for nearly all gun shop requirements . . . from reaching inside a small action and inserting a small part, to holding red-hot screws while being blued by the oil-heat method. Insist on the steel varieties and not the cast-iron models found in dime stores and discount houses. Those manufactured by M. Klein & Co. are the best I have used, although I'm certain that other good brands are available.

Adjustable combination pliers have been around a long time. They are a common household tool and have been used for everything from driving tacks to pulling teeth, but they have a definite place in the gunshop. In general, a slip joint holds the two parts of the pliers together so that the jaws can be opened or closed to hold large or small objects. Most adjustable combination pliers have two cutting edges at the back of the jaws for wire cutting, but their main purpose is for gripping—like holding a small part against a grinding wheel.

Longnose pliers—often called "needlenose pliers"—are used with small objects in hard-to-get-at locations, such as starting the replacement of a pin or spring inside of an action. The tips of these pliers are easily bent if they are misused and they should never be used for loosening or tightening a screw or nut. Starting them, yes; but tightening them, no!

Other types of pliers similar to longnose pliers include roundnose pliers, half-roundnose pliers and flatnose pliers. All three types are used for similar situations as the longnose pliers.

Side-cutting pliers are used in gunsmith work for cutting wire—like black iron stove pipe wire used to hold barreled actions and parts while hot bluing—and other small wire-type items. Their use, however, on hardened steel or heavy material will quickly nick or dull the cutting edge.

Pump pliers (often called Channel-Locks) have a quick adjustment for widening or narrowing the jaws to hold various materials, especially round objects. The interlocking tongues and grooves on the two parts of the pliers enable the jaws to be moved closer together or farther apart.

Self-adjustable locking pliers act as a small portable vise. These pliers have a toggle and floating wedge arrangement that automatically adjust the

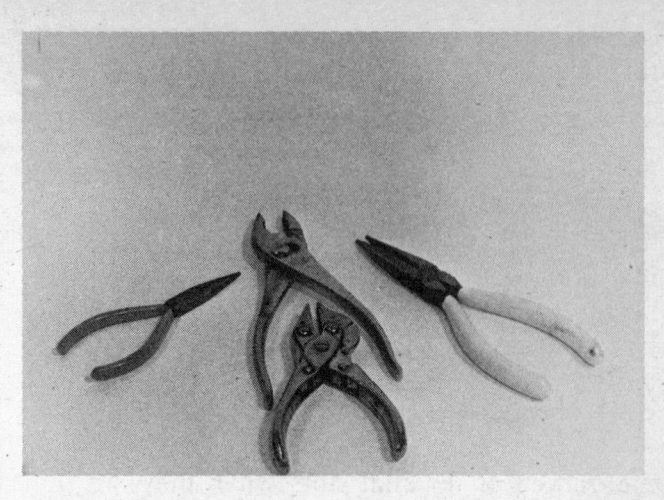

A good selection of pliers is imperative. The assortment shown is used daily.

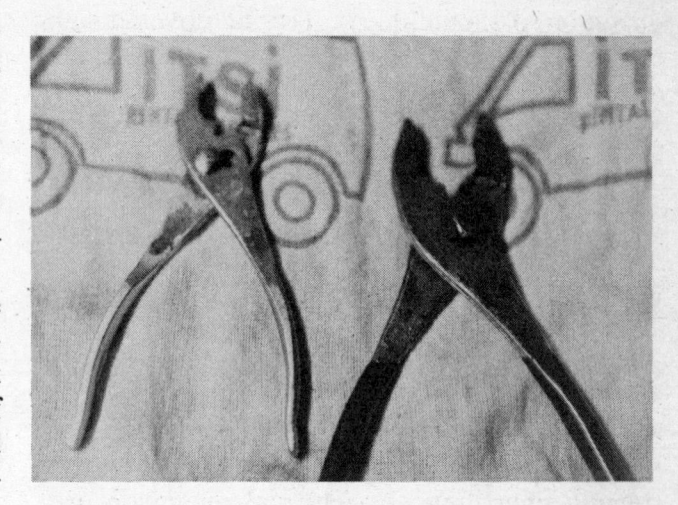

Common, adjustable "combination" pliers can be purchased almost anywhere. Several sets in various sizes are a must.

Combination pliers come in handy when it comes to holding any small part against any buffing or grinding wheel.

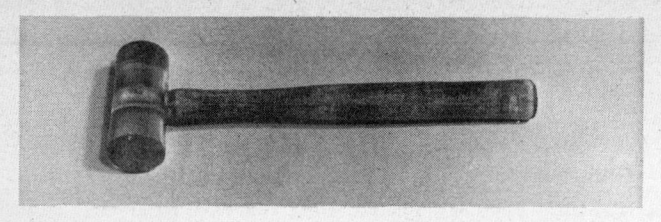

A no-mar hammer should be one of the first items purchased by the gunsmith.

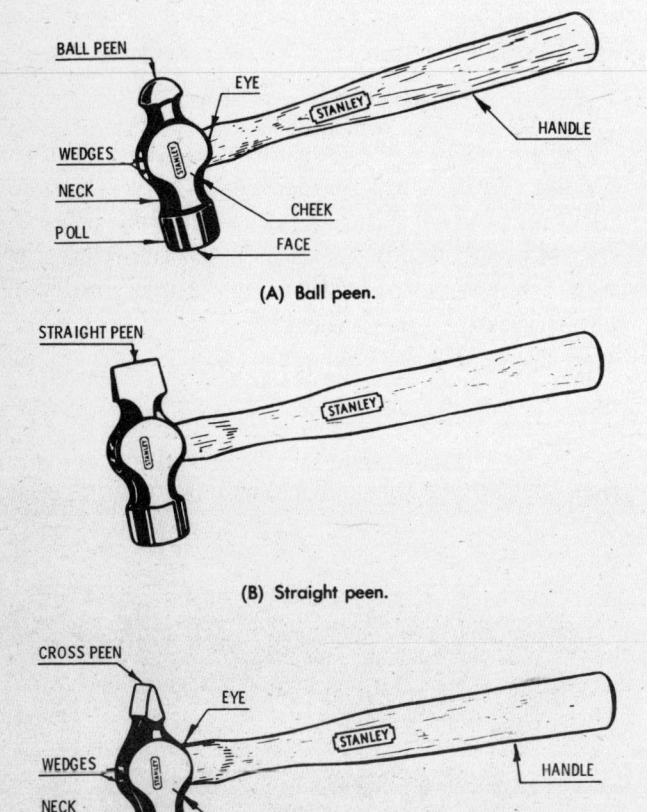

(A) Ball peen.

(B) Straight peen.

(C) Cross peen.

(Above) This illustration provides apt descriptions of the different types of peening hammers frequently used by gunsmiths.

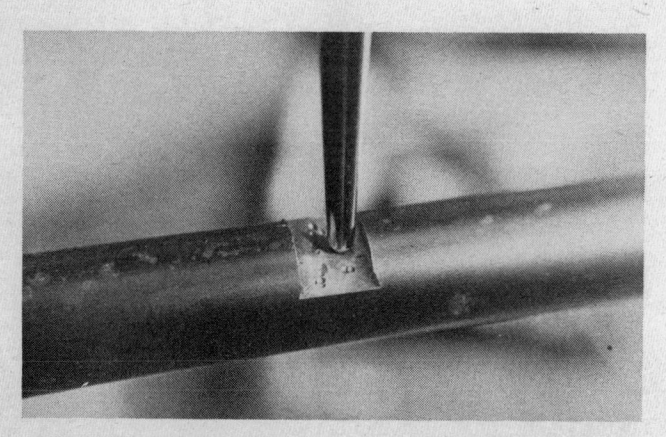

jaws of the pliers to the size of the object they are being used on. Pressure on the handle then enables the jaws to lock around the object very tightly and remain in this position until reverse pressure is applied to release the vise grip.

The variety of cutting and gripping pliers just discussed come in a number of sizes and each has a specific purpose. Any of them can be ruined if they are used for the wrong job.

Hammers

Hammers will find a variety of uses in benchwork: driving pins; installing or removing sights; seating inlays; peening dovetail sight bases to tighten sights; and a host of other jobs. One of the first hammers purchased by the gunsmith should be a no-mar type. These nylon, rubber or leather-headed hammers may be used for a multitude of jobs around the shop where you have to pound but don't want to mar the metal or wood you are working on. Of the several sizes available, you'll probably want to get the 1" diameter tip size first. You can also purchase a brass hammer tip that will screw into the 1" no-mar hammer. When this is used in combination with a no-mar plastic, nylon or phenolic tip, it makes an excellent all-purpose gunsmith hammer.

Metal working hammers may be classified with respect to peen as:
1. Ballpeen.
2. Straightpeen.
3. Crosspeen.

They are used mainly to hammer metal; that is, to indent or compress it, to expand or stretch, that portion of the metal adjacent to the indentation. One use of peening hammers is to tighten dovetail sights. Remove the sight base and lightly peen the top of the dovetail slot—forcing the overhang downwards to grip the sight base tighter. Marred metal areas can sometimes be peened back into their original condition if care is taken; and, of course, a gun part—such as a bar or shaft—may be straightened by peening with the convex portion of the hammer.

You may eventually find need for a wooden mallet and also a rawhide mallet for pounding on parts where none of the other hammers seem to

(Left) If you have a dovetail slot that's loose, you can tighten it up by lightly peening the overhang of the slot downward. This will provide a firm grip on the sight base.

work. The wooden mallet will be useful in tapping wood chisels for carving and stock inletting, and the rawhide mallet will be helpful when trying to loosen stubborn gun parts. You'll also find the rawhide mallet handy for several other uses.

Bench Vise

Eventually, every hobbyist and professional gunsmith will want a heavy machinist's vise. However, this is sometimes not practical for the beginner. One reason is the lack of a good sturdy workbench. Obviously, if the bench will not stand the strain, a heavy vise is not much good. If the work area has to be temporary—like on the kitchen table—then a portable vise should be purchased.

One completely portable vise goes by the trade name Vacu-Vise. This vise fastens instantly to any non-porous surface with super vacuum power. To attach, merely apply slight pressure to the top of the vise and push the side lever down. It then acts as a "third hand" in any gunsmith's shop, kit or on the range.

The Versa-Vise is also very popular in the gun repair trade. It gives both vertical and horizontal holding positions and also rotates in a full 360° circle in either position. The vise automatically locks in the desired position when the jaws are clamped tight. Serrated pipe jaws for round objects up to 1½" diamter are provided as well as a built in anvil.

Gunsmith's Knives

The gunsmith will eventually need several kinds of knives in his shop—especially if he is involved with much wood work. I personally like a set of Xacto knives as they fulfill over 90% of my cutting needs; that is, cutting rifle slings, cutting holes in recoil pads (to get to the screw slots) and many other applications.

The Versa-Vise is one of the most useful items a gunsmith can have. It turns a full 360° in either the upright or laid-flat position.

A set of Xacto knives will find extensive use in the gun repair trade. Every gunsmith should have one.

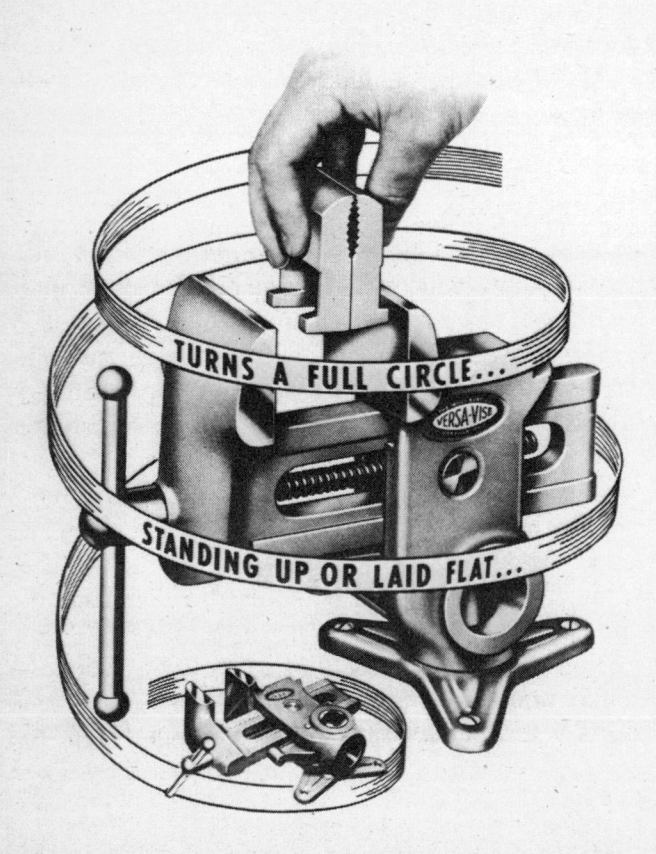

One of the most common uses for the Xacto knife in the gunsmithing trade is for cutting clean screwdriver slots in recoil pads.

Sight-Base File

A sight-base file comes in mighty handy for widening dove-tail slots in gun barrels without the danger of deepening the slot or damaging any edges not being worked on. This type of file is always a true parallel 3-square file with only one side doing the cutting. The other two sides are smooth or safe. Being a true parallel file you have absolute control over the angle of the dovetail. Every gunsmith—either hobbyist or professional —should have one of these files in his tool kit.

Pillar File

The pillar file is considered the standard gunsmithing file since they are parallel as to width, but taper somewhat in thickness toward the point.

PILLAR FILE

Both edges of the pillar file are safe so cuts may be made right up to the faces without undercutting the sides of the work.

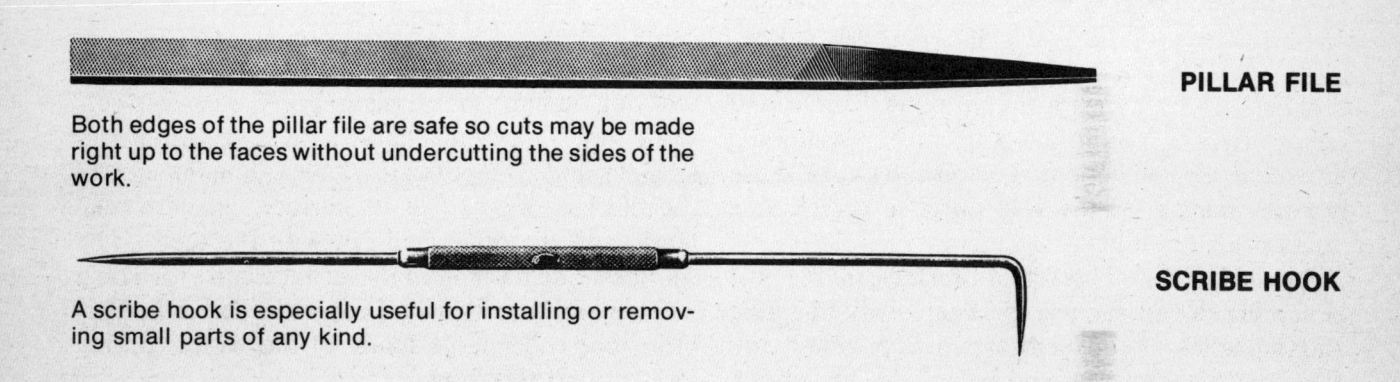

SCRIBE HOOK

A scribe hook is especially useful for installing or removing small parts of any kind.

Both edges are safe so cuts may be made right up to the faces without undercutting the sides of the work. These files are made in narrow and extra-narrow patterns and are usually double-cut. Pillar files are especially useful when fitting new parts to firearms.

Scribe Hook

Anyone anticipating assembling and disassembling firearms will quickly learn the value of a scribe hook. It's especially useful whenever small inside springs are to be installed or removed or for slipping out or locating small parts of any kind.

The scribe portion of the instrument is used for marking metal such as a shotgun bead sight shank that protrudes into the bore. In this case, the sight bead is removed after having been marked, and then cut off (preferably with an emery cutting wheel used in conjunction with a Moto-Tool). The sight bead is then reinstalled and polished flush with the bore with a felt polishing tip.

Brushes

Besides conventional bore cleaning brushes as described in Chapter 6, the gunsmith will want to obtain a selection of toothbrushes for getting down into actions and for cleaning other hard-to-get-at-places. The bristles should be rather stiff and should be solvent-proof. Brownell's Inc. carries an M-16 cleaning brush that has been tested in practically every oil and solvent available on the market with no damage to the bristles. They cost less than a dollar and are an exceptionally good, practical cleaning brush for use on your bench or in the field.

A stainless steel brush is of special value for cleaning hardened grease and dirt from parts and actions. I also find much use for mine when bluing firearms by the hot-water method. The .005"

A scribe hook is also handy for engraving "trim lines" on parts that are too long. A good example is this shotgun sight bead that's protruding into the bore

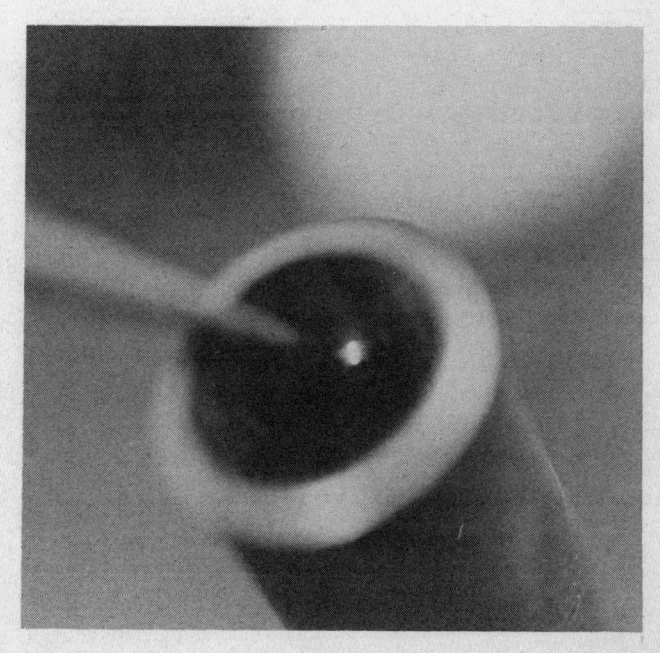

15

Toothbrushes are excellent cleaning devices for getting down into hard-to-get-at-places.

hand-tied stainless steel wire varieties are excellent for carding off the rust in hard-to-get-to-areas.

You'll also want one of the old-time scrub brushes—the kind with the wooden handle and hemp bristles. You'll find it useful for scrubbing down barrels and actions. I also keep one of these brushes handy for the sole purpose of cleaning tanks prior to bluing.

An old fashioned horsehair brush is still the best bench brush you can use to sweep away fine dust and particles—keeping the gunshop bench top clean and free from grit and grime that can scratch the finish on firearms. The brush part should be about 8" long with about a 5" handle. It should also be fully set with about 2" of black horsehair bristles.

Wood Rasp

The 4-in-1 hand rasp is a good first tool for working on gun stocks, pistol grips, etc. This versatile tool is made in a half-round style with parallel sides and no taper in thickness. The flat side of the file has one-half of its surface cut with rasp teeth, and the other half cut with file teeth. The rounded side has half of the surface cut with a rasp section and the other half cut with file teeth. This little tool will handle many of the woodworking jobs around the shop.

India and Arkansas Stones

India and Arkansas stones are needed in the gun shop for precision trigger and sear work, accuriz-

The stainless steel brush shown is exellent for both cleaning hardened grease from parts and for carding off rust during hot-water bluing.

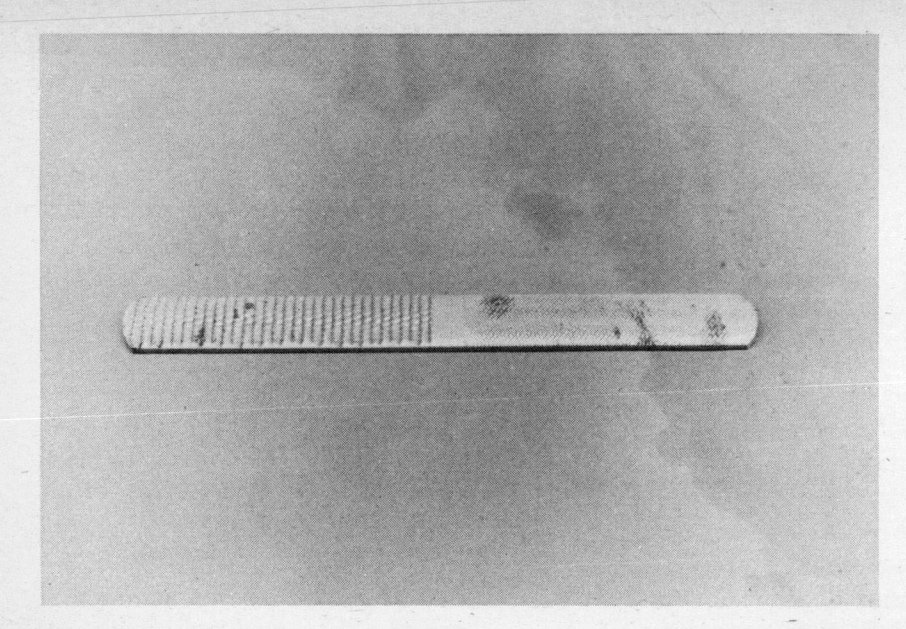

This 4-in-1 hand rasp is a good first tool for working on gunstocks, pistol grips and the like.

ing, close fitting and for other parts where fine stoning is needed. Arkansas stones are also used extensively for sharpening gunsmithing tools such as knives, chisels, gravers and other precision cutting tools. Each grade of Arkansas stone has a special sharpening application as recommended below.

Washita: Most rapid cutting stone. Used to start edges on knives, and by wood carvers, commercial knife sharpeners, butchers and sportsmen who desire a keen edge in minimum of time. It will sharpen a knife to the point where you can shave hair from your arm.

Soft Arkansas: Best general purpose stone. Produces and maintains very sharp, polished edges on all knives and tools. Smoother, even sharper edge than from Washita.

Hard Arkansas: Touches up and final-polishes an already sharp edge. Sharpening with this superb stone takes a little while longer, but the truly polished, razor sharp edge is well worth the effort.

Black Hard Arkansas: Supreme ultimate in a finishing whetstone; used on already sharp blades by the perfectionist. Final step in sharpening high quality cutlery or straight razors.

The sizes and grades listed are those stones I personally prefer to use, plus the ones most often seen on the benches of gunsmiths, knifemakers and woodcarvers. Each stone is hand cut with a diamond saw, then carefully finished and graded. To protect the precision ground cutting surfaces, each stone usually comes in a nicely finished and varnished cedarwood box.

(Above) A hard Arkansas stone is being used to hone a trigger sear to provide a smooth trigger pull. A set of these stones is a must.
(Below) Arkansas stones are often used to sharpen wood carving chisels and other similar cutting tools found on the gunsmith's bench.

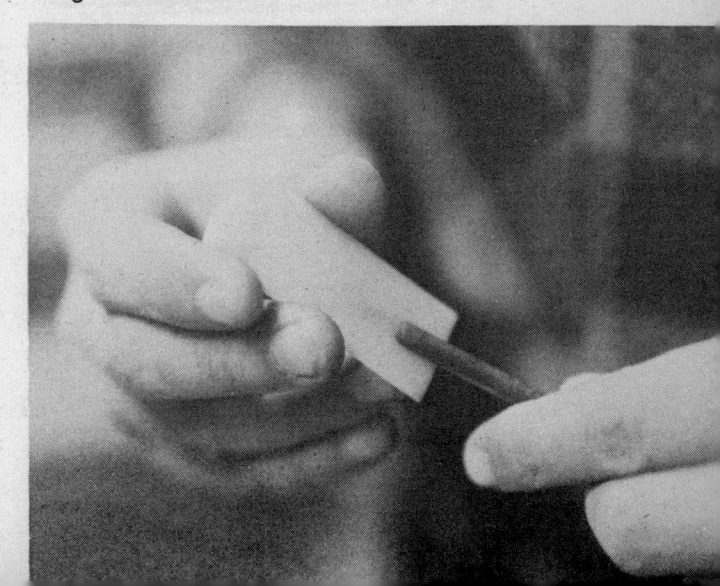

Allen Wrenches

The gunsmith will need a complete set of Allen head bits in both English and metric sizes. One good set is offered by Chapman which fits their screwdriver set handle and extension. This assortment contains 11 Allen head bits from 1/16" to 5/16" and 6 metric Allen head bits along with 1/4" square drive adapter.

Most telescopic sights—especially as sold by the discount houses, etc.—use Allen head screws, primarily for the scope mounts. I remember one scope repair that should have been relatively simple. However, I didn't have a metric Allen tip and wound up grinding down an inch Allen tip (the next size larger than the metric size) until I had a fit. Therefore, a ten minute job took nearly two hours!

You will probably see more and more metric Allen tips in use in the firearms industry, so be sure you have a set of both types of Allen wrenches. They are inexpensive and you'll find many daily uses for them around your shop. Set screws for handloading equipment are also of the Allen type.

Miscellaneous Tools

The tools previously described are the bare minimum with which you can perform gun repairs. You'll also quickly find that this set is incomplete and more tools will be needed as you progress in the field. This is especially true when you start disassembling firearms. Certain firearms will require specialized tools, for without them, assembly and disassembly steps can be difficult. One example is removing the retaining caps on Winchester Model 12's and similar shotguns. A retaining cap wrench will greatly simplify the removal. The extra wide tips of this wrench fit the slots in the cap exactly; it's available from Brownell's Inc.

If you're a professional (or intend to be one) a big part of your business will be working on Colt handguns. A special Colt tool is made for remov-

Brownell's Basic Gunsmithing Kit consists of a good selection of tools ideal for the hobbyist or professional. At the top is a brass/nylon headed hammer; to the left is a pair of needle nose pliers with a pair of parallel pliers just below. Underneath the hammer is a Magna Tip screwdriver and bits. Below the screwdriver set and to the right and left can be found such items as jeweler's screwdrivers, pin punches, Allen wrench set, bench knife, screwchart, scribe hook, starter punches, drift, honing stones, M-16 brush, spring vise, a file and a 4-in-1 hand rasp.

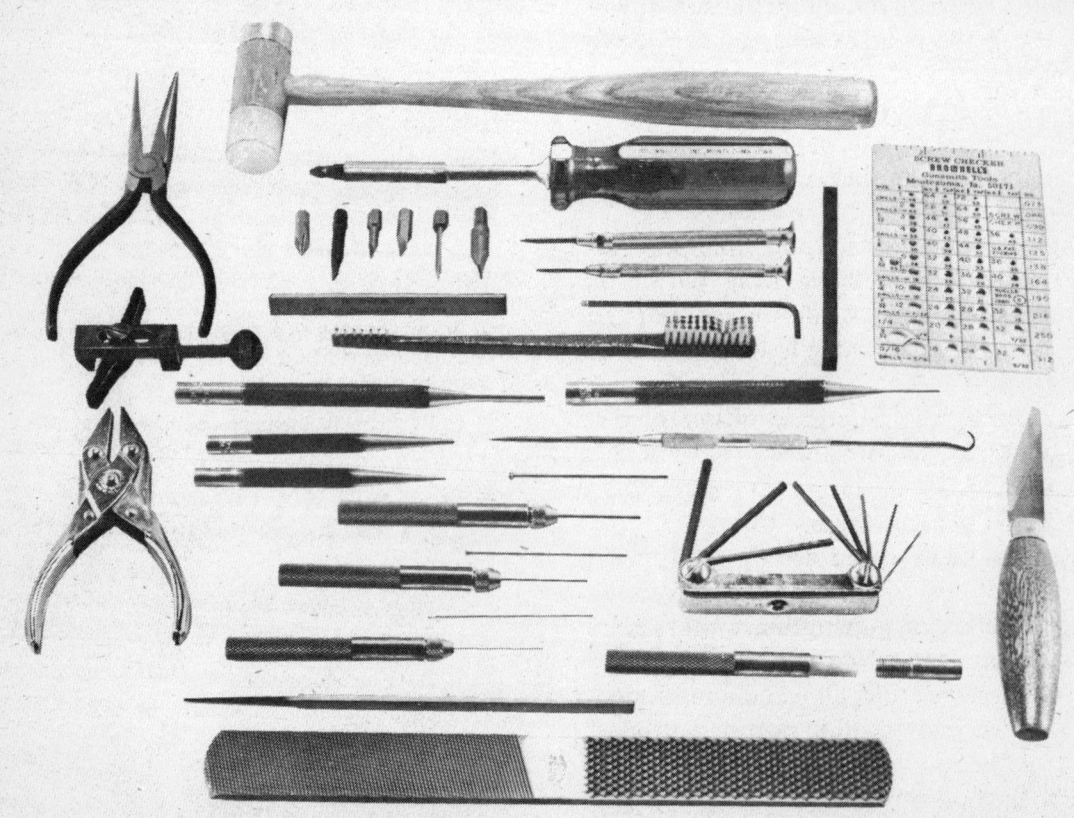

ing the ejector from the cylinder prior to bluing, polishing or servicing—it's darn handy. This tool also makes it easier to remove or install tight .38 or .45 auto bushings.

Bolt extractor pliers will also be appreciated when you begin fighting the removal and installation of a stiff extractor on an Enfield, Springfield, Mauser or similar bolt.

A lot of other service tools for special models of firearms can be found in the gunsmith's service manuals provided by firearm manufacturers. In fact, these catalogs should be one of your first "tools." They have helpful troubleshooting information, assembly and disassembly instructions (plus schematic drawings) and much, much more helpful data. You'll also want *The Encyclopedia of Modern Firearms Parts & Assembly* compiled by Bob Brownell because, according to the Dec. 1959 issue of *The American Rifleman:*

"The publication of this outstanding work is an event of great importance for the gunsmith,

When removing the pump handle retaining cap on a Winchester Model 12, use the special tool shown—Brownells can provide one.

Brownell's Assembly/Disassembly Tool Kit will make gun repair a lot easier, as you'll have a good basic set of assembly/disassembly tools to start off with. At the top is a nylon/brass headed hammer; just below the hammer is a Magna-Tip screwdriver and bits. To the left of the hammer is a set of parallel pliers, below those a spring vise and a Colt pistol wrench. Tools to the right of the spring vise and Colt wrench include: M-16 brush, pin punches, stones, screw chart, drift, bench knife, files, jeweler's screwdrivers, bolt spring extractor pliers, Model 12 wrench and a speed-head wrench. Tools like these help conserve the gunsmith's most valuable resource — time.

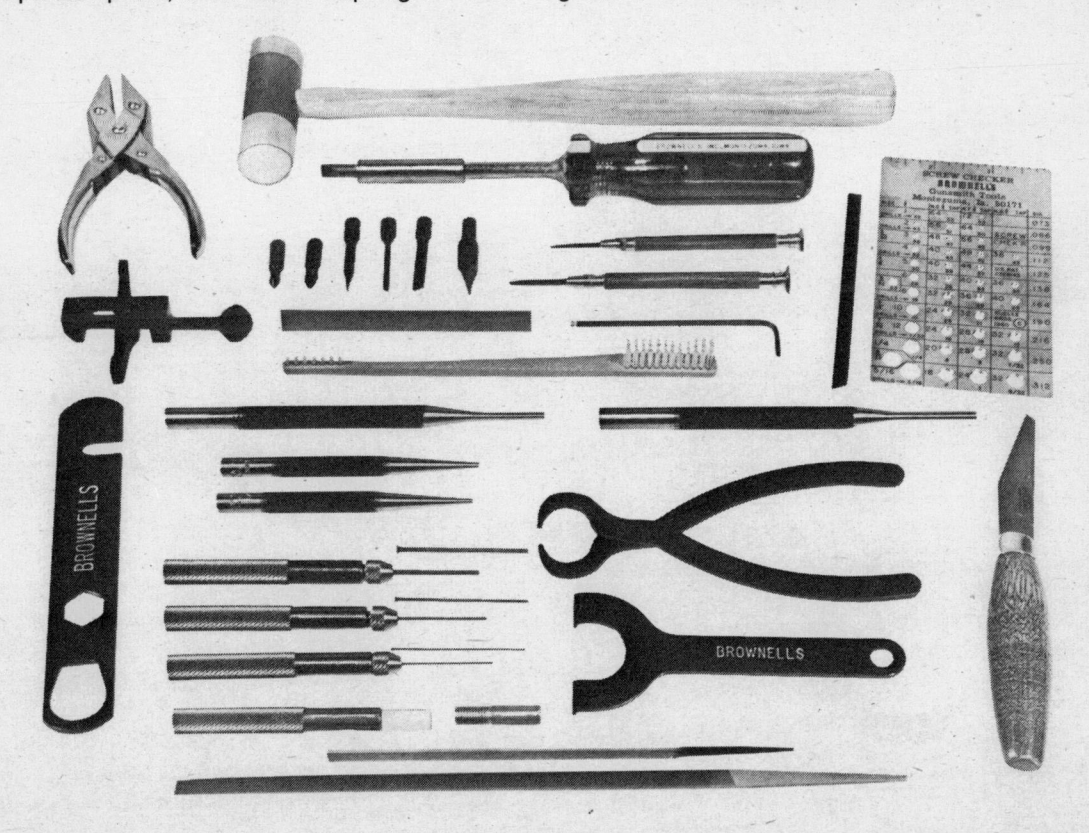

19

This Colt tool is very helpful in removing the ejector from the cylinder prior to bluing, polishing or servicing.

the firearm hobbyist, and serious gun workers in the small arms field . . . something that every gun enthusiast and firearms hobbyist will want, and that every gunsmith will find to be an indispensable tool of his trade."

I concur. There is hardly a day that goes by that I don't need to use this reference for some reason—assembling a firearm, looking in the diagrams to see what parts are missing from a firearm in for repairs, troubleshooting data, and much much more. It's paid for itself in my shop time and time again.

While we're on the subject of books, I'd suggest you take a long, hard look at Chapter 23, *Gunsmith's Library*. In that chapter you'll find a thorough list of superb titles devoted to the subject of gunsmithing. Many, if not most of those books, should be near your workbench for fast reference. I find mine indispensable.

Bolt extractor pliers will be appreciated when removing and installing extractors on an Enfield, Springfield, Mauser or similar bolt action rifles.

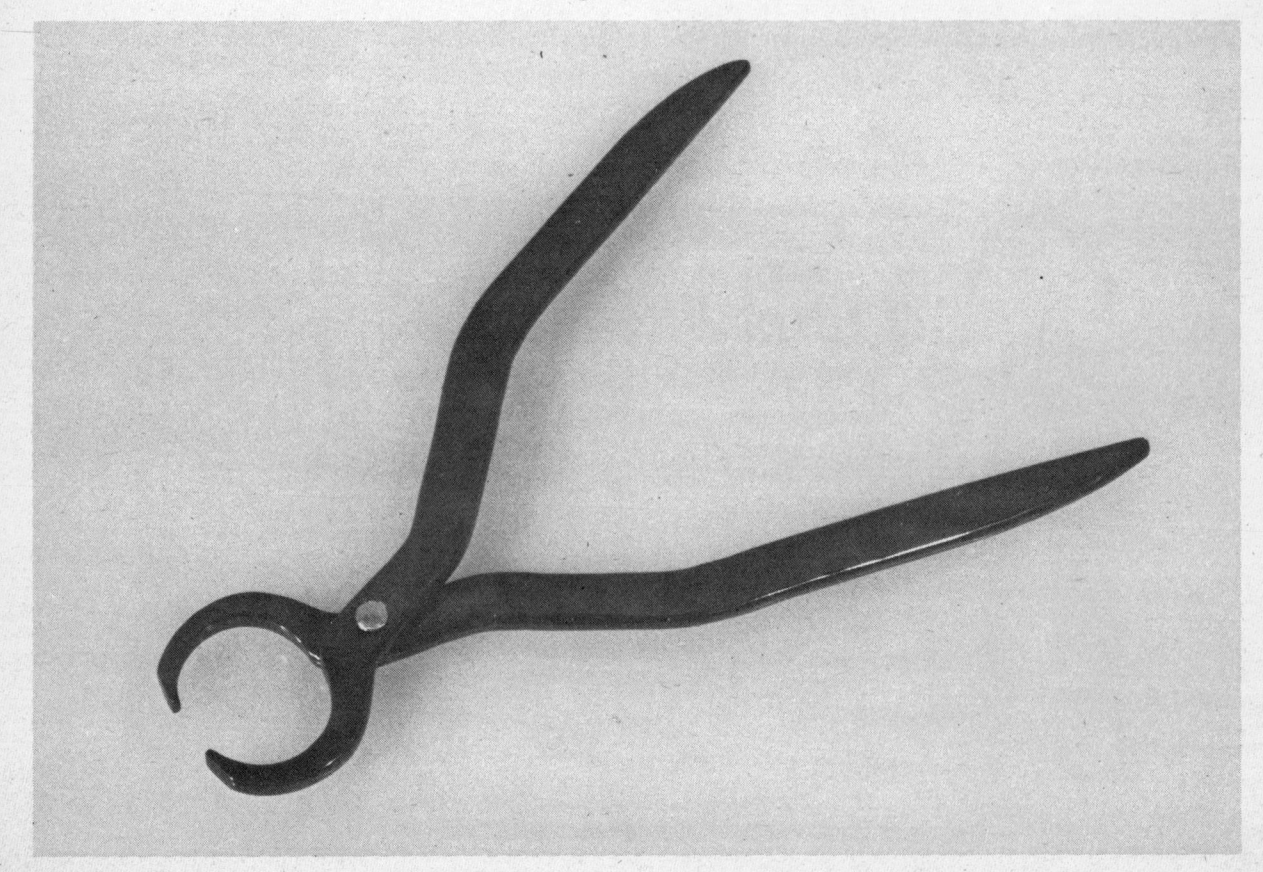

2
A PLACE TO WORK

WITHOUT a doubt, everyone who tinkers with guns needs a shop. The professional, of course, needs the shop for his livelihood and while the hobbyist may save a little money on his own gun repairs, the home shop is noted more for the pleasure it offers.

There are at least ten good locations for a gun shop. There are countless ways to create space where there seems to be none. But in planning a location for a gunshop, you must first decide what type of work you will be performing. For example, if you plan to get your Federal Firearms License and work on guns for others, one room or area in the home must be set aside exclusively for the gun business. If it's in the basement, the room can't also be used for a recreation room nor can Mommy do her ironing in this area. The space must be devoted entirely to gun business.

On the other hand, if you plan to work on firearms only for yourself, you can locate the "shop" any place you like—even in your living room!

Shops for gun work involve troubleshooting, stock finishing, rebluing, stock checkering, cleaning, rebarreling, chambering (just to name a few), and, again, the person must decide just what types and how much of this work he plans to do. One gunsmith may specialize in metal work— doing rebarreling and rechambering jobs mostly. Then his shop will be centered around a lathe and perhaps a milling/drilling machine. Another may specialize in stock work, requiring mostly woodworking tools. Another may want to do only rebluing, and so on. However, the average gunsmith will perform a variety of work on firearms covering the entire field. He may have to farm out some of his lathe work (because he can't afford a lathe at this time) but he's expected to be able to handle most jobs that come along.

Basement Shops

Most home gunshops are located in the basement. This location has several advantages over other locations and the few drawbacks can be usually overcome. The chief advantages include:

1. Easy to heat in winter.
2. Cool in summer.
3. It's out of the way of most family activities.
4. It's quiet and it can be made relatively soundproof from the living area.
5. If you have to, you can leave it messed up overnight without worrying about guests seeing it.

The basement area also has several disadvan-

Fluorescent fixtures are normally the best light source for gunshops. Get the best you can afford—it will save your eyes.

tages, but as mentioned previously, most can be overcome. Most basement areas (as finished by the builder) are poorly illuminated. This gives a dark, dingy appearance. So, if the basement is the area chosen for the shop location, one of the first projects should be the installation of adequate lighting. Fluorescent fixtures are ideal. However, if an acoustical T-bar ceiling is used, you may want to go with recessed fixtures—either incandescent or fluorescent.

One of the major disadvantages of a basement is dampness which of course, creates rust problems. To overcome this problem, epoxy waterproofing may be applied to basement walls from the inside and then foam boards can be used to insulate basement walls and check dampness. A good dehumidifier is added insurance.

Flooding is another problem with some basements that can be a disaster. However, if the home owner will grade all slopes away from basement walls, repair all gutters and downspouts, and install a good sump pump, the chance of basement flooding is greatly reduced.

Another major problem with basement areas (especially those in older homes) is the low ceiling height. Many basement ceilings are only about 6'10" above the floor. This not only gives a cramped-in feeling but also causes trouble with guns, tools and other items accidentally hitting the ceiling as you're working on them. Cove lighting around the perimeter of low ceilings will give the affect of a higher ceiling; it's also a very good indirect lighting method for general illumination. Lowering the basement floor or raising the ceiling are expensive operations and are not (usually) economically feasible in this day and time. It would be better to utilize another area in the home or else build a new shop in your backyard.

One gunsmith near Berryville, VA opened a professional gunshop in the basement of his home. A separate outside entrance and show windows were installed and the interior was completely finished. A partition separates the showroom from the shop area where all phases of gun work are performed. The show room walls are lined with a gun rack which is always full of new and used guns which are for sale. Other shooting items such as reloading manuals, reloading components and other firearm accessories are also on display. The shop contains a bench lathe, drill press, barrel vise and hundreds of other useful gunsmithing tools. A firing range was built in back of the shop for testing weapons by the gunsmiths and also the customers.

This shop has several advantages. One is that of low overhead; that is, a separate place of business does not have to be leased or built and otherwise maintained. Secondly, someone is usually at home at all times which discourages intruders. Having a place of business in one's home is also convenient. For example, if business is slow, the owner can mow his grass or perhaps paint the wood trim or any number of other activities normally performed at home while waiting for customers to come. The chief disadvantage of such a setup is being bothered by customers after closing hours. A gun owner, for example, may decide that he must have a particular firearm looked at in the evening—after regular business hours. If the gunshop were located away from one's residence, chances are the customer would not bother to call at the gunsmith's home. However, with the shop in one's home, it's very tempting for the gun owner to merely go to the front door and knock, even though the gunshop may be closed. This is good for business, but hell on one's privacy.

If you're building or buying a house in which a basement workshop is planned, here are a few things to look for:

1. The basement walls should be built of concrete blocks at least 12 blocks high. Many are built only 11 blocks high and this produces a ceiling about 7' high which is too low for a good gunshop.
2. Be sure the basement is waterproofed correctly. In general, the exterior block walls should have a coating of cement plaster as well as a heavy coating of asphalt waterproofing compound over this. The first two or three courses of block should be of the solid type and a line of drain tile placed in a bed of loose gravel should be installed around the basement footings to lead off excess water.

In remodeling a basement for a workshop area, try to rework all plumbing pipes and electrical cables so that they are run between joists instead of below them. Some warm air ducts may also be run between joists, but some will be too large for this type of installation. Those which are too large to be run between joists should be run at the perimeter of the basement and then boxed in to give more head room.

Attic Shops

Attics are probably the worst places to put a gun shop around the home. They are often hot in summer, cold in winter and short on head room. Add to this the difficulty of transporting materials to and from the attic, plus the noise and vibration that carries down into the living area and the disadvantages are quickly realized.

Of course, if there is no other place available, these disadvantages can be somewhat remedied. First of all, insulation in the walls, roof and floor will help to keep a more controlled, comfortable temperature and muffle noises. An attic ventilating fan will reduce attic temperatures considerably as will the installation of several windows if they're currently absent.

Noise and vibration produced by power tools can be overcome by mounting them on rubber mats and/or rubber washers. Tightly sealed attic doors will also help retain the shop noises in the attic and also cut down on dust escaping into the living area.

Garage Shops

A gunshop in a garage is one of the best places to locate it. Although garages are often drafty and hard to heat in winter, they can be made into excellent shops having advantages that other areas in the home cannot offer. First of all, a garage shop lets you work into the wee hours of the morning, usually without disturbing anyone in the home. If it's located far enough away from the house and other neighbors, even power tools can be operated without bothering anyone. You don't have to worry about fumes from hot bluing and other operations smelling up the home, and if you are faced with leaving a temporary mess, no one is going to care.

Even if you still plan to use the garage to park your cars, there are ways to also use it as a shop. The nearby floor plan, for example, shows a two-car garage with a large workbench worked into a nook on the side of the garage. A hinged, fold-down bench may also be used, but this of course requires that the bench be cleared before it can be folded out of the way.

The ideal set-up is to use one-half of a two-car

**WINDOWS
(typical of 6)**

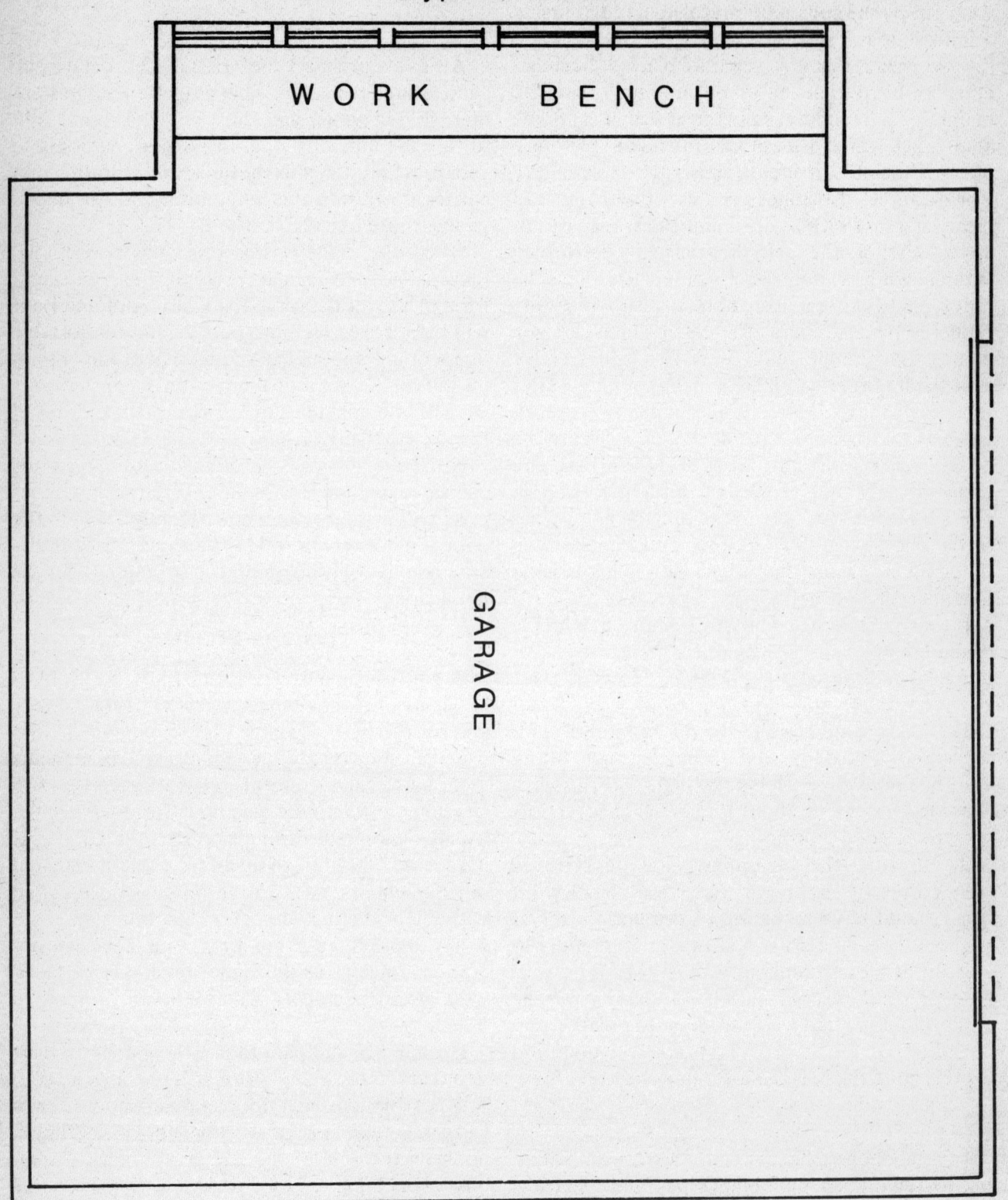

WORK   BENCH

GARAGE

This floor plan of a two-car garage has a large workbench installed in a nook on the side of the garage.

garage as a shop and the other half for parking a car. If you still want shelter for a second car, build a carport—it's much cheaper than building an enclosed shop.

Even if you don't have a garage on your property, and you're an apartment dweller with no other possibilities for locating a shop where you live, look around town for the possibility of renting a garage. Then set up your shop in this rented structure and work away in your spare time.

Outbuildings

My own home has no basement, no garage and my attic space was converted into an office some years ago. Therefore, my only possibility—or so I thought—was to build a shop in my backyard. First of all, I got hold of some plans for a two-car garage (with storage space above) that matched our Dutch Colonial home, but when I received the bid from a local contractor, I knew this garage would have to wait—$21,000 is a lot of money to spend for a garage!

The next possibility were two outbuildings that I had considered too far gone to save. One had

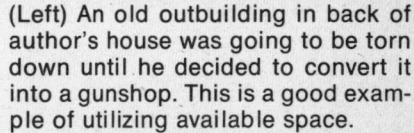

(Left) An old outbuilding in back of author's house was going to be torn down until he decided to convert it into a gunshop. This is a good example of utilizing available space.

(Above) Once the grape arbor was removed, and the brush cleared away, the outbuilding started to show promise as a gunshop.

The first chore was to jack up and level the building.

Then, the interior of the building was stripped of all the junk and the entire building was hosed down with water.

The author's next chore was to start framing the old outbuilding and install the electrical wiring.

Inexpensive paneling and a plywood floor was installed; and, a U-shaped workbench was put in along with fluorescent lighting, cabinets, tools, etc.

Although not complete when this picture was taken, it didn't take long for the area to become filled up with gun repairs.

been used at one time as a smoke house and the other for a meat house. In fact, they still had the smell of Virginia hams when I moved to this farm. But when I received the bid of over twenty thousand dollars for a garage shell, I decided to take another look at these buildings.

My first step was to tear the old grape arbor down and jack up the building to level it. All the junk that was in the building when I moved on the property was then removed and the building interior then thoroughly washed down with a garden hose. I then decided upon a layout (after several tries on my drawing board) and started the electrical wiring and the insulation of the sidewalls. Inexpensive panelling was then erected, while 3/8" plywood was laid on the floor to level it and to better accept the tile flooring.

A U-shaped workbench was then constructed as is described in Chapter 3, fluorescent lighting installed, cabinets, tools, etc. No, I'm not quite finished with the shop at this writing. I'm beginning to paint the exterior and build tool racks above the benches, but I'm really in no big hurry since I'm able to use the shop now. It will just be more convenient when all the drawers and shelves are completed.

The other building was half torn down before I decided to leave it for awhile. This building houses my hot-bluing operation. The cracks in the boards provide excellent ventilation!

Porches

Does your home have a porch that is seldom used? If so, you can probably convert it to a very good shop with comparatively little expense. In most cases, the roof, floor and at least one wall is already there so all you have to do is fill in the other two or three walls, add a workbench and you're ready to start working.

Since the walls that are added will usually be exposed to the weather, be sure to insulate well. The floors and ceiling should be considered also. If you can't get to existing void spaces to install insulation, consider having insulation blown in—

after boring holes to reach the void spaces between studs.

Conventional framing can be used to enclose the open walls of a porch, but perhaps jalousie windows would provide a better arrangement. A jalousie window consists of a series of operable overlapping glass louvers which pivot in unison —usually by a crank-and-gear system. Such windows are best used in southern climates, where maximum ventilation and flush exterior and interior appearance is desired. These windows may be arranged so that an entire wall—from, say, a foot below the ceiling to two feet above the floor —is constructed of windows.

Spare-Room Shop

A possibility for apartment dwellers is a spare room—like an extra bedroom that hasn't been used since Junior decided to tie the knot. Such a place, however, is not without drawbacks. Apartment rooms are difficult to soundproof, which will definitely limit your activities to certain hours each day. Can you imagine what your neighbors would say if you started your 1 hp buffer/grinder at 2 AM? If you weren't evicted, you'd certainly get the cold shoulder from all your neighbors the following day.

You will also have the problem of tracking debris into the living area of your home, but probably not any worse than tracking dust in a basement shop. Just provide a rug at the room entrance to clean your feet well when you leave. A tight-fitting door will help eliminate dust and chemical odors from the room and also cut down on the noises to the rest of the apartment.

The main advantages of a spare-room shop are lighting and electrical outlets are already provided. Such rooms are also heated and air conditioned for greater comfort than if you selected your garage or outbuilding for the shop location.

Closet Shops

Highly productive gun-tinkering shops have been hung on the back of a closet door, with a workbench that folds down from a neat-looking wall panel, but this is not the ideal situation— although it is a beginning. You won't be able to do too many repairs requiring power tools, but with a little Moto-tool or ¼-inch electric drill with attachments, you could make trigger repairs and adjustments, install sights, do touch-up bluing and a host of other minor gun repairs.

One person I know, built a sawhorse-type bench with an elevated section at one end, on which he secured a bench vise. A small piece of plywood with a 2x4 screwed into its bottom about center provided a work surface. The 2x4 was gripped in the vise to hold the plywood securely while using it as a work table. The person's weight on the sawhorse provided extra rigidity while working. A checkering cradle could also be secured in the vise, and gun stocks could be checkered while sitting on the sawhorse. Tools were stored on the back of the closet door, and the sawhorse with its attachments was stored in the closet when not in use.

In mild climates a carport may be used for a work area. Tools can be kept in a storage wall or closet at one end of the carport and can be pulled out and used on the platform. Many homeowners use this set-up for storing table saws and lathes, so why not use the same set-up for gun repair work.

Trailer-Shops

If you can't find space in your garage or basement for a suitable work shop, and you don't want to lay out a pile of cash to construct a new outbuilding on your property—especially if you're renting—consider a small travel trailer. Sometime ago, I was able to purchase a used travel trailer for less than $1000. It was about 25 feet long and 8 feet wide. The existing LP gas range provided all the heat I needed for the hot water bluing operation, and the bedroom area made an excellent bench location. Of course the ingenious built-in drawers, cabinets, etc., provided me with all the storage space needed for tools and materials. The gas-fired furnace heated the area snugly, and it really was an ideal set-up.

If you choose to go this route, I'd suggest substituting the small 20-pound gas tanks that come with most Rv's with larger LP gas tanks if you don't plan to move it often. It doesn't take long to use up the gas in the small tanks and nothing is quite as discouraging as finding yourself out of fuel right in the middle of a bluing operation.

3
A WORKBENCH FOR EVERYONE

WHEN THE hobbyist gunsmith begins to think of graduating from the tool-box/repair-kit stage to a full-fledged workshop, his first thoughts undoubtedly turn to a suitable workbench. Unfortunately, there are not very many commercial workbenches to choose from—and those that are available will make your pocketbook look like a sieve.

The next alternative is to build one, but again, workbench plans designed expressly for gun repair work are few and far between; or else the benches are so complicated that it would take a complete woodworking shop to put them together.

The workbench ideas given in this chapter are of simple—yet functional—design and most can be built with conventional hand tools in a relatively short period of time. The reader should find one design that will come close to filling his immediate needs—and at a price he can afford.

Basic Bench Requirements

In general, a workbench should be 30" wide and from 5' to 12' long. Don't skimp on the length, however, because you'll soon find that there is really no such thing as too much bench space—it will become cluttered in a very short time.

The height of the workbench will vary depending on your height. My own workbench is 33½" high and suits me fine. However, you may want yours anywhere from 30" to 35". Above all, the bench must be sturdy and firm. You can not do your best work if the bench moves every time you take a file stroke, or tap a drift pin out of its hole. Therefore, the workbench should be amply reinforced and legs and top should be made of heavy timber.

In addition to the main workbench, it is nice to have an auxiliary bench for special projects. A description of one such bench follows and will come close to fulfilling all of the requirements for an auxiliary workbench. In small shops, this bench will also suffice as a main bench, and although the legs are constructed of 2x4's, the plywood bracing makes it very sturdy.

The exploded drawing seen on the next page shows that the frame is made of 2x4s, solidly interlocked and secured with glue and ¼"x3" FH wood screws. The top consists of two layers of ¾" plywood with one layer of ⅛" hardboard nailed to the top layer of plywood with finishing nails; the shelf also consists of ¾" plywood (only one layer). For maximum rigidity, ⅜" plywood is nailed to the backs and sides. With this arrangement, and with the legs anchored to the floor, the table will not budge under almost any treatment you may want to subject it to.

To begin, lay out the diagram for the top pieces

WORKING PLANS FOR A WORKBENCH

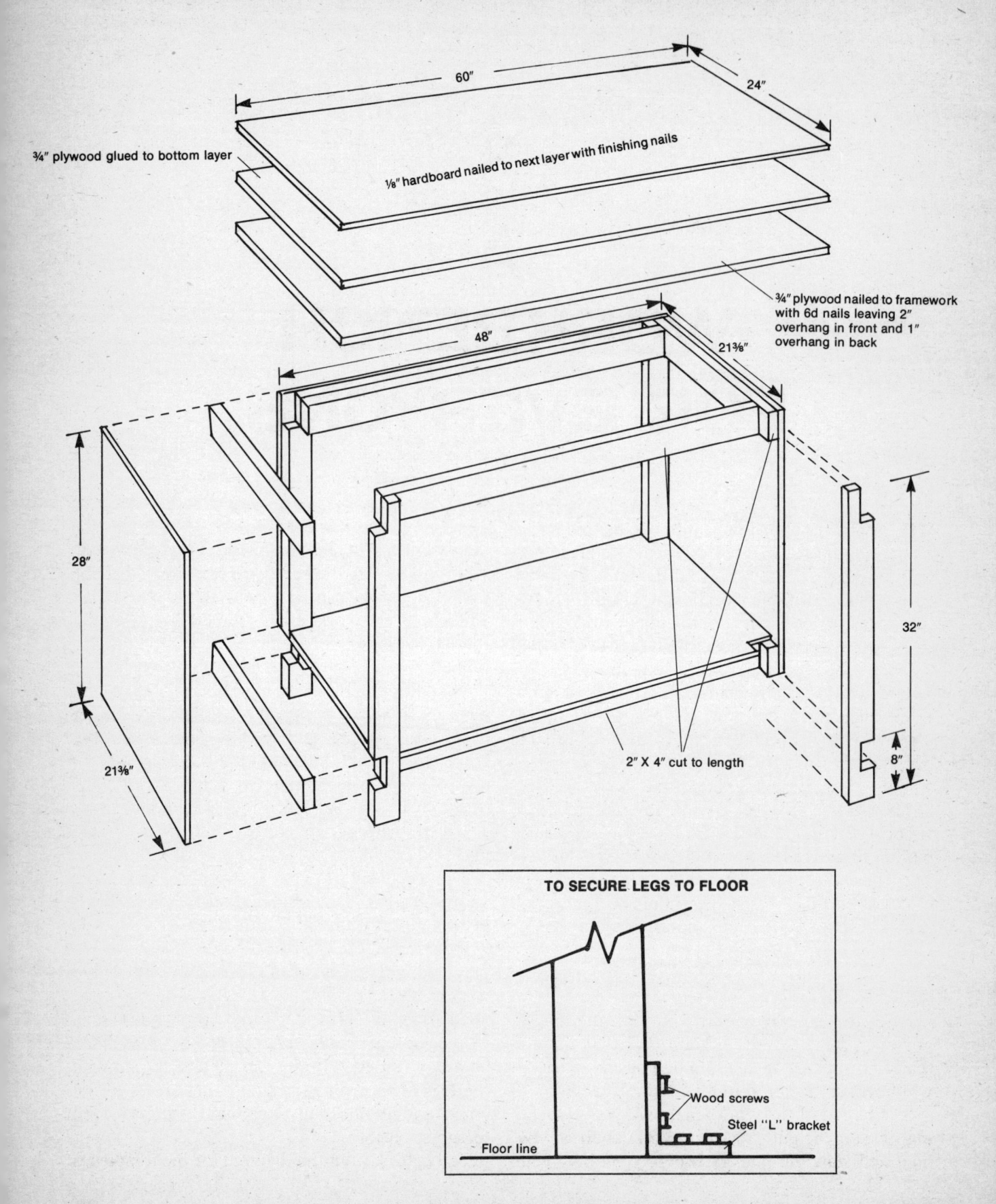

60"
24"
¾" plywood glued to bottom layer
⅛" hardboard nailed to next layer with finishing nails
¾" plywood nailed to framework with 6d nails leaving 2" overhang in front and 1" overhang in back
48"
21⅜"
28"
21⅜"
2" X 4" cut to length
32"
8"

TO SECURE LEGS TO FLOOR

Wood screws
Steel "L" bracket
Floor line

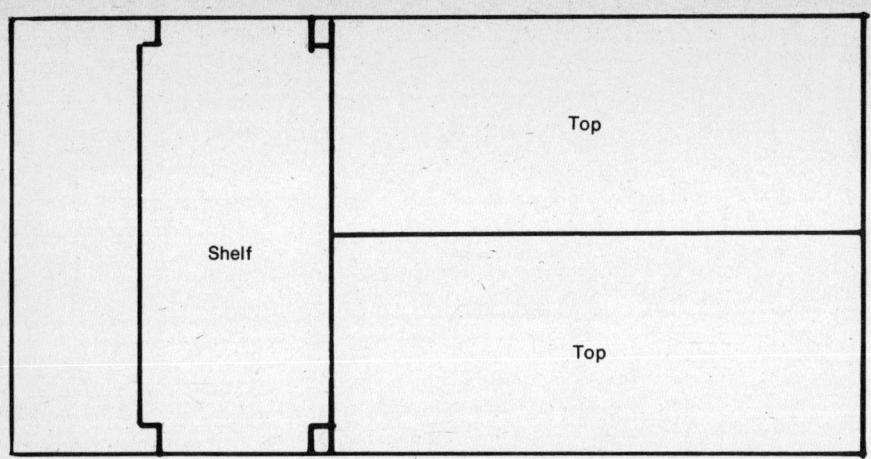

Here is the layout of the ¾" plywood pieces for the basic workbench.

and shelf on a piece of 4'x8'x¾" plywood. Use a straightedge and square for the lines, and then cut out the various pieces with a hand saw.

Next cut all 2x4s, notching the legs as shown in the exploded drawing. Mark and drill screw holes as indicated and then assemble the two end frames with glue and wood screws. You may want to countersink the screw holes for a neat appearance. Join the two end frames with the four long 2x4s, again using glue and wood screws.

Insert the lower shelf as indicated after notching all four corners to fit the bench legs. Nail and glue them in place. At this point, the work should be taking the form of a work bench.

Continue by marking the cutting diagram on the ⅜" plywood for the sides and back—again using a straightedge and square. When they are cut out, nail and glue these panels to the sides and back as shown.

Now nail and glue the lower ¾" top panel to the top rails of the frame, followed by the next panel and the sheet of ⅛" hardboard (nailed only). Keep all of these panels under pressure (using C-clamps) until glue dries.

You could probably get away without nailing the top plywood panel and hardboard (using only glue), but when nailed only, the ⅛" hardboard top may be removed in case it became stained, scratched or damaged.

A simple tool rack, such as the one shown in the

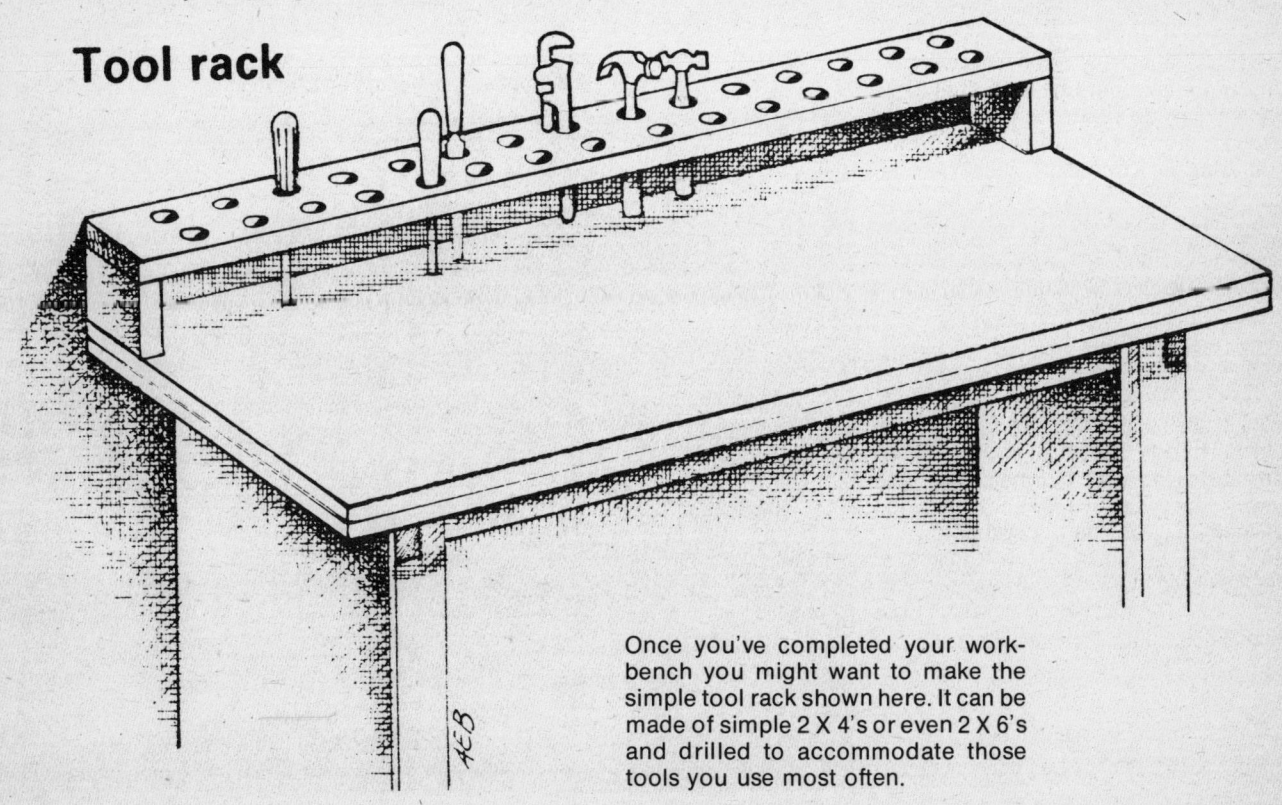

Tool rack

Once you've completed your workbench you might want to make the simple tool rack shown here. It can be made of simple 2 X 4's or even 2 X 6's and drilled to accommodate those tools you use most often.

31

Shelving unit

Front doors

(Above) Shelving is often a handy addition to any bench. The shelving shown can be made of ¾" ply or 1" shelving boards of sufficient width to suit your own needs.

Other handy storage sources are prefabricated wall cabinets that are usually a snap to assemble and darned easy on the pocketbook.

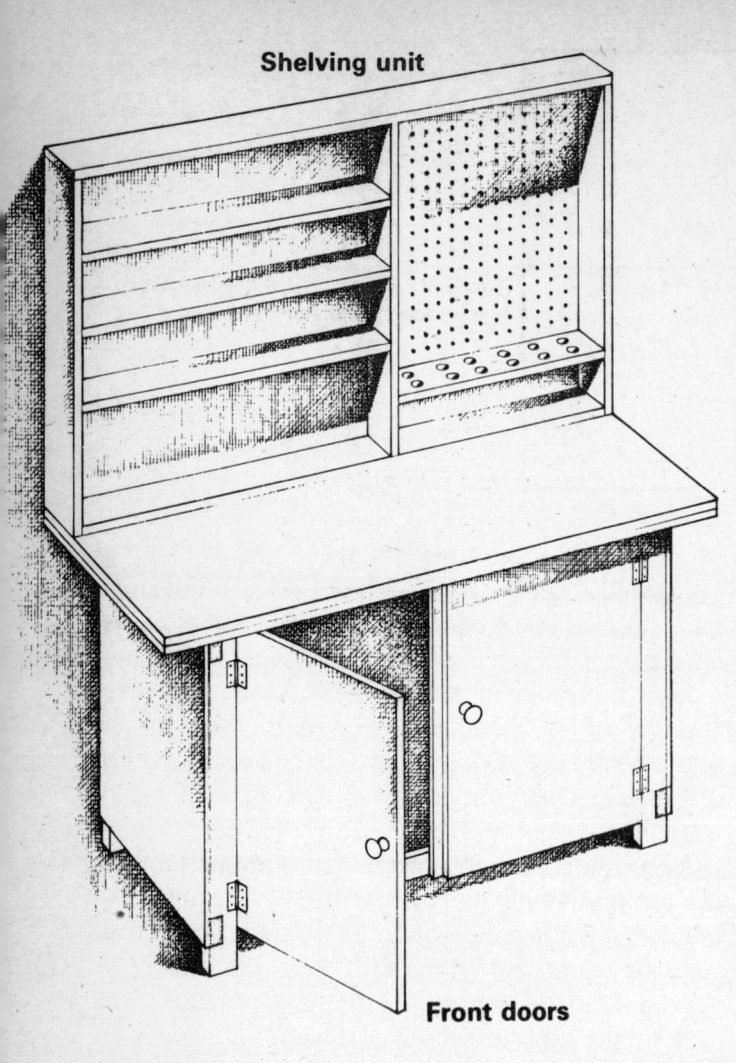

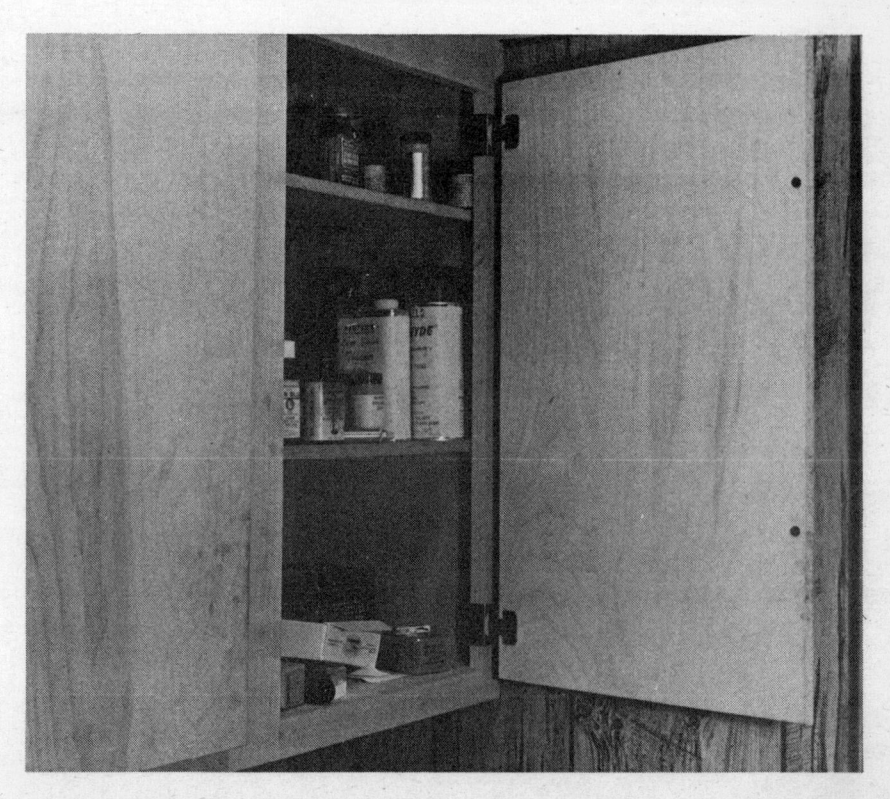

diagram may be added to the top of the bench (at the rear side) for a useful addition. This rack may be constructed of either 2x4s or 2x6s and drilled any way you like to accommodate screwdrivers, drift punches, wood chisels and similar tools.

If you prefer shelves over your bench, a shelving unit may be hung on a wall directly in back of the bench or mounted to the bench top. The top, sides, and shelves may be made from ¾" plywood or 1" shelving boards of a width to suit your needs. A pegboard area is also handy for tool hanging. The overall size of the unit, spacing of shelves, etc. can be varied to suit your needs.

At one time I had a bench vise fitted at the left front corner of the bench and the entire setup served me well for all types of gun repair over a period of several months. However, when I setup my new shop and constructed a new U-shaped built-in workbench, the bench just described was put in my bluing room where it is used mainly for hot water bluing operations.

Wall-Mounted Workbench

My current shop area is approximately 9' x 13' in size and due to the small area, I had to make every inch of space useful. To do so, I designed and constructed a U-shaped workbench to ac-

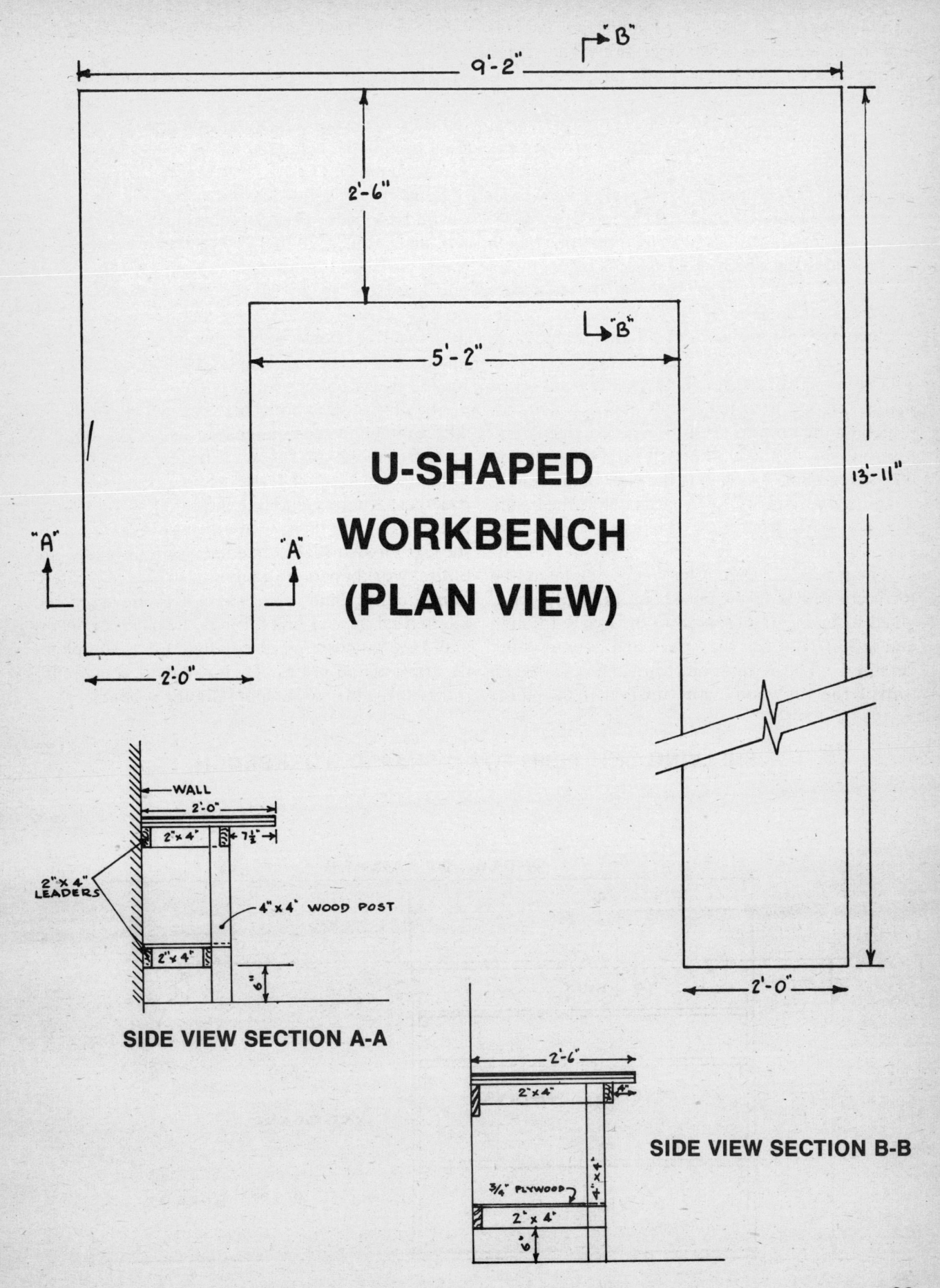

U-SHAPED WORKBENCH
(PLAN VIEW)

SIDE VIEW SECTION A-A

SIDE VIEW SECTION B-B

33

commodate my reloading equipment, power tools and for general gun repair operations The design can be modified to fit practically any size area as may be required.

The basic dimensions of the U-shaped workbench are shown in the illustration. Note in the plan and elevated view that the counter top consists of two different widths: 30" wide for the main section of the bench (under the window) and 24" wide for the side wings. Note also that this bench is wall-mounted which required less labor, materials, and time to complete as compared to a free-standing workbench.

Once the pieces are cut to the dimensions shown, nail a 2"x6" board securely fastened to the wall studs. Also secure a 2"x4" board in the same manner, along with the length of the bench, for attaching the bottom shelf to. These ledgers support one side of the workbench very securely and also saves using 4"x4" legs in the back of the bench. Framing consists of 2"x4" boards, while the bench legs are made from 4"x4" timber. All joints are secured with ¼"x4" lag screws.

When the basic framing has been completed, the top is constructed from two sheets of ¾" plywood, glued together, and secured to the bench framing and ledger with finishing nails and counter-sunk lag screws. The ¼" masonite top is then secured on top of the plywood with finishing nails. This hardboard is really not necessary, but it facilities clean-up since it is smooth, hard and relatively impervious to oils and solvents. Should the top become stained or damaged, merely replace it with another relatively inexpensive piece of hardboard; thus, saving the wooden bench top and protecting it from damage.

Drawers and plywood doors may be added, if desired, for neat storage of tools and supplies. You will also want shelving for storing and arranging tools, parts, and components. Your own ingenuity and available space will determine the best arrangement. A typical over-bench shelving set-up utilizing 1"x8" boards with space for pegboard is illustrated, or use the design previously described for the free-standing workbench.

My shop utilizes both shelves and wall cabinets. The cabinets were obtained at a very reasonable cost from one of the mail-order houses, and although unassembled, they were quite easy to put together. After assembling the cabinets, all that is left to complete them is to either paint or varnish the exterior surfaces. In fact, you can make an entire workbench utilizing these prefabricated components that are designed to be used as kitchen cabinets. Look through the pages of Sears and Montgomery Ward catalogs for a complete description and prices. Then decide if you would rather take this route than building a bench.

SHELVING UNIT PLAN FOR U-SHAPED WORKBENCH

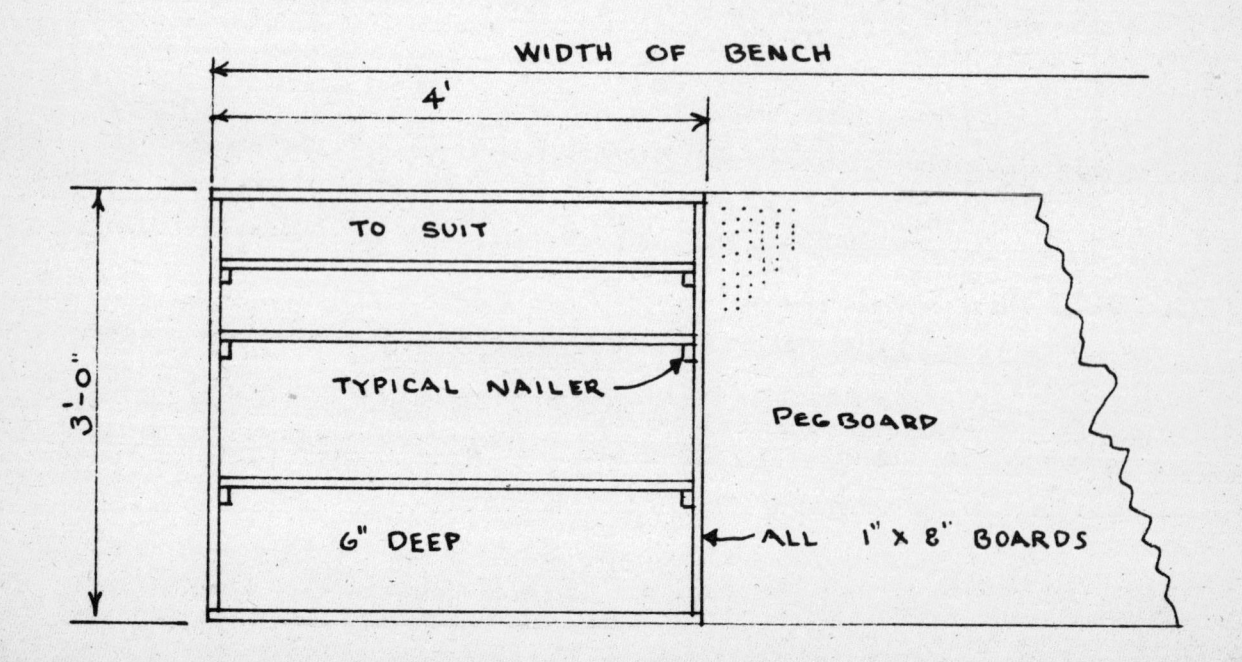

Apartment Workbench

Apartment dwellers in cities are usually handicapped by not having sufficient space in which to do gun repairs. However, it is possible to have a complete workshop in a handsome cabinet that looks like a respectable piece of furiture. John W. Sill, editor and publisher for Outdoor Life/Popular Science Books designed and built such a cabinet when he was cramped for space in his New York apartment. The details of construction are shown in the illustration. While this mini workshop was designed primarily for small woodworking projects, it may easily be adapted for gun repair work.

The hinged top opens to display an ample assortment of gunsmithing hand tools which are held securely in place by hold clips fastened to the bottom of the ¾" plywood top. The narrow panel on the front of the cabinet hinges outward and up to provide access to the 24"x27¾" workbench top which is supported by rollers fitted into slots as shown in the drawing. Stops cut from 1"x2" wood blocks keep the workbench top from coming all the way out from the cabinet while 2"x2" screw-in legs are used to support the work surface.

A raised platform on the bottom shelf of the cabinet can be used to house power tools such as an electric drill motor and Moto-Tool. Note also that an electric cord runs through a hole cut through the bottom to a power outlet. A 24"x18" drawer may be used for other heavy tools while the inner sides of the cabinet doors hold bits, blades, sandpaper and other gunsmithing supplies.

John Sill also designed a frame that is supported by a pole and cross arm that holds plastic sheeting over the workbench for controlling saw dust when sanding. Holes cut at the proper position in the plastic provide access for hand and electric cord for power sander. You will want to reinforce these holes with heavy masking tape. You may also want

PLANS FOR AN APARTMENT WORKBENCH

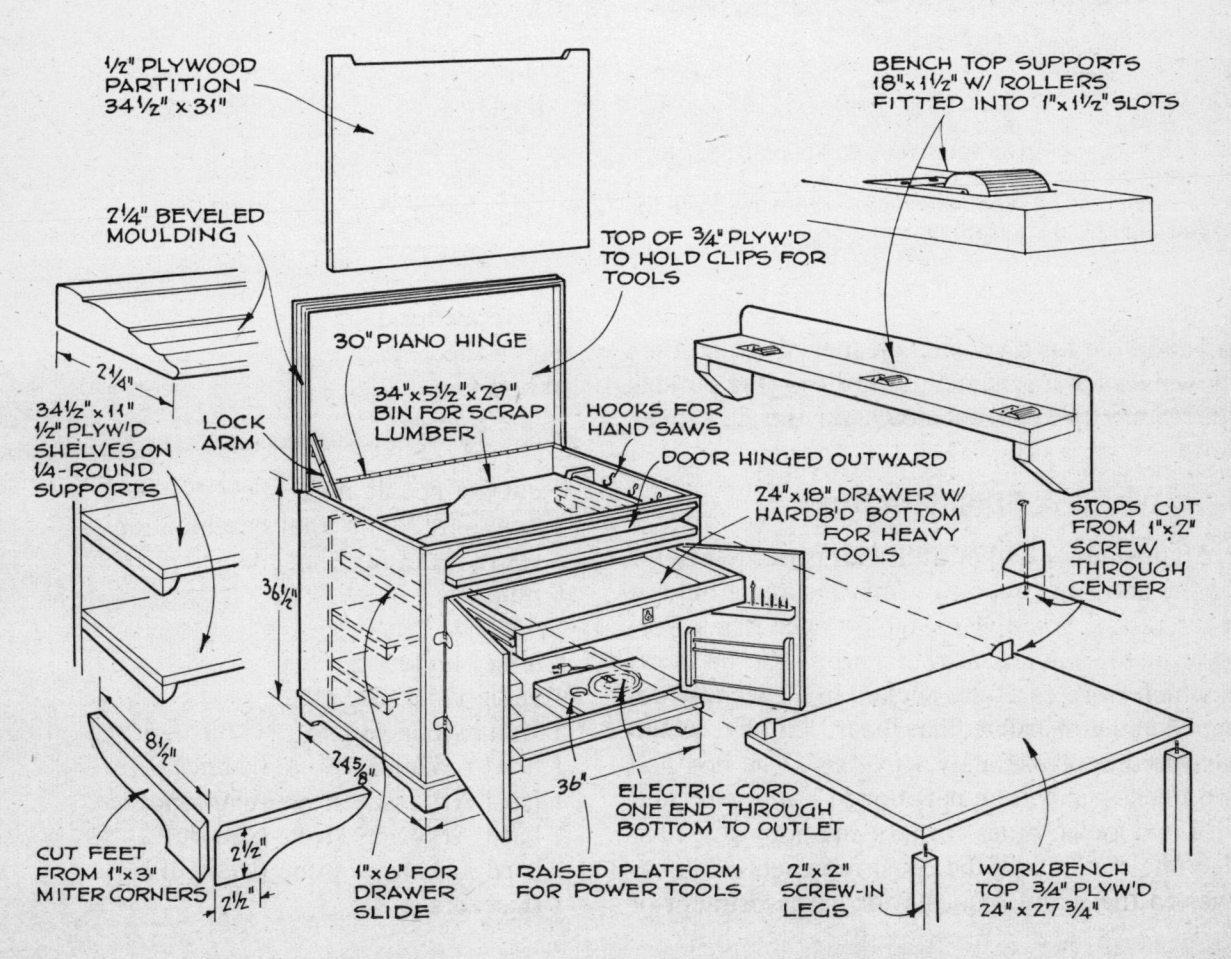

Here's a good look at an apartment workbench made from the plans. As you can see, once the unit is finished you've got a very practical, and handsome, work-spot. Note the hinged top and the assortment of tools.

to cut a hole for a vacuum cleaner hose and then allow the vacuum cleaner to run during the sanding operation; this will cut down on the dust even more.

A Shop in a Box

A gunsmith's tool or utility kit is necessary for repairs and adjustments of firearms in the field or at the range. Some years ago Stoeger Arms Corporation offered a gunsmith's utility kit, all items of which were carefully packed in a specially designed and constructed hardboard kit box, which measured approximately 16"x9"x6". The box had two decks—each one partitioned—and was built with two locks, brass corners and a luggage handle. The contents of the chest represented an answer to the many requests for an assortment of tools and equipment necessary to maintain and make all minor repairs and alterations of firearms. The kit was prepared primarily for use by the gunsmith on the range, or for repairs in the field, but it also contained sufficient materials to satisfy the home requirements of the amateur gunsmith and repairman. An idea of the completeness of the tools and accessories are seen from the following list:

Stock polisher
Stoegerol
Barrel grease
No. 1 patches
No. 4 patches
London Oil finish
Noshine
Tutchup Bluer
No. 1 barrel restorer
No. 2 barrel restorer
X-ring paste
Stockwax
Rustoff
Steel wool
Emery cloth
Carbide lamp
Carving tool set
Swiss needle files
Hand vice
Magnet
Jeweler's loupe
Sportsman's stone
Set of jeweler's screwdrivers
6" screwdriver
8" screwdriver
10" screwdriver
Knife file
Wood rasp
Scale rule
Calipers
1 curved needle nose pliers No. 888
1 heavy-duty slip joint combination
1 short chain nose mechanics pliers
6 punches
Scriber
Christy knife
1 India stone round
1 India stone square
1 hard Arkansas stone (round)
1 hard Arkansas stone (diamond)
1 hard Arkansas stone (square)
1 hard Arkansas stone (triangular)
1 tweezers

PLANS FOR A "SHOP IN A BOX"

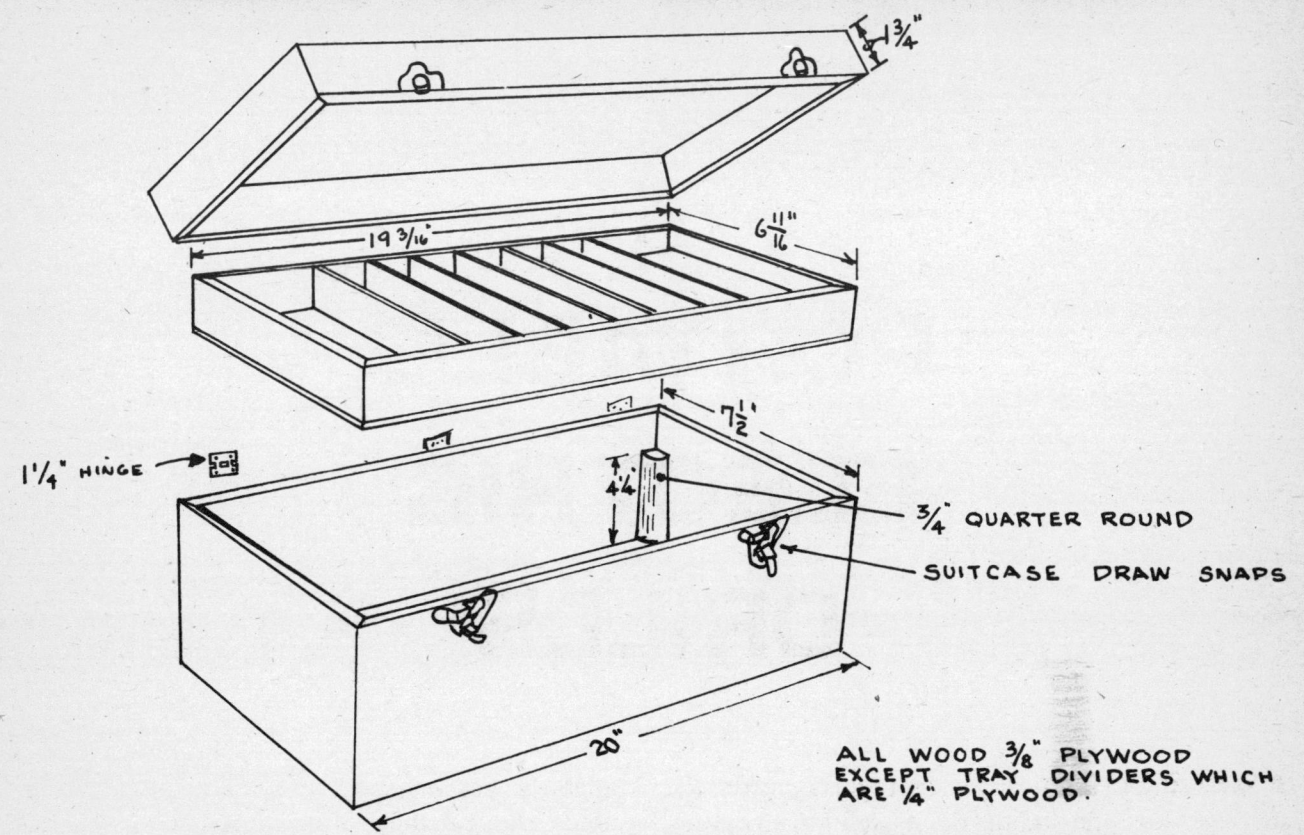

Most gunsmiths have a sturdy tool box—it not only keeps the tools organized, it keeps them protected. The plans shown may be modified to suit your own needs; however, the plans (if followed) provide a box similar to the old Stoeger tool kit the author favors.

1 .22 pistol rod
1 .38 pistol rod
1 rifle and shotgun rod
1 hammer
1 bull dog end cutting nippers

A similar kit may be made up by anyone using current cleaning materials, cold bluing solution, and the tools as described in the list. I would also add one other tool—the popular Dremel Moto-Tool with several accessories. If electric power is not available in the field or on the range, you can still use the tool if you have an automobile close by. An apparatus that runs AC/DC (universal) equipment from DC outputs of cars, trucks and other vehicles equipped with alternators is available at a very reasonable price. Besides operating many power tools such as saws, drills, Unimat 3 lathes, it will also operate appliances such as refrigerators, hot plates and lights.

One model offered by Montgomery Ward and called the Auto/Pod provides 3,750 watts of power at 120 volts DC. To operate this device, connect it to the car's electrical system as per instructions supplied with the kit. Start the engine and plug in the power tool. The tool will receive 120-volt DC power directly from the car's alternator.

A kit to contain your tools may be obtained from several places. You may wish to build your own using the plans above. You can also check the mail-order catalogs for their line of tool boxes. Some tool box/kits are designed on the order of an attaché case for a real neat appearance. Several compartments are provided to contain practically any tool you may wish to carry.

4

PORTABLE ELECTRIC DRILLS

IF YOU should ask what power tool is considered the most versatile and the most useful in any gunshop, the answer from most experts would probably be the electric hand grinder such as the Moto-Tool manufactured by Dremel. However, if you should ask these same gunsmiths what would be the *one* power tool they would keep if they had to get rid of all others, the answer would have to be the portable electric drill motor—with the many available accessories.

Once the gunshop is equipped with several other power tools such as a good drill press, a disc sander, bench grinder and a Moto-Tool, the portable electric drill will probably take a back seat and be used infrequently. But until this time occurs, the portable drill should be the hobbyist's first power equipment without reservation.

Portable electric drills vary in size and horse-

Portable electric drills are suitable for many gunsmithing jobs; it's one of the handiest tools you can purchase.

power rating, but the most common sizes are those that take shanks up to ¼" or ⅜" diameters. The tool is equipped with a trigger switch and most have a locking pin that holds the trigger ON until disengaged. Some even have a speed control and can be reversed. Chucks are of the *geared type* that require a special key for opening and closing.

One problem in using a portable drill with a metal housing is the danger of electric shock, especially when working around damp areas like a basement floor. This is where the third grounding prong on the plug cap comes in handy. If properly connected, by means of a third grounding wire in the cord, to the frame of the drill, a ground fault in the metal housing will cause the circuit breaker, fuse or other means of over-current protection in the main electric panel to trip or blow, or otherwise open the circuit. Many portable drills are now equipped with heavy-duty plastic housings to prevent the user from coming into contact with electric shock. In most cases, these drills do not have a third grounding wire in the cords or caps.

A good choice for the gunshop would be a drill motor that will accept ⅜" diameter shanks and has a variable speed from 0 to 1200 rpm or faster. Such a drill motor will cost you a bit. Less expensive ones can be obtained but you're going to get what you pay for.

Polishing Shotgun Bores

One of the most frequently encountered problems with a shotgun barrel is the scratched or pitted bore. Removing these defects must be done with care lest the choke be damaged.

To correctly polish a shotgun bore, the barrel(s) is (are) first removed from the receiver and inserted in a vise with padded jaws to enable the polishing head to be inserted from the breech end of the barrel. If the shotgun happens to be one of the rare non-takedown types, the polishing can be done from the muzzle end as explained later.

A shotgun barrel polishing head is available from Frank Mittermeier, Inc.. This head comes attached to a 34" long steel rod, which is chucked in an electric hand drill. The head consists of slots to fasten four polishing strips centrally. When the head is revolved at a rapid speed, centrifugal force forces the strips of polishing cloth to the walls of

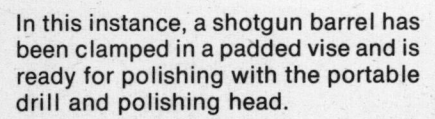

In this instance, a shotgun barrel has been clamped in a padded vise and is ready for polishing with the portable drill and polishing head.

the bore. Only the ends of the strips touch the bore; this allows air to freely circulate inside of the bore which in turn prevents overheating the barrel.

Coarse polishing strips should be used for scratch removal while fine strips or crocus cloth should be used for polishing. The strips are easily changed by unscrewing the slotted bolt, removing the old strips, and then inserting new ones before tightening the bolt.

To polish, chuck the polishing head and steel rod in a portable drill motor; then insert the polishing head in the breech end of the barrel, and start the motor. The polishing head (with polishing strips attached) is slowly pushed forward and back through the bore.

Shotgun barrel polishing heads usually hold several strips (4, in this case) of polishing cloth. The head comes attached to a 34" steel rod and the entire unit is available from Frank Mittermeier.

When it is necessary to insert the polishing head in the muzzle of the barrel, carefully push the head all the way down the barrel to the chamber area before starting the motor. Also finish up in this area and pull the head out with the drill motor OFF.

If the polishing head described herein is not available, fair results can be obtained with a conventional cleaning rod chucked in a drill motor with crocus strips inserted through the eye in the cleaning tip. Many shotgun barrels have also been polished by wrapping steel wool around a cleaning brush (attached to a cleaning rod) and then revolving the assembly through the bore with a drill motor.

Installing Rifle Slings

Sling studs are normally placed at varying distances apart, usually between 26" and 28", with the rear stud located about 3" from the toe of the stock.

If no studs have been previously fitted to the stock, two holes will have to be drilled to accept the studs and swivels. In general, the rear stud screws directly into the wood, while the front studs require a special retaining nut which presses firmly into the wood of the forearm so as not to protrude against the barrel. Therefore, the front hole must be drilled completely through the stock; both holes must be countersunk.

An excellent swivel installation tool kit is available from B-Square Co. This kit enables sling swivels to be installed quickly on any stock without risk of damage. The "V" jig has a hardened drill guide bushing and will automatically locate the $5/32"$ diameter drill (furnished with the kit) the correct distance from the fore-end or from the toe.

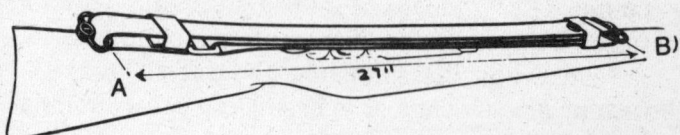

For best results, sling swivels should be located approximately 27" apart, the rear stud (A) about 3" from the toe of the stock.

When it comes to accurately installing sling swivels, the B-Square swivel installation kit is superb. Not only does the kit assure accuracy, it speeds up the entire swivel-installation process.

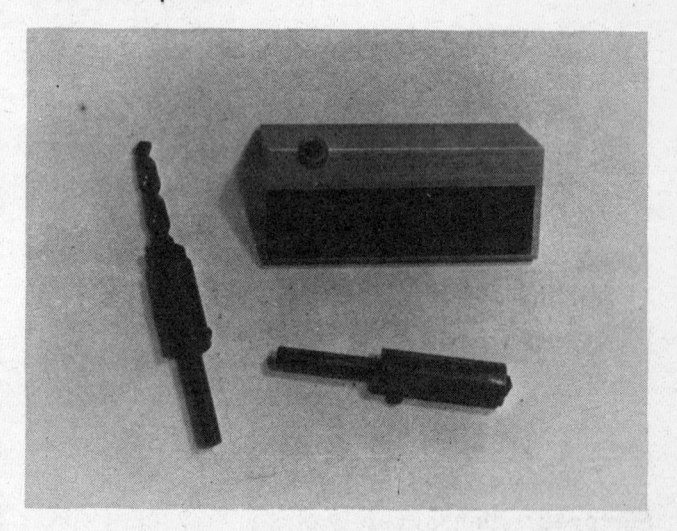

Furthermore, it will guide the drill on the exact center of the stock edge or in the exact center of the barrel channel.

To install the rear swivel turn the rifle upside down and clamp it in a suitable padded vise—a Decker gun vise works nicely for this job. Place the swivel jig over the edge of the stock so that its end is flush with the butt; this puts the pilot drill about 2½" from the butt. Insert the $5/32"$ pilot drill in an electric hand drill and align the swivel jig to drill a hole approximately 1" deep.

Exchange the $5/32"$ pilot drill for the $7/32"$ diame-

40

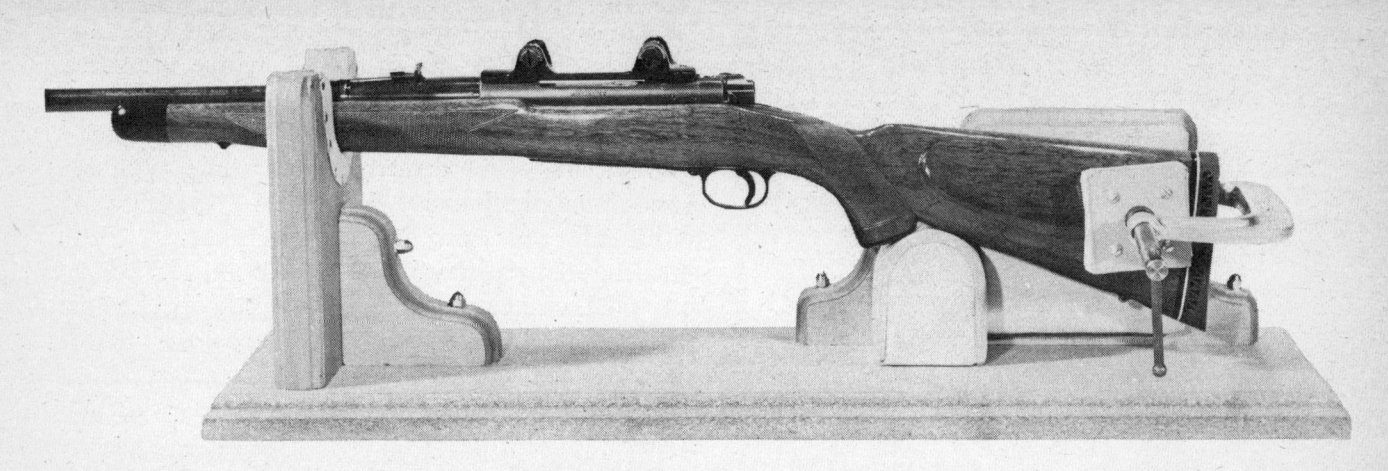

(Above) One of the author's favorite "tools" for many gunsmithing chores is the Decker Vise. As shown, it's perfect for bore cleaning or scope mounting. By inverting the rifle and clamping it in place, the Decker Vise is perfect for sling swivel installation.

ter safety counter-bore and counter-bore the $5/32''$ hole just drilled. This last operation provides for the unthreaded portion of the swivel screw.

Before inserting the swivel screw into the gun stock, it should be dipped in linseed oil to seal the wood and bind the fibers. Then, using a swift punch or a common nail as a wrench, screw the swivel screw into the gun stock until its cross hole is correctly positioned when tight down against the stock. Never use the swivel itself as a wrench.

To install the front swivel screw on most one-piece rifle stocks, remove the barreled action from the stock and clamp the stock in a padded vise so that the barrel channel is *up*. Place the swivel jig in the barrel channel with the "V" down. Its end should be flush with the fore-end tip so that the drill will be approximately 2½" back from the tip. The jig is designed to center the $5/32''$ pilot drill in the barrel channel, so use this drill in the drill motor and hole completely through the gun stock. Then enlarge this hole with the No. 10 safety drill which will counter-bore for the swivel nut all in one operation. Again, coat the counter-bored hole with linseed oil and press the swivel screw nut into the counter-bore. A small amount of Loc-Tite should be placed on the screw threads before tightening the swivel screw into the nut. Use a drift punch or a nail to tighten. Be sure that the front swivel installation is permanent; an improper installation can greatly affect accuracy not to mention the damage that could be caused to the gun should it be dropped.

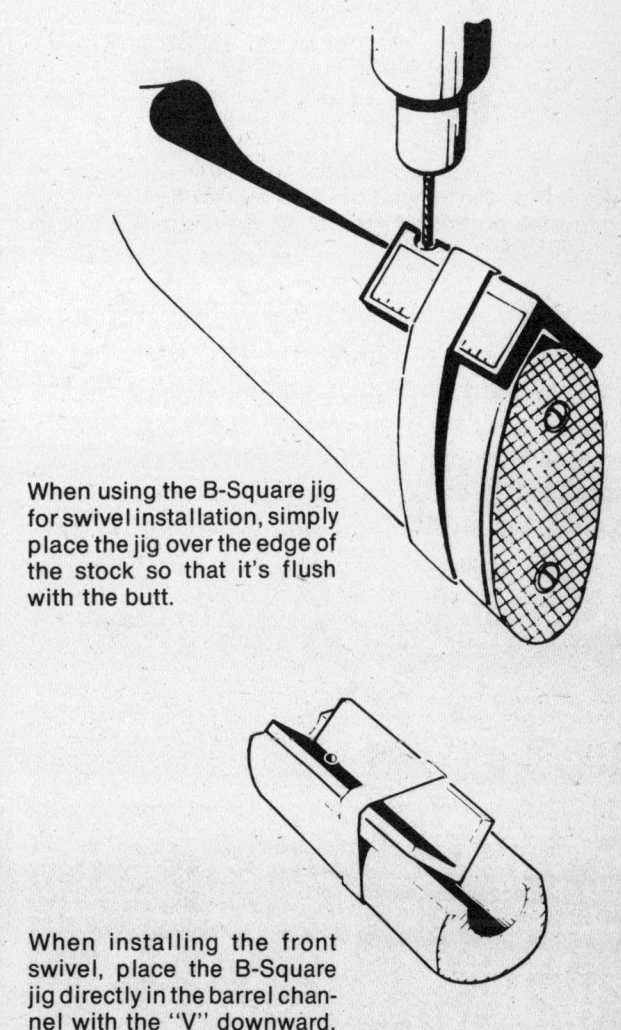

When using the B-Square jig for swivel installation, simply place the jig over the edge of the stock so that it's flush with the butt.

When installing the front swivel, place the B-Square jig directly in the barrel channel with the "V" downward.

Installing Recoil Pads

A disc sander attachment is available for portable electric drills and will find much use around any gunshop that does not have a combination belt and disc sander. One use of the disc sander is for working down new recoil pads to fit the stock.

In most cases, some of the stock will have to be

Adding a recoil pad is a job most gunsmiths will be called to do. A Dem-Bart layout guide is perfect for accurately scribing the portion of the butt to be removed prior to pad installation.

cut off prior to installing the pad. If the stock "feel" is right with a conventional hard rubber butt plate and you want to add a thicker recoil pad, first measure the thickness of the two pads, subtract the difference, and this will be the amount to cut off. One word of caution. A stock that feels long may not be as long as it feels. Therefore, cut off only about 1/8- to 1/4-inch at a time until the gun feels right and shoulders properly.

Once the amount to be cut off has been determined, mark the distance with some type of scriber and depth gauge. I find that a layout guide is ideal for this marking. Although designed for insuring that checkering patterns come out properly positioned and truly parallel to the top line of the fore-end, when the arm is laid across the butt of the stock and the scriber adjusted to score a line around the butt, a true parallel is assured for use as a guide for sawing.

Before sawing, however, apply masking tape around the butt of the stock, even with the scribed line. This will prevent the wood from splintering and will also act to protect the stock finish when the recoil pad is worked down.

You may secure the stock in a padded vise and make the cut with either a hack saw or a regular hand saw, but a deep miter box is better and cleaner cuts can be obtained if you use a hack saw. Regardless of the type of saw you use, it should be fine-toothed with at least ten teeth per inch to minimize splintering.

After sawing off the end of the stock, true-up the surface with a rasp, but be careful not to cause splinters, shorten the stock or bevel the edges. Make sure the pad selected is large enough to

(Left) When removing a section of buttstock for recoil pad installation, be sure to mask off the area of the stock immediately adjoining the cut-line. (Below) The masking tape will help prevent splintering or marring during the actual cutting of the stock and the final shaping of the pad.

permit the bottom plane of the stock to continue through the toe of the pad. You may also want to apply Prussian blue or some other marking material to the inside surface of the pad before the preliminary mounting of the pad. When removed, the color transfer and lack of color on the wood indicates high spots which should be corrected for a perfect pad/butt contact. In other words, those spots on the stock butt that show color should be trimmed down.

To mount the pad, scribe a line down the exact center of the stock butt, from heel to toe. Then center the pad in position on the butt and mark the top screw hole with an ice pick or similar sharp object. Drill a starter hole 1" deep with a ⅛" bit on the centerline and as near to the mark made by the ice pick as possible. Depending upon the size of screw, widen the hole enough so that the threads of the recoil pad screw will make firm contact with the wood; make this second cut about ½" deep, then insert the top screw, position the pad and tighten it down.

Now mark the bottom screw hole in the same manner as the top hole, before loosening the top screw and swinging the butt plate aside so that the bottom hole may be drilled. Tighten down both screws and with a sharp scribe, trace the outline of the stock on the inside of the recoil pad. This line is for the disc sanding that follows.

Secure the electric drill in a vise or drill bench stand so that the sanding disc, chucked into the drill, is readily accessible. Then remove the recoil pad from the butt of the stock and remove all but about ⅛" of the recoil-pad material on the outside of the scribed line. Be absolutely *certain* that you leave enough material on the toe so that the plane of the stock may be continued when you finish up the fitting. Leave this part of the shaping until later.

The rough-shaped pad is then remounted on the stock and tightened down. Make sure that sufficient masking tape is still on the stock to help prevent scratching or marring the stock or finish. You may even want to apply another layer of glass tape over the masking tape for further protection. Install a fine sanding disc on the drill, and finish trimming the recoil pad until it is exactly even with the stock. For the last few thousandths of an inch, you might want to switch over to a fine-toothed file to insure accuracy; or perhaps to garnet paper wrapped around a file.

The B-Square Co. of Fort Worth, Texas, offers

USING B-SQUARE'S RECOIL PAD JIG

When using a B-Square recoil pad installation jig, the procedure is as follows: (1) Carefully centering the pad on the butt of the gun, scribe a line on the pad that follows the outside dimensions of the butt. Next (2), place the butt pad upside down on the jig; and (3) set the toe and heel angles with a square prior to final disc sanding.

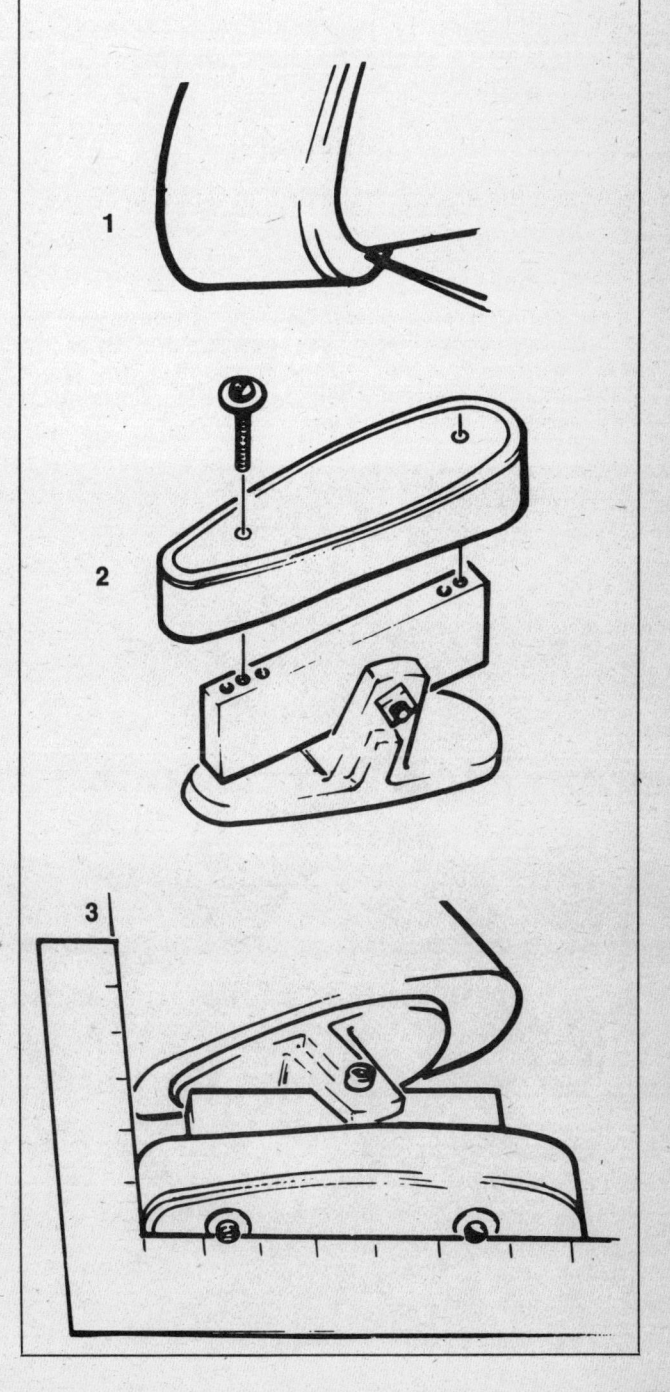

a recoil pad jig that makes installing a recoil pad easier and with less risk to wood damage. To use, just scribe the exact outline of the stock butt on the pad back and place it upside down on the pad jig. Set the toe and heel angles with a square and completely finish it by sanding with a disc sander as described previously. You can do a perfect job every time with absolutely no risk to a gun stock. All shaping and finishing is done completely off the stock.

The pad jig comes with complete illustrated instructions. These instructions are easy to follow and are detailed step-by-step. They will show you how to fit the gun to the shooter, how to cut off the stock, how to shape the pad, and many other useful details.

Jeweling

When the electric hand drill is set up in an inexpensive drill press—available from most tool supply houses, hardware stores, etc.—the little drill becomes an altogether handier tool. One of the operations consists of jeweling bolts for rifles and shotguns.

Jeweling is a form of decorating the metal surface in a series of fine concentric circles on a polished surface. Its purpose is decorative, but it provides a wear indicator and a possibility of "holding oil" for protection. It's a relatively simple operation and adds class to fine guns. The process is done with many different devices such as rubber abrasive rods (pencil erasers will work fine), dowels with abrasive paper glued to the end, or a fine wire brush "charged" with oil or abrasive compound.

When jeweling bolts, it is recommended that a specially designed fixture be used to hold the bolt to be decorated. The fixture containing the bolt is

If you don't have a disc sander, you can purchase the appropriate accessories for your portable drill. By securing the drill with sanding attachments in a vise, you'll have a sturdy sanding unit perfectly suited for finishing off any recoil pad installation job.

One of the most common jobs a gunsmith will get requests for is bolt-body jeweling. The bolt jig shown holds the bolt securely and insures the job will be accurately and attractively done. (Jigs such as this one can be obtained from any of the major gunsmith-tool houses.)

placed on a drill press table so that the bolt body is centered under the jeweling tool which is held in the drill chuck. The bolt is coated with abrasive compound; then the pattern may be started at either end of the bolt, but each row of concentric circles must start from the same end. The drill motor should run at medium speed as it is brought down onto the bolt. Then the fixture is moved approximately one-half diameter of the circle and again the brush is brought down to overlap spots on the surface of the bolt. This continues for one row, then the bolt is rotated approximately one-half circle diameter and the process repeated. This continues until the bolt has been fully jeweled in the areas desired.

Scope Mounting

The electric hand drill is also a valuable tool for mounting scope sights on rifles—especially when used in combination with a drill press and the scope jigs offered by B-Square. One such B-Square jig is made for the Winchester Model 94. This jig accurately locates the holes for Weaver side mount bases on the Winchester Model 94 lever action rifle. It is precision made and has four hardened No. 28 drill jig bushings correctly spaced to match the Weaver base and provides for its shoulder. It automatically locates (without measuring) the mounting holes to provide clearance with holes already in the gun. A clamp bolt, nut and special washer are provided to hold the jig to the gun while drilling.

When drilling holes for scope bases, use a new standard high speed drill bit for each job as this will save time. The shorter screw machine drill bits are best since the longer ones tend to wander. Use cutting oil sparingly. The holes should be of the proper depth to allow the holes to be tapped, but *not* so deep as to protrude into the bore, chamber or other undesirable area.

Use a new tap for each job as this is cheap insurance against a broken off tap in the drilled hole. Three or four flute hand taps should be used as these are stronger than the 2-flute types. The 2-flute taps will also cut oversize if not guided. Use a special tapping oil such as Tap Magic supplied by Brownell's Inc. Tap Magic prevents any weldment of any type metal to the cutting tool. It permits the tool to cut freely and produces a finer chip with a minimum of galling and friction. The extremely high rate of evaporation of Tap Magic also makes it act as a refrigerant, thus keeping the tool cool, sharp and cutting.

Some guns may have to have their hardened receivers annealed before you're able to drill them. Polish the spot(s) to be drilled—usually an area the size of a dime—and proceed to heat the polished spot with the tip of a needle point acetylene torch. Heat the spot until the metal turns dark blue. Remove the torch and, with a piece of 400 wet or dry sandpaper, polish the blue spot (while hot) with a few quick strokes till the blue is removed. Repeat the process. About the third time around, and after you've given the blue spot a few quick strokes with the 400 wet or dry, you'll notice that after you knock the blue off, the polished spot will suddenly turn blue again. This lets you know the annealing job has been completed and the receiver's ready for drilling.

Once the receiver is drilled and tapped, provisions must be made so that the scope tube can be clamped without bending, binding, twist-

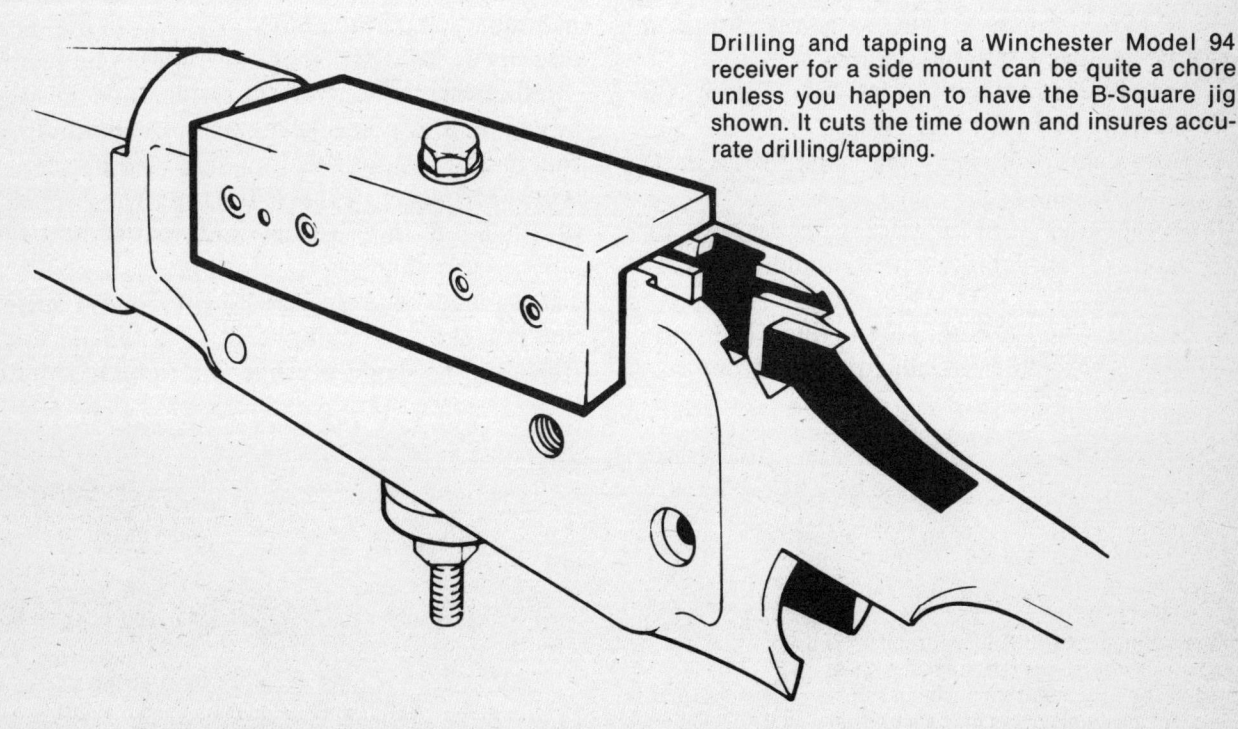

Drilling and tapping a Winchester Model 94 receiver for a side mount can be quite a chore unless you happen to have the B-Square jig shown. It cuts the time down and insures accurate drilling/tapping.

ing, collapsing, etc. Any deflection will change the point of impact and any change in temperature will change the stress and deflect the scope. Therefore, it is important that the scope be mounted without any stress or strain. Since high magnification scopes require the most corrective adjustment in mounting, only the Redfield and the Leupold type bases and rings will be considered. To install scopes in these type mounts:

1. Install base without bending. Tighten with perfect fitting screwdriver. Any chemical screw retention liquid is considered a "crutch" and if it is a good screw (and threads are correctly tightened) it will stay tight. Most important, it can be removed without damage.
2. Install rear ring with slight "play" so it will be partially self-aligning.
3. Lubricate front ring "key" and install in its base "key hole."
4. Rotate and/or oscillate ring in its base by using a lever until it is just free enough to turn by hand only.
5. Remove the top halves of the rings. Place the scope in the saddles by adjusting the front saddle until the scope is free to enter and "touch bottom" completely.
6. Replace caps, lightly tighten screws and align cross hairs.
7. Tighten all cap screws even and tight with a screwdriver that *fits*.
8. Bore sight and line up scope using base windage adjustment screw. Finally adjust both windage and elevation using scope's internal adjustments.

It is important to use only a minimum of the scope's internal adjustment to prevent stress and strain. If the scope is strained by excessive internal adjusting, re-machine or re-adjust the base to attempt to zero the scope using its mount only.

When using Weaver type rings and bases, no adjustment is possible other than shimming, and this method is not recommended for professional work. However, if this is the only way, use a pair of small tin snips to cut and shape the needed shims—use thin brass shim material. Be sure to cut a piece wide enough to offer good support, yet not show from under the scope or mount. Place under scope in rings and tighten down.

Often times, you'll find yourself in a position where you'll need some shim stock for jobs such as scope mounting. A small pair of tin snips are ideal for cutting up brass sheeting when shim stock is needed.

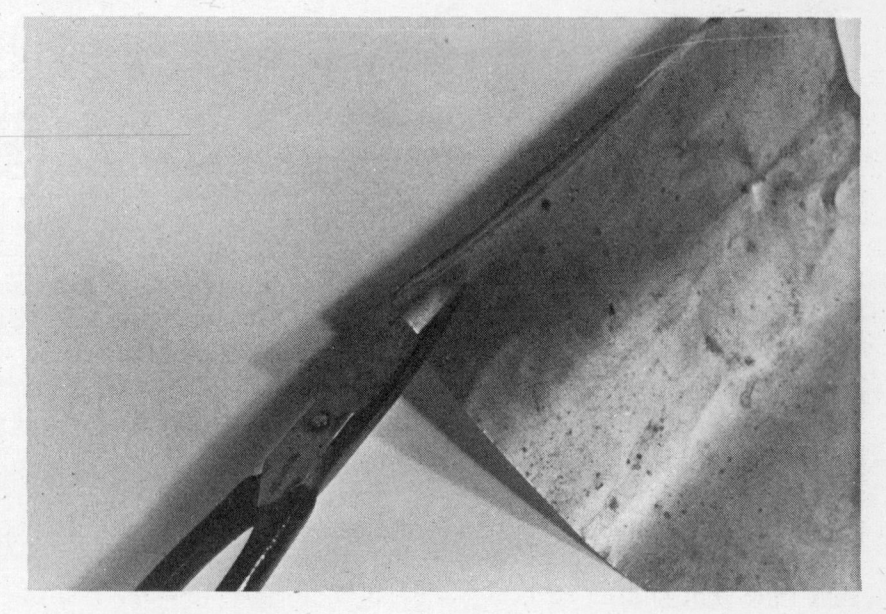

—5—
THE THIRD HAND

THE BENCH VISE should be one of the first tools considered by anyone who anticipates working on firearms. Without a good vise even the better mechanics are near helpless when it comes to some types of gun repairs.

A vise is a clamping device, usually consisting of two jaws which close and open on a threaded shaft which is turned by a lever. Most attach to a bench and are used for holding a piece of work firmly. There are a great variety of vises used by gunsmiths and a description of each follows.

Vises

Pin Vises

A set of pin vises is useful for holding rods and pin stock for filing. They are also useful for holding scriber points, small files, taps, drills and the like. A hole extends through the set manufactured by Starrett® so that wires or a rod of any length may be held. The handle is reduced in size so that it may be rapidly rotated between the thumb and finger when filing small work. The jaws are hardened and close fitting, and with a few turns of the binding nut a firm grip may be obtained with them. The handle and binding nut on the set shown are nickel plated. The entire set will handle work from 0 to .187".

A similar vise, the *screw head polishing vice*, is

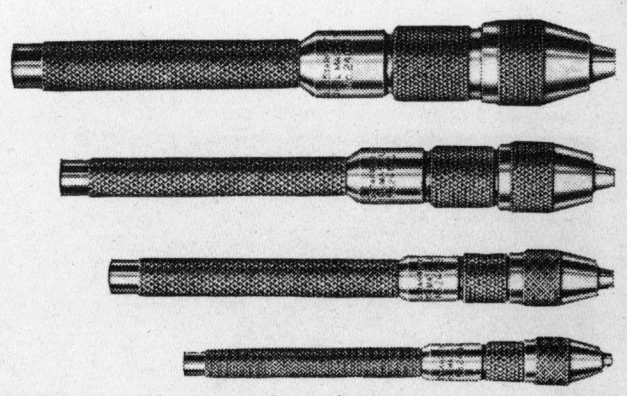

A set of pin vises are useful for holding rods and pin stock for filing.

A screw head polishing vise is used to hold gun screws and pins while polishing on a buffing wheel.

used to hold gun screws and pins while polishing the screw heads to get them ready for bluing. Obviously, this tool saves burned fingers not to mention those screws that snap out of the fingers while they're being polished and become lost in the shop. This particular vise will handle screws up to ¼" in diameter. To "load," merely loosen the chuck, insert the screw (thread end first) and the screw head is exposed for polishing. This vise may also be used for holding screws while they are being blued by the heat/oil-dip method as described in Chapter 9 on bluing equipment.

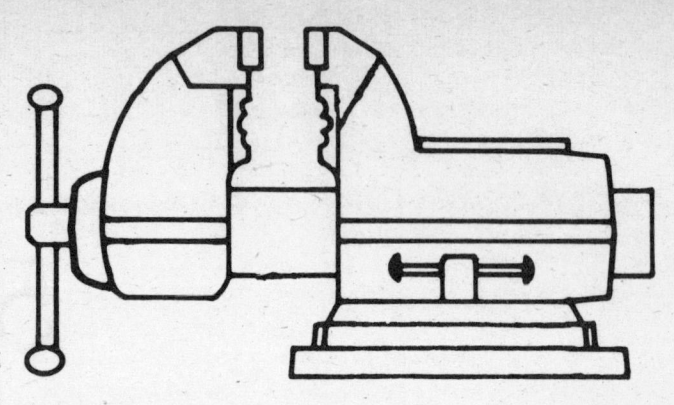

Eventually the gunsmith will need a heavy machinist's vise for the type of work he'll be called upon to do.

Combination Vise

The combination vise is ideal for home workshops and will also find use around professional shops that are not too demanding. This vise is furnished with replaceable steel serrated jaws, an anvil surface, auxiliary jaws for clamping round stock, an anvil horn for forming and bending and a swivel base with locking clamp and handle.

Eventually the gunsmith will need a heavy *machinist's* vise. These almost indestructible vises have been a favorite of the serious gunsmith for longer than most of us can remember. If you select a machinist's vise that is strong and heavy enough, it will also double as a barrel vise if a few accessories are added. Clamp two hardwood blocks in the vise and drill a hole at the joint of the smallest diameter of a tapered barrel. Then contour the hole to the barrel shape (you may need

A combination vise is ideal for home workshops as well as gunshops.

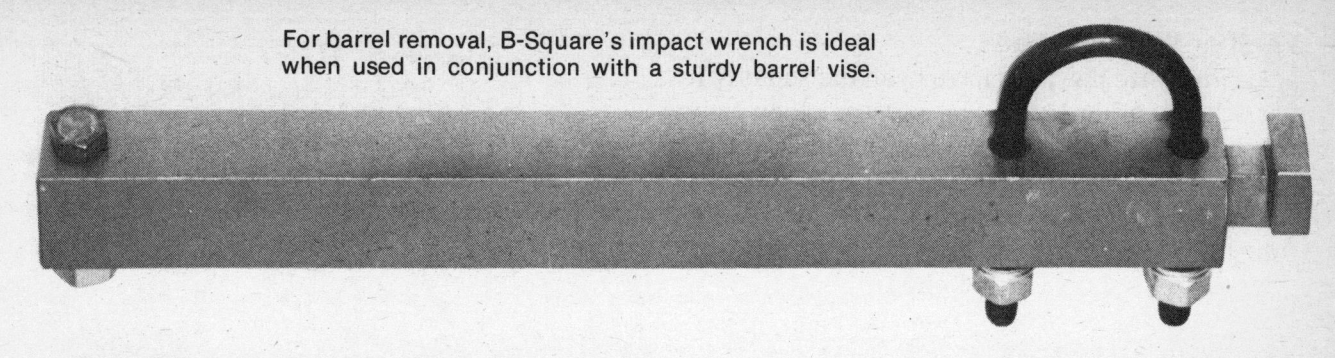

For barrel removal, B-Square's impact wrench is ideal when used in conjunction with a sturdy barrel vise.

several such blocks). Powdered rosin is then sprinkled onto the barrel to prevent it from slipping and the barrel is clamped between the two blocks which are held by the vise jaws.

Once you have the barrel tightly clamped in the vise, you'll need some type of wrench to grasp the action securely without damaging the finish on the action. The B-Square action wrench is designed especially for this job. This wrench consists of a heavy steel bar made to fit both flat-bottomed and rounded receivers. For flat-bottomed actions, the flat part of the wrench bears against the flat bottom of the action; if the action is rounded, the clamp ring fits into the bottom grooves.

Some barrels are nigh onto impossible to remove, but the application of some penetrating oil will help tremendously. Once the wrench is secured to the action, tests have shown that a single impact blow with a 5-lb. hammer against the wrench will often loosen a barrel when brute force will not.

Another wrench that will work on some barreled actions is the type that's designed for working on PVC (plastic) pipe without marring the pipe. If a piece of 2-in. pipe, about 5' long, is wedged over the short pipe handle, the leverage provided will remove a number of pistol and rifle barrels. However, if the barrel has rusted to the receiver, as is often the case with old military rifles, chances are you're going to break the web "jaws" before loosening the barrel. Due to the price, however, this little wrench is worth a try—especially for the hobbyist. It's available from Brookstone Tool Company and costs about one quarter of a standard barrel wrench.

Versa-Vise

I've seen this vise advertised in the *American Rifleman* way back when I was still hunting with my Daisy Red Ryder BB gun. It is easily the most universal vise ever built for the hobbyist or a second vise for the professional gunsmith. The Versa-Vise gives both vertical and horizontal holding positions and rotates in a full circle in either position. The vise automatically locks in any position when the jaws are clamped tight for holding the workpiece at the most favorable position when filing, grinding, polishing, soldering, etc. Such vises, however, are not designed for rough treatment and should be used only as a second vise for gun repair work.

Vise Accessories

To prevent marring of blued metal surfaces as well as wood finishes the bench vise should be equipped with removable copper, brass, lead, leather or wood vise jaws.

Special wrenches designed for PVC pipe can also be used on *some* gun actions for barrel removal providing the barrel has not rusted to the action.

Leather Vise Jaw Pads

Leather vise jaw pads have been the standby to use when working with gun parts or other items that are subject to marring. The pads may be glued to the vise jaws or may be backed with masonite providing removable pads that rest on the vise frame slide. Of course, they may be used as separate pads as shown in the photo.

Lead Vise Jaw Faces

Lead sheets are easily shaped to fit your precision machinist vise or heavy shop vise jaws. They prevent rough vise jaws from marring delicate or polished parts while holding them firmly in place. They also help to hold parts so they will not slip at a lower vise-jaw pressure.

(Above and left) Leather vise jaw pads are indispensable when working on gun parts that are subject to marring.

Slide-on Rubber Jaws

The Dremel vise can be set up with slide-on rubber jaws that protect easily marred items you may be working on. Similar protection is offered by the nylon jaws on the swivel vise. Either pair of these jaws must be removed or protected with wood blocks before applying heat to any part being held in these vises.

Wood Jaws

Jaws made from ¼" plywood will come in handy around the gunshop for holding specific items

Bronze vise pads are generally shaped from 60-to 40-degrees of angle and make excellent working jaws for all types of bench vises.

Bronze Vise Jaws

Bronze jaws are best shaped at 60- to 40-degree angles to make perfect working jaw faces for your heavy bench vise, drill press vise or precision machinist vise. They may be readily formed to fit any vise top contour and they prevent marring of parts being held. Such jaws also act as a heat sink (draws off heat) when holding parts to be heated. They are available from Brownell's in three lengths—3", 4" and 12".

(Left) Slide-on rubber jaws, as found on this Dremel D-Vise, are used to protect easily marred items.

(Below) Jaws that are made of materials such as nylon or rubber must either be removed or protected with wood blocks before applying heat to any part being held in the vise.

without marring the finish. You can make a set from scrap lumber. Such jaws give a little firmer grip than leather and offer about the same degree of protection.

Octagon Barrel Holding Vise Jaws

Aluminum holding jaws can be made to fit any conventional bench vise, and should be specially machined with a "V"-shaped groove that matches the angle of octagon barrels. Two self-adjusting pins keep the holding jaws in alignment in the vise. Such jaws are highly recommended for safe, strong, non-slip holding of any octagon barrel that needs to be locked-up securely in the vise to be worked on.

CUT TO WIDTH OF VISE JAWS

NOTCH TO FIT VISE

¼" PLYWOOD

As can be seen here, it's pretty easy to make a set of vise-jaw pads from ¼" plywood.

Super-Hold Vise Jaw Pads

Brownell's recently offered a set of superhold

51

B-Square octagon barrel holding jaws are made to fit any conventional bench vise. They are particularly handy for the gunsmith who does a fair amount of black powder gun work.

vise jaws that are made of new space-age elastomerics that grip the work piece and hold it securely without any slipping, marring or straining. They don't even require excessive clamping pressure to insure a non-slip grip. The pad material was developed for missile launch tube liners, so it is obviously tough and does not readily impregnate. They'll give years of useful service.

Each pad measures 3"x4" and is permanently bonded to ¼" aluminum plate that measures 5"x4" wide. They may be custom fitted to your vise by notching the bottom of the plate for the adjusting bar on the vise. Two types are available: *Red*—for wood, plastic, and other soft materials. *Green*—for metals and other hard materials.

Drill and Bench Vise

A drill vise is a very versatile tool with unlimited uses. It may be secured to a rotary compound table or clamped into a conventional bench vise for holding work firmly at any angle for cutting, drilling or filing. The jaws of this vise have one cross groove and one perpendicular groove for holding round work, yet these grooves do not effect flat work.

The drill vise is an absolute must for positioning and rigidly holding work that must be drilled with wobble-free precision and accuracy. The jaws on the vise pictured are 2⁷⁄₁₆" wide and have a maximum opening of 2½". It will tilt up to 90 degrees.

Rotary Compound Table

The rotary compound table provides compound slides as well as rotary feed in one compact unit. Cross-feed screws are ½" Acme thread, and provide transverse and longitudinal travel of 4¼". Cross-feed dials are 1" diameter, graduated in

This drill and bench vise is a very versatile tool with unlimited uses around the gunshop.

thousandths. The rotary feed dial is 1¾" diameter, and is calibrated in 3 minute intervals. Such a table makes possible the finest of precision drilling as the three adjustments will center the drill exactly. For scope and sight work it is unequalled, and when used in combination with the drill and bench vise described above, provides an even more versatile arrangement. Detailed indexing operations may be found in Chapter 16, Milling Machines.

Practical Applications

The following are a few of the practical uses of vises—of different types—in the gunshop. While the list is not nearly complete, those listed should stir the imagination enough to bring to light many other uses that may be applied daily to gun work. Remember that nearly all work in the gunshop requires the work to be held in a certain position, and the vise—or its kin—is necessary for most of them.

Bore Sighting

Bore sighting is essential for quickly adjusting a telescopic sight. By doing so, you'll be putting the first test shot "on paper." Here's another use for the bench vise.

Obtain some leather vise jaw pads to prevent marring the firearm when it is tightly clamped in the jaws of the vise. A bore sighting kit like the Bushnell Bore Sighter is ideal for the gunsmith who must bore sight a variety of different rifle calibers. This kit comes with three expandable arbors which provide exceptional flexibility where several different calibers are involved. With these arbors the user can bore sight the full range from .22 to .45 caliber. The smallest arbor fits any bore from .22 to .270 caliber; the middle-sized arbor fits any bore from 7mm to .35 caliber, and the largest fits bores from .35 to .45 caliber.

To bore sight a rifle, place the gun in a padded vise and select the proper arbor from the kit. Make sure the expandable tips are completely closed by turning the arbor's locking nut counter-clockwise as far as it will go. Insert the small end of the arbor

In this instance, a bolt has been secured in a padded vise and is ready for any number of gunsmithing chores (trigter-pull improvement in this case).

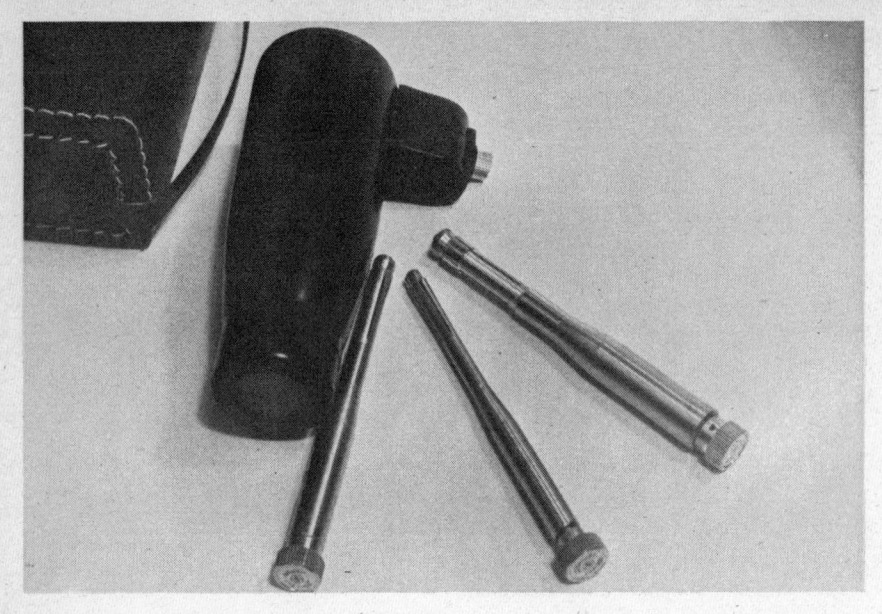

Bushnell Bore Sighter makes quick work out of sighting in scopes.

When bore sighting any rifle, be sure it's firmly tied down. The rifle being bore-sighted here has been secured in a padded vise.

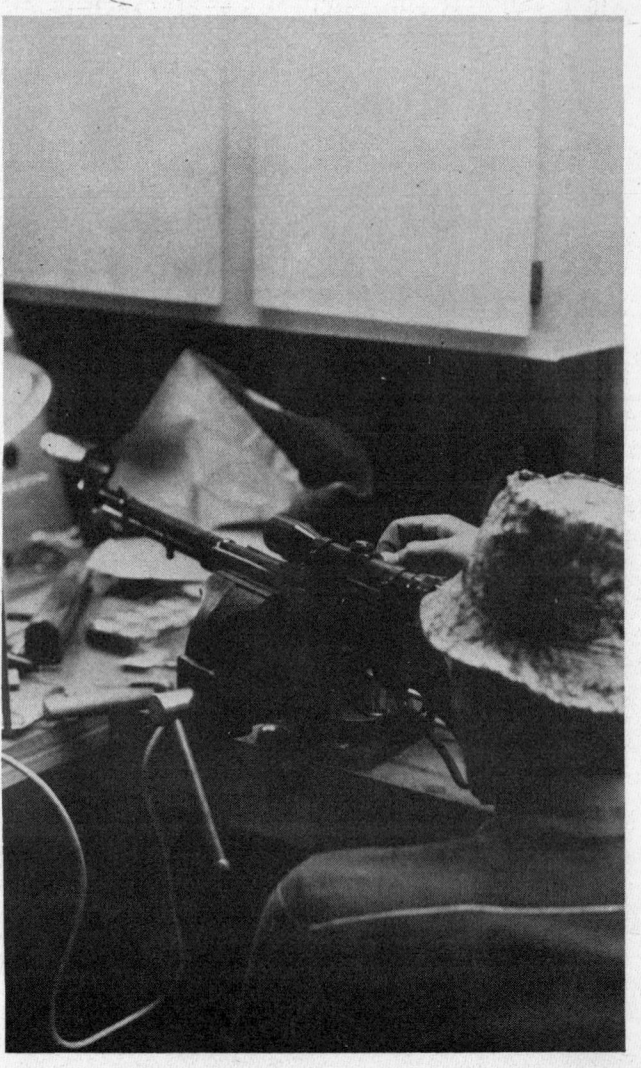

into the bore sighter mount with the locating spot down, so the end of the clamp screw will bear against the flat surface. Turn the screw clockwise until it is finger-tight to hold the arbor and bore sighter in position.

Now, with the bore sighter in an upright position, gently insert the arbor into the barrel and push it forward carefully (so as not to damage the lands) until the muzzle rests against the tapered section of the arbor. With the arbor locking nut loosened and while looking through the scope, swing the bore sighter to align the vertical grid lines with the scope reticle. When aligned perfectly, turn the arbor locking nut clockwise until the arbor holds firmly to the bore; the expandable tips prevent the bore sighter from turning of its own weight.

Remove the caps over the adjustment mechanism on the riflescope and sight through the scope. Move the elevation and windage adjustments until the reticle aligns with the crosshairs of the graduated grid reticle in the bore sighter. For best results, the bore sighter should be held close to a well-lighted area such as a window or an adjustable lamp. You are now ready for sighting-in on the range.

To remove the arbor from the barrel, simply loosen the arbor locking nut and push inward to retract the tips; pull the unit from the barrel.

For rifles or handguns with iron sights, secure the bore sighter into the bore as described before. Then, viewing through the rear sight, adjust the sights to align with the crosshairs on the graduated

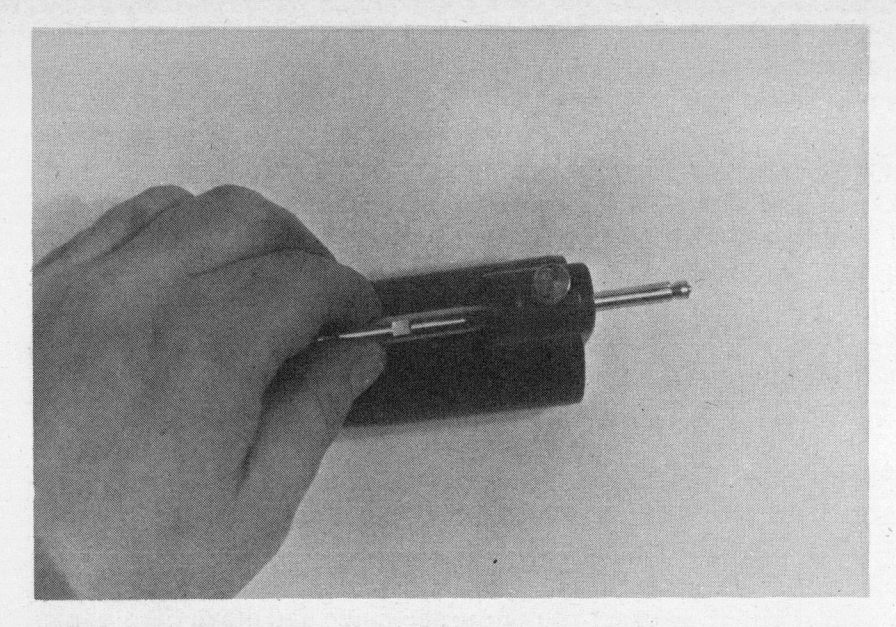

When using the Bushnell Bore Sighter, insert the small end of the arbor into the bore sighter mount with the locating spot down, so the end of the clamp screw will bear against the flat surface.

With the bore sighter in an upright position, carefully insert the arbor into the barrel and push it forward gently until the muzzle rests against the tapered section of the arbor.

For best results when using any optical bore-sighting device, an adjustable lamp should be used to illuminate the bore-sighter grid.

grid reticle in the bore sighter. When you have completed the bore sighting as described previously, the iron-sighted firearm is ready for sighting-in on the range.

Using the scope or iron sight adjustments, you can make correction for bullet drop at a specific distance provided the trajectory of the specific load is known. Each graduation on the bore sighter grid is equivalent to 4 inches at 100 yards. But watch what you're doing as this is as confusing as looking through a twin-lens reflex camera—everything is opposite from what it seems. For example, when the scope reticle is above the grid center, the firearm will shoot low. When below the grid center, the gun will shoot high!

How many times have you started to drill and tap a receiver for a riflescope and couldn't find a flat place on the gun to level it before drilling? One solution to this problem is to use only the bore sighter's arbor—inserted into the bore—and you've got a ready-made flat surface to place your small machinist's level on that will be exactly in line with the bore.

Smoothing Up Trigger Pulls

In most cases, trigger pull may be smoothed to the point where it feels lighter by simply honing all bearing surfaces to reduce friction. These surfaces include the cocking piece sears and trigger sears. When these surfaces are honed smooth, the apparent trigger pull weight will usually be reduced. Begin by mounting the trigger sear in a vise with jaws that are protected with leather pads. Polish surfaces with a hard, rectangular Arkansas stone held at a right angle to the sear surface. Be *extremely* careful not to change the angle of the original sear (unless it is incorrect when you start) or to bevel or round the edges. Usually, a *few light strokes* is all that is necessary.

You'll want to check your work frequently with a magnifying glass to make certain you're not rounding the corners or removing too much metal. Any rounded edges that may be present should be trued up or flattened with a soft, faster cutting Arkansas stone first, and then polished with a hard stone.

A cocking piece may also be secured in a vise and polished. Work at a right angle to the notch—using a hard Arkansas stone. Be sure to follow the exact contour of the notch and move the stone in as straight a line as possible. Again, don't round the edges or remove too much metal.

(Left) A Bushnell bore sight arbor is perfect for leveling a rifle prior to drilling and tapping holes for mounting a scope.

Soldering on New Sights

When soldering on a new front sight ramp—using the techniques described in Chapter 11, Soldering and Welding—both the barrel and the sight base must be securely held in place during the operation. One of the best ways to hold the parts to be soldered is to use wooden blocks in the vise jaws to hold the barrel securely, and then use a 3-V clamp to hold the ramp in place for soldering

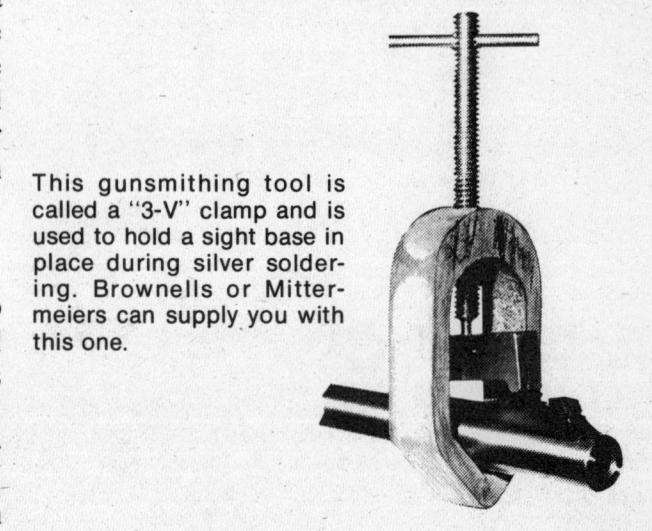

This gunsmithing tool is called a "3-V" clamp and is used to hold a sight base in place during silver soldering. Brownells or Mittermeiers can supply you with this one.

56

as shown. Note that the front clamp foot rests on the flat surface on the top of the ramp while the rear clamp foot rests on the barrel.

When mounting a new front sight ramp, it is absolutely necessary that the ramp be aligned correctly and centered on the barrel. Use a square and level to true up the barrel/action assembly as the barrel must first be straight in the vise before you can line up the sight. Once the barrel and action are straight and level, the ramp is aligned and then secured by soldering as described in Chapter 11.

Fitting the Shotgun Stock

Proper stock "pull" is one requirement that is vitally important to the shotgun owner's shooting proficiency, yet few shooters understand what it is, or why a stock may either fit right when it is purchased or have to be lengthened or shortened to fit him personally. To find the correct pull for a shooter, he must be measured—the Brownell Pull & Drop Gauge is the tool to use. This gauge is designed to accurately, easily and quickly measure the pull and drop of the gunstock and the pull of the shooter's forearm-trigger-finger.

To measure the shotgun stock, mount the gun in a vise with padded jaws and then place the Pull and Drop gauge in proper position as indicated by the directions that come with this handy tool. The zero mark at the inside of the ring bored in the gauge should be aligned exactly with the edge of the gun's trigger (the edge that your finger rests on). Then the length may be read directly by moving the slide snug against the butt plate.

Characteristics of improperly-fitted stocks include shooting to either the right or left of a target. For example, if the stock is too short, chances are you'll shoot to the right; if too long, you'll shoot to the left of the target. Recoil will also be felt differently when the stock is improperly fitted.

The drop at the heel of a stock is another important area to consider for fitting shotgun stocks to a particular shooter. Heel drop is the distance between the heel of the butt and a line extending straight back from the sighting plain of the barrel. The Brownell gauge is also used here to measure the drop of heel while the shotgun is firmly secured in a vise with padded jaws.

When the stock has to be lengthened or shortened, the vise is used to hold the stock for cutting or to install a recoil pad as discussed elsewhere in this book. Here is a list of other operations where the vise should be used:

1. Assembling and disassembling guns of all types.
2. Removing stuck cases from rifle chambers.
3. Removing burrs from action feed ramps.
4. Cleaning firearms.
5. Hand fitting new barrels to revolver frames.
6. Securing barreled actions for chambering or freeboring.
7. Holding barrels for chamber cast or lapping.
8. Holding metal guide bar while wrapping spring wire to make magazine spring.
9. Stock work/checkering.
10. Inletting gun stocks.
11. Shaping gun stocks.
12. Repairing gun stocks.
13. For holding guns and parts for nearly all gun repair work.

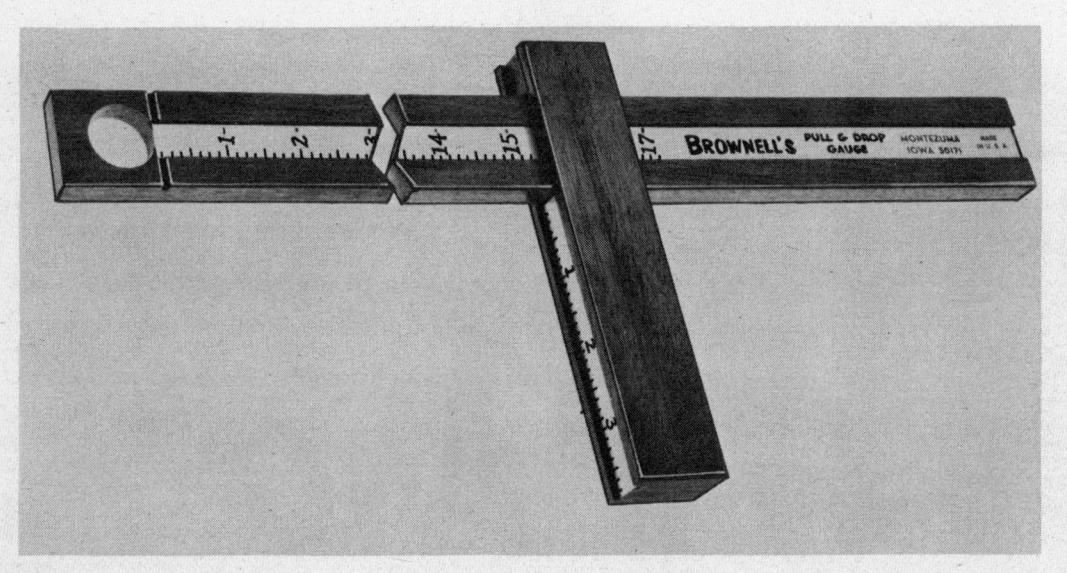

Brownells Pull and Drop gauge is the sort of tool that will come in handy if you plan on doing any amount of stock work.

6
RX FOR LONG GUN LIFE

BENCH REST shooters have known for years that a well cleaned bore is imperative in attaining the ultimate in rifle performance. Gunsmiths know that the cause of 90% of malfunctions in autoloading rifles and shotguns is due to dirt and/or corrosion in the action, chamber and/or gas piston. Proper cleaning and care of a firearm is also an important factor in extending its usefulness and preserving its appearance. Other reasons could be cited, but these should suffice to convince every gun owner that his guns should be cleaned periodically—both at home, in the field or on the range.

Cleaning Tools

Cleaning kits are available on the market for cleaning rifles, shotguns, handguns and black powder weapons. Most contain a cleaning rod, a

A simple commercial gun cleaning kit is suitable for the general gun cleaning chores most gunsmiths will encounter.

A silicone impregnated cloth is excellent when it comes to rust prevention or the removal of finger prints.

bronze bristle brush, slotted patch tip, patches, powder solvent, gun oil and gun grease. These kits are fine for cleaning guns in the field or on the range, but the average gun owner will need more equipment for thoroughly cleaning the guns at home.

For general field cleaning with the kit, soak one of the patches with powder solvent (bore cleaner) and place it through the slotted tip on the cleaning rod. Insert the tip into the barrel (preferably from the breech end) and run the patch the full length of the barrel and return. Repeat this operation many times—usually 15 or 20. Then use a dry patch to dry the bore. Keep changing patches until the last one comes out clean. Finish the bore cleaning by lightly oiling a clean patch and running it up and back through the bore.

Stubborn bores will require the use of the bronze bristle brush. Soak a patch as before with bore cleaner and run it up and down the bore until it is saturated with the bore cleaner. Remove the slotted patch tip from the cleaning rod, insert the brush and dip it in the bore cleaner. Push this brush up and down the bore about a dozen times to loosen all dirt and grime. Finish up as before by drying the bore with clean patches until the last patch comes out clean.

The outside of the gun should be wiped off with a Silicone cloth. This cloth prevents rust and corrosion and also removes finger prints and eliminates salt spray damage. This cloth may also be used on wood.

Cleaning Rods

In general, cleaning rods are made of wood (hickory), aluminum, or other metals such as brass or steel. Most are made of sectioned aluminum and are fine for shotgun and pistol rods, but I've

Sectioned aluminum cleaning rods have a tendency to bend and/or break from the pressure needed to force cleaning brushes/patches through most barrels. As a result, I'd suggest you keep a sturdy 1-piece rod near the workbench.

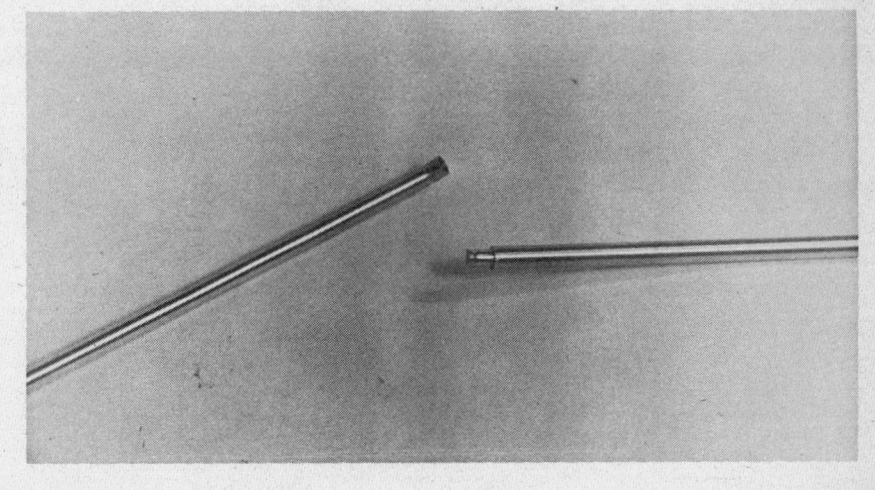

SINGLE SLOTTED TIP

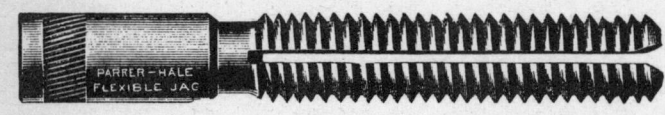

FLEXIBLE JAG

PLAIN JAG

ROLL JAG

BRASS BRUSH

Here's a good selection of common cleaning rod tips. From top to bottom: single slotted tip; flexible jag; plain jag; roll jag and a brass bristle brush.

broken several over the years when used in rifles. They have a tendency to bend and break at the joints from the pressure needed to force the proper-size cleaning brushes through the barrel.

Cleaning rods for use on rifle and pistol barrels should have swivel handles so that the rods revolve freely, allowing the patch or brush to follow the rifling of the barrel. Without this rotation, the patch will drag at right angles across the lands and will eventually destroy the sharp edges of the rifling. A shotgun cleaning rod does not require a swivel joint since the bore is smooth.

Cleaning Accessories for Rifles and Pistols

Several types of cleaning tips are commonly used on rifle and pistol cleaning rods. The single slotted tip is the simplest and holds onto a patch under all conditions. The patch used with these tips should be of such a size as to require about 4 pounds of pressure to force it through the bore of the rifle or pistol. Slotted tips do sometimes jam when reversed inside the bore; also, the cleaning action is often one-sided, permitting the bare sides of the tip to rub the bore.

The plain jag tip gives uniform cleaning action and reverses perfectly inside the barrel. The patch sticks to the tip as long as it is inside the barrel, but will come loose should the tip be pushed beyond the muzzle or chamber. A pointed jag tip has the advantage of centering the patch before it is in-

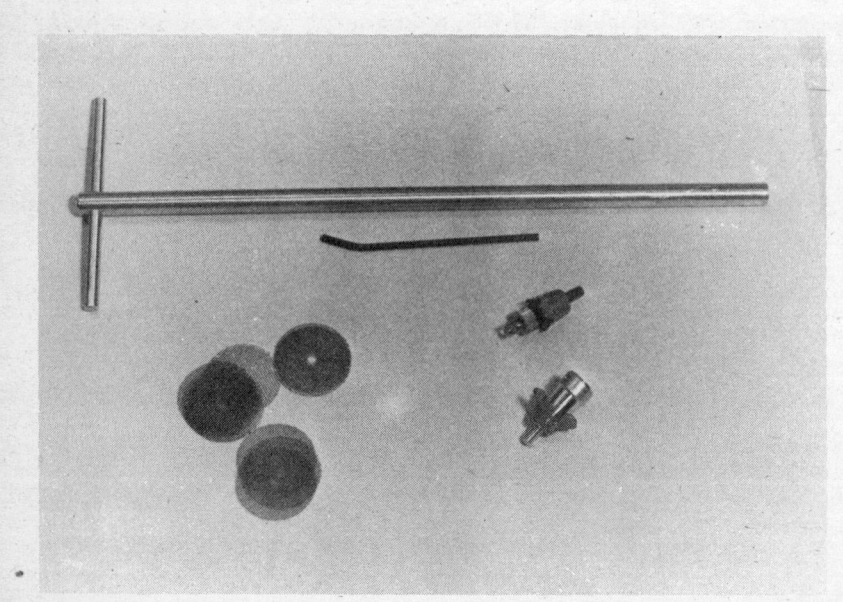

The Lewis Lead Remover has long been recognized as the best tool for cleaning out badly leaded bores.

To assemble the Lewis rod, pass the rod body through the barrel and screw the cone tip (C) through the brass cloth patch (B) into the rod body (A). You then bend the patch back over the taper of the screw cone tip and you're ready to remove lead from a revolver's forcing cone using the tip shown.

serted in the bore.

For cleaning rifles and pistols that have to be wiped out from the muzzle end, the roll jag tip is far safer because the patch does not have to be dragged in. Consequently, the rifling is preserved instead of being worn away at a most vital spot.

Other than powder fouling, the shooter must sometimes give consideration to metal fouling. This is a deposit of metal left by the bullet in the bore. If lead bullets are used, the problem is more specifically designated as "leading." Even the best match ammunition will cause leading in the finest target handguns and this leading can affect accuracy to a disastrous degree. However, a perfect cleaning job on handguns can be accomplished in a few minutes with a Lewis Lead Remover distributed by L.E.M. Gun Specialties. This tool will remove lead from the forcing cone, chamber(s) and bore with ease.

In revolvers the forcing cone (or bullet seat) may be cleaned by first swinging the cylinder out of the firing position and then inserting the handle (with the tip and cloth patch removed) through the barrel from the muzzle end. Screw the cone tip with attached cloth patch into the handle hand tight. Hold the revolver with fingers around handle and thumb through the frame, and with the right hand, pull the cone tip and patch snug into the forcing cone. It won't go very far, so don't get excited if you think it's not going in. Holding this pressure, turn the handle in a clockwise direction four or five turns; then push the cone back and examine the brass cloth patch. If the forcing cone is badly leaded, repeat this operation after flipping the lead off the patch with the thumb nail, pocket knife or similar object.

Clean the revolver barrel with the rubber tip unit. First remove all grease and solvent from the barrel. Then insert the handle through the barrel from the muzzle end as before. Screw the rubber tip with formed brass cloth patch into the handle hand tight and examine the knurled nut to see that

(Top) Be sure to firmly hold the revolver when pulling the cone tip and patch of the Lewis Lead Remover into the forcing cone.

(Above) When using the Lewis Lead Remover to clean out the cylinders of a revolver, be sure to insert the rod from the forward end of the cylinder.

61

it is backed one-half turn away from the rubber portion of the tip to allow the assembly to turn with the rifling. Hold the revolver as described before and pull the tip through the barrel, allowing handle and tip assembly to turn with rifling. Repeat this operation until all lead is removed.

Revolver cylinders may be cleaned in a similar way to the barrel; that is, insert the handle from the forward end of the cylinder, screw the rubber tip with formed brass cloth patch into the handle. Hold the cylinder with the left hand and pull the rubber tip with formed patch into the cylinder. When the tip engages the front end (reduced diameter) of the cylinder, begin turning in a clockwise direction.

The brass cloth patch should be good for several cleanings. Should it become clogged with grease and lead, it may be cleaned with lighter fluid and a toothbrush. If any of the above operations tighten either tip too tight to release with the fingers, a key is provided to loosen them.

Cleaning Accessories for Shotguns

The shotgun cleaning swab is useful for oiling the bores or applying powder solvent, but they must be kept clean as otherwise much harm can be done by the fouling on the wool swab neutralizing the preserving powers of the oil. The brass or bronze bristle brush of the proper size for the bore is used to remove as much of the fouling and powder residue as possible by pushing it down and back through the bore 4 or 5 times. The slotted tip is then used to hold patches to remove all the debris that has been loosened. Several patches should be used until the last one comes out clean. Then oil a clean patch and run it through the bore several times.

Metal fouling in shotgun barrels or any condition of rusting or pitting can be removed (usually) by mechanical methods as the smooth bore permits almost any type of polishing. The flexible brass jag, for example, was designed for cleaning shotguns with a patch. The patch is slipped into the slot of the jag and wrapped around it; the slot imparts a measure of flexibility, which causes the patch to press evenly on the bore thereby squeezing the oil into the pores of the steel. The flexible slot also permits the jag to be compressed by the

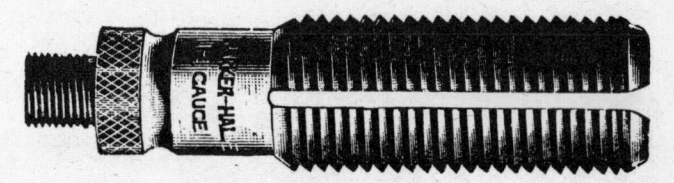

This slotted, flexible brass jag is ideal for cleaning shotguns when used with a patch centered in the slot.

These rod tips (for cleaning shotguns) are, from left, a brass bristle brush, single loop tip and the cotton mop or swab — be sure to use the proper gauge of brush loop or mop.

A slotted jag is also perfect for holding abrasive paper when polishing out shotgun bores.

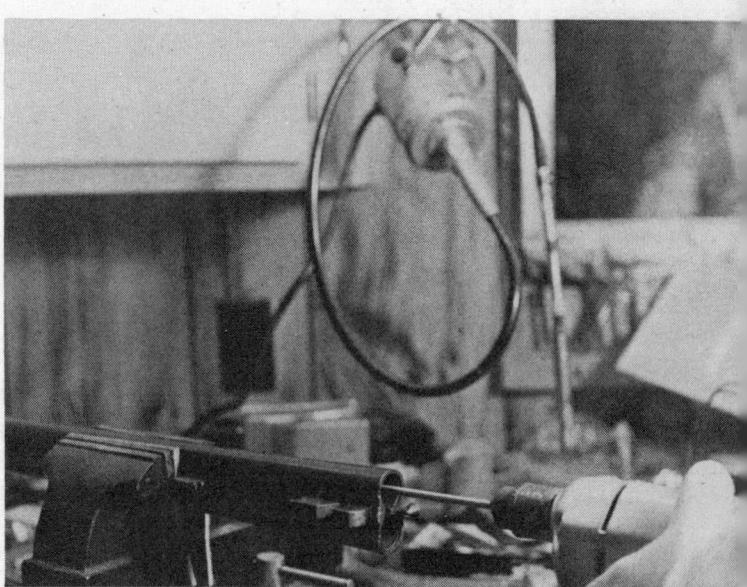

choke thus ensuring a thorough cleaning of the bore throughout its length. This jag is also ideal for holding abrasive paper strips when you have to polish shotgun bores. For faster results, attach the jag to a metal cleaning rod, cut the handle off so that it will fit into the chuck of a drill motor, and polish the bore. Steel brushes and polishing heads designed expressly for the purpose of polishing shotgun bores are available.

The leather shotgun bore polisher shown here is built up of seven buff leather discs that absorb polishing materials such as Clover abrasive compound, and aid in repolishing the bores of shotguns that have been neglected. Since no metal touches the bore, they can be used on the most expensive shotguns without fear of damage.

Leather-washer bore polishers are perfect for putting the final touches on any shotgun bore — only the leather washers touch the metal.

Holding Guns for Cleaning

Cleaning operations may be greatly simplified if some type of vise is used to hold the guns. One such vise is the Decker Shooting Vise. When used properly, all scratching, marring, etc., are eliminated as the Naugahide covering the sponge padding is all that comes in contact with the gun.

The entire base may be permanently mounted to a table or else temporarily secured with C clamps. This tool will quickly pay for itself if only used in bore cleaning. However, the vise has many other uses. For example, a rifle may be inserted in the vise in an inverted position for loosening and tightening guard screws. A semi-inletted stock may be secured in the vise while fitting a barreled action. This vise is unsurpassed for bore sighting. By removing the two cap nuts that secure the rear section, the vise becomes a completely adequate substitute for a zeroing rest—provided a sandbag is used under the butt stock.

Of course, rifles and shotguns may be clamped in a standard bench vise, but care must be exercised in exerting too much clamping pressure and the jaws of the vise must be well padded.

Gun cleaning can be made one heck of a lot easier by using the Decker Rifle Vise. It holds the rifle or shotgun firmly in place and you thereby run less risk of damaging anything with a fast-moving cleaning rod.

Professional Gun Cleaning

A good part of the professional gunsmith's business consists of cleaning guns for customers, usually before and after the regular hunting season in the fall. For such cleaning, special equipment and cleaning solutions are needed.

The simplest and quickest setup is to use a clean bluing tank to hold the cleaning solution. The plastic tanks supplied by Birchwood Casey are ideal. You will also need brushes of various

The Decker vise is also well suited for bore sighting.

63

types to get to the hard-to-reach places. Toothbrushes, baby bottle brushes and the like should be purchased just for gun cleaning.

A fast, efficient soak cleaner for guns and parts that is non-hazardous, non-flammable, odor-free and not too expensive is called d'SOLVE Gunsmith Cleaner and is available from Brownell's Inc. The grimiest parts left soaking in a bench tray of d'SOLVE while doing other work on a gun come out clean, ready to dry, oil and assemble. Used as a brush-on cleaner, actions and chambers are rapidly rid of crusted dirt and grime. Wiped on, it's an excellent pre-cleaner for touch-up bluing.

Add a can of WD-40, with needle applicator, and you're all set for cleaning. Squirt WD-40 onto the gun and parts and let it soak for a couple of minutes while you're mixing one part d'SOLVE to 5 parts water in the clean bluing tank. Mix enough to thoroughly cover the gun and all parts. Now place all the parts in the solution and let soak for several minutes. The WD-40 will have started loosening the dirt and dissolving the grease, and the d'SOLVE will finish the job. Use the tooth brush to get any stubborn grime off the parts. Of course, *all* wood should be removed from the gun prior to soaking in the cleaning solution.

After the parts have been cleaned thoroughly, dry all the parts and lubricate them with a good gun oil or give the entire gun a light coat of WD-40.

If you want to go a bit further, nothing beats

The Water Pic®, with its fluid reservoir filled with cleaning solution can be used for cleaning out dirt and debris from any action. (Don't use the family unit for the shop!)

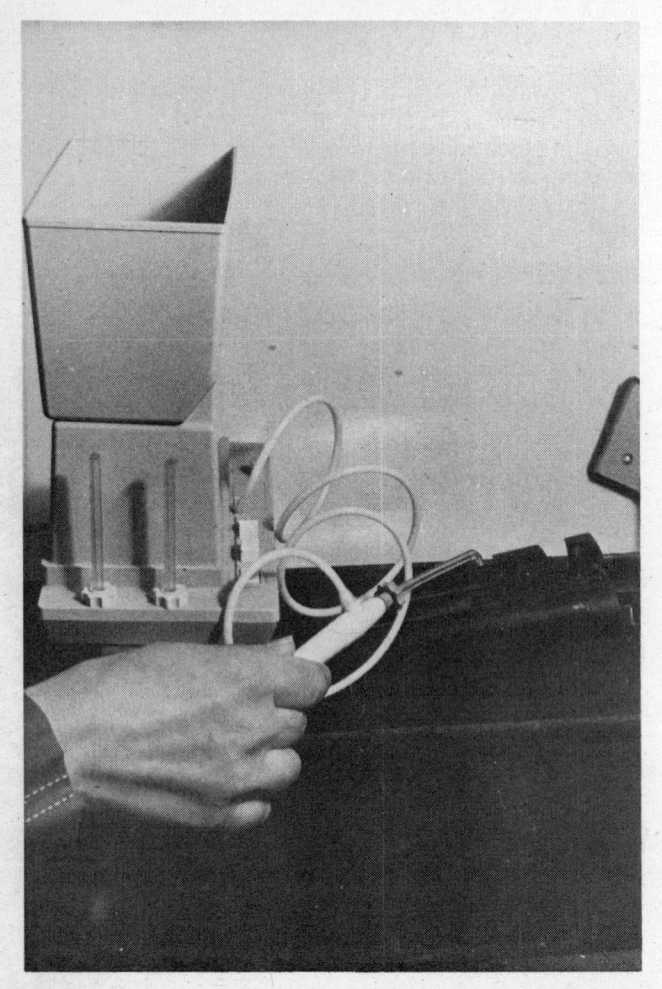

When cleaning guns, put a light coat of WD-40 or other quality gun oil on the metal parts to be cleaned. Allow the oil to soak in for a few minutes. This "soaking" will help loosen grime and make overall cleaning an easier chore.

compressed air for blowing gun parts clean. Once the parts are lifted out of the cleaning tank, all the loose grime is quickly blown out with a compressed air gun set at about 50 psi of pressure. The air gun is also a quick way to dry parts.

A friend, Alan Eldridge of Potomac Arms Corp. in Alexandria, Virginia suggests using a Water Pic® for cleaning guns—the same kind that a lot of us use for cleaning our teeth! With this gadget sitting next to the cleaning tank, fill the reservoir

(Left) If you've got a rust-removal problem, a soft-wire carding wheel mounted on a buffer can remove a pile of rust in a hurry; however, consider this approach to rust removal carefully unless you're working on small, unseen parts. If you take *great care*, spot rebluing may not be necessary when removing small amounts of rust from exposed metal parts.

(Below) Fingerprints can leave a chemical deposit on metal that will, in time, provide an unwanted coating of rust. Keep a silicone impregnated rag on hand for wiping down guns after they've been handled.

with the cleaning solution, turn the spray gauge to high, and go to work on the gun parts and action. The tiny, forceful jets of cleaning fluid will do wonders for cleaning them properly. The only problem that I can see with this method is you must be careful what you run through the Water Pic as some chemicals will obviously ruin the mechanism.

One of the most difficult problems confronting the gunsmith is removing heavy rust without damaging the bluing. The best first attempt is to coat the area with WD-40 and rub vigorously with a rough towel to scrub the rust off. The process is repeated until a clean patch wiped over the surface comes up clean. If a lot of rust is present, use No. 0000 steel wool dampened with WD-40, rubbing lightly until the rust is removed.

If you run into deep heavy rust that the steel wool won't remove, try using a soft wire carding wheel on your buffer. If care is taken, you can remove quite a lot of rust without harming the blue underneath.

When all else fails, and it seems that no other way but removing both the rust and blue will solve the problem, I take a piece of No. 0 steel wool and dip it in a container of Brownell's OXPHO-BLUE and rub the rusted area vigorously with the solution-soaked piece of steel wool. The chemical (in most cases) goes through the oil on the gun, removes the rust and blues the steel underneath to replace whatever was removed by the steel wool.

7
FILES AND THEIR KIN

Files

FILES are simply metal cutting tools with a large number of cutting teeth. They have many uses, and consequently, there are hundreds of types of files available. With a full assortment of files in the workshop, an expert gunsmith can make practically any tool necessary from scrap metal as well as parts and other metal work.

The cuts made across the face of a file to form the file teeth are either fine, course or some degree in between. In general, the coarser the file, the more metal it removes with each file stroke, and consequently, the rougher it leaves the filed surface. Naturally, a coarse file is normally used for rough cutting a part and the part then finished with a fine-cut file.

When only one series of parallel cuts has been

Files are primarily designed as metal-cutting tools that have a large number of cutting teeth.

taken across the face of the file, the file is known as a *single-cut file*. When two series of cuts are used, it is known as a *double-cut file*. In addition to single- and double-cut classifications—and their coarseness—files are classified according to their shape and purpose. For example, they may be *flat, triangular, square, half-round,* etc.

Due to the numerous styles and types of files, it is difficult for the amateur to even begin selecting a set that will handle most of his gun repair work without overbuying. The brief description that follows should be of some help.

Pillar file: This type is considered the standard

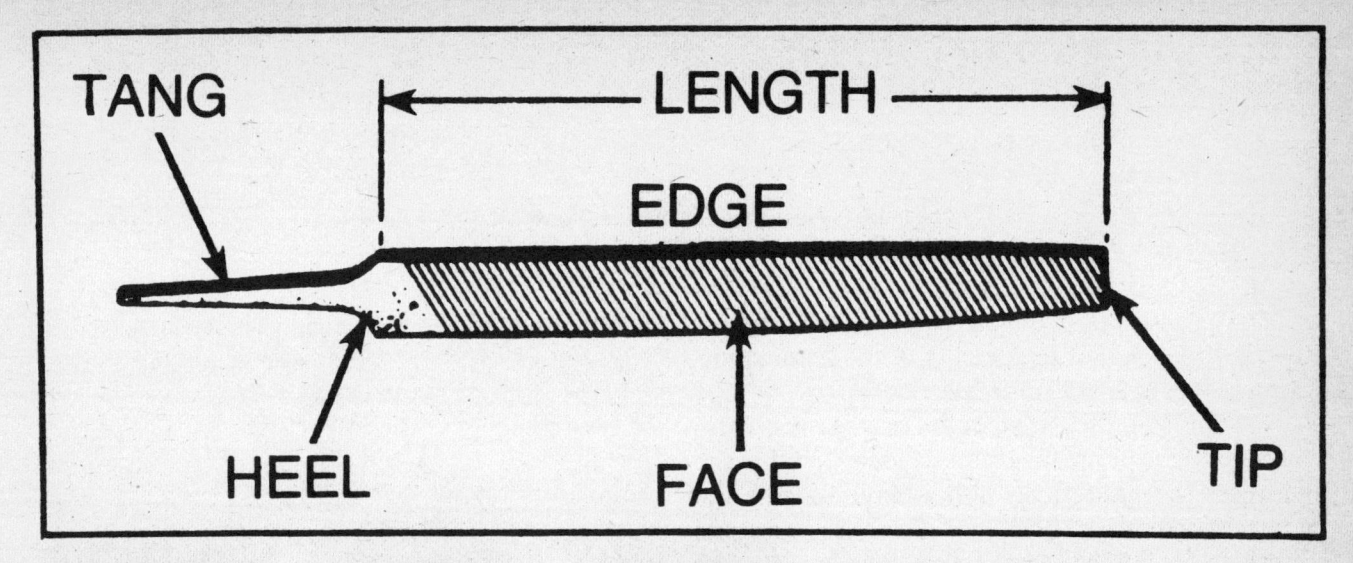

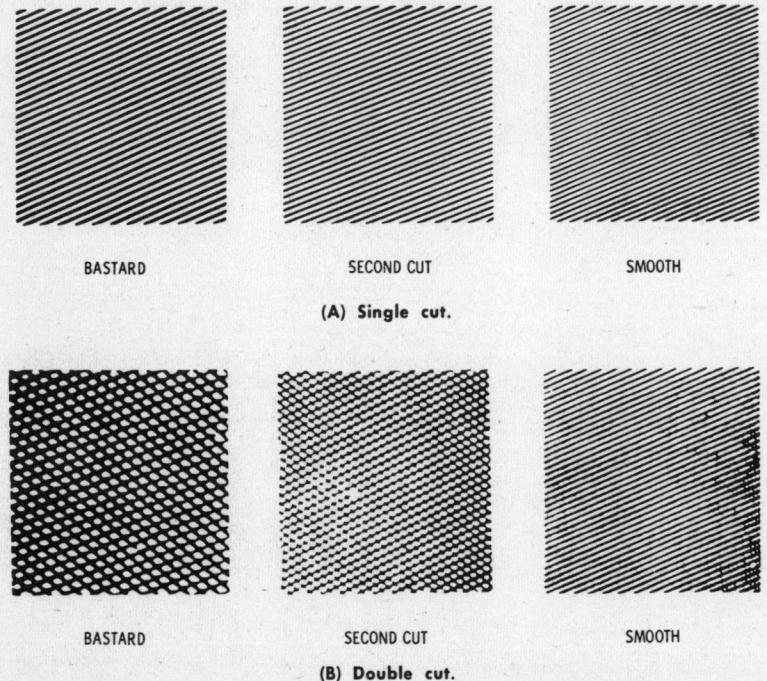

(Above) Parts of a typical file.

Files have either single- or double-cut file teeth. When only one series of parallel cuts appear on the face of the file, it is known as a *single-cut file*. When two series of cuts in a cross-hatch pattern appear on the face of the file, it is known as a *double-cut file*.

gunsmithing file and many jobs can be done with it which could not even be attempted with standard files. A pillar file is parallel as to width, but tapers somewhat in thickness toward the point. They are "safe" on both edges so that a cut may be made right up to the faces without undercutting the sides of the work. Number 0 is the coarsest and is used for fast removal of wood or untempered soft metal. The Number 2 cut is good for final fitting of fine parts and the like. Number 4 cut is very smooth and is for finishing. They are double-cut and are applicable to general gunsmithing work, especially in connection with fitting new parts.

Round file: Common cuts for round files are 00 to No. 4. The coarser size (00) is used for fast removal of metal or as a rasp to slightly enlarge or adjust accessory holes in wood stocks. Cuts 2 and 4 are for adjusting screw and pin holes, scope mount holes, fine cuts on tightly curved parts and all types of parallel round cuts.

Lathe file: The lathe file is rather heavy with about twice as much slant on the teeth as a standard file. This characteristic produces a sort of shearing cut and is excellent for filing old rough military rifle barrels as they turn in a lathe.

Hand file: Hand files are parallel in thickness from the heel to the middle, and are tapered, as to thickness, from the middle to the point. This type of file will find many uses around the gunshop for dressing, striking off, shaping, cleaning up and

The lathe file is rather heavy with about twice as much slant on the teeth as a normal file.

removing all types of metal. This should be one of the first files added to your list of tools after purchasing a No. 2 cut pillar file.

Mill file: Mill files are parallel in thickness from the heel to the point and usually tapered so that the width at the end equals about three-fourths the width of the stock. They are also made of equal width and thickness throughout their length. The teeth are ordinarily single-cut, bastard; however, they can have rows of teeth that cross each other in somewhat of a diamond or cross-hatch pattern. In this case, it's a double-cut bastard mill file. Other cuts include No. 2 cut and smooth. This file is used in the gunshop for lathe work, draw filing and for filing brass and bronze.

Knife file: This type of file, with its narrow knife-blade type section, is ideal for getting down into sharp angles and tight corners where no other file will reach. The teeth are double-cut, and normally come in three sizes—bastard, 2nd cut and smooth.

Barrette file: This is another type of file designed for getting into tight places; that is, coming right up to right angles, working over dovetails, slots, and other tight or critical areas where precision work is a must. Common cuts include No. 0, No. 1, etc.

Needle files: A set of needle files should be in every gunshop as they will find regular use. The set pictured consists of 12 assorted files in four types: equalling, square, three square, and half round. Cuts are medium and fine.

Sight base file: The sight base file is specially designed to safely widen or cut new dovetail slots for sight bases. It's a true parallel, 3-square file with only one side cutting; the other two sides are safe (smooth). This means the file can be used to widen dovetail slots in gun barrels without danger of deepening the slot or damaging the edge not being worked on. Since it is a true parallel file, absolute control is had over the angle of the dovetail—very difficult, if not impossible, with any other type of file.

Screw head file: Gunsmiths are often called upon to make or alter a screw slot, and for this purpose,

Every gunshop should have a good set of needle files on hand. This particular set has 12 assorted files.

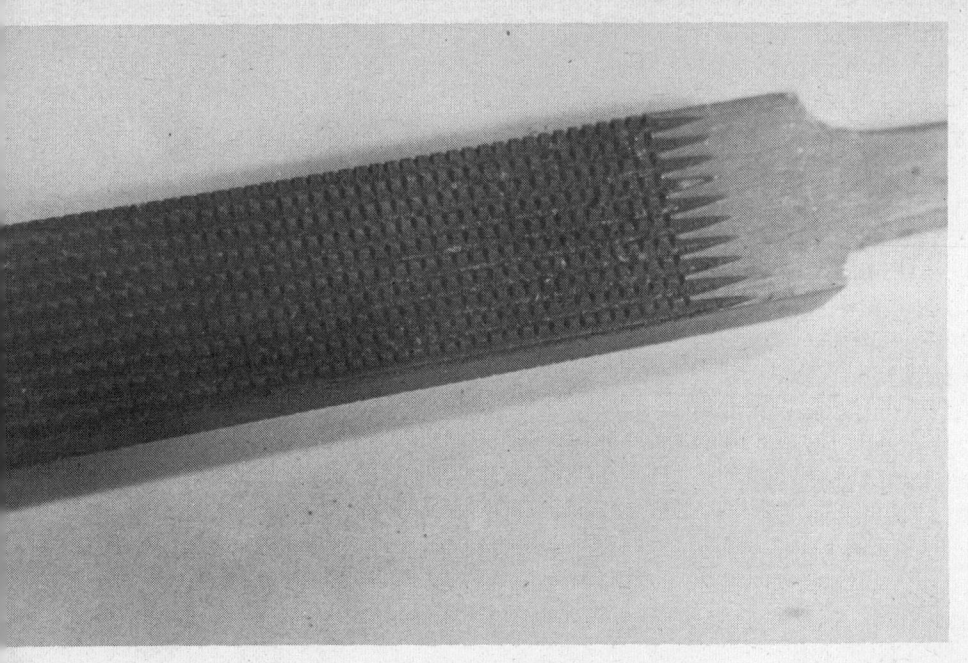

Metal checkering files are used for checkering hammer spurs, pistol grips and a host of other gun parts.

a screw head file is hard to beat. Such files cut only on the edge because the wide flat sides are safe or smooth. Therefore, the screw head will not be damaged during filing. Three slot sizes are commonly available for perfect width every time: .043", .035" and .027".

Clock maker's file: Did you ever wonder how those tiny screw slots in many European firearms could ever be touched up except with a gnat's hair? Clock maker's files are ideal for that purpose. Brownell's sell a No. 5 (fine) cut clock maker's file with or without tang. These are especially useful for the European-type "V" screw slots.

Metal checkering files: These files are used for checkering hammer spurs, back straps or fore straps on pistol grips or serrating ribs. They are manufactured in sizes from 20-75 lines per inch.

To file, position the work so that it's about level with the elbows for light work, and a bit lower for heavy work. Right-handed persons hold the file with the right hand, thumb on top of the handle, fingers below.

Filing may seem to be an easy operation, but nothing could be farther from the truth. First of all, filing depends on the motion of the hands for the cutting action and without a means of guiding the tool, which is always the case, it is difficult to move over the work with the correct pressure and in the right direction. The only way to obtain proficiency in filing is to practice using proper methods.

To file, the correct position and method of holding the file must be learned. Position the work so that it's about level with the elbows for light work, and just a bit lower for heavy work. The feet should be about eight inches apart and at a comfortable angle to each other. The left foot should be parallel with the file. Right-handed persons

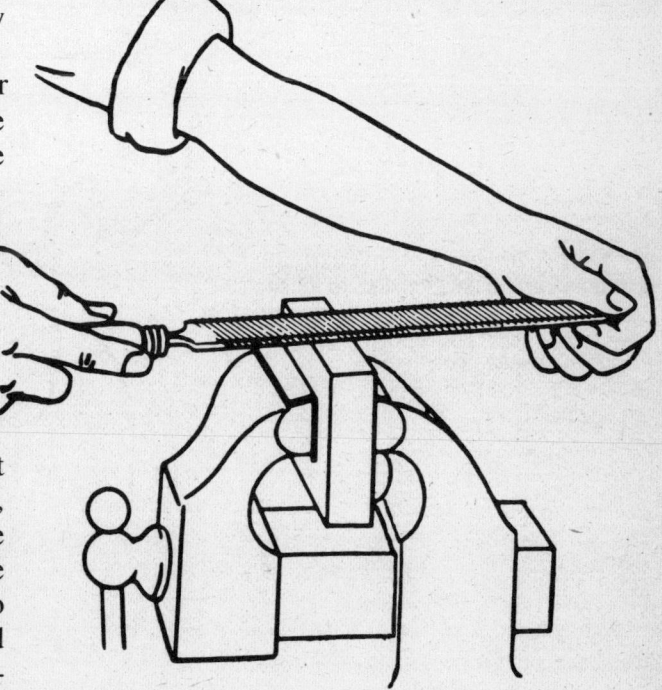

69

should hold the file with the right hand—thumb on top of the handle and the fingers below. When the filing action begins, pressure should be exerted on the forward stroke only as pressure on the return stroke produces no cutting action and tends to dull the teeth which are pointed toward the end of the file.

The gunsmith will often be called upon to remove tool marks from rifle barrels and other gun parts. This operation is commonly accomplished by draw filing. To perform this operation, grasp the file by the ends and move the file sideways across the work. This produces a smooth finish and removes tool marks when a second cut or smooth file is used. A single-cut file is better than a double-cut file, as it is less likely to scratch the surface of the work.

The ultimate finish on gun parts such as old rough military barrels is to start with a coarse file and continue using successively finer grades of file, finishing with a smooth or dead-smooth file, according to the degree of finish desired. This procedure is sometimes called "striking" in the trade.

Use padded vise-blocks and secure the barrel, barreled action, or whatever you're working on in the vise. Select a wide, and very fine cut file unless the barrel is very rough, then use a coarse file to start out. Use the file in both hands and run every stroke the full length of the barrel, maintaining a constant firm pressure, so that the file takes a cut both ways. Don't make the cuts too deep, however, just enough pressure to barely make the file take hold is all that is necessary. Neither should the pressure be too light as this will scratch the metal rather than cut it.

When the correct pressure is applied to the work, the cuts will be relatively even, with no flats visible on the surface. However, the flat spots will be there nonetheless and will have to be removed by polishing as discussed in Chapter 9 on bluing.

Keeping the file clean is the key to smooth, clean cutting. Use a file card or a stiff steel brush (like the one shown) to remove metal chips from the teeth. Before actually using the file, it's a smart move to rub a piece of chalk over the teeth—this makes the cleaning job a lot easier.

Working down and smoothing rough surfaces can be accomplished in less time when a special draw file is used. This is the way you should hold the file for best results.

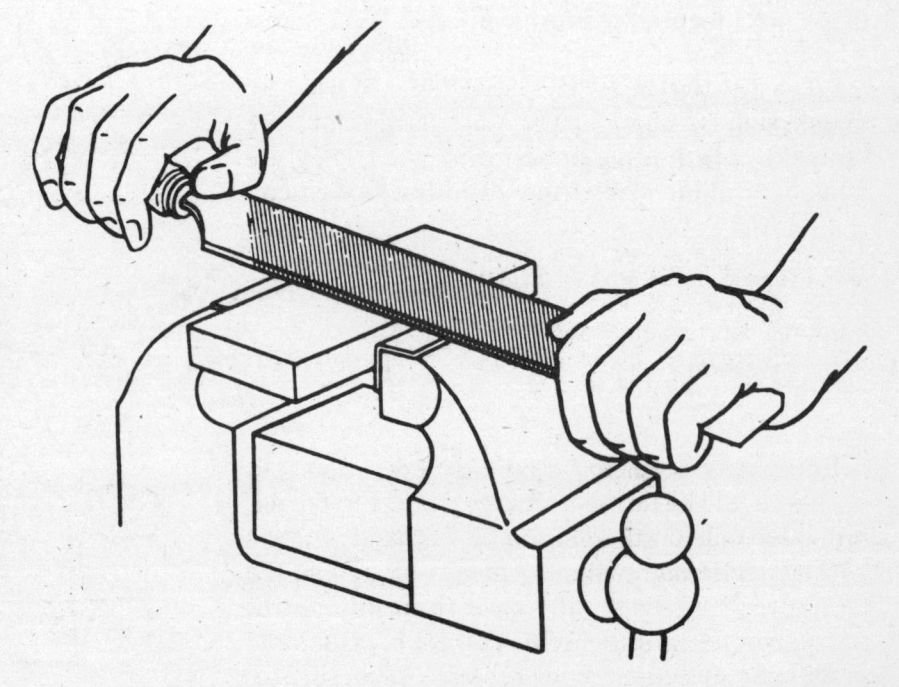

Of course, when the barrel is turning in a lathe and draw filed, much less polishing is necessary.

Particles of metal often remain in the teeth of the file, and they either reduce the cutting qualities or scratch the work. Keep a piece of chalk handy, and chalk the cutting side of the file all over at frequent intervals to prevent the metal build-up. Also use a stiff brush or a file card frequently, for cleaning the file thoroughly. Then re-chalk and continue the operation. Frequent pinning or clogging of the teeth can sometimes be prevented by using oil on the work when filing; that is, on steel, but *never* on cast iron as grease on the latter material tends to cause the file to slide over the work without cutting into the metal.

Working down and smoothing rough barrels can be accomplished in less time when a special draw file is used. A barrel draw file is available from Frank Mittermeier, Inc., and has the following features:

1. Its usefulness is not limited; it can be used on single and double barrel guns, on straight and taper barrels and close to fixed sight bases, ribs and places otherwise inaccessible.
2. Its concave shape means elimination of nearly all "flats" thus doing away with most cross-polishing.
3. Its 3½" length allows a firm grip and for those preferring to mount it to a wooden handle, there are two countersunk screw holes.
4. Its circular cut teeth work fast and are spaced at the right intervals to prevent pinning and with its nasty deep scratches.
5. It's the greatest tool for working down and smoothing barrels when a lathe isn't available.

Files Used in Rebarreling Work

In rebarreling either a rifle or handgun, many times the barrel can not be turned snug by hand so that it is within ¼ of a turn of coming to alignment. When this occurs, metal must be removed from either the barrel shoulder or the action shoulder. This operation can be accomplished by careful filing with a safe-edge file. Begin the operation by masking the barrel threads with tape. Then, use some type of marking element—like smoke, chalk or inletting black—to mark the surface of the barrel to be filed. With the barrel held securely in a vise, use short, overlapping file strokes to work completely around the barrel shoulder until all of the marking disappears. Remark the surface and repeat the operation. Then try the barrel on the action or frame. If it does not fit, repeat the filing operation until it does, but be extremely careful not to take too much metal off the barrel shoulder. Furthermore, be *extremely* careful to maintain squareness of the shoulder. In the event that too much metal is removed, use a machinist's hammer with a smoothly polished face to peen the barrel shoulder until the barrel fits snugly.

Another common use for a double-cut smooth bastard file is for squaring and leveling the muzzle surface of an amputated barrel. To shorten a rifle barrel, mount the barreled action in a vise, trueing up the entire assembly with a level. If you can't find a level spot on the barrel or action, use a bore sighter spud without the optic bore sighter and you can then level the bore with a conventional small machinist's level. This will help assure a right-angle barrel cut.

Measure, mark and scribe the cutoff point on the barrel. Then, making sure the cut will be perfectly square, saw off the barrel with a hacksaw, using a standard, good quality, hacksaw blade with about 18 teeth per inch. After sawing, smooth and crown the muzzle end with a metal file. Finish up by removing metal burrs turned inward toward the bore; polish and blue by conventional methods.

Hacksaws

Since hacksaws are cutting tools, a description of their use is in order. The best hacksaw frame is

In this case, the author is sawing off a portion of damaged muzzle with a hacksaw. This "tool" is one of those "must-have" items for every gunshop—don't be cheap, buy the best you can afford.

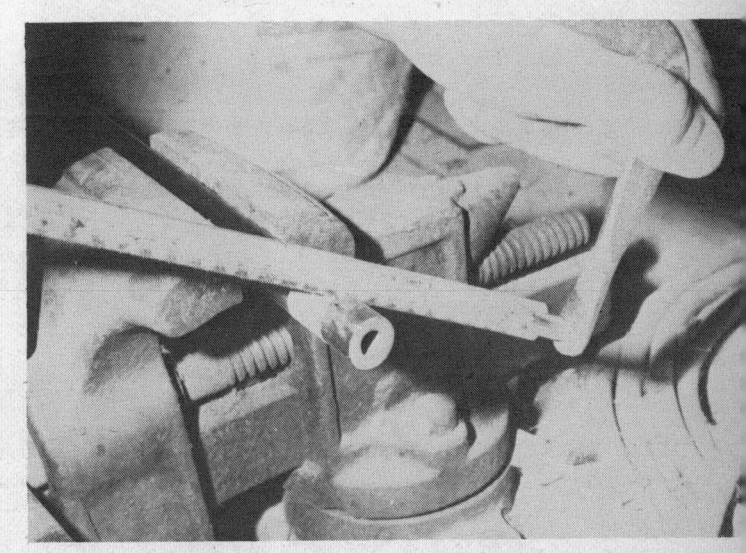

When any muzzle has been cut off, you won't have to do a lot of squaring-up (left) if the barrel was cut cleanly. Smoothing the face of the cut (below) with a file is your next step.

not expensive, so only the best should be purchased. It will be used a great deal around the shop. Likewise, only the best tungsten high-speed hacksaw blades can be expected to hold up for all kinds of gun work. A quality hacksaw frame will help eliminate blade twist or wobble. The blade may be inserted in a conventional manner for cutting stock down to the surface and may also be inserted for cutting flush with the surface.

The choice of teeth per inch on the blades will depend on the type of work the saw is used on. In general, the thinner the material to be cut, the higher the number of teeth. Soft material requires fewer teeth per inch than hard material. (Round, wire-type hacksaw blades are also available for cutting wood, metal, plastics, tile, rubber, linoleum, leather, etc. The roundness of the blades also permits a cut along any line that can be drawn.)

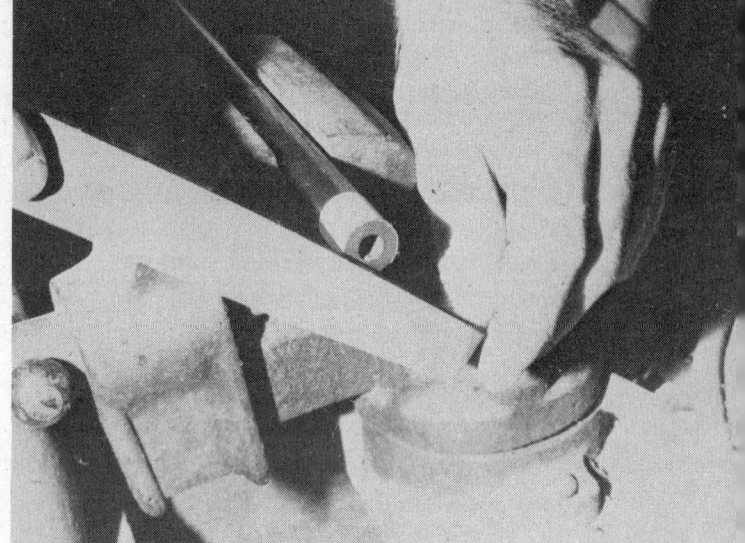

When sawing, the workpiece must be held securely in a vise and positioned so that the cutoff is near the vise jaws to prevent shattering. To start a

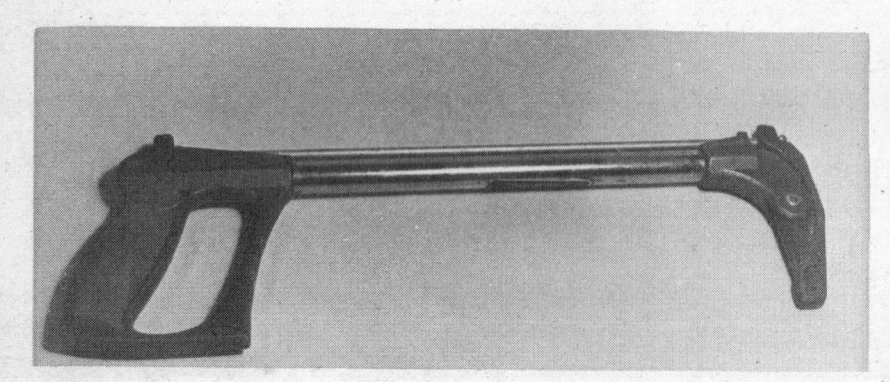

This particular hacksaw frame (above) is called the "Challenger" and is available from Brownells. With this frame design, the user can cut metal stock in a conventional manner (top right) or adjust the blade to cut in a horizontal position (bottom right). (Drawings courtesy of Brownell's Inc.)

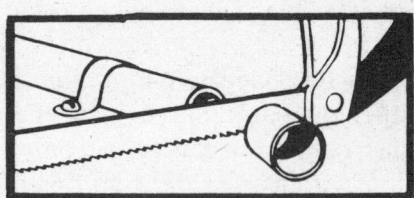

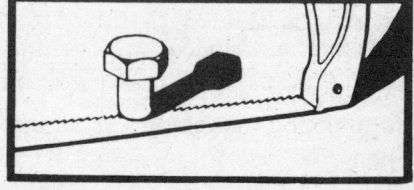

To start a cut with the hacksaw, use the thumb as a guide and saw slowly using short strokes until the cut is started. (Courtesy Diston, Inc.)

A deep hacksaw frame will come in handy when slicing through a large workpiece. A good example would be the removal of a portion of butt stock prior to the installation of a recoil pad.

This diagram shows the proper stance and working height when using the hacksaw. (Courtesy Diston, Inc.)

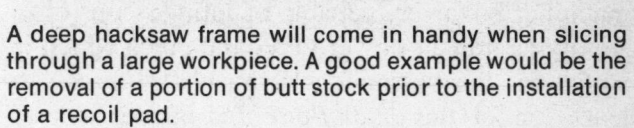

cut, use the thumb as a guide and saw slowly with short strokes until the cut is well started. As the cut deepens, grip the front end of the frame firmly and take a full-length stroke.

Face the work while sawing with one foot in front of the other and approximately 12" apart. Pressure should be applied on the forward stroke only because the blade only cuts on the forward stroke. On the backstroke don't let the teeth drag as this will dull the teeth and may cause the blade to break.

Besides cutting metal, I also use a hacksaw to make fine, splinter-free cuts in wood—such as when sawing off a portion of a butt stock to install a recoil pad. Masking tape is first applied to the stock, the exact amount of wood to be removed marked, and then the cut is made. The only drawback is that the hacksaw frame is too shallow to make this in one cut. Therefore, a cut must be started on both the top and bottom and it is very difficult to align the cuts exactly. However, this problem can be overcome by using a hacksaw with a deep frame. Such a frame permits a deep enough cut so that the blade will only have to be started once when sawing through a butt stock.

Wood Files

Wood files and rasps are similar in design to metal files except that they are obviously used (only) on wood. They are certainly kin to metal files in all respects—the main difference being that wood files have coarser and different shaped teeth. Woodworking equipment is covered in detail in the next chapter.

Engraving Tools

Every gunsmith, gun lover or craftsman—no matter what his other calling—has the soul of an artist. This personal creative urge can be easily directed into the highly remunerative field of gun engraving through the proper learning techniques and much practice. This statement does not mean that anyone can become an expert engraver overnight. On the contrary, master engravers are the product of skill, devotion and hard work—tempered with a will for perfection. There is a machine, however, capable of infinite control in supplying impact power to a hand piece which is suited for the beginner who hasn't a lifetime to learn, or for the quality-oriented master who is production minded. It's called the Gravermeister and is manufactured by GRS Corporation. It's regulated through a foot pedal which serves the same function as the foot throttle in an automobile. Control is so precise that with the proper tool chucked into the hand piece, the operator can vary the power in ranges from stipple engraving on delicate crystal to the task of hogging out metal from a steel die.

Delicate control of speed and power of this machine makes it ideal for gun engraving. It moves gravers, liners, beading tools, files, stones, etc., effortlessly in ranges from cutting steel dies to the delicate task of carving and finishing jewelry. Bright smooth cuts are obtained in both ferrous and precious metals. The alternating vacuum and pressure system does not permit the hand piece to heat as happens if operated by air pressure alone.

Florentine and matt finishing will be the types most used on gun engraving. Such finishes are applied with a tool installed on the Gravermeister called a liner, which is essentially a flat graver with equidistant V-shaped grooves cut into the bottom to produce parallel lines. Liners are categorized by width and number of lines per tool. The lower the width number, the narrower the tool; therefore, a #14-6 and a #18-6 would both cut six lines, but the #14 would be closer spaced because of its narrower width. Many different width and line combinations are available, but the liner generally favored by gun engravers for florentining is the #18-10.

Florentining consists of cutting crossed sets of lines. First, all of the lines in one direction are cut; then cross lines are applied at the preferred angle. A somewhat similar effect can be obtained by dragging the tip of the liner across the desired area. This action produces lines with no material removal. The stroke-speed setting and the speed with which the Gravermeister is pulled determine the spacing effect. If you drag the tool at a constant speed, increasing the stroke speed results in closer spaced lines.

The liner is sharpened the same as a flat graver; that is, the face of the tool is held at about a 45-degree angle and like most gravers should be polished after sharpening. In addition, the tip of the liner should be gently wiped a time or two on a sheet of crocus cloth to remove burrs thus permitting polished cuts.

In talking with Don Glaser, President of GRS Corp., I understand that few people have been able to take the tool and start turning out work rapidly without some personal preliminary instruction from someone who is familiar with the tool's operation. However, Don tells me that many have started engraving only after an hour's time when they got started right with some personal guidance.

The machine is like a piano. Those people who show an interest in the instrument and practice religiously start producing faster. Those who aren't willing to practice don't seem to do very well. Therefore, if you decide to purchase one of these machines, you'll do well to purchase several engraver's practice plates from Brownell's Inc. They sell cheaply in lots of five plates, so you can practice, practice, practice for very little money.

The tool itself is of very little use without certain other tools. First of all, you'll need an engraving block. One such block is offered by GRS and was designed by a master engraver who was tired of block movement when making precision cuts. This massive, 28½ pound engraving block is a

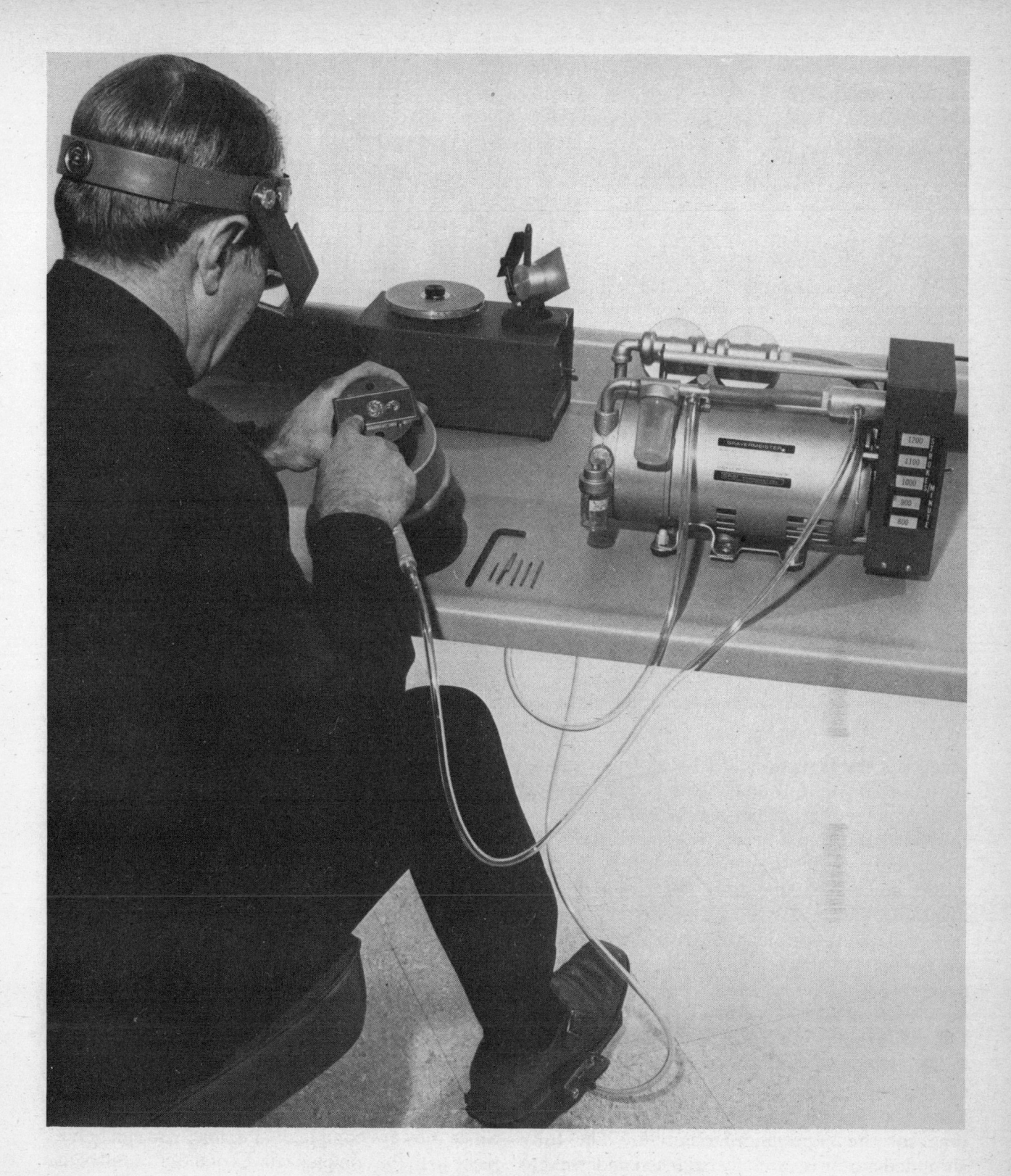

If you can afford the cash outlay, and have a *sincere* desire to enter the field of engraving, you might want to consider the Gravermeister engraving system. Many professional engravers have adopted this machine as it greatly speeds up production. Before buying *any* engraving equipment, the novice should consider his own artistic talents (and temperament) and try to discuss the field of engraving with someone who is experienced in the art.

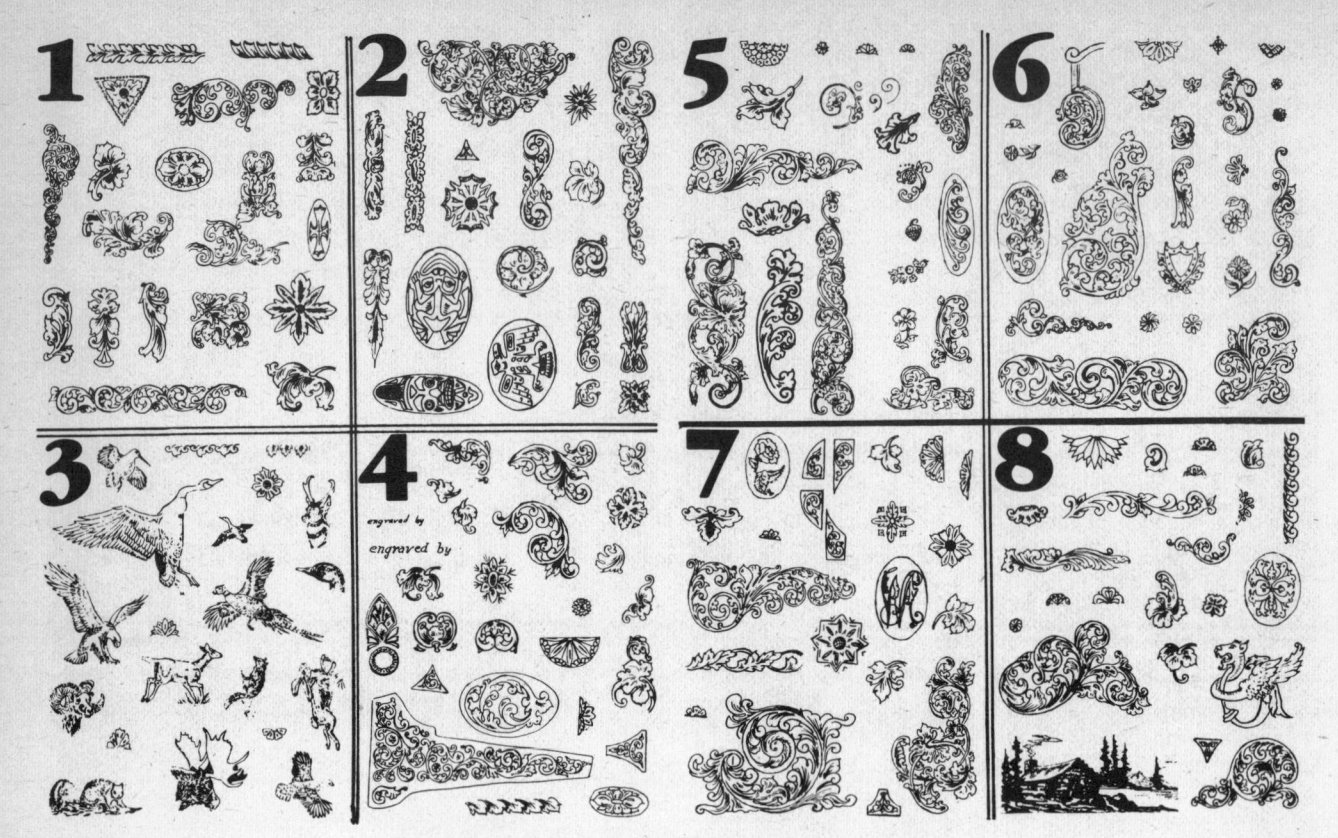

Gravermeister has a totally new concept in engraving pattern layout. Each numbered square has around 20 different design segments which are easily tranferred to the metal surface you wish to engrave.

precision, stable work-holder for all engraving including heavy cutting and chipping. The fully adjustable pivot drag will never develop looseness as the radial and thrust needle bearing between the crown and ball uses the entire mass of the block to absorb any undesirable shock or force on the cutting tool.

Besides an assortment of gravers, you'll need some means of sharpening them, as the tools will have to be sharpened often. The power honing tool—also offered by GRS—is ideal for this use. The power hone tool sharpener provides the same benefit for the task of sharpening that the Gravermeister does for engraving. It is faster and easier for the beginner to learn and saves valuable time for the experienced engraver. The fully shrouded motor is carefully balanced and trued to turn the 4" silicon carbide stone, or the long-lasting, fast cutting 600 grit diamond lap smoothly and without wobble. The 115-V, 60 Hz motor rotates the stone at a smooth 200 rpm for fast, no-heat tool sharpening. High position of the stone gives ample clearance to sharpen all graver points and tip angles. Flat top surface provides ideal platform for combined use with the GRS sharpening fixture to maintain consistent angles.

The Graver Sharpening Fixture provides accuracy for sharpening the tools. It enables gravers to be located exactly every time, assuring that your tool will cut the same after each sharpening.

The example provided above shows a totally new concept in engraving pattern layout designed by GRS Corp. Each numbered section contains about 20 individual design segments or motifs which are molded into a transparent rubber-stamp material. You simply cut out the pieces you need to make up the final design you want to lay out on the gun you are working on; ink them on a standard ink pad and transfer the inked pattern to the metal. Since they are completely flexible, you can bend a piece to fit the complex curves of the gun; and being transparent you can butt one segment correctly to another one and see that you are getting it right.

When properly sharpened chisels are used, the Gravermeister can also be used for stock carving. Sharp, rapid blows of the machine render smooth, polished cuts in all kinds of wood. For relief carving on wood, first layout the design. Next, with a

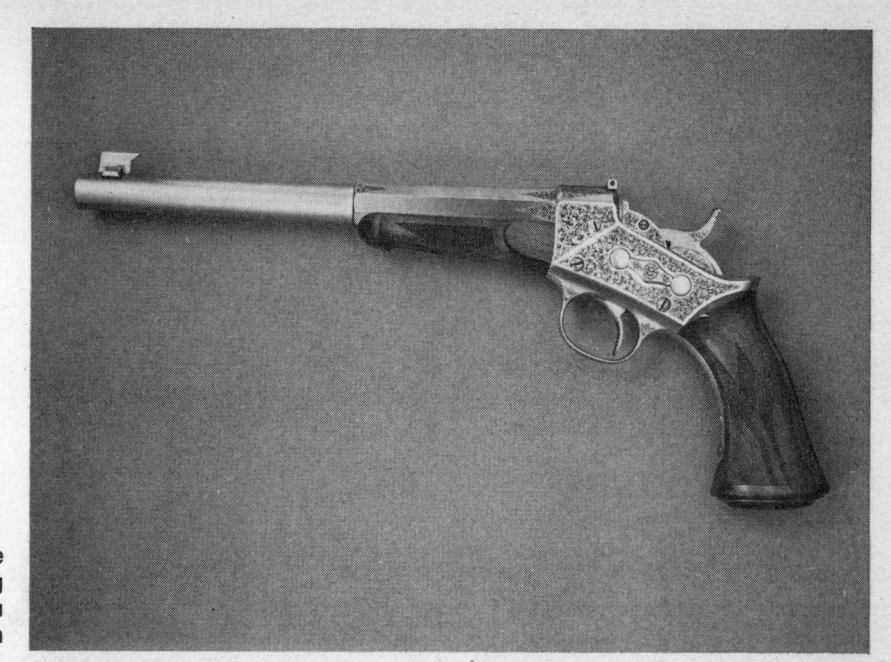

Engraving, such as the coverage shown on this Remington rolling block pistol, is a real work of art. You can be assured that the gentleman who did this job didn't do it overnight. A degree of artistic talent, the ability to take constructive criticism and more than a modicum of patience are necessary to pursue a career in engraving.

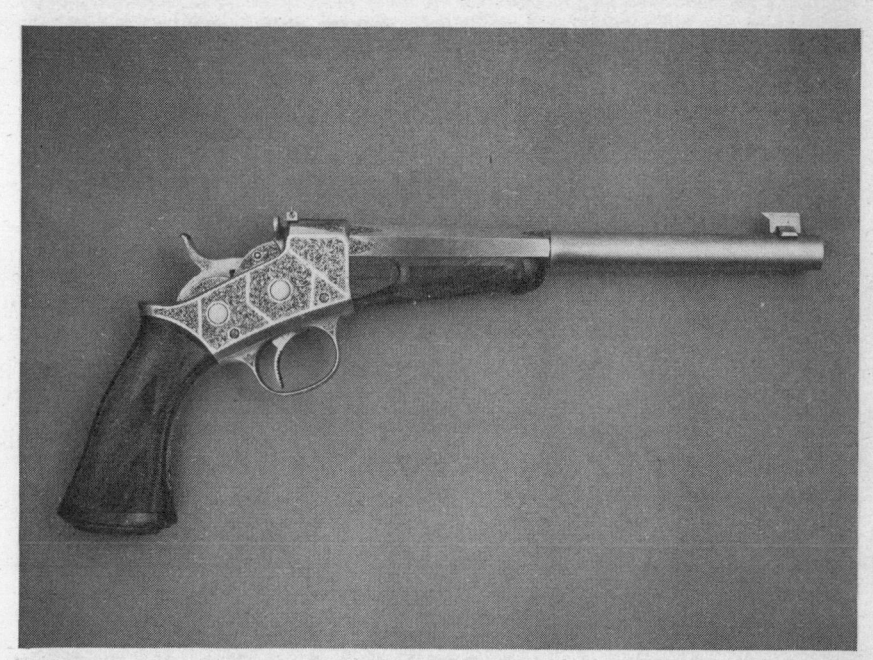

scalpel-like chisel gripped in the hand piece, follow the design outline backwards, not forward as one would in a normal cutting manner, at the same time applying power to the hand piece. Depth of the cut depends on the power supplied to the hand piece. Insert a scoop or gouge into the hand piece chuck and remove the background. As in metal work, the background can be stamped with a variety of punches, which of course are held in the jaws of the hand piece. Rasps, files and cutters held in the hand piece speed up the work without compromising control.

For wood carving, this machine can be very useful for stock designs and the process may not be as difficult as one might imagine. Stan de Treville offers decal carving patterns that are easily applied to the gun stock, where they provide outlines and guidelines for use in carving.

Just because you have a pattern, don't install it on your favorite, most expensive gun stock and start carving away until you have gained some experience. It would be a smart move to buy two patterns of the same design and try the first on an old, broken or otherwise useless gun stock. When you have gained confidence in your carving ability, use the other pattern on a good gun stock.

8
WOODWORKING TOOLS

THERE ARE many, many special woodworking tools available to the stock maker which you'll eventually want in your shop to speed up the stock finishing procedure. These include chisels, gouges, bottoming tools, rasps, inletting tools, curl scrapers and the like. You can, of course, stock up all at one time, but for openers, Frank Mittermeier's stock finishers kit will handle most of your needs. This set consists of one 8" smooth cut cabinet rasp for shaping and smooth finishing the stock; a chisel and two gouges to cut away the extra wood during the semi-inletting of the action and trigger guard; a bottoming file for flat bedding the action; and, a barrel inletting rasp, to shape the barrel channel to the exact dimensions of the barrel is also included. The kit also comes with sandpaper for a smooth exterior of the stock and three checkering tools—one each single, 2 line and

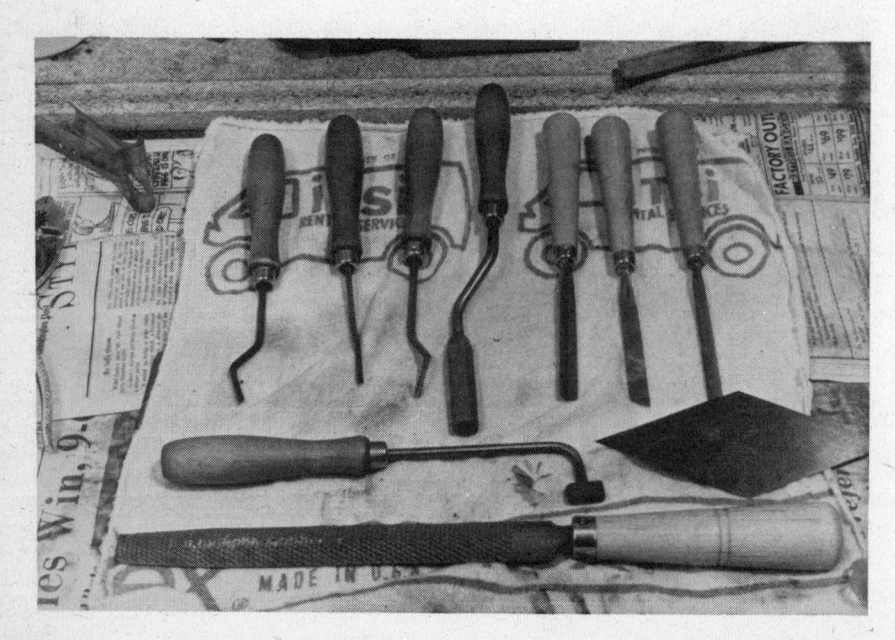

All of these woodworking tools are available from Frank Mittermeier — it's called the Stock-Finisher's Kit.

border tool. A diamond shaped lay-out template of the checkering pattern and full instructions on the whole procedure of inletting, shaping, finishing and checkering of the gun stock completes the set.

This kit contains all the tools necessary to completely finish a semi-inletted/finished stock. You can of course start with a walnut blank and do all the "bull work" yourself, but a lot of time can be saved if you start out on a semi-finished stock. Even if you have the time, you'll want to have several semi-finished stocks under your belt before attempting a complete stock from scratch. To do the latter satisfactorily, much talent and experience is necessary. On the other hand, anyone with a little patience and knowledge of what has to take place, can expertly stock a rifle or shotgun

is necessary to achieve the best results. In doing so, it is suggested that a spotting compound be used to indicate where the metal parts are touching; this provides a "map" to show the stockmaker where the excess wood must be removed.

The spotting compound commercially available is called Prussian blue inletting black such as the type sold at Brownell's, Inc. You can also make your own by mixing Vaseline with lamp black oil paint, obtainable at any hardware store. The main point for the beginner to realize is to proceed with caution—removing only a little wood at a time. Remember, once the wood is gone it *cannot* be replaced. If you do remove too much wood, you'll be faced with having to build up that area with epoxy or some type of wood filler.

When it comes to tapping barreled actions into a semi-inletted stock, use a No-Mar hammer like this one.

with one of the semi-inletted and approximately shaped blanks as offered by Bishop, Herter's, Fajen, and a host of others.

In general, the manufacturers of semi-finished stock blanks offer the blanks in two different ways: 1) for a standard model gun, they inlet the barrel channel to match the standard barrel; and 2) for a re-barreled gun (or an action that is commonly re-barreled), they generally provide a ½" barrel channel. The final inletting of a semi-finished stock is a relatively simple matter, and if executed with a little care, even the most inexperienced gun craftsman can achieve professional results.

Constant fitting of the metal parts to the wood with slow and careful removal of the excess wood

To begin work on a semi-inletted stock, tighten the action down into the stock, allowing the barrel to settle down as far as it will go into the barrel channel. Because of the excess wood, this won't be very far. Outline the outside contours of the barrel and receiver; this will tell you how high your barreled action is riding in the stock. A *gouge* is used for preliminary shaping and deepening of the barrel channel and then a barrel inletting rasp is used to complete the channel. Final smoothing is accomplished with sandpaper wrapped around the inletting rasp.

Any excess wood at the sides of the receiver is removed with a small chisel. Then coat the bottom of the barrel and the receiver with spotting compound before it is carefully placed in the stock and

STOCK REFINISHING

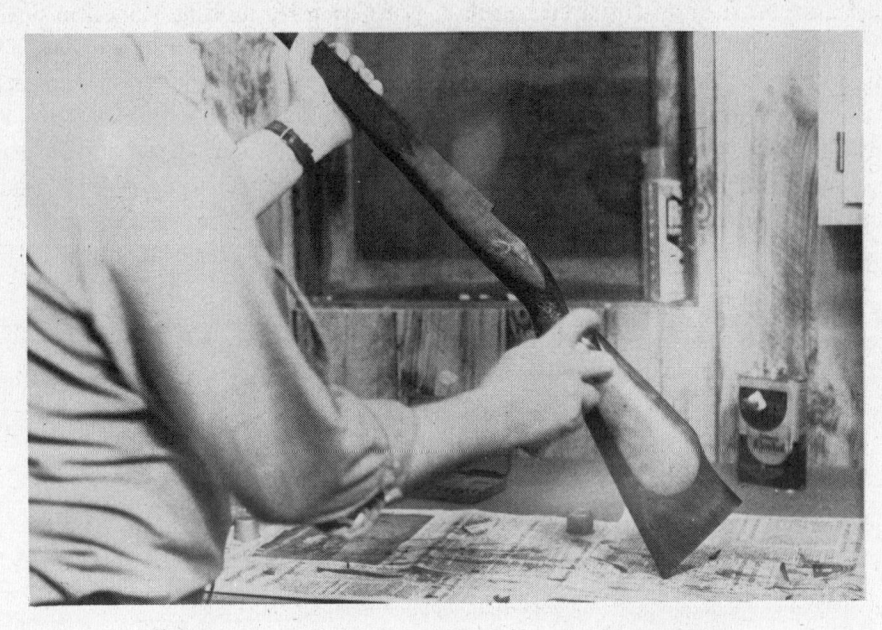

(Above and below) Old stock finish can be easily removed by using commercial preparations available from any paint store or gunsmith supply house. When removing finish from areas covered with checkering, a toothbrush will help make the job a lot easier.

If you're faced with removing the oily finish from old military stocks, mix a few ounces of whiting (available at most paint stores) with some AWA 1-1-1 and paint a thin layer onto the stock. As the solvent penetrates the wood, it dissolves any impregnated oil and brings it to the surface where it is absorbed by the whiting.

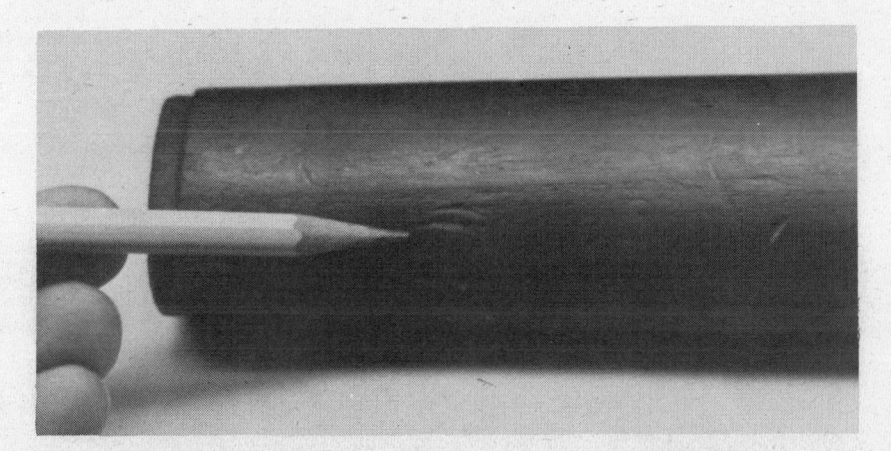

Once the old stock finish has been removed, any surface dents may be removed by applying a hot soldering iron to a dampened cloth placed directly over the dent. If the dent is severe, you may have to repeat the operation until the dent is raised completely or has risen to a point where a small amount of sanding will do the rest.

Before applying a new finish stock defects must be repaired. All of these stock defects may look hopeless, but, they can all be corrected by carefully splicing new wood to old. When splicing, great care should be taken to match up the grain flow of the new piece of wood to the grain flow of the stock itself.

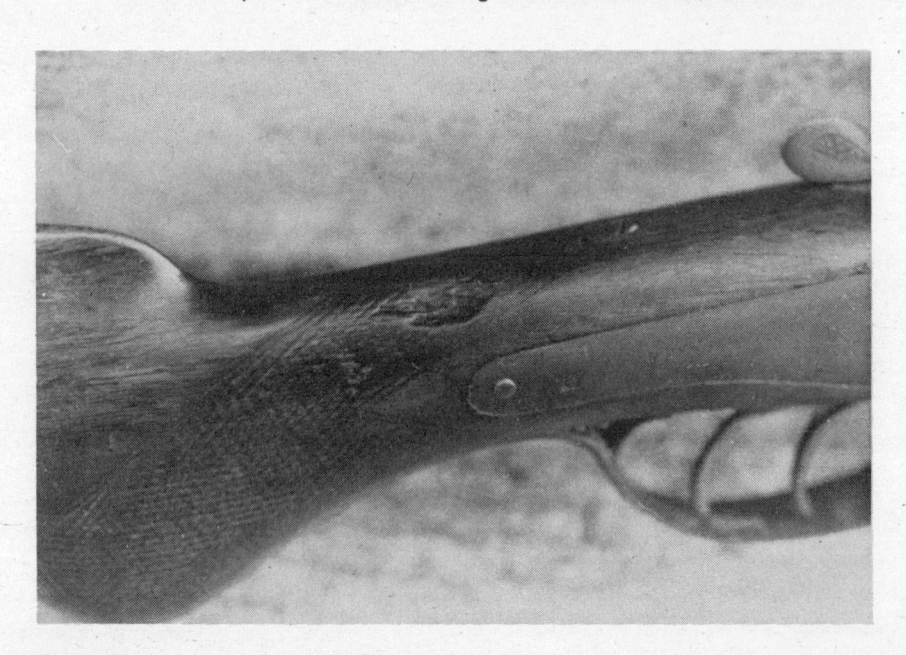

(Left) The range of popular stock finishes seems almost unlimited. The choice of which finish to use is often a matter between you and the man whose stock is being refinished.

(Below) After sanding and filling has taken place its time to select the finish you (and your customer) want and proceed following the instructions that come with the finish. In this instance, Birchwood-Casey's Tru-Oil is being used and applied with the hand. Applying an oil finish by hand makes the oil "stretch and flow" evenly.

As the coats of stock finish are applied, they must be given a proper place to dry out. A "drying closet" can be constructed out of plywood. A light bulb located at the bottom of the closet will help speed the drying time.

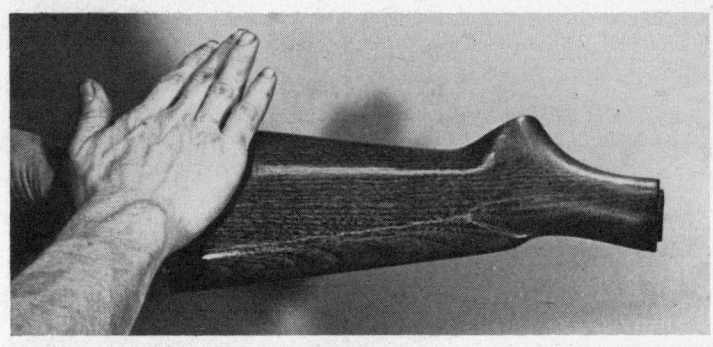

Depending upon the type of finish you use, you may find that the instructions advise sanding in between coats. If this is the procedure you are following, be sure to get a "Tac Rag" from one of the gunsmith supply houses. The Tac Rag is used to wipe down and remove sanding dust in between coats of finish.

This stock has received three coats of finish and is ready to be rubbed out. One of the most popular stock rubbing compounds is rottenstone. It can be found at any hardware store.

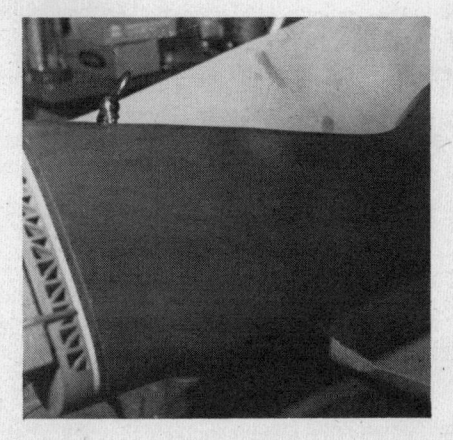

83

tightened down. The receiver should be tapped solidly into place with a plastic hammer. You then carefully remove the entire barrel/receiver assembly. Any irregularities or high spots, as indicated by the spotting compound, should be removed with a small chisel so that the action fits snugly into the wood. As the job progresses, the proper tool to be used should become obvious. Final touch up and cleaning is done with a bottoming file. Lastly, it should be said that most suppliers of semi-inletted stocks can provide explicit instructions for inletting their stocks. Certainly, that information can prove invaluable in using the tools described.

Checkering Tools and Equipment

Basic checkering tools are simple and inexpensive. This fact may lead one to believe that the process is just as simple. Checkering isn't difficult if you have patience. If you don't, you'll find the project impossible.

The basic tool used to checker wood is the "V" cutter which is used to cut the first or master lines. The other checkering tools used are the 2-line spacer and the border tool. The spacer tool determines the size of the checkering; that is the number of lines per inch. Generally, the 12, 14, 16, 18 and 20 lines-per-inch checkering is the most

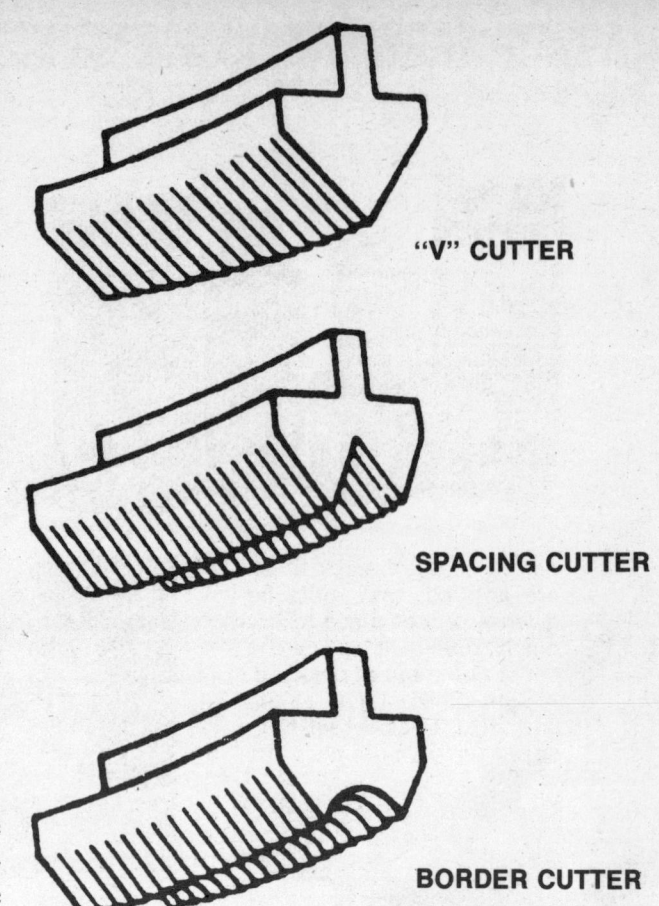

If you plan on doing any amount of stock work, chances are you'll want to get some checkering tools. The three basic cutting tools you'll need are (from top to bottom) the "V" cutter, a spacing cutter and a border tool.

Once the border of a checkering pattern is cut, take the 2-line spacer and, starting at the end of a border line, move the spacer forward in short thrusts, moving in one direction.

When cutting your borders, the use of a 2-line border cutter will provide you with a wide, concave border that's quite attractive.

working with the 2-line spacer, start at the end and work the spacer forward in short thrusts. Cant the tool enough to keep one row of teeth in firm contact with the line previously cut. After finishing the spacing in one direction within your checkering pattern, follow the same procedure in the other direction. When the spacing is complete, a second pass over the lines is performed with the spacer tool to remove the remaining wood.

On the second pass, cut the line deep enough so that the crest of the diamond will be nearly to a point. Keep brushing the saw dust out of your work as you progress because it can be very deceiving when it fills the diamonds or the grooves in between. A bordering tool may be used to obtain a wide, concave border if one so desires.

You may want to lay out your own patterns—perhaps using the book, *Checkering and Carving of Gunstocks* by Kennedy (Stackpole Books)—or use decal patterns as supplied by Stan De Treville. Stan has about two dozen different patterns from

To start the checkering job, use a straight edge (or French curve where appropriate) and knife to outline the border on the stock. Once this has been done, take a single-edge checkering tool and deepen the cuts made with the knife.

common on rifle stocks. The 20, 22 and 24 lines per inch are common on shotgun stocks.

In general, a checkering pattern is outlined on the forearm and pistol grip (both sides) of the stock and the outline and master lines are then cut with the "V" tool. This first pass should not exceed more than ½ the finished checkering depth. Now,

very simple to complex designs. All can be ordered direct or from gunsmith supply houses.

When using the patterns, it may be desirable to make minor modifications so that the design will fit better on certain gun stocks. This is accomplished by shortening or lengthening the designs by overlapping or filling in respectively. Design modifica-

After using your 2-line cutter in one direction, reverse field and cut the lines once again. When the spacing is complete and even in both directions, a second pass over the lines will cut them to full depth.

then swab smooth with a piece of cotton and wipe off excess water. Let it dry before attempting to checker.

At this point, three basic styles of checkering may be used. *American checkering* is the type most generally used on gunstocks made in the United States. In this type the lines are first scored lightly with a spacing tool starting with the "guide lines" on the decal pattern and working in both directions until the design is completed. The lines are gone over again with a "V" tool—as discussed previously—which deepens the cuts and bevels the edges of the diamonds. *English checkering* is similar to American checkering except the "V" tool is not used, leaving the diamonds flat on top instead of pointed. *French or Skip-line checkering* is most frequently used on fine custom made guns as it gives a more distinctive look than ordinary checkering. It is achieved by using two different width spacing tools. In the example shown, a regular spacing tool is used to cut three lines, then a spacing tool with twice the width is used to cut one line; then three more regular width lines are cut and so on. The effect may be varied by changing

tions of this type are limited only by the creativity of the user.

To apply the decal pattern, cut the decal pattern sheet apart so that the forearm pattern and both grip patterns are separate. Soak them in water just long enough for the decal to begin to loosen from the backing paper. Dampen the areas on the gun stock where the designs are to go, and apply the decal by carefully sliding them off the backing paper into the desired position. Make sure the patterns on each side of the stock are in alignment,

(Below and right) Checkering patterns or templates help simplify the layout of any checkering job. A wide variety of decal patterns are available from Stan De Treville.

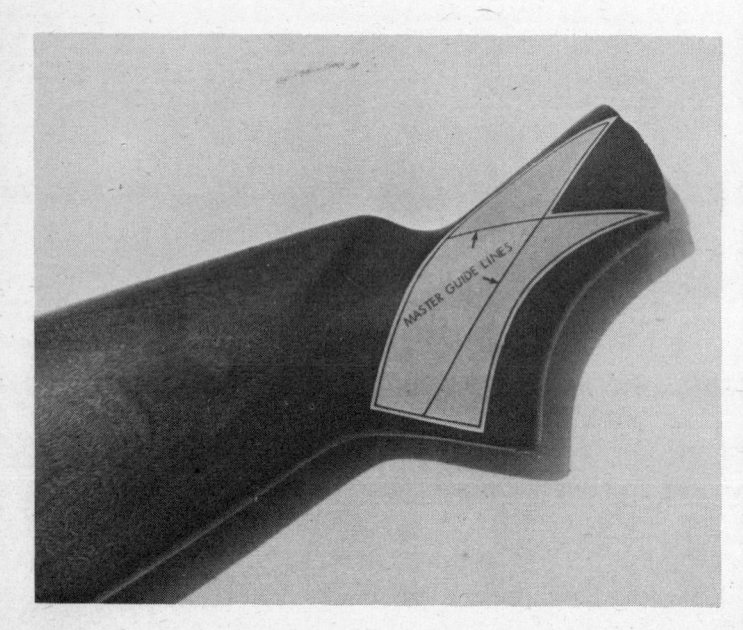

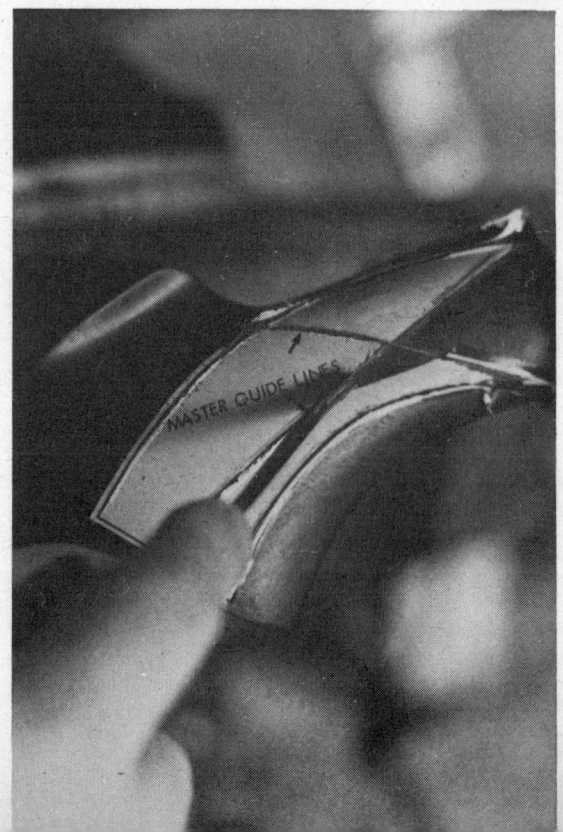

AMERICAN CHECKERING   ENGLISH CHECKERING   FRENCH CHECKERING

The most commonly found checkering styles are (from left to right) American, English and French — the latter referred to in this country as "Skip-line" checkering.

the number of regular lines cut, the number of lines skipped or both.

Once the checkering job is completed, place a damp cloth over the checked area. Then press a piece of Scotch tape firmly over the area and peel up; the tape will pick up the tiny pieces of decal which are left sticking to the wide flat-topped diamonds in a skip-line checkering job.

To start the checkering job, use a straightedge (or French curves where the lines curve) and knife to cut the border lines and the guidelines on the decal. Then use a single cutting tool to deepen the cuts made with the knife. Make certain that these initial lines are precisely cut as they will be your "guide" for all other lines cut in the pattern.

If hand checkering tools are used, the spacing cutter is then used to cut parallel lines to the guidelines as discussed previously. However, there are at least two types of power checkering tools on the market that will make the job go a little faster. The Burgess Vibro-Tool is an excellent tool to have around the gunshop. Besides the checkering tools, other accessories include engraving points, saw blade, abrasive point for frosting glass and sharpening tools, wood chisels, etc. Frank Mittermeier furnishes special checkering heads to fit the Vibro-Tool, and regardless whether you use the hand checkering tools or the faster MMC Power Checkering Head, you'll want the Vibro-Tool to checker up to border lines. Since the tool requires no back-and-forth motion, the cutter may be worked up precisely to border lines without overcutting.

For most checkering jobs, the Vibro-Tool should be used on its HI position; that is, 7200 strokes per minute. This speed gives a smooth even hum and is best for the delicate work of stock checkering. There is also a "Depth-of-Stroke" adjuster that controls the length of the stroke from a minimum of zero to a maximum of over ⅛-inch. To lengthen the stroke, turn the knob counterclockwise.

Power checkering tools can be helpful if you end up doing any volume of checkering work. The Burgess Vibro-Tool is very useful, especially when cutting near border lines.

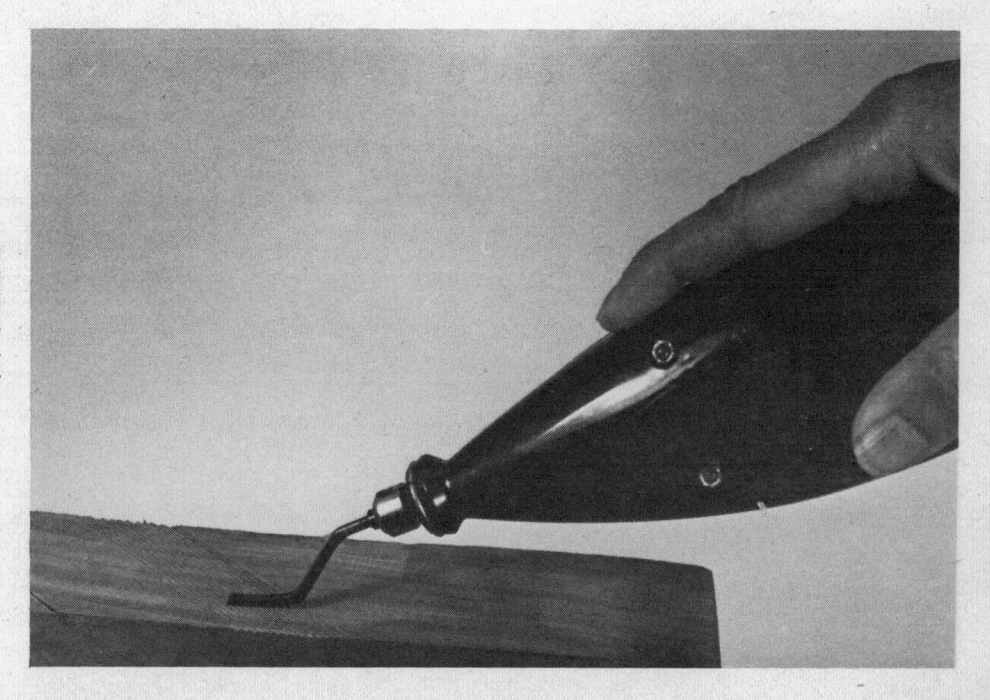

One of the most popular power checkering tools is made by MMC — it's used by many shops where checkering production is high. Above is a shot of the handle and power head; to the left is the entire unit, complete with motor.

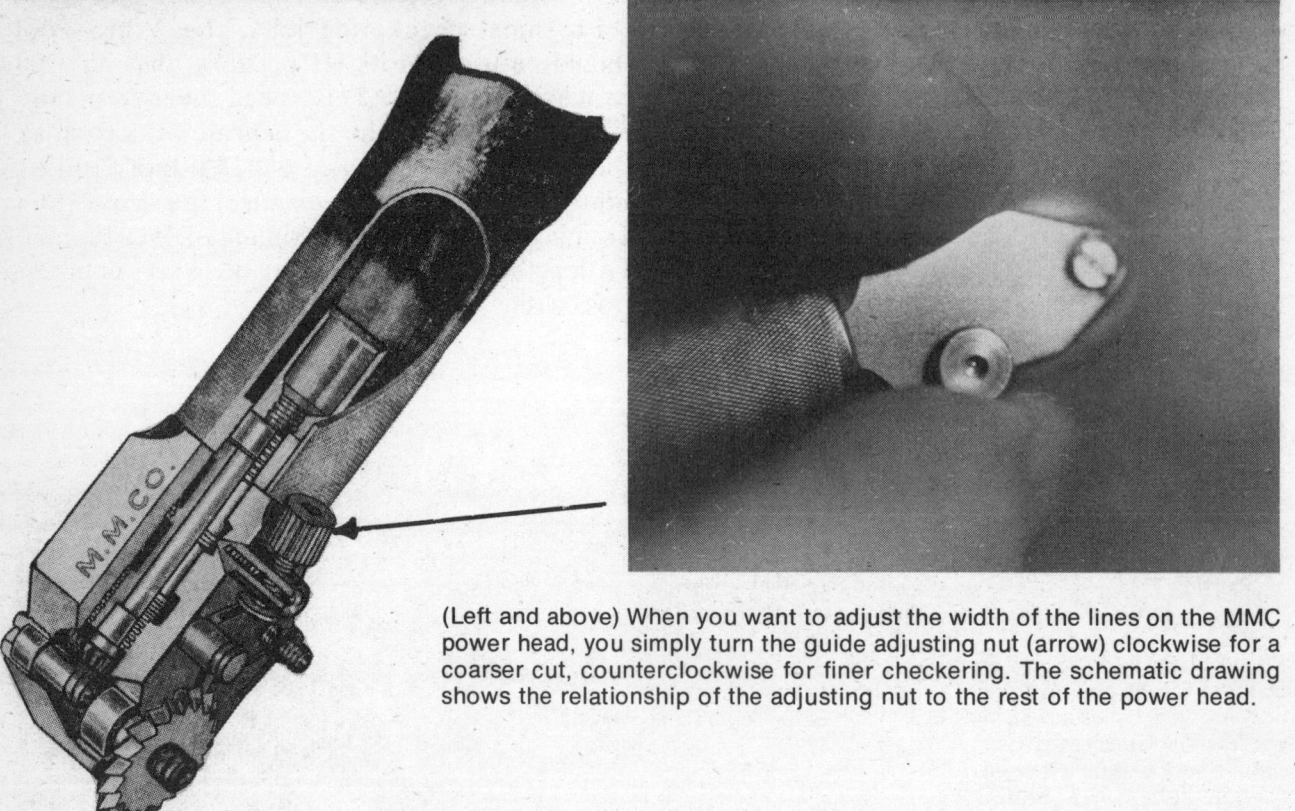

(Left and above) When you want to adjust the width of the lines on the MMC power head, you simply turn the guide adjusting nut (arrow) clockwise for a coarser cut, counterclockwise for finer checkering. The schematic drawing shows the relationship of the adjusting nut to the rest of the power head.

Maximum finger control of the tool may be had by holding it like a pencil, but for checkering, the tool should be held more firmly. Don't bear down too hard, as this will only shorten the stroke somewhat and tire the hand. Let the tool do the work for you. Also make certain that the stock is secured firmly in a checkering cradle or vise (in the case of small pistol grips, etc.). Always experiment with a piece of scrap material before trying out the Vibro-Tool on a new job.

One of the most popular power checkering tools in the industry is one developed by Bob Sconce of MMC. The outfit consists of a power checkering head and a Foredom industrial grade CC motor,

The handle of the MMC checkering unit is knurled just above the power head to provide a firm, sure grip.

flexible shaft, rheostat and a hand piece. The checkering head is a beautiful, precision high-performance instrument that has proven to be a popular money maker for anyone who checkers guns—whether he be manufacturer, full-time stockmaker, gunsmith or serious hobbyist. The fast, true-cutting operation, non-fatiguing ease of handling and simplicity of adjustment makes any checkering job a pleasure.

The checkering tool is set and tested at the factory for 18-lines-per-inch checkering. However, it may readily be adjusted to cut any other width checkering from 16 to 24 lines per inch by turning the guide adjusting nut clockwise for coarser and counterclockwise for finer checkering. Special thin cutters are even available for cutting checkering finer than 24 lines per inch. The depth adjusting screw should be adjusted so that the guide, when depressed, is level with the cutter. The width of checkering is set by experimenting on a piece of flat scrap walnut and measuring with a screw-thread gauge.

The guidelines should be cut to full depth as discussed previously. The remaining lines may be cut to full depth on the first two or three passes by tilting the head slightly to the left while making the passes. Subsequent lines will be cut to full depth and will require little, if any, "finishing up" with a

The width of checkering with a power tool should be set by experimenting on a piece of flat scrap walnut and then measuring the results with a screw-thread gauge.

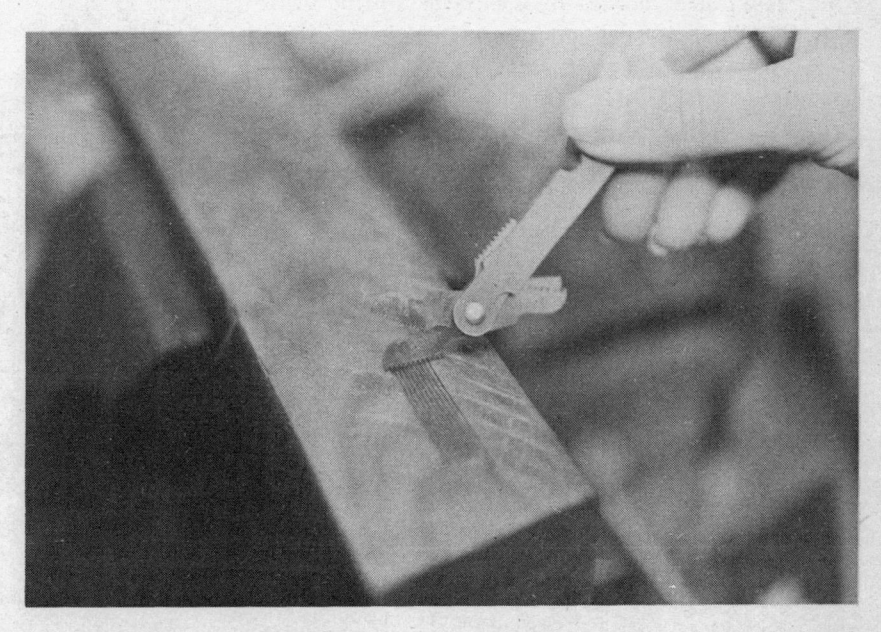

89

hand tool. Of course, the proficiency of the operation comes with practice.

The speed at which the machine is operated is determined by conditions such as width of checkering, hardness of wood, and speed of the operator. Sufficient speed should be maintained to avoid chatter but excessive speeds accomplish nothing and might cause the cutter to heat. Too low a speed can cause the load on the flexible coupling to exceed the manufacturer's design and cause trouble.

If this is your first attempt at using the MMC Power Checkering Tool, don't expect to get a professional job the first time around. I experienced trouble in getting even lines the first few minutes of experimenting. However, like practically all new tools I have used, a few hours practice has made its use second nature. Again, practice on scraps of flat and curved pieces of walnut until some skill in manipulating the tool is acquired. Then you'll be ready to tackle a checkering job on a quality piece of walnut.

Miscellaneous Checkering Tools

You'll need some type of device for holding the gunstock firmly without damaging the finish and which permits the stock to be rotated or positioned at almost any angle for easy checkering. You can build your own like the one shown or from plans in *The American Rifleman* or other gunsmith books, but you'll probably do better by buying Brownell's Checkering Cradle. (This cradle sells for very little, and if you value your time at all, you won't come close to building one for twice the amount.) The Brownell Checkering Cradle is simple in design, low in cost, of rugged wood construction and highly practical. It's adjustable to hold stocks up to 33" long. Stocks are held firmly without marring the finish, yet turning of the stock is permitted as the work progresses. It can be bolted to a bench or secured in a vise, the choice is yours.

I've experienced some difficulty in holding shotgun butt stocks in this device as the butt sometimes slips in the plastic holder. However, if you remove the existing wing nuts and screws and replace this with pointed screws you'll solve the problem.

Magnifying Visor: An optical glass binocular magnifier of 1½ to 2½ power is a big help in preventing overruns and for doing some of the more intricate checkering and carving. The most popular among gunsmiths is the OptiVISOR distributed by Brownell's. It magnifies 1¾ times at 14 inches. The next most popular size is the type that magnifies 2½ times at 8 inches.

Xacto Knife: Xacto knives have various shapes of blades available to make them very useful for cutting guidelines and for doing much of the carving on the fancier patterns.

Set of Small Carving Tools: Small chisels and gouges of various shapes are very useful in carving the small circles and scrolls found in some of the more ornate designs. Included in the category of carving tools is a *layout guide* and a checkering *pounce wheel*. The former insures that your checkering pattern comes out properly positioned and truly parallel to the top line of the fore-end as well as exactly matching the position of the pattern on the other side. The marking quill is fully adjustable to mark both top and bottom lines of the pattern,

When doing *any* checkering, you should be sure that the stock being worked on is securely held. A stock cradle is the answer; and, they are available from any of the gunsmith supply houses.

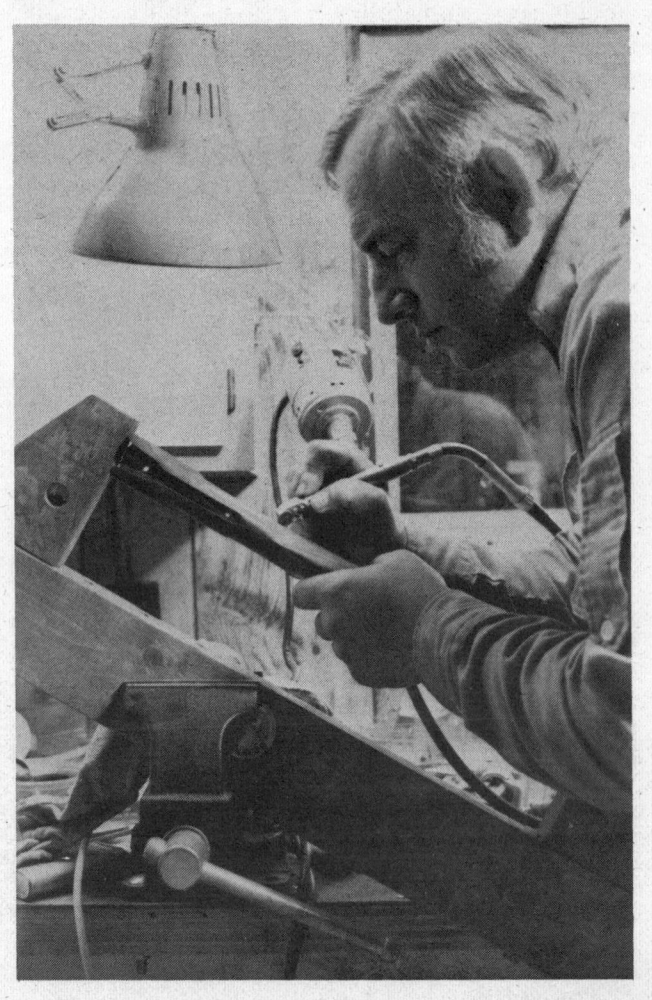

PLANS FOR A CHECKERING CRADLE

If you need a stock cradle and don't want to spend the money for a ready-made version, you can follow these plans and build your own.

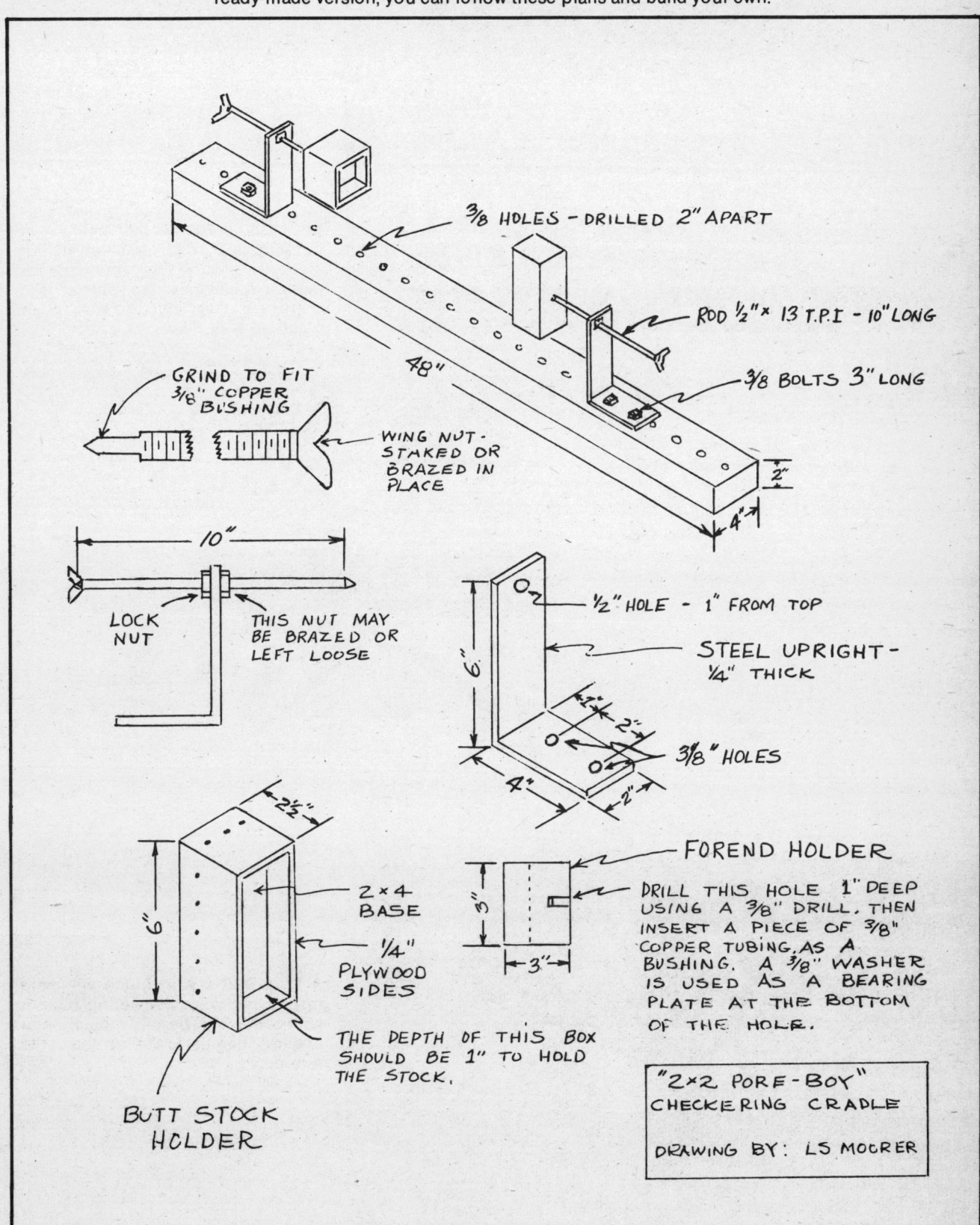

3/8 HOLES – DRILLED 2" APART

ROD 1/2" × 13 T.P.I – 10" LONG

48"

3/8 BOLTS 3" LONG

2"

4"

GRIND TO FIT 3/8" COPPER BUSHING

WING NUT – STAKED OR BRAZED IN PLACE

10"

LOCK NUT

THIS NUT MAY BE BRAZED OR LEFT LOOSE

1/2" HOLE – 1" FROM TOP

STEEL UPRIGHT – 1/4" THICK

6"

4"

2"

3/8" HOLES

2½"

2×4 BASE

6"

1/4" PLYWOOD SIDES

THE DEPTH OF THIS BOX SHOULD BE 1" TO HOLD THE STOCK.

BUTT STOCK HOLDER

3"

3"

FOREND HOLDER

DRILL THIS HOLE 1" DEEP USING A 3/8" DRILL, THEN INSERT A PIECE OF 3/8" COPPER TUBING, AS A BUSHING. A 3/8" WASHER IS USED AS A BEARING PLATE AT THE BOTTOM OF THE HOLE.

"2×2 PORE-BOY" CHECKERING CRADLE

DRAWING BY: L.S. MOORER

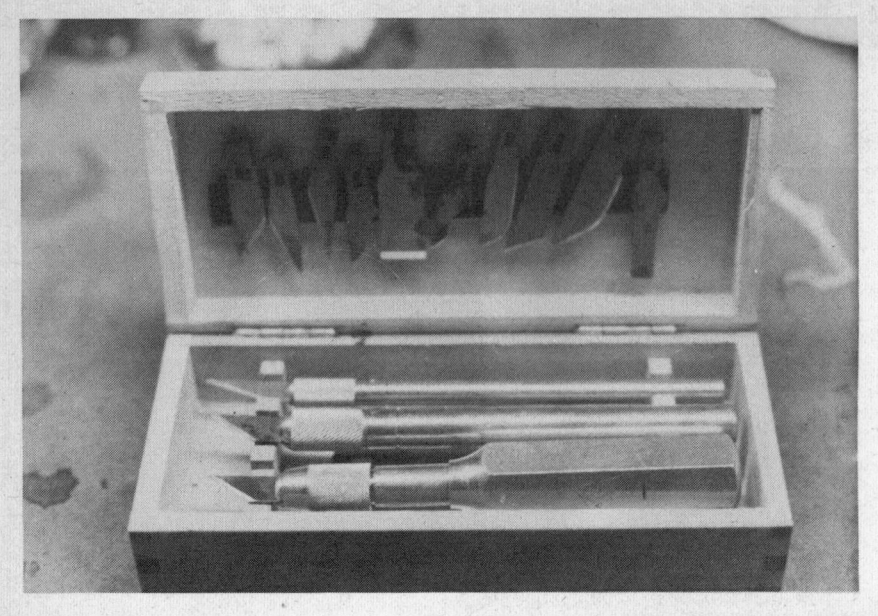

(Left and below) One of the most useful "tools" a woodworker can have in his shop is a set of Xacto knives. For checkering work, they are handy for cutting guidelines. As you can see there are a variety of Xacto knife blade profiles.

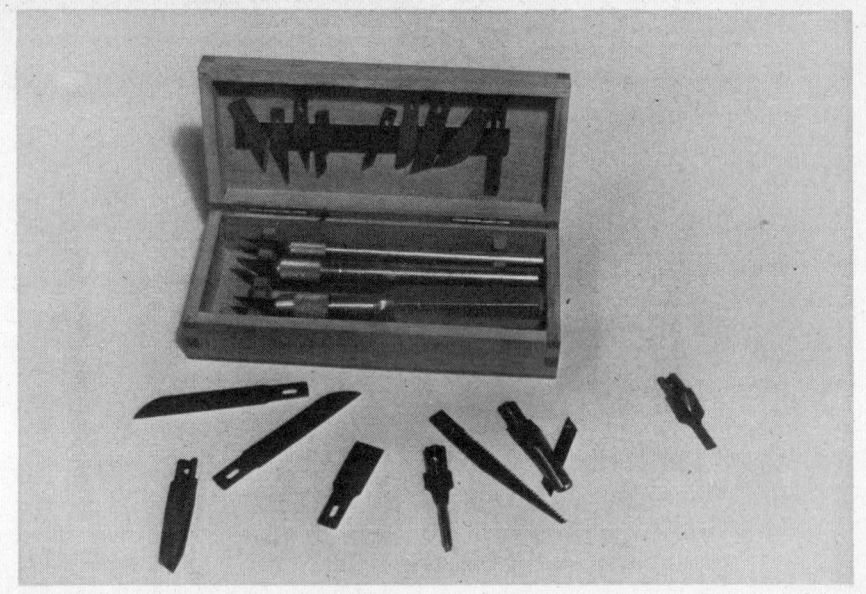

A Dem-Bart layout guide will help insure that your checkering pattern will come out properly positioned and truly parallel to the top line of the fore-end.

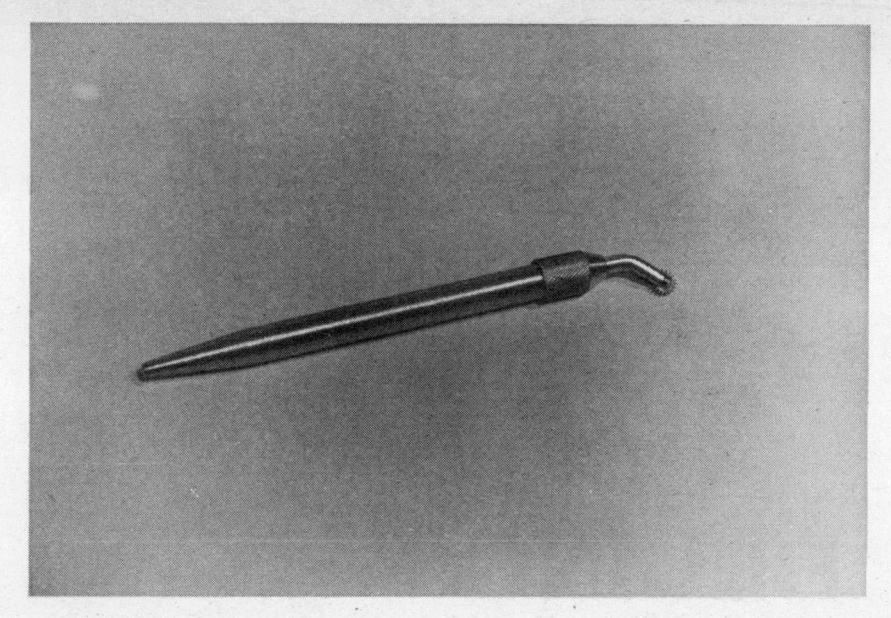

When laying out checkering patterns, or marking the lines on a checkering template, the checkering "pounce" wheel comes in handy. By first running this tool along the desired border lines, you will get a series of equally-spaced dots that serve to lay a path for your first border line cutting strokes.

and the fixed arm is long enough to lay across the flats of the widest barrel channel.

The checkering pounce wheel is perferred by many for transferring patterns from paper drawings (or the Stan De Treville decals) to the stocks. With a little practice, you'll discover that by drawing the tool along, you can follow tight curves and sharp angles. The results are a series of deep, fine, easy-to-follow dots in the wood, which are a good guide for the knife or gouge to follow.

Needle or Pattern Maker Files: These small files will come in handy for truing-up checkering and for finishing carved surfaces. Veiners, for example, are excellent for making curved lines, *fleur de lis* or any border work. They are also used for border clean-up at border junctions.

Checkering rifflers are used by many gunstock checkerers and stockmakers for pointing-up checkering, cleaning up damaged or old checkering and for border work. The No. 131 riffler offered by Brownell's has a 3-square shape, cutting a perfect 60° angle, and it will make the finest hair-line cut at the bottom of the diamond grooves.

Bent needle files that are "V" shaped and bent at 90 degrees are used to point-up 90-degree diamonds and normally come in medium or fine cut. The back of the file should be "safe"; that is, will not cut.

Three-square bent needle files are used for pointing-up new checkering and cleaning out old. This is the favorite of stock checkerers for getting true, sharp diamonds. Most are available in three cuts: *coarse*—for cleaning out old checkering; *medium*—for pointing up new diamonds; and *fine*—also for pointing up new diamonds.

You'll want to purchase needle file handles for use with all your files. Good needle file handles help the file become a part of your hand. They also help to control the direction of cuts and eliminate canting.

—9—
BLUING EQUIPMENT

FEW gunsmithing projects can be as rewarding as the bluing of firearms. First of all, as the guns are dismantled, the operating characteristics of the guns become instilled in one's mind. Further handling of the more popular guns soon leads the gunsmith to know—almost instantaneously and without thinking—just what parts are worn, broken or need replacing. This knowledge is obviously invaluable when troubleshooting firearms.

Also, few operations are more pleasing than to see a rusted and badly-worn firearm turn into a thing of beauty with rich, blue-black finish instead of the reddish rust. For those who are not familiar with the bluing operation, the process seems like magic; that is, turning a worn firearm into one that looks brand new. But for the person doing the bluing, he knows that the process was not a magic act. Rather, it was accomplished by knowing what he was doing, a masterful job of polishing all the surfaces true and bright, keeping the corners sharp, and not funnelling the screw holes. Furthermore, he made absolutely certain that all parts were thoroughly cleaned with a degreasing solution before bluing. The results were rewarding—a perfect blue-black finish on the steel that will last for years to come.

For cold bluing, you'll need some 3-0 steel wool, cold blue solution, clean cotton swabs, a degreaser and some quality gun oil.

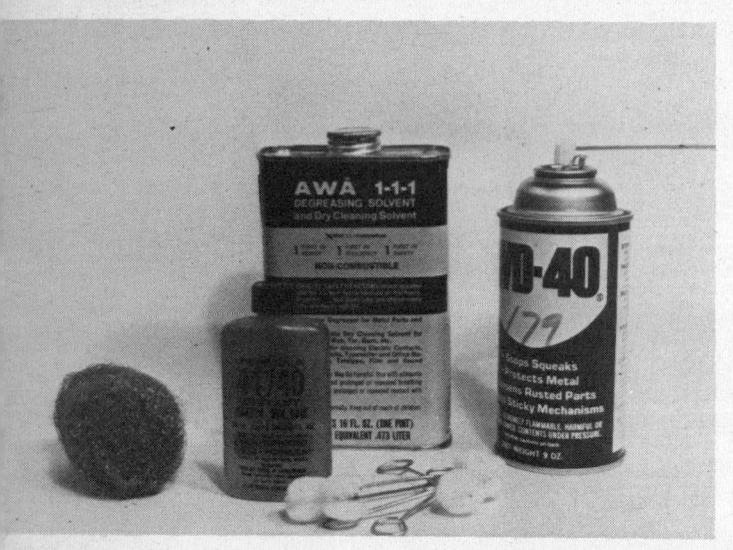

Cold Bluing

There are dozens of cold or instant bluing solutions on the market that will blue or blacken gun metal. Some are superior to others, but all of them will produce good results if care is taken. Regardless of the bluing solution used, you will need a cleaner-degreaser solution, steel wool, applicators and for other than touch-up jobs, a blue remover cloth. One of the best kits on the market is supplied by Birchwood Casey and called Perma-Blue Kit. This kit contains everything needed for a quick touch-up or a complete rebluing job. It is also one of the easiest bluing solutions to use. It gives a deep blue-black finish with few problems.

The equipment shown is essential for good cold bluing results. Rubber gloves should be worn to keep finger prints off the metal parts and to avoid any possible skin irritation. The large wire ring-handled dauber-type swabs are excellent for applying the blue and rust remover, the cleaner-degreaser and the cold blue solution. Steel wool is used for removing rust, scouring, polishing and burnishing the metal surfaces of the firearm. The oil is applied for lasting protection from rust. All of these supplies are available from Brownell's.

To cold blue a firearm, first clean all parts to be blued with a cleaner-degreaser to remove all grease, oil and dirt. This cleaner may be one of the commercial cleaner-degreasers like those manufactured by Birchwood Casey or any of the substitutes for old-fashioned carbon tetrachloride (such as chlorothene). Wood alchohol may also be used to clean the metal surfaces. Once clean, wipe the surface of the metal dry.

The old blue is removed with a liquid blue and rust remover such as those supplied by Herter's, Brownell's, Birchwood Casey, etc. Use a piece of steel wool to apply and scrub all parts to be reblued. However, before using the steel wool, it must be thoroughly degreased with RIG III (or some other suitable degreaser) as most steel wool comes from the factory soaked in oil to prevent rusting.

Once most of the old blue is removed, brighten all areas to be blued with abrasive cloth (320 followed by 400 wet and dry sandpaper strips will work nicely). Work around the barrel from the muzzle to the breech with a rapid "shoe-shine" motion—removing as many rough spots and pits as possible.

Once again clean all of the metal parts with the cleaner-degreaser and afterwards do not touch any of the metal parts, not even with the rubber gloves if at all possible. Apply the cold blue with the swabs in long even strokes. Do this as quickly as possible and try not to let the bluing solution run all over the metal; *it should be carefully applied,* not splashed on. After the solution has worked about one minute, it should be wiped off with a clean, oil-free cloth. Polish the reblued surface with clean (degreased) steel wool and then reapply the bluing solution at least three times to obtain a rich dark blue and to thoroughly cover all areas.

After the desired results (depth of color) have been obtained, oil the metal thoroughly with a good gun oil or Birchwood Casey's Sheath Take-Along—a polarized rust preventative which neutralizes the corrosive action of moisture, sweat and salt water. It drys to a thin, non-gumming film.

For mere touch-ups, good results can usually be obtained by just degreasing the metal and applying the cold blue until the area blends in with the surrounding metal. Of course, wipe clean and oil.

One of the disadvantages of cold bluing is the difficulty in obtaining an even finish over the entire surface. Streaks and uneven surfaces are common if great care is not taken. Birchwood Casey offers an immersion cold blue kit that greatly simplifies

If you plan on cold bluing an entire rifle or shotgun, you might want to consider buying a Birchwood-Casey cold blue immersion tank. It will help to make a neat job out of a chore that can sometimes become a shade messy.

the process and eliminates streaks and uneven surfaces. The kit comes with a plastic tank and the necessary chemicals and materials to blue 10 or more guns. All parts are dipped in the chemicals rather than applying them with swabs as discussed previously. The operation, however, is otherwise similar to the conventional cold bluing process. The result is an even, rich blue-black finish that closely resembles the color obtained from the hot bluing salts method.

Even professional gunsmiths are finding a use for this cold blue kit. Double barreled shotguns and those with soft soldered ribs are seldom blued by the hot-dip process as the chemicals react on the solder to soften it. A time-consuming rusting process is normally used—requiring several hours (if not days) to complete the job. This cold bluing immersion kit enables these jobs to be performed in a short time with good results.

The plastic tank that comes with this kit is also excellent for using blue and rust remover solutions prior to hot bluing.

Professional Hot Bluing

The hot bluing method is used by all leading firearm manufacturers in their finishing operations. It is also the common method employed by gunsmiths doing a large volume of bluing jobs. The resulting black oxide finish is handsome, extremely durable and "takes" well on modern steels. At this point it should be stated that the bluing process is an oxidization process intended for ferrous metals (steel) only. Many of today's firearms utilize aluminum components. A good example is Smith & Wessons Model 39, 9mm autoloader. The frame of that pistol is made of aluminum alloy. It *cannot* be blued by conventional cold or hot blue methods. In fact, any attempt to *hot blue* any aluminum alloy part will result in that parts total destruction. When it comes to "bluing" aluminum, *don't*.

If you're not sure if a part is aluminum or steel, keep a small magnet handy and you'll get your answer fast. (Blackening aluminum is covered further on in this chapter.)

The steps required to perform this steel bluing are as follows:

1. Remove old finish.
2. Polish all surfaces to be blued.
3. Clean metal surfaces in hot alkali cleaner.
4. Rinse in cold water.
5. Suspend parts to be blued in bluing solution.
6. Rinse in cold water.
7. Soak in hot soluble oil *or* boil in water for about 10 minutes and then oil all surfaces thoroughly.

The following are the essentials for a good professional quality blue job:

Polishing Equipment: A two-wheel buffer with one cutting wheel and one finishing wheel is a minimum set-up for polishing metal parts to be blued—if the operation is to be handled on a profitable basis. Many firearms have been blued with hand polishing only, but the time involved prohib-

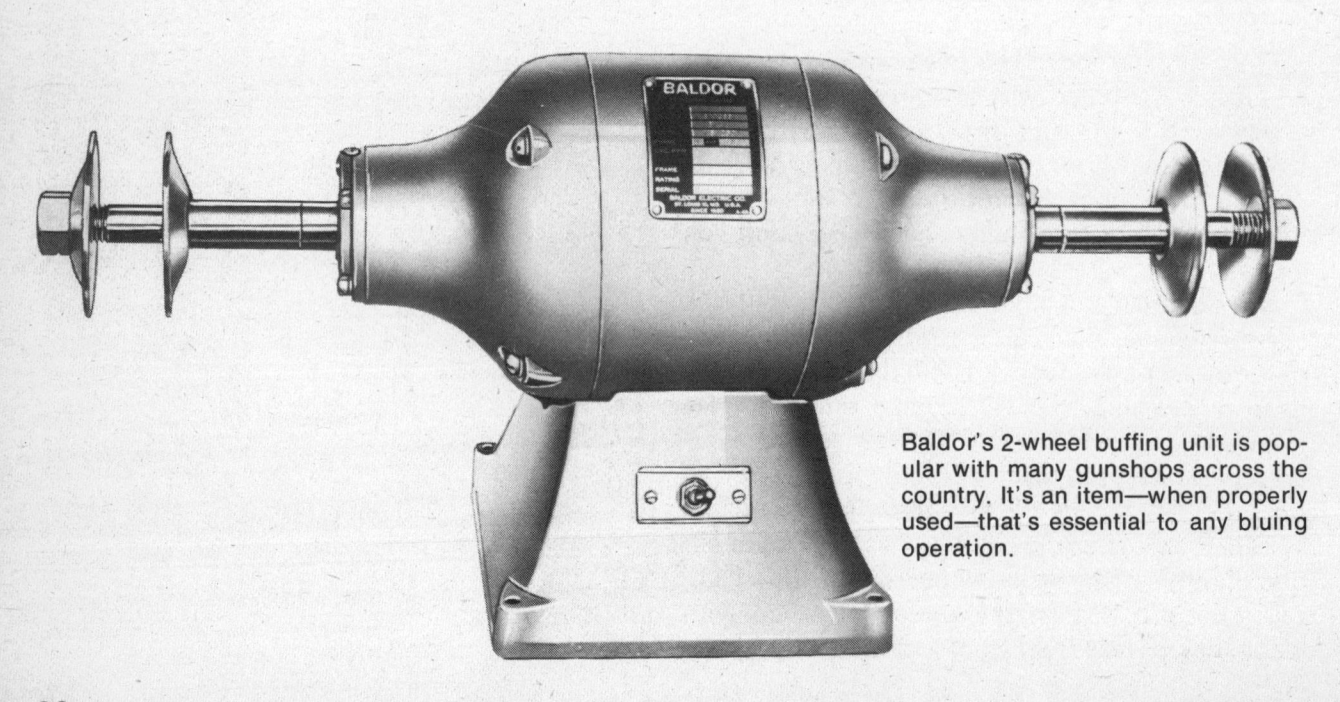

Baldor's 2-wheel buffing unit is popular with many gunshops across the country. It's an item—when properly used—that's essential to any bluing operation.

its its use in this day and time.

The Baldor buffer seems to be the most popular for use in gunshops. For the professional shop doing a substantial business, a 1 HP motor at 1725 rpm is recommended. For an occasional bluing job, a smaller buffer will give complete satisfaction as will a muslin buffing wheel attached to a conventional bench grinder or even a drill motor held in a vise.

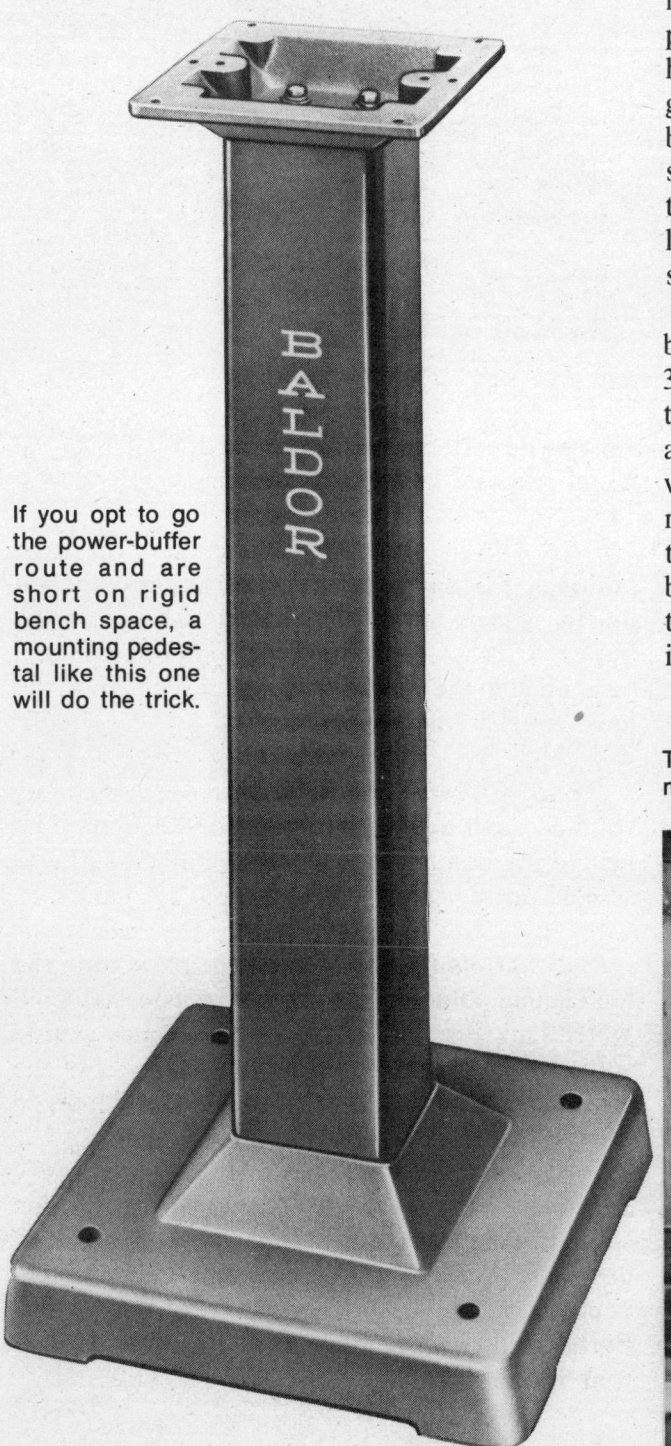

If you opt to go the power-buffer route and are short on rigid bench space, a mounting pedestal like this one will do the trick.

A heavy cast iron buffer pedestal will help keep the buffer perfectly steady during operation and gives free access to both polishing wheels for best polishing results. The ideal mounting location is away from walls so that both shafts are exposed for full 360-degree polishing on all parts of guns including barrels and receivers.

My own buffer consists of a modified bench grinder obtained from Montgomery Ward. It is mounted on the corner of my work bench to expose the left-hand shaft of the grinder. The left-hand grinding wheel was removed, as well as the guards and 6" and 8" buffing wheels are used for buffing. The speed of the shaft is 3600 rpm. This setup gave me a combination buffer/grinder that takes up little space and didn't cost me an arm and leg. For the occasional bluing job, I consider this setup to be ideal.

A very satisfactory finish for hunting guns may be obtained by using 3 stitched muslin wheels and 3 loose muslin wheels on the buffer. On one end of the buffer's double shaft, place 3 stitched wheels and on the other end, place the 3 loose muslin wheels. Before applying any polish, however, make certain that the wheels are in proper condition to receive the polish. A crystolon rubbing brick may be used for dressing, cleaning and/or truing felt and muslin wheels. These bricks are ideal for breaking in new muslin cloth wheels prior

The author's own metal polishing system is simply a modified bench grinder complete with buffing wheel.

(Above) When your buffing wheels become overloaded with buffing compound, you will have to dress them down a bit. A crystolon rubbing brick is perfect for the job.

(Right) When applying polishing compound to a buffing wheel, the best way to do so is to get the wheel running full tilt, then, after turning the motor off, apply the compound until the wheel stops.

to applying the first application of polish.

With the wheels in shape, start the buffer and bring it up to full speed; then shut it off. As the wheel speed is slowing down, touch the tube of polishing compound to the wheel until it stops. Several applications will give a smooth even coating, which should be allowed to dry about 5 minutes prior to using. Grit size 140 should be applied to the stitched wheels and 240 grit to the loose muslin wheels.

The buffing wheels are now ready for cutting and polishing, but in doing so, be careful at all times not to round corners on frames and actions or to funnel screw holes. Either lowers the value of the firearm and is certain to curtail future bluing jobs for you.

The hot bluing method is used by leading firearm manufacturers in their finishing operations and is also the common method employed by gunsmiths doing a substantial volume of bluing jobs. The resulting black oxide finish obtained by this method is handsome, extremely durable and "takes" well on modern steels. Simply put, it's a professional finish.

The steps required to perform the hot bluing operation are as follows:

Remove Old Finish: A rust and blue remover, such as the type offered by Brownell's, is the easiest and fastest way to remove the old finish. Follow directions carefully and don't leave the metal parts in the solution too long.

Polish All Surfaces: A very satisfactory finish for hunting guns may be obtained by using 3 stitched muslin wheels and 3 loose muslin wheels on the buffer. Grit size 140 polishing compound should be applied to the stitched wheels and 240 grit to the loose muslin wheels.

Clean Surfaces in Hot Alkali Cleaner: A cleaning solution such as Dicro-Clean No. 909 should be heated in one of the tanks and all metal surfaces soaked in this compound for about 15 minutes.

Rinse in Cold Water: Remove the parts from the hot cleaner solution and quickly transfer to a cold water tank for rinsing. Scrub thoroughly with a soft (not metal) bristle brush to remove all of the cleaner, making sure that all parts are submerged at all times.

Suspend Parts in Bluing Solution: Bluing solution should be kept at a temperature from between 285 degrees F. to 292 degrees F. and the parts suspended in this solution from 15 to 30 minutes. Parts should *not* be allowed to touch sides or bottom of tank.

Rinse in Cold Water: Again, rinse the parts in

cold water. Make the transfer from the bluing tank to the cold water rinse as quickly as possible.

Boil Parts to Stop Bluing Action: The parts may be soaked in a hot oil solution or boiled in water for about 10 minutes and then oiled.

More detailed directions accompany the bluing salts and these should be followed exactly as instructed. Salts are available from Brownell's; Knife & Gun Finishing Supplies; or Heatbath Corp.

plete and includes 100 pounds of Nickel Pentrate bluing salts, 25 pounds of Pentrate Cleaner, rubber gloves, a thermometer, water soluable oil, water reservoir and splash guards. This outfit and the polishing equipment described previously will put you in business immediately. All that is left to purchase is a tank or two of bottled gas for fuel.

Of course you will still need to acquire some experience. You may be lucky and have your first attempt come out perfectly, but if you're like me, my first attempts were like playing a slot machine

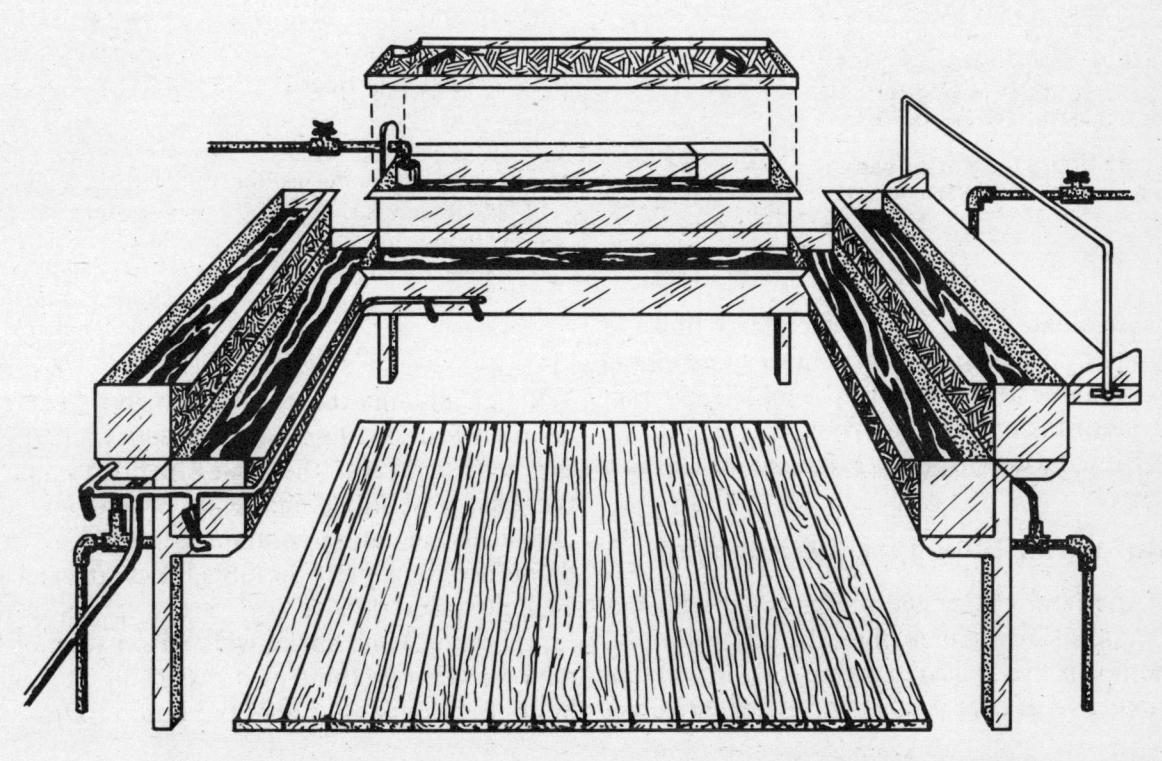

The multi-tank bluing setup is the most professional way to go about any hot-bath bluing operation. In this setup, each tank has its own water and heat source. Multi-tank bluing operations insure thorough degreasing, rinsing and bluing steps.

The initial equipment required to set up a bluing operation on a professional basis will cost approximately $1200 to $1500. Some gunsmiths have blued firearms for much less money, but to do the job right, you're going to require about $1200 worth of equipment.

There are two basic ways to go about setting up for bluing firearms: You can purchase 6 individual 6" x 6" x 40" long tanks, build your own frames and then have pipe burners installed under four of them. The other way is to order a complete bluing unit (requiring very little installation time) from Heatbath Corp. Their 6-tank model is shipped com-

in Vegas—I never knew just what color the metal was going to be next. They came out green, plum, red, and some even blue-black, but eventually I got the hang of it and haven't had a failure in quite some time.

You'll need an area of at *least* 8' x 8' for your bluing and buffing operation and the area should be away from your normal business or shop area because of the harmful effects of the bluing fumes; that is, odor and the ability of the fumes to rust any metal that it should come in contact with.

Pure water is another necessity for good bluing jobs—especially when using the hot water method

In his own shop, the author has installed a Heatbath 6-tank bluing outfit.

discussed next. Some of the chemicals that are found in city water prove harmful to some bluing solutions and cause less-than-par jobs. I use rain water that runs off my shop roof, catching it in a barrel from the downspouts. Fifty gallons will go a long way!

Hot Water Bluing for the Hobbyist

For the hobbyist or the professional who has only an occasional gun to blue, the hot water bluing method is the easiest to set-up for and with the least expense. If care is taken, an excellent velvet blue-black finish will result.

You can get by with one tank for this method, but you'll obtain better (and faster) results by using three separate tanks—two of them with heat. One tank is used to degrease the metal parts as discussed previously; one tank is used for rinsing parts, and the third is used to boil water to bring the parts to a temperature to accept the bluing solution.

The basic formula for bluing guns by the hot water process was developed in the late 1800s and consisted, basically, of sodium and potassium nitrates, potassium chlorate, and bichloride of mercury, mixed in distilled water. If you'd like to mix your own, or have it mixed by a local chemist, here's what you need.

750 grains	(avoirdupois weight)	Mercuric chloride
1000 grains	"	Potassium chlorate
1200 grains	"	Potassium nitrate
300 grains	"	Ferric chloride
150 grains	"	Cupric chloride
300 grains	"	Sodium nitrate

Weigh and mix these chemicals in a clean glass jar then heat 1700 cc's of distilled water to 130 degrees F. and pour the heated distilled water into the glass jar containing the six previously-mixed chemicals, agitating continuously until all ingredients are completely dissolved. Let cool and after 24 hours, add 175 cc's of sweet spirits of niter (ethyl nitrate) and shake well. Place solution in a dark glass bottle (blue or brown) and let stand 24 hours before using. Label the bottle *POISON*.

When using the "hot-water" bluing method you will need the following items: a clean glass jar, cotton balls, steel wool, rubber gloves, degreaser, carding wheel, stainless steel brush and some Herter's Belgian Blue.

If you don't care to go to all the trouble, commercial bluing solutions are available. Herter's Belgian Blue is excellent; so is Brownell's Dicropan IM and Stoeger's Yankee Blue, although the latter is becoming hard to find. All of these solutions may be used for the hot water method of bluing firearms.

Besides bluing tanks and a source of heat, the equipment needed for the hot water bluing process is as follows:

Dicro-Clean No. 909: Used to remove all grease, traces of bluing compound and dirt. It is added to water and brought to a temperature of approximately 180 degrees F. before submerging parts to be cleaned.

Glass Jar: To be used to heat the bluing solution. It is suspended by an iron wire in a corner of the hot water tank and the bluing solution poured directly into it.

Herter's Belgian Blue: Bluing solution used for the hot water method of bluing firearms.

Swabs: Used to apply the bluing solution to the metal. The large wire ring handles on the swabs make it easy to flood the surfaces with the solution after they are heated in the hot water.

Stainless Steel Brush: Used for carding (removing rust) from hard-to-get-to places on the guns.

Steel Wool: Used for general carding of metal surfaces.

Carding Wheel: Used on the electric buffer for carding metal surfaces.

Rubber Gloves: Used to protect hands from chemicals and hot surfaces; also protect metal surfaces from finger prints. Many experts of the past have recommended white cotton gloves to handle guns during the hot water bluing process, but this writer has found cotton gloves to become soiled quickly. Rubber gloves are best.

Clean water and an appropriate amount of the Dicro-Clean No. 909 is added to a tank and the metal parts boiled for about 15 minutes.

Meanwhile, a tank of clean distilled or rain water is being heated in another tank. The clean jar containing the bluing solution is suspended in one corner of the tank so that part of the jar is underwater. Be careful not to let any of the water in the bluing tank splash into the jar to mix with the bluing solution.

After the cleaning period is completed, remove the parts from the cleaning tank and quickly transfer them to the rinse tank, and then immediately into the hot water tank. The water must be kept at a slow, rolling boil from here on out. Nothing else will do. The parts should be suspended from iron wires from above or else placed on U brackets within the tank. Just be sure that none of the parts touch the sides or bottom of the tank. If they do, "hot spots" and blotchy bluing will be the result. Small parts may be individually suspended by wires or else placed in a wire basket which is then suspended in the tank.

Let the parts boil for a full 15 minutes the first time to insure an even heat throughout. Then remove the largest part from the tank and shake excess water from the metal. If the surfaces do not dry immediately of their own heat, put the part back in the tank and let it heat for at least another 5 minutes (the part is not hot enough). When the part is hot and dry, set the part on clean V-blocks, on clean paper, or suspend the part in mid-air with wire. Then quickly, before it cools too much, dip a swab into the hot bluing solution and dampen the swab. Don't "load" the swab, just dampen it. Then swab the solution on the hot metal with long, light strokes, avoiding runs and puddles. Allow the fluid to "work" about five minutes and then return the part to the hot water tank for another five minutes. Again remove the part and swab

When cleaning/degreasing prior to using the "hot-water" method, the author uses a small, portable tank and heat source. In this instance, a set of barrels is being readied for a 15-minute boiling hot-water bath in a solution of degreaser and water.

more of the solution onto the hot metal surfaces. Do this to each of the other parts in turn, returning that part to the hot water tank after the solution has been allowed to work for about 4 or 5 minutes. Reheat and apply the solution twice to each part. The bluing solution should dry almost instantly upon application.

Following the second application, you'll see a grayish coat, flecked with rust, forming on the metal. Now, before returning the part to the hot water tank, rub it briskly lengthwise with fine 00 steel wool. Use the stainless steel brush to get into tight places. As the gray disappears you'll see a blue-black finish begin to develop. Then put the part back into the tank.

Once the barrels have been removed from the final bath, you may want to finish the job off by lightly using a soft-wire carding wheel along the barrel's exterior.

Following the second application of Herter's Belgian Blue, the set of barrels are rubbed briskly with fine steel wool to remove the rust formed by the bluing solution. (Note the use of rubber gloves.)

One way to remove annodizing from aluminum parts is to use some steel wool and alcohol.

Continue this process as many times as necessary to obtain the finish desired. Five or six passes should be sufficient for most metals. When you have obtained a satin, blue-black finish, return all parts to the hot water tank and boil for at least 15 minutes to halt all of the rusting process. During the final few passes, you may want to use a soft wire carding wheel on your buffer to card the rust from the parts. Oil all parts thoroughly and the job is finished.

Blackening Aluminum

Some trigger guards and other parts on modern firearms are made of aluminum. The bluing methods previously described will not blue aluminum, and therefore, some other means of blackening the metal must be used. One method is to use Brownell's Aluma-Hyde which is a spray-on lacquer which gives the appearance of bluing.

To refinish an aluminum gun part, use steel wool

After removing the old finish from an aluminum part, you can apply a couple of coats of Aluma-Hyde. It provides an attractive finish that's almost as tough as the original annodizing.

saturated with alcohol to remove the old finish. Then apply the Z/C primer on all surfaces and allow to dry. Follow with two light coats of black lacquer. The result is a beautiful, tough, scratch resistant, semi-gloss finish that wears almost as well as the original anodizing. The color is also a close match to the original.

Engraving Inlay Kit

Gold Lode, Inc., offers a 23 kt. gold engraving inlay kit that enables you to enrich all engravings with genuine gold. Each kit contains enough gold to do one or two lavishly engraved firearms and the steps are simple. The kit contains Agent No. 1, brush, cloth, dropper and a jar of gold crystals,

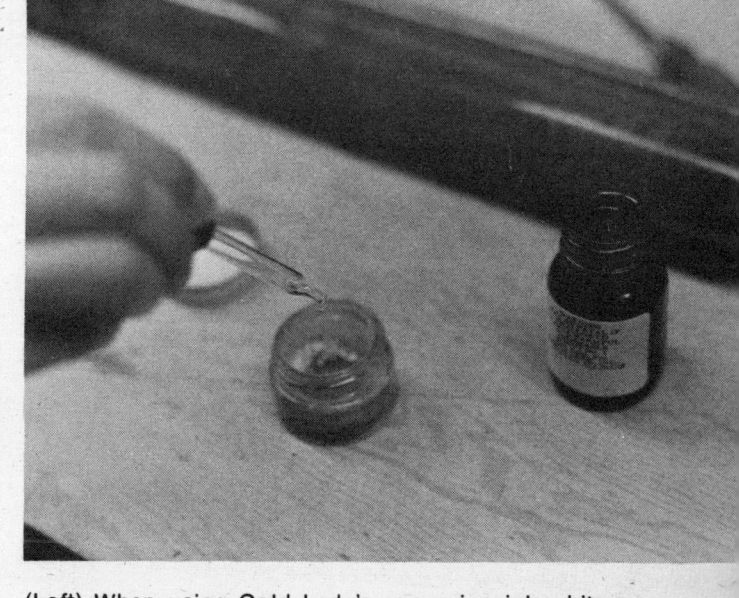

(Left) When using Gold Lode's engraving inlay kit you must first remove all grease and dirt from the engraved recesses to be filled.

(Above) Your next step in using the Gold Lode kit is to add about 40 drops of that kit's "Agent No. 1" to the gold mixture that's provided.

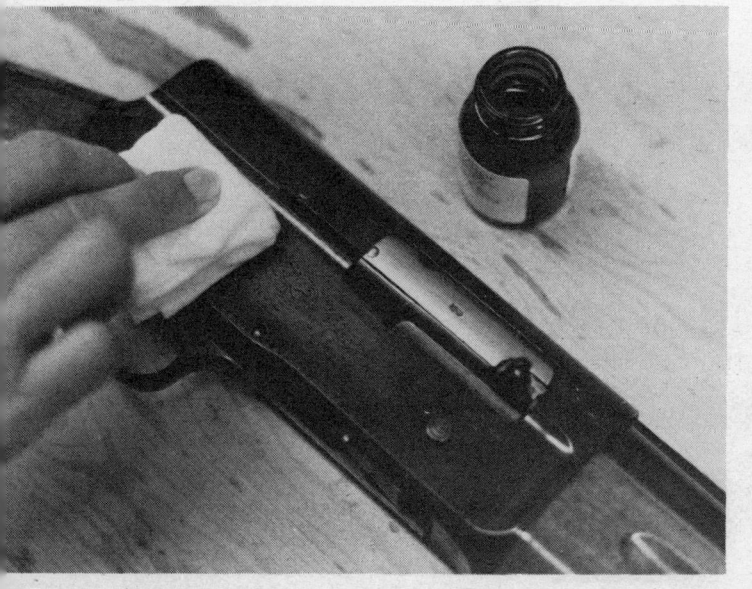

everything necessary for a complete job.

Using the soft cloth and Agent No. 1, carefully clean the engraved areas, removing any grease or dirt. Then add Agent No. 1 to the gold mixture (about 40 drops) and mix with the brush to a smooth mixture. (Work with the mixture on the thin side.)

Brush a thin coat of gold over a section of the engraving and before it dries work the gold into the

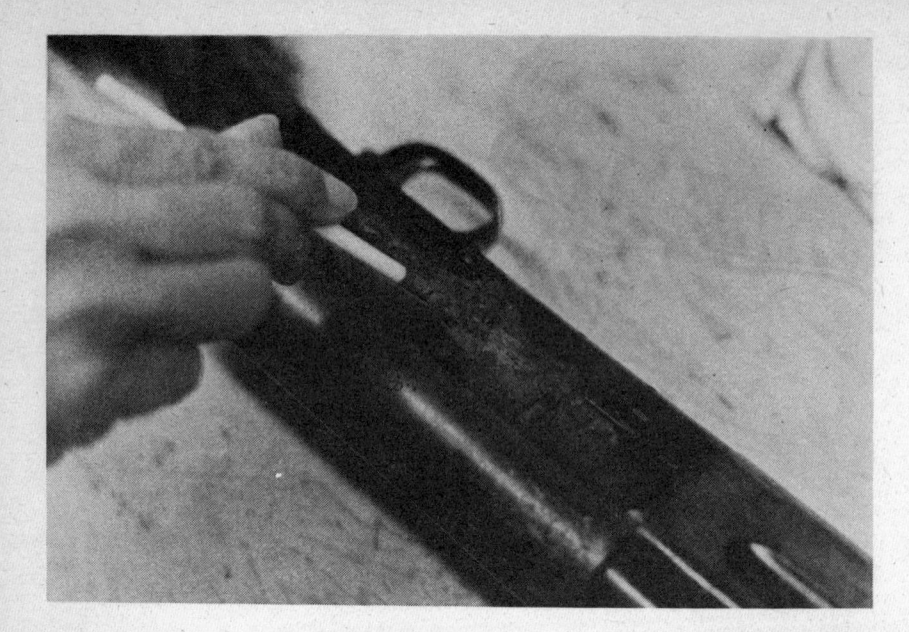

Next, brush on a thin coat of gold over a section of engraving.

(Below) After the gold coat has been applied—and before it dries—work the gold mixture into the engraving as shown.

engraving with the index finger. Repeat this operation until all of the engraving is filled.

Wrap a portion of the wiping cloth around your index finger and dampen the cloth with Agent No. 1. It is important that the cloth is damp only. You can be sure of this if you apply the dampened section to a piece of paper towel to remove the excess. Gently work your finger and dampened cloth over the engraved area to remove the gold from the smooth sections leaving the gold in the engraving. A felt block is provided with the kit to be used in the same way as the cloth to remove the gold from the hard-to-get-at areas.

After you have completed the entire area, inspect for any spots that might have been missed.

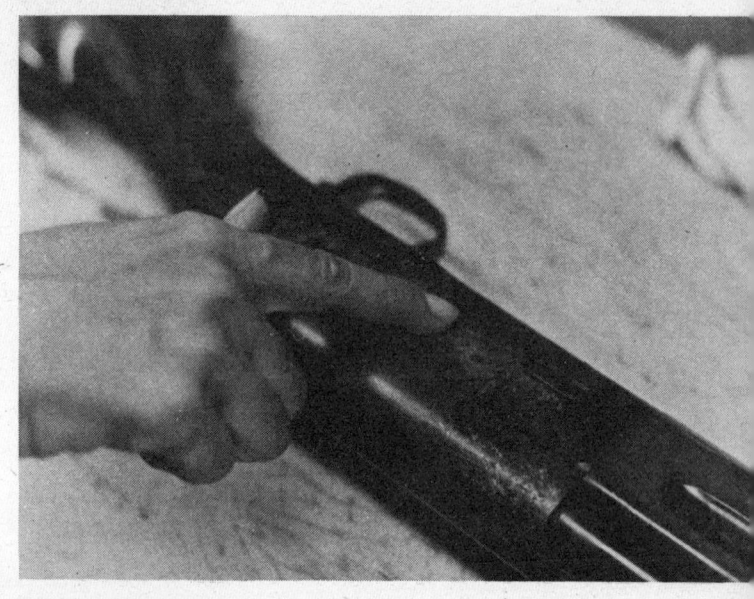

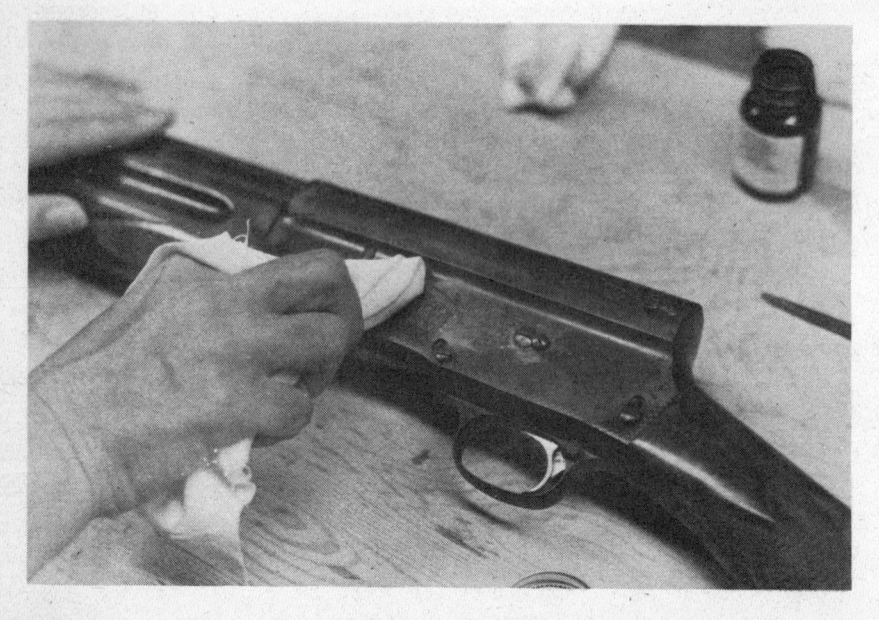

Now that the gold mixture is fully into the engraving, take a cloth dampened with Agent No. 1 and lightly go over the engraving to remove excess gold mixture from the surrounding non-engraved surfaces. Once the excess mixture has been removed, allow the inlaid areas to dry for about 30 minutes and finish up by polishing with a soft cloth.

Here, the Texas Plater's nickel plating apparatus has been set up and is ready to go.

Allow the inlaid area to dry for 30 minutes and then polish with a smooth cloth.

Plating

Many firearms—especially handguns—are nickel plated for appearance and to protect the metal surfaces. Conventional methods of plating are often beyond the reach of the average gunshop and many gunsmiths bypass this operation. However, there is one kit, offered by Texas Platers, especially designed for the gunsmith. All you need, besides the kit, are three 1½-volt ignition batteries. The batteries are connected in series with the negative terminal connected to the gun or part and the positive (+) terminal connected to the brush holder or handle. The brush is then dipped into the solution (nickel, gold, brass, etc.) and merely brushed onto the surface. Of course, all surfaces must be clean—just like before bluing a firearm—and several coats will have to be applied to obtain a durable finish.

Parkerizing

Parkerizing has long been the metal finishing process used by the armed forces since it is highly rust resistant and wears longer than most hot bluing processes. The old method consisted of boiling the parts to be finished in a solution of Parko Powder composed of specially prepared powdered iron and phosphoric acid. During the process, minute particles of the gun's surface are dissolved and replaced by insoluble phosphates which are rustproof. The result is a slight etching of the surface, giving a dull, non-reflecting finish.

To Parkerize a firearm, you will need a stainless steel tank large enough to accommodate the gun parts; a thermometer that will measure up to 180°F (± 5°F) and a measuring cup (graduated in ounces) and a pair of tongs with at least 8" handles.

Degreasing Parts: Clean grease and oil from parts with gasoline, perchlorethylene (dry cleaning fluid) or mineral spirits.

Rust or Scale: Rust or scale must be removed by dry abrasive blasting using glass beads. If you don't have the equipment, most automobile body shops will do this operation for a small fee. Glass bead all parts until a chrome look is obtained and no dark spots remain.

When using the Texas Plater's kit, you get a quality finish by simply brushing on the plating solution as shown.

105

After the abrasive blasting, do not handle parts with bare hands as this will leave body oil on the parts and cause spotting. Use rubber gloves, just as for bluing, for handling parts. Treat the parts as quickly as possible after abrasive blasting—never more than 3 hours.

If you don't have a sand blasting machine and the glass beads, an alternate rust or scale removal method will work with reasonably good results. Use a 50/50 solution of muriatic acid and water in a plastic or glass container. Place the parts to be parkerized in this solution, and while keeping all parts submerged, brush off all rust and scale, using a bristle brush. Do not, however, leave the parts in the acid solution for a prolonged time as the acid will dissolve the metal parts.

Remove the parts from the acid and immediately rinse in running water for not less than 30 seconds and not more than 1 minute. Then immediately place parts in the treating solution. Do not let the parts dry after the rinse. As with any chemicals, wear safety goggles or a face shield and avoid contact of acid with skin.

Treating: Prepare enough solution to cover all parts sufficiently at a concentration of 4 ounces of parkerizing solution per gallon water (3% by volume). Put the solution in the stainless steel tank and bring the solution to a temperature of between 160 and 170 degrees F. The parts are placed in the solution with the tongs, taking care not to touch the parts with the bare hands. Allow the metal to react, turning the parts periodically so as to get an even treatment. However, be careful not to agitate the parts where they will rub or grind against each other.

The parts should be left in the solution for about 40 minutes, maintaining the prescribed temperature at all times. Then remove the parts with the tongs and immediately rinse in cool running water for one minute. Drain excess water and dry with a clean absorbent cloth. Once the parts have dried, immediately dip them in a light oil or spray the part with WD-40. Wipe off excess oil and the job is completed.

The bath can be used as long as the solution is clear. A cloudy solution indicates depletion of its active ingredients. However, once the solution has cooled, do not attempt to reheat and use. If you'd like to try the process described above, the solution is available from Marion Owens in Greenville, SC.

Slow Rust Bluing

All of you have probably seen the TV advertisement where an American car is supposed to look so much like a much more expensive European car that it fools an entire police escort. Well, I happen to own the American version and my brother owns the European car, and while both cars do look similar, from a distance, a closer examination quickly reveals the higher quality of workmanship in the more expensive model. The same is true with gun bluing methods.

For the past 40 years, all firearm manufacturers and professional gunsmiths have turned almost 100% to the caustic nitrate hot bath method of bluing firearms since this method is much faster and gives more uniform results than any other method known. Furthermore, labor is cut to a minimum and fairly good results may be obtained if an expert polishing job is done and the salt bath is maintained at the correct temperature. However, the initial setup is generally too expensive for the amateur with only a couple of guns to blue from time to time, and the dangers of the bluing solution is too risky for use in the home. It'll ruin floor tile, take enamel off the kitchen stove (the prime source of heat for bluing in the home), eat through leather shoes and wool clothing, and cause blindness if any of the solution should splash in your eyes. In my opinion, it's a method that should be left strictly to the professional.

On the other hand, any gun owner who is willing to spend from 8 to 12 hours of hard work, and about $50 cash can obtain a rich, velvet blue-black finish that will surpass any of the factory jobs by using the cold-rusting process. This is not the same method as the "instant" or "touch-up" bluing solution. It's a slow, cold-rusting process used only on expensive rifles and shotguns.

It's difficult to explain the difference in the cold-rusting process from the hot bath bluing method, but once you have compared the two side by side, no other type finish than the cold-rust process will seem satisfactory. For durability, it can't be beat; it resists wear better than any other type of bluing known. To prove this to yourself, compare a modern firearm that has seen, say, 10 years of normal use to the one that was manufactured around the turn of the century when the cold rusting process was used by many of the manufacturers. Chances are, the older gun will have more remaining blue than the modern firearm.

Materials Needed for Slow Rust Bluing

If you have a bench vise and two water-tight metal containers large enough to hold the gun parts, you'll be able to blue several guns for a relatively small investment. You could buy two 6" x 6" x 40" bluing tanks but to save quite a bit of money you can substitute with two 3" x 6" x 36" chicken feeding troughs—available at your local farm supply store. Just make sure that the tanks are made of ferrous metal or stainless steel; don't buy galvanized tanks.

A 10" mill bastard file and file card is needed if the gun has rust pits, nicks, scratches, etc., too deep for the abrasive paper to remove. Otherwise, these two items can be eliminated. The method of applying the bluing solution can vary, depending on your preference, from cotton balls, to ring-handled dauber-type swabs, to small sponges. If you choose the easy-to-find cotton balls, you'll also need a pair of needle nose pliers to hold them.

Purchase three sheets each of the following grit of aluminum oxide (open coat) abrasive paper. If your local hardware or automotive supply store doesn't have them, order them from Brownells: 80 grit, 150 grit, 240 grit, 320 grit. You'll also need three sheets each of 400 and 500 grit silicon wet and dry paper for the final polishing.

A package of 00 steel wool and stainless steel brush made of .005" hand-tied stainless steel wire is necessary for carding the rust from the gun. Most steel wool, however, comes from the factory soaked in oil to prevent rusting and this oil must be completely removed before using it to card the rust from the gun.

Most experts recommend wearing clean white cotton gloves during the bluing operation to insure that your hands, which contain oil, will not come into contact with the gun metal. White gloves are fine for the boiling and application process, but tend to become rather soiled during the carding operation. For this reason, I use rubber gloves during the carding process after they have been thoroughly degreased in the degreasing solution along with the gun parts. There are several good degreasing solutions on the market, but a can of household lye (sodium hydroxide) will do the job just as well. If you use a commercial cleaner, follow the directions on the package.

A source of heat can be the kitchen range, but to keep on good terms with your wife, you'll do better to take the work to the basement or garage and use a camp stove or gas hot plate.

Draw filing light rust off of shotgun barrels is acceptable; however, remember that those tubes are thin and you can only go so far without weakening the barrel itself. Also, you should remove any dents with a dent removing tool, not a draw file — those shotgun barrels are thin.

There has been a lot of controversy over the effects of ordinary tap water on the bluing job. Chemicals added to city water supplies are said to have an adverse effect on the final results. "Hard" well water can also do the same thing. I've always used cistern water for my bluing jobs and this is about as pure as you can get outside of distilled water. You might try catching 8 to 10 gallons of water the next time it rains by placing plastic dish pans out in the yard; or if you want the purest, distilled water may be purchased at your friendly drug store.

Another way to get pure water is to have your pharmacist get you a water "deionizing column." A deionizing column is nothing more than a clear plastic cylindrical container packed with purification crystals. There are couplings at either end for surgical tubing; and, you simply run tap water (slowly) through a column into a clean receptacle —a gallon jug works well. Deionizing columns come in various sizes; the larger the column the greater the expense. If you plan to do a fair amount of bluing the money spent will be worth it.

(If your pharmacist bridles at acquiring a deionizing column for you, don't be surprised—

that's probably how he makes his "distilled" water. Just assure him you're not going into competition with him and you'll notice the color return to his face.)

You'll need some tapered dowels to plug the bore of the barrel and also some gun grease to lubricate the inside of the barrel to prevent it from rusting during the bluing process. You can mix your own bluing solution from chemicals available from your local drug supplier, but you'll be money ahead if you buy a solution from Dixie Gun Works already mixed for the purpose.

Now that you have all of the materials at hand, get ready for some hard work, but keep remembering that you are getting the best blue job that can be obtained.

proper polishing of a bolt action rifle; a little more for a pump or double barrel shotgun.

Roy Dunlap points out in his book, *Gunsmithing,* that a hand-polished gun of course, looks better than a power polished one, since corners and angles can be maintained with no loss of profile. A rather surprising fact is that an excellent final finish can be obtained on metal polished by hand, while metal polished by power to the same apparent finish before bluing will not turn out as well.

The first step is to completely disassemble the gun down to the last screw and drift pin. If you're unfamiliar with the take-down procedure, exploded views and instructions are available from the manufacturer on modern arms. The *Gun*

Prior to bluing, be sure to remove any dovetailed parts from the barrel, slide or action assembly. If you leave those parts in place, the bluing solution will work its way in between the dovetail and the part it holds. The solution may oxidize the sightblade to the dovetail, making later removal or adjustment difficult, if not impossible.

Polishing

Aside from keeping the metal surfaces free from oil, polishing is the most important step in obtaining a rich, velvet finish on your gun. Without proper polishing, you might as well forget bluing the gun and leave it as is. The coloring of the metal will never cover up pits, scratches, and the like. The surface of the metal must be perfect before the bluing solution is applied. Nothing less will do.

Most professional shops utilize power buffers for polishing, but most hobbyists will have to do the polishing by hand. So much the better! Only by hand polishing can all contours, lettering, markings and square edges be properly preserved. About 5 hours of hand polishing is required for the

Digest Book of Exploded Firearm Drawings and Brownell's *Encyclopedia of Modern Firearms Parts & Assembly* are two good sources, as well as the new *Gun Digest Firearms Assembly & Disassembly* series. For guns with no printed instructions, I'd suggest making notes as you disassemble the gun and perhaps even taking close-up photos of intricate parts. You'll then have some reference to go by when you're reassembling the firearm.

Wipe each part clean and examine for wear and to insure that no aluminum alloy parts are present. This can easily be determined by using a toy magnet. If the magnet doesn't react, then the part is nonferrous—aluminum, brass or similar alloy— and these parts should be set aside with other parts

Prior to any bluing, inspect the gun for any major pitting. Depending upon the depth and coverage, you may want to remove the pitting with a draw file.

not to be blued by the cold rust process. Steel parts normally not rust blued are springs and other small parts not visible when the gun is assembled.

With all the parts to be blued in one pile, thoroughly clean each one with a solvent such as acetone AWA1-1-1—the safe substitute for carbon tetrachloride. Start with the barrel or the barreled action, and clamp this assembly in a padded vise. Care must be taken, however, not to "clamp down" too hard and damage the gun parts.

If the gun requiring bluing has rust pits, nicks or scratches that are too deep for the abrasive paper to remove, use a 10″ mill bastard file to smooth all metal surfaces. With the tang of the file in the left hand, and the tip in the right hand "draw" the file on the metal toward yourself over the surface to be smoothed.

The amount of pressure used on the file is very important; too little will only scratch the metal, while too much will clog the file and also cause scratches. On the return stroke, do not let the file touch the metal; cutting should be done only on the "draw" stroke. In other words, with the file positioned at the most distant spot on the barrel, draw the file smoothly toward you using enough pressure to smooth the metal without scratching it. At the end of the stroke, lift the file from the metal and sort of arc it back to its starting position; then again use pressure and draw the file toward you. Repeat this procedure until all pits and scratches are removed.

Heavy nicks in gun barrels can sometimes be peened back into shape prior to polishing; however, draw filing is usually the answer.

The barrel is now ready for cross polishing to remove the many "flats" that will be left after draw filing. With a pair of scissors or your bench knife, cut a strip of 80 grit abrasive paper about 1½" wide (cut the long way) and polish with a shoe-shine motion. Your first few strokes will reveal the flats left by the draw filing. Continue this operation over the entire length of the barrel with the 80 grit paper until all of the flats disappear, and the barrel looks like it has just been "turned down" in a metal turning lathe. You may have to use several pieces of the abrasive paper to obtain this polished condition.

Cut a 1½" strip of the 150 grit paper and fold it as shown below. With the open edges in the direction of the axis of the bore, commence polishing the barrel lengthwise. Continue polishing in this manner until all cross polishing marks from the previous operation are removed.

Those procedures are repeated alternately with each next finer grit until the final "draw" is completed with the 500 grit silicon wet and dry, i.e.: 80 grit—cross polish; 150 grit—draw polish; 240 grit—cross polish; 320 grit—draw polish; 400 grit—cross polish; 500 grit—draw polish. (With the silicon wet and dry paper, apply a drop of oil to the paper when polishing.) Insure that all polishing marks from the previous polishing are removed before proceeding to the next finer grade of paper.

Once the barrel is polished, the position of it in the vise is reversed, and the receiver is polished in a similar manner, but make certain that the newly polished areas are well protected from the vise jaws. Heavy leather padding offers good protection. Then continue with the trigger guard, trigger, floor plate and other parts. Most of the smaller parts, however, are most adaptable to cross polishing all the way because of their configuration, and not lengthwise polishing. Just make certain that all polishing marks from the previous grit size are completely removed before using a finer grit size. Protect all of the newly polished surfaces from rusting with a light coat of oil until you are ready to apply the bluing solution.

Screw heads are best polished by securing them in a screw holder, and then using a power buffing wheel (with different size grits) for polishing. If a buffing wheel is not available, insert the screw in the chuck of a ¼-inch drill motor (held in a vise) and while the screw is rotating, lightly run a fine file over the head to remove any dings or minor pits. Complete the polishing in this manner with

After removing any old finish, and the pits or dings are dressed out to your satisfaction, you can start to polish the parts with 80-grit paper. The author suggests using the shoe-shine approach when polishing barrels or other parts with contoured surfaces.

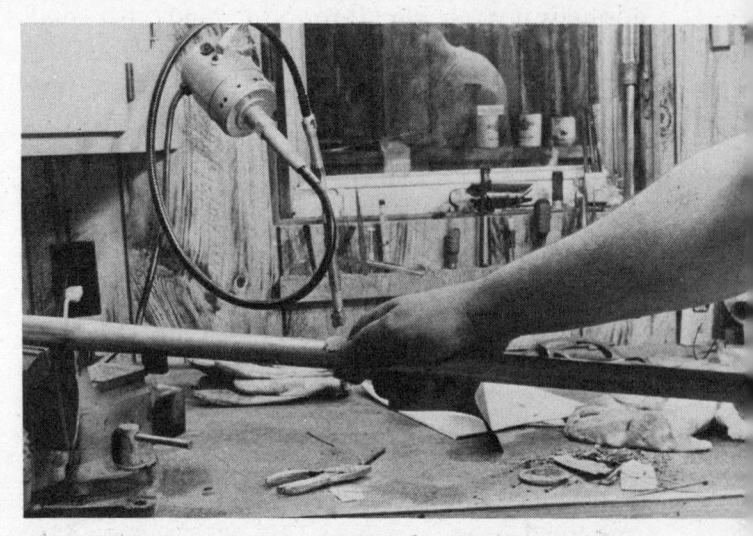

When polishing metal in a lengthwise direction (above), fold the abrasive cloth in this fashion (below) for best results and control.

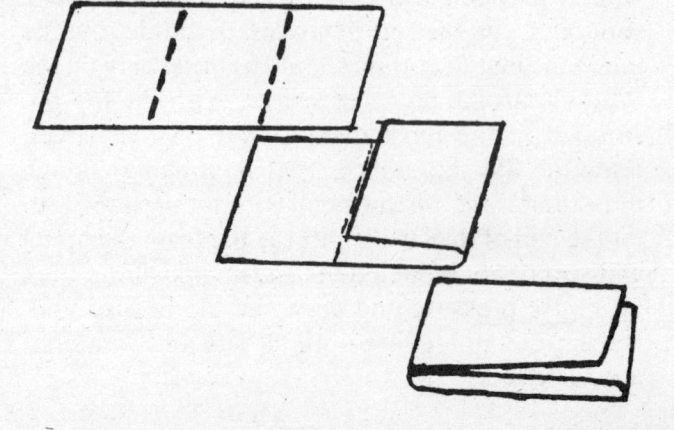

Besides eye protection, the gunsmith should wear a filter mask when polishing off old blue or rust.

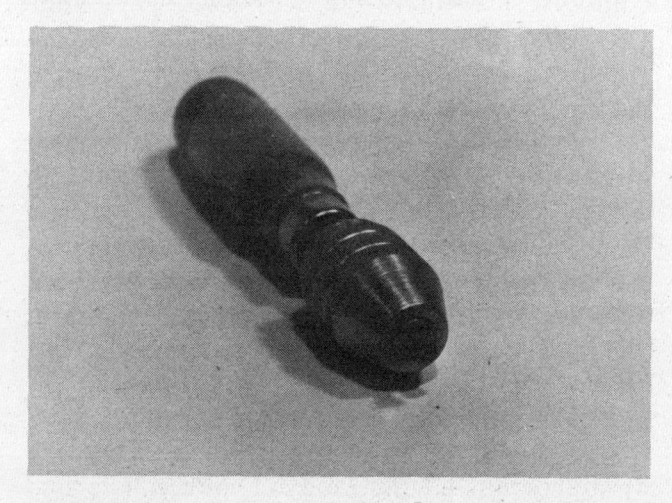

Screw heads are best polished by securing them in a screw holder and then using a power buffing wheel.

The polishing job on this reblued barrel still shows some buffing marks; however, some customers may not want, nor be willing to pay for, a blue job with a high degree of polish. It's all a matter of personal choice.

the different grit sizes of abrasive paper. The gun is now ready for bluing.

In using this or any other method of bluing gun metal, it is very important that the metal be absolutely free of all grease, oil, foreign matter, etc. Furthermore, once the procedure starts, be careful not to touch any of the parts to be blued with your hands, or with anything that could transfer foreign matter to it, or you may have to start the procedure over. Many experts recommend wearing absolutely clean white gloves during the entire bluing operation, but I have found these to quickly collect dirt and grime during the carding operation and prefer to wear clean rubber gloves instead.

Once more, clean all parts to be blued with a solvent such as AWA 1-1-1. Wipe out the bore thoroughly, then coat the inside of the bore lightly with a heavy gun grease—a thin coat of RIG works well. Tap the wooden plugs tightly into each end of the barrel so that the bore is water tight and the heat of boiling water will not cause the air in the bore to expand and blow the plugs out. A piece of black iron stove pipe wire should be attached to each wooden plug and then both wires attached to a wooden hanger—a broom handle will do the trick— to suspend the barrel in the boiling water and to hang the barrel while applying the bluing solution. On the small parts such as screws, a small spool of No. 22 iron wire (available at any hardware store) will be adequate.

Fill each tank with enough water to completely cover all parts. To the cleaning tank, add a cleaning solution such as Brownells Dicro-Clean No. 909 according to instructions on the package, or conventional household lye (sodium hydroxide) in proportions of 2 tablespoons of lye per gallon

111

The "hot-water" and "slow-rust" methods of bluing are the only ways to blue old double barrel guns that have had their barrels and ribs joined by soft soldering.

of water. Either of these solutions will degrease the parts to be blued. Insert all parts into the tank and suspend them so that none touches the bottom of the tank. Bring the solution to a boil, and leave the parts in the boiling solution for about 15 minutes. After this, immediately transfer the parts into the tank containing the clean boiling water. Let the parts remain in the clear water for two minutes, then remove them and hang them up to dry and cool. At this point, the hands must never touch any portion of the metal which is to be blued. Also make certain that the clean boiling water is kept at a hard, rolling boil—nothing else will do.

When the parts are dry and cool, take a clean cotton swab, saturate it with the bluing solution, and squeeze out any excess solution from the swab. With long even strokes, and moderate pressure, swab the solution over all areas to be blued. Do *not* use an excessive amount of solution. After all areas have been covered, hang the parts in a damp, humid place for 24 hours to rust. I hang guns to be blued in this manner in my utility shower. Using a rubber drain stopper, I fill the shower base with about 2 inches of water and then suspend the gun parts across the top of the shower stall with a broom handle so the parts hang down inside the stall.

After 24 hours, one of the tanks is again filled with clean water and brought to a rolling boil. Then all of the rusted parts are returned to this tank to boil for about 15 minutes. After boiling, they are hung up to dry and cool, but before completely cool, all accumulated water droplets in contours, screw holes, etc. are blown away. When cool, all of the oxide covering (rust) is removed with new, clean (grease free) steel wool. For tight places, I use a clean stainless steel brush. This process is called "carding." This first carding may give you any color from a light gray to a light blue; it may be splotched, or it may be uniform. Don't let any of this bother you. Each succeeding pass will deepen the color and make it more uniform. When all parts are thoroughly carded with steel wool and the brush, repeat the application of the bluing solution; that is, boiling, applying the solution, rusting, boiling and carding as before.

The number of passes necessary to obtain the desired depth and uniformity of color will depend on the hardness of the metal. You may get by with as little as 3 passes on .22 caliber rim fire rifles, or it might require as many as 10 or 12 on nickel steel shotgun barrels, but let's say that the average will be 5 passes. After the metal reaches the depth of color desired, give the just-carded parts one more carding, this time with a steel wool pad saturated with an oil such as WD-40. Don't be afraid of wearing the bluing off with steel wool—it's so tough that you won't phase it with 00 steel wool.

When the job is completed, you'll agree that it was hard, meticulous, work, but if you did your part, you'll also agree there is no bluing job equal to this method.

—10—
THE MULTI-PURPOSE MOTO-TOOL

MOST gunsmiths would be lost without their Moto-Tool and the dozens of accessories and attachments that go with them. In fact, I would dare say that this is the most useful and the most used of any tool in the gunshop—with the possible exception of the screwdriver.

There are various sizes of the Moto-Tool, but mine happens to be the Dremel No. 380 variable speed Moto-Tool. The built-in variable speed control brings out the full versatility and workability of the Moto-Tool by matching motor speed to the job at hand. The speed dial on this unit gives instant, positive control from 5,000 to 25,000 rpm permitting more accurate, precise grinding on all materials from soft woods to the hardest steels and alloys. It incorporates a heavy-duty combination of ball and oil impregnated bronze bearings with a .9 amp motor.

The smallest Dremel tool is their No. 260. It's a compact, palm-size versatile tool that is at its best with light delicate work. The 270 is the middle size and the 280 is the largest. The 370 and the 380 are variable speed versions of the 270 and 280 models.

The best way to buy one of these Moto-Tools is in kit form. For a bit extra, you get a 34-piece accessory set consisting of a good universal assortment of most-used items at a big savings over purchasing them separately. Rather than describ-

The speed dial on the Dremel No. 380 Moto-Tool gives instant, positive control from 5,000 to 25,000 rpm.

ing all of the accessories and attachments available for this Moto-Tool, let's get right into the nitty-gritty of gun repair and put some of them to use.

Installing Shotgun Bead Sights

It may seem like a simple matter indeed to unscrew an old shotgun sight bead from the muzzle of the barrel and then, just as easy, screw in a bright new silver or gold one in its place. Not so! When you start shooting away, chances are the barrel is going to split or even be blown completely off if the threaded shank of the sight is allowed to protrude down into the bore. The result is almost as bad as if the barrel were tightly stuffed with cleaning patches.

The installation of a shotgun sight bead is certainly within the reach of almost any shotgun owner provided he has access to a few simple tools (the Moto-Tool being the handiest) and more important, follows certain procedures. I've never run across a shotgun bead that gave any problems when it was being removed; most unscrew easily. However, if you should run across a stubborn thread, don't hesitate to use a good penetrating oil like Liquid Wrench. Apply the lubricant as per the instructions on the container, wait about 15 minutes, and then try removing the sight with conventional pliers.

Should you accidentally wrench off the bead from the threaded shank, or if the bead is already off when you start the project—eliminating any gripping surface—the old threaded shank will have to be drilled out and a new thread tapped. You're probably going to have to drill and tap a new hole anyway because most shotgun sight beads come in two sizes, 3 x 56 and 6 x 48 and these seldom fit factory drilled sight threads . . . or at least this has been my experience. Out of 30 or 40 guns that have been in my shop this year for new bead installations, I'll bet not three out of the bunch had either a 3 x 56 or 6 x 48 thread.

When drilling, use short screw machine drills as long ones tend to wander. Also use a B-Square barrel sight drill jig if available. To use the jig, merely "square-up" the barrel under the drill bit, place the jig on the barrel and line up the jig hole and bushing with the sight hole in the barrel (or the spot where the hole is to be drilled if no hole exists). Tighten the jig clamp and you're ready to start drilling, without using a center punch and with no further measuring. Since you'll be using either #45 or #31 drill bits, the Moto-Tool can be used to drill the hole if you wish.

Tap the hole with hand taps of 3 or 4 flute—preferably with the use of a tap guide. The guide—available from Brownell's—is expensive but is well worth the price. It insures the tap is perfectly square with the hole to be threaded and works on contoured or flat surfaces. Use a special tapping compound such as Tap Magic. Do *not* use conventional cutting oil.

With the sight hole drilled, tapped, and cleaned,

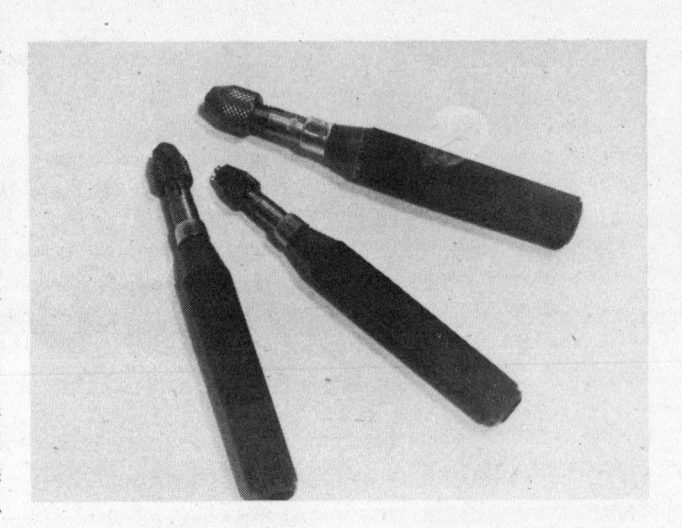

Shotgun sight installers like the ones here are available from any of the gunsmith supply houses.

When the shotgun bead is installed, take a scribe hook and mark off the protruding portions of threaded shank—this mark will serve as the cut-off point and insure that the bead shank doesn't extend into the bore.

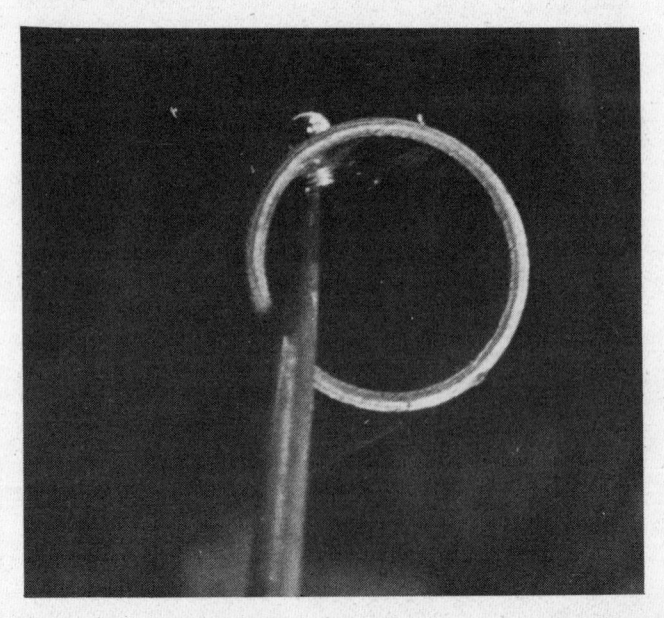

be sure to select a bead with the proper size thread. This may seem like a silly statement to make, but many persons have gotten the threads mixed up and tried to install a bead with the wrong size thread. In doing so, you'll end up with a jammed sight. Select one too small, and you have a sight that wobbles and will eventually work out or else protrude down into the bore.

Once the proper sight has been selected (proper thread, finish, size, etc.) start the sight by hand or with a special shotgun sight installer as offered by a number of gunsmith supply houses. Run the threads to full depth, and then scribe a line on the shank threads where they are flush with the inside of the bore.

Remove the sight and cut the shank off at the scribed line. This is best accomplished with the Moto-Tool using a narrow emery wheel. These wheels work similarly to large industrial abrasive cutting discs and will slice through the threaded sight shank in seconds. This cut-off wheel will also find a lot of use in shaping new parts and truing up the slots in screws. Be sure to buy plenty. They're cheap and although tough, they do break frequently. While doing the cutting with the Moto-Tool and cut-off wheel, the sight may be held in the sight installer and the holder clamped in a small vise, for additional rigidity. The cut-off wheel will make a fast, smooth cut.

Once again, install the sight into the threaded hole. If you have the slightest amount of projection into the bore, remove the bead and smooth up the remaining shank with a small file or emery polishing wheel in the Moto-Tool. Reinstall the bead and finish up with a cloth polishing tip coated with 140 grit polishing compound until the shank is *exactly* flush with the contour of the bore. If you've done your final trimming properly, your inside-the-bore polishing will be a quick 2 or 3 second job and you won't damage the choke.

If the old screw comes out easily and you can find a sight that exactly fits the existing screw hole, then a new hole will not have to be drilled and tapped; the entire operation should not take longer than 15 minutes. If you have to drill and tap, the job may take another 10 or 15 minutes. If the procedures just given are followed, the job is easy and perfectly safe.

Polishing for Rebluing or Plating

Any gunsmith that does rebluing or replating will find the small Moto-Tools with their cloth polishing wheels and tips indispensable for getting into tight places like trigger guards, triggers and similar irregular, close places. The cloth tips are impregnated with polishing grits—the same as you use on your regular buffing wheel. You also apply the abrasive on the tiny felt tips just about like you do on the larger wheels; that is, turn the motor on to about half speed (12,000 rpm), then turn it off and quickly push the felt tip against the abrasive, allowing it to stop the rotation of the Moto-Tool.

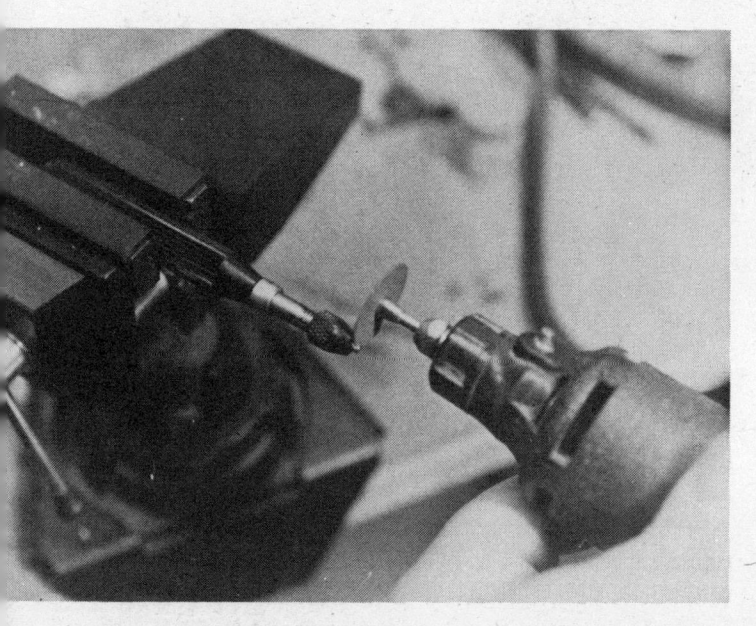

After the bead threads have been marked for cutting, you can remount the bead in a sight installer, secure the installer in a vise, and cut the thread to the desired length.

Here, the new bead has been properly trimmed and installed.

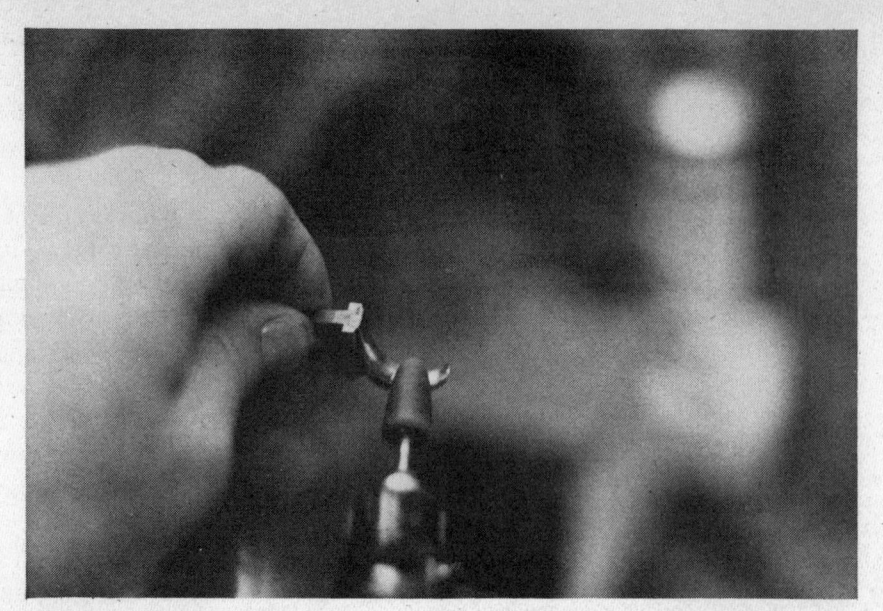

Polishing hard-to-get-at areas like triggers and trigger guards is made easy through the use of a Moto-Tool.

With the sanding drum attached to the Moto-Tool, you can easily remove excess material on butt plates quite quickly and easily.

more easily removed when using a speed of around 25,000 rpm.

The sanding drums and discs that come in the 34-piece kit are also good for polishing metal—although the name leads one to believe that they are to be used only on wood. The sanding drums are useful on wood, but they will also cut and polish metal. The inside of a trigger guard is one place you will find them invaluable. The thin disc will allow you to reach into tiny cracks for polishing and smoothing. You will also find hundreds of other uses for these sanding wheels, discs and polishing tips. For example, for minor fitting of a

The replacement grips on this revolver (prior to finishing and installation) were rough shaped with a Moto-Tool.

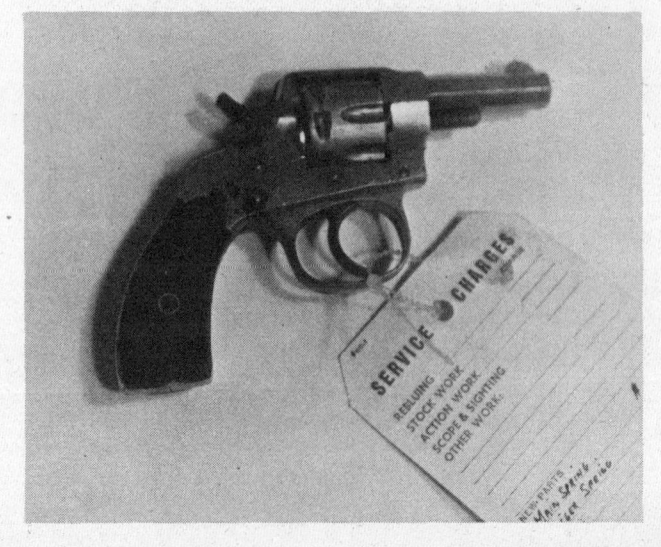

This allows the wheel to fill with abrasive compound and prevents excessive throw-off. However, when performing this operation, as in polishing, remember to wear safety goggles or glasses. The tip traveling at 12,000 rpm can throw grit and sparks all over the place. I've been hit a few times in the face, and from the sting I got on the cheek, I'm sure eye damage would have occurred if it had hit my eyes.

When using the Moto-Tool to polish parts prior to bluing, you don't have to use very heavy pressure, just a light touch will usually do the job. Also, I've found that you get smoother results when you use the higher speeds; it also cuts more quickly into the old finish. Nicks and pits are also

butt plate—where only a very small amount of material needs to be removed—the sanding drum attachment is very useful. If the operator uses care, no taping of the finished stock is necessary. With the sanding drum rotating at high speed, excess material on the butt plate can be removed very rapidly and accurately in only a few minutes.

The hard rubber grips on the old Hopkins & Allen, .22 rimfire handgun shown here were rough-shaped entirely with the Dremel 380 tool using a sanding drum. A fine sanding disc (or drums) can be used for final finishing although these particular grips were finished by hand.

Need to de-burr a delicate piece of metal where it's necessary to constantly observe the part being polished? Again the Dremel tool comes in handy. A round polishing head can, for example, be used to remove burrs on small parts such as rimfire cartridge lifters or extractors. These and other jobs are performed easily with the Dremel tool as very little setup time is required, and the smallness of the tool gives the operator a special "feel" unobtainable with the larger power tools.

There are also special attachments suitable for use with the Dremel tool that are available from other sources. Dental burrs or drills, for example, are excellent for cutting very tiny grooves in wood or steel and you can obtain all you want for nothing! A dentist must use only very sharp drills when working on teeth and must discard them when they become only slightly dull. Even the dull drills discarded are probably sharper than your average tool bit and these drills can be had for the

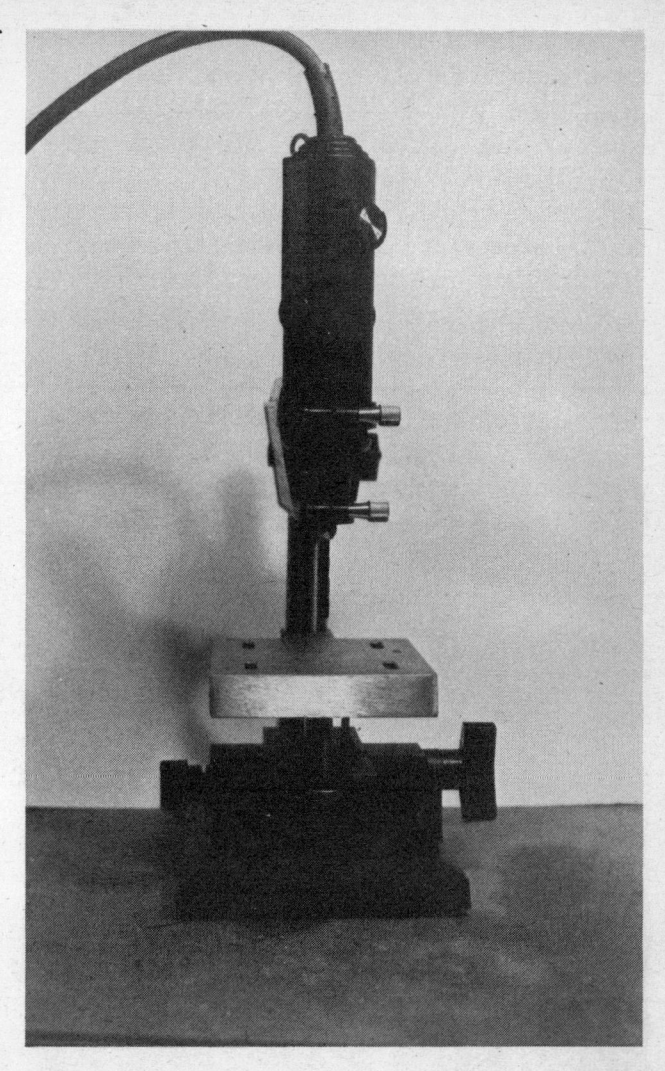

One accessory Dremel offers for the Moto-Tool is a handy drill press frame. It's most useful for small, delicate drilling jobs.

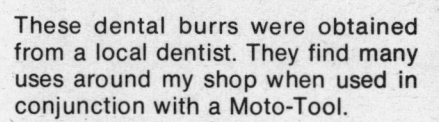

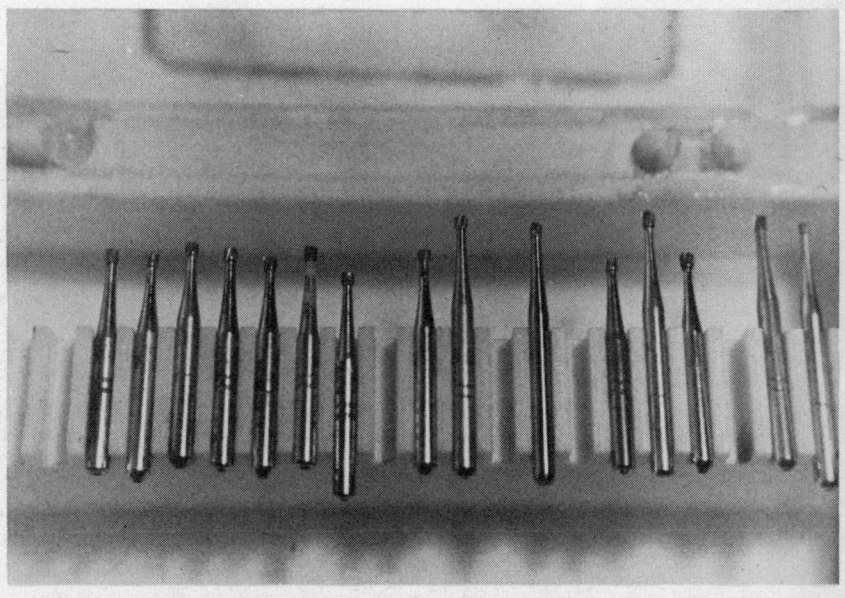

These dental burrs were obtained from a local dentist. They find many uses around my shop when used in conjunction with a Moto-Tool.

asking. The next time you're at your dentist, ask him to save all the old burrs or drills. Believe me, they'll come in handy. The dental burrs I obtained from my own dentist would cut through screw steel like the steel was hot butter, yet they were supposed to be dull. I didn't have the proper size chuck collet to accept the ultra-small shank—although they are available from Dremel—so I merely wrapped one layer of electrical tape around the shank and they fit perfectly.

One application of dental burrs is cutting a new slot in a screw that had the screw head broken off. The most recent example was an F.I. Mauser that was brought into the shop with one of the scope base screws broken. Of course the screw could

When drilling Springfield, Arisaka, Enfield (or similar) receivers for scope bases, the B-Square drill jig will accurately align mount-hole spacing.

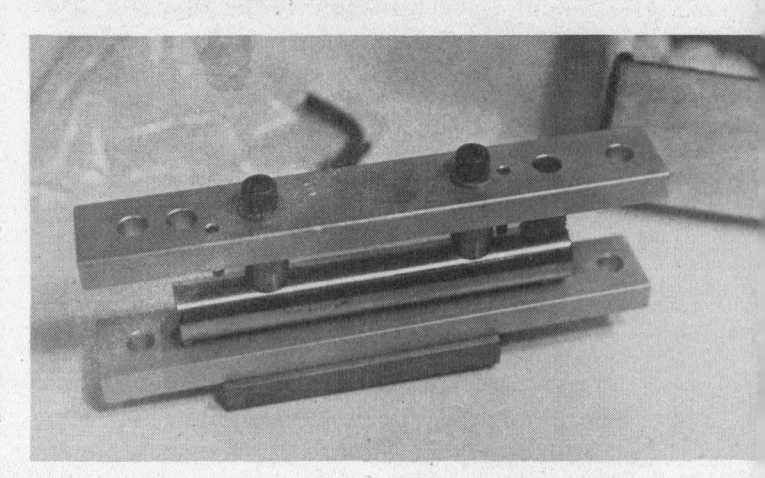

Lathe set-up for bolt-face opening with the Dremel Moto-Tool; lathe dog holds plug, threaded to replace bolt sleeve; tailstock center in firing pin opening centers bolt body. Steady rest must be positioned between bolt lugs and extractor collar; back off tailstock and move toolpost held grinder into place.

Completed lathe set-up for opening bolt face, with variable-speed Moto-Tool grinder in toolpost; compound feed handles grinding depth; crossfeed controls amount of bolt face opening.

When using any power tool, it's a smart idea to securely tie the work piece down. This is especially true when working on larger assemblies, or, the entire gun as shown here.

have been removed by drilling a $^{17}/_{64}''$ hole in the center of the broken screw and then using a screw extractor to remove the screw. Such extractors have left-hand spirals that grip the metal inside of the drilled hole and allow right-handed screws to be unthreaded without damaging the threads. This of course takes a certain amount of setup time, and since I was rushed this particular morning, I merely laid the rifle in a Decker gun vise and grabbed my Moto-Tool. I used a magnifying glass to examine the work as I cut a new screw slot in the top of the broken screw and then used the appropriate size screwdriver to back the damaged screw out.

One word of caution. This operation sounds simpler than it actually is. It takes a lot of patience to guide the tiny dental burr straight across the top

119

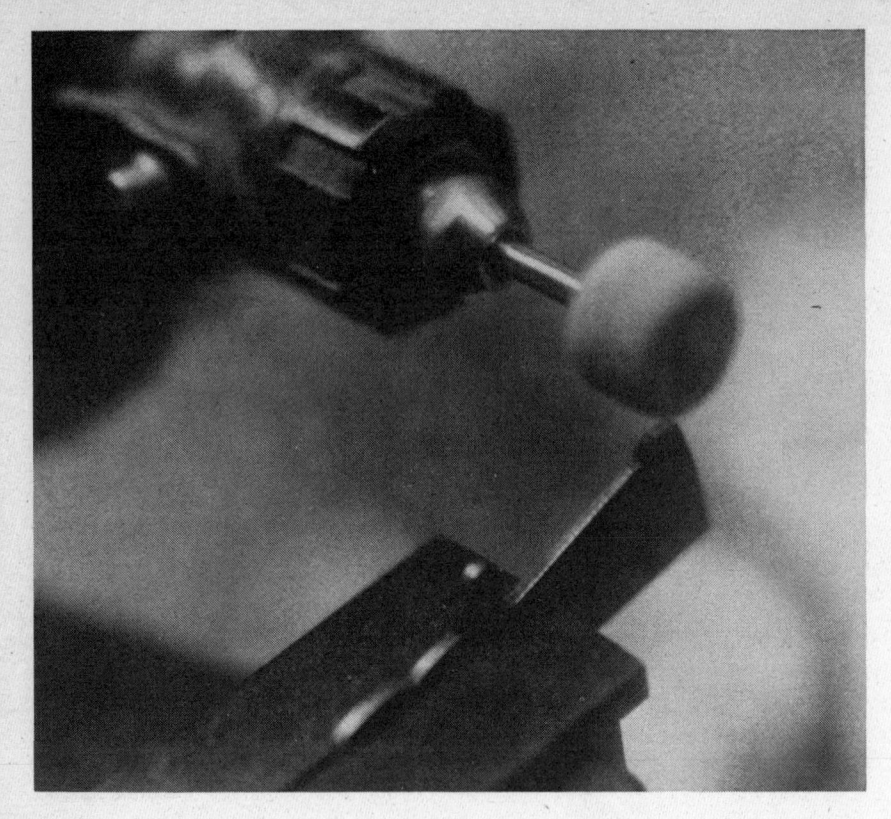

In this instance a Moto-Tool is being used to polish off a burr on a rimfire cartridge lifter.

of a broken screw, so I'd advise practicing on a few old screws first. Also make sure the hole is deep enough for the screwdriver blade to get a firm grip. If the slot is too shallow, you'll wrench it off on the first try.

It is possible to make a template for cutting new screw slots and then use the Dremel router attachment. This will make the job easier. However, if you have to go to all this trouble, you might as well drill a hole in the broken screw and use a regular screw extractor.

Polishing Odd Contours

Many polishing accessories are available for the Moto-Tool that will easily polish the short, small and shielded surfaces found on rifles and shotguns. The basic polishing accessories consist of felt polishing wheels (½" and 1" diameter); felt polishing tips (⅜" diameter); a ⅞" diameter polishing wheel impregnated with fine emery (ideal for polishing metals); a 1" diameter cloth polishing wheel for polishing all metals and plastics; a polishing point impregnated with emery for polishing metals; and, No. 421 polishing compound to apply to polishing wheels and tips. Other felt bobs, both mandrel mounted and unmounted, are available for the Moto-Tool; (just specify ⅛" mandrel) which can be sized and shaped as needed. All may be used to polish such surfaces as the inside of trigger guards, and the endless other contours impossible to reach adequately with the big conventional buffing wheels.

Wire and bristle brushes in various shapes and sizes are also available for use in the Moto-Tool and are excellent for removing rust and corrosion as well as polishing metal surfaces. The wire brushes are especially suited for carding hard-to-reach places when bluing guns by the hot-water method.

Notching Stocks for Bolt Handles

When altering a military bolt to allow a scope sight to be mounted on the action, the stock usually has to be notched to accept the lower-fitting bolt handle. These cuts can be made with the Moto-Tool using ¼" x ⁷⁄₁₆" rotary files of cone, ball, or tear-drop shape mounted on an ⅛" shank.

To notch the stock, mount it securely in a vise with padded jaws or use a Decker gun vise. The action should be stripped with only the bolt body remaining and the assembly then placed in the stock. The bottom 30 degrees of the bolt handle should be coated with inletting black before the bolt is lowered, and pressed firmly against the stock several times to leave a dark print. Remove the action and bolt from the stock and start the

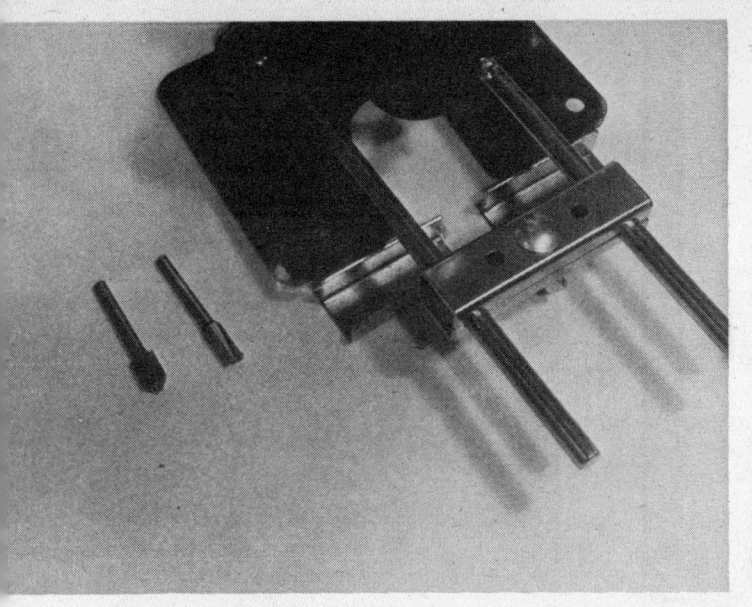

The Moto-Tool is also capable of small (wood) routing jobs. The routing bits shown are just a sample of the available bits from Dremel.

In this case, a Dremel Moto-Tool router attachment is being used to inlet new side locks on this old, exposed-hammer shotgun.

grinding-inletting work. Take only small amounts of wood from the stock at a time before repositioning the action and bolt in the stock, and sharply lower the bolt onto the handle notch already started. Repeat these operations until the notch is deep enough, and of the correct fit so that the bolt will barely clear the wood as it bottoms against the metal of the action. There must be a slight clearance between the bolt handle and the wood, because if there isn't, the recoil of the firearm may cause the stock to crack or split at this area.

Router Attachment

An inexpensive router attachment is available for the Dremel Moto-Tool that easily mounts to the tool. It has a calibrated depth-control adjustment for precision routing and shaping. The edge guide can be quickly removed for free hand and surface routing. The fence adjusts from 0 to 3¾".

You'll find many uses for the router attachment if you do much stock work. They're excellent for gouging, countersinking, and roughing-in stock fore-ends and other work on gun stocks, such as inletting shotgun or muzzle loading side locks.

11

SOLDERING AND WELDING

PERSONS working on firearms will soon discover that they need equipment and a working knowledge to perform silver soldering and brazing—especially when working on some of the older firearms where parts are absolutely not available; or when you get into some of the more exotic conversions and alterations.

When using any form of heat on firearms, extreme caution must be used. Barrels, actions and other parts are subject to heavy stress when fired and all are heat treated when manufactured to withstand the pressure. Any application of heat on these areas can deteriorate the original hardness and can then render the firearm dangerous. The most critical area is around the chamber; that is, the barrel area in the immediate vicinity of the chamber, the action, and the bolt face. Therefore, a front sight ramp, for example, can be silver soldered with relative safety around the muzzle of a rifle, but heat applied farther back—like when welding on a new bolt handle—can mean trouble if certain precautions are not taken.

Soldering Equipment and Its Uses

Soft soldering—generally with a lead-and-tin alloy—has very little use on firearms. The process

(Below) Soldering irons have been used for decades to perform soft soldering on all types of metal.
(Right) This electric soldering gun may be used for small soft soldering jobs as well as removing dents from gunstocks when used in conjunction with a wet rag.

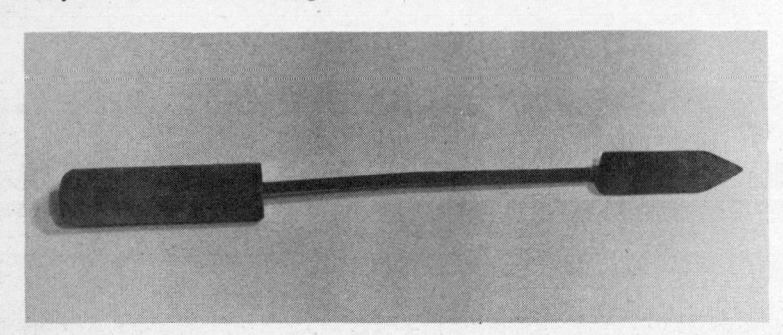

When bluing small parts by the heat-and-dip method, first dip the parts to be blued into a container of conventional gun oil.

requires as much skill and care as silver soldering; has much less strength than silver soldering; will contaminate hot bluing solutions quicker than silver solder; and is nearly as expensive as silver solder. The only advantage that I can see in soft soldering is that it requires less heat than silver solder and therefore can be controlled better in tight areas.

Soft soldering may be performed with soldering irons, electric soldering guns or a controlled gas flame such as the Bernz-O-Matic propane torch. Of these three heat sources, the Bernz-O-Matic torch will find the most use around the gunshop, not only for soldering, but for many other uses where a source of heat is required.

One use of the propane torch is for bluing small gun parts like screws and drift pins. This method is especially useful when replacing one screw or pin and not bluing the whole gun; or when using the hot-water method of bluing. It is extremely difficult to blue smaller parts by the hot-water method, and the oil-and-heat method is perfectly acceptable for small parts.

To blue small screws and pins, polish the parts as usual. Then dip the part in a container of oil (conventional gun oil will work fine). Heat the part until the oil is burned off and the part is a deep blue. Then quench in oil to cool. Repeat the process until the desired color is achieved.

A propane torch is also useful when repairing dents in gunstocks with shellac sticks. These shellac sticks are available from Brownell's and come in an assortment of colors including white,

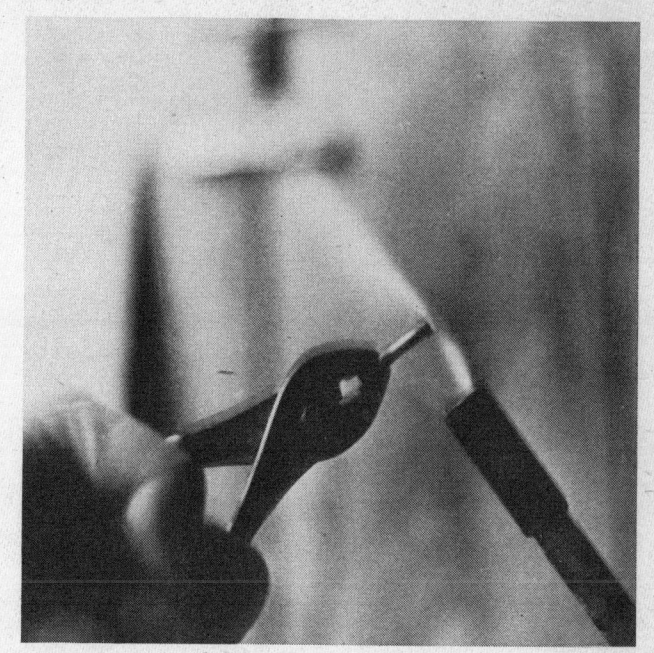

Heat the part until the oil is burned off and the part starts to turn a deep blue.

ivory, transparent, medium walnut, light walnut, dark walnut, circassian walnut and black.

The ideal tool for this work is a pallet knife. You can make one by taking an old table knife (preferably one with an insulated handle) and cutting the blade down to about 3 inches. Round off the end on your grinder and taper it slightly from the handle to the rounded end. Remove the burrs and polish the blade until you have a smooth, flexible tool.

Hold the knife in the flame of the propane torch

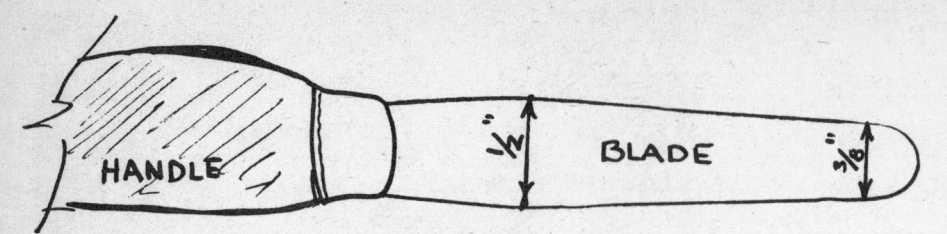

Dimensions for making a pallet knife to use on stock repairs.

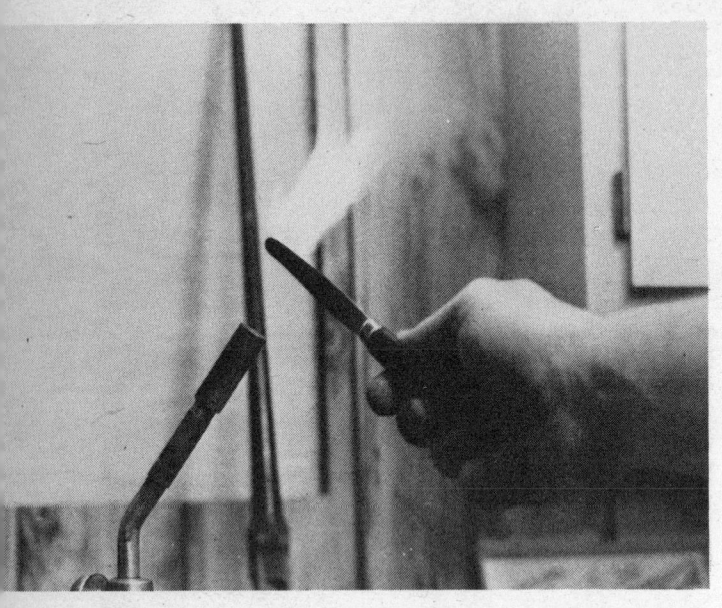

Hold the pallet knife in the flame of the propane torch (above) until it's hot enough to melt the shellac when pressed against the end of the shellac stick which can be seen to the left of the knife (below).

until it's hot enough to melt the shellac when pressed against the end of the shellac stick. When a small quantity of melted shellac has formed on the end of the blade, immediately wipe it across the area to be repaired. This is best done by turning the blade so the melted shellac will be on the bottom of the blade and then, holding the knife at a 45° angle, draw it over the scratch, dent, tool mark, crack, etc. The motion should be quick yet gentle. If the first pass doesn't completely fill the defect, repeat.

When the shellac has thoroughly hardened, sand down to the level of the stock and finish in the same manner as you would for the wood itself. The shellac repair will have a glossy appearance and is best used on stocks with a glossy appearance. (A London oil finish will show the repairs more readily.)

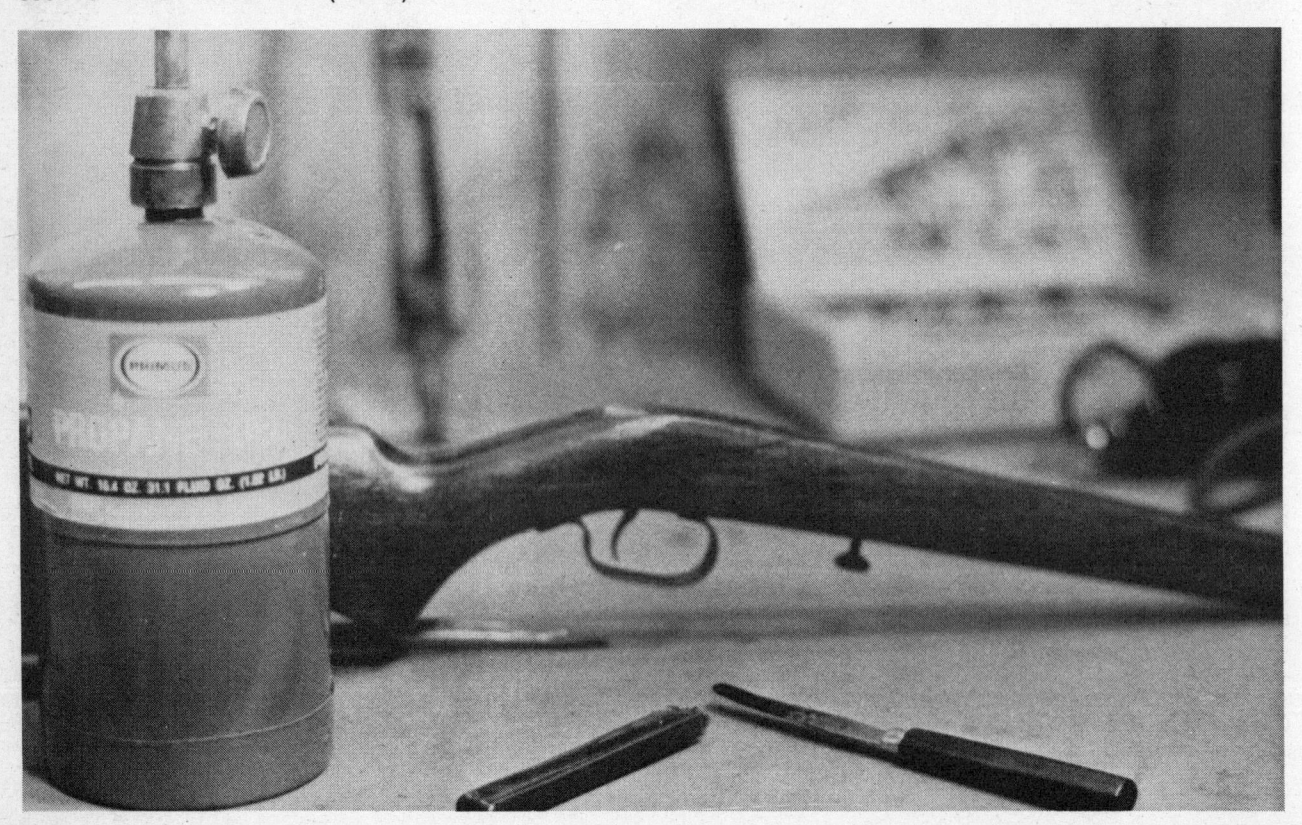

The gunsmith's first propane torch should be one like the Bernz-O-Matic. This brand was my first, and since it has served me so well, I haven't had any need to try another. When using this type of torch, light in the following manner:

1. Open valve ¼ turn.
2. After five seconds, close valve.
3. Light match, lighter, or spark lighter. When using the latter, open the valve 1 full turn and ignite ½-inch away from the nozzle.
4. Open valve slowly until pilot flame is lit.
5. For the hottest, most efficient flame, adjust the blue flame so that it is 1 to 1½ inches in length.

The lightweight steel cylinder of fuel has a self-sealing valve that pops shut when you thread off any burner unit to replace it with another. Extra cylinders may be stored indefinitely without any loss of fuel.

If you don't want to be bothered with changing the cylinders so often, a propane shop torch kit is offered by RIDGID. A unique design and construction of burner assembly and nozzle propels the propane/air mixture with a high-velocity whirling action to produce a very hot, pointed flame that actually encircles the work you are heating.

This torch is ideal for both soft and silver soldering jobs and provides a 2600-degree flame for brazing also, although it is not recommended for brass brazing. The assembly attaches to a tank of LP gas, available from your local bottle gas dealer. A 20-pound tank is recommended unless you anticipate moving the apparatus very much. Then a 10-pound tank should suffice.

The Bernz-O-Matic torch will find the most use around the average gunshop. Besides soldering, it can be used for bluing small parts, melting shellac sticks to make stock repairs, and a number of other jobs.

Silver Soldering

Experience is the greatest teacher when it comes to soldering, but there are a few guidelines that can be useful to the beginner. The main concern should be with the basic principles. In general, silver soldering is the process of uniting two pieces of metal by means of an alloy having a melting point of between 1000 degrees F. to 1150 degrees F. (depending upon the type of alloy used). When applying the silver solder, it should be spread evenly over the work to be joined, and when so applied, its holding strength is surprisingly high—25,000 PSI strength or more!

Of the various techniques available, the one known as "sweating" is the most value to the gunsmith. This process enables sight ramps to be soldered to barrels, ribs may be attached, even barrels of side-by-side and over-and-under shotguns are joined together by experts using this method of soldering. Broken parts may be repaired and many other jobs around the gunshop may be candidates for silver soldering.

The equipment needed for this operation is simple. You'll need only a propane torch, a file or scraper for cleaning the surfaces, suitable solder, a felt or woolen rag for wiping joints, and, some small clamps for holding the work. That's just about all that's needed. Just about, but not quite! One of the most common problems encountered by the beginner is making the solder stick to the surface. Chances are you're going to have the whole mess form into little shiny balls and roll everywhere except where you want it. To solve this problem, you'll need some type of soldering flux.

Dyna-Flux solder flux is available from Brown-

125

When soldering a front sight ramp on a barrel, first position the ramp in place and then secure it with a C-clamp.

ell's and promotes smooth, even solder flow that results in neat, professional looking and stronger solder joints. This type of flux is formulated with a special wetting agent that works through capillary action to assure total coverage of work surfaces. It is for use on practically all metals but aluminum. This flux is excellent for all soft solders and Brownell's Hi-Force 44 solder which contains 4% silver and 96% tin. More importantly, it shows no effects when immersed in hot bluing solutions.

For true silver soldering, AMCO 45 silver brazing flux is recommended. This is a creamy brush-on paste that will not separate, harden or crystallize. It wets the surfaces, removes oxides and prevents oxidation. The heat range is in the neighborhood of 850 to 1600 degrees F. It may be removed with warm water. Another problem is when the solder flows on surfaces where it is not wanted. A common talc crayon may be used on areas where the solder is not wanted. Merely rub the crayon around ramps, bases, etc., and the solder will not stick to any area rubbed with it. It washes off with soap and water or detergents.

Here's one method of soldering a front sight ramp on a rifle barrel. Position the ramp in its proper position on the rifle barrel and hold it firmly with a C-clamp. Double check the ramp for proper alignment, etc., and then mark around the lower edges of the ramp with a scriber. Remove the ramp, and polish the area within the scribed boundaries with a Moto-Tool using a polishing tip and 240 polishing compound. Tin the barrel within these scribed lines, and wipe off excess solder with

Mark around the lower edges of the ramp with a scriber. Then remove the sight and polish the area within the scribed lines.

Once again secure the sight in place with a small clamp and then heat the area sufficiently to melt the solder.

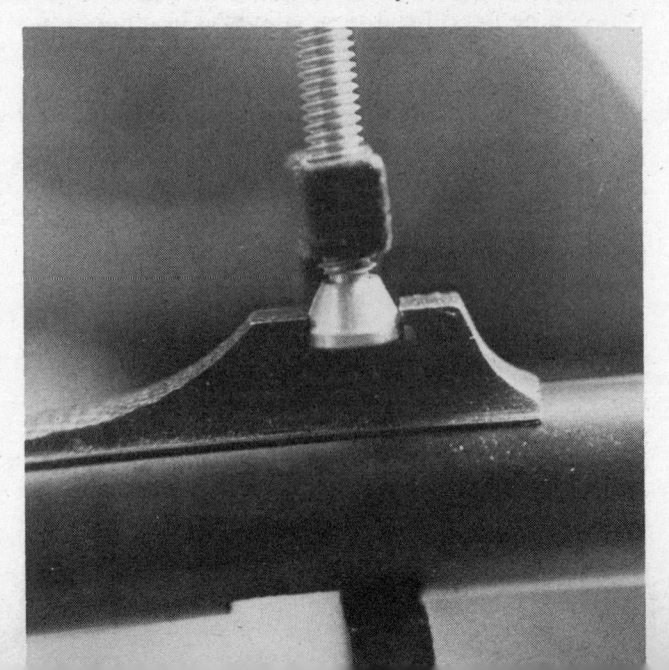

a wool or felt rag. Then tin the underside of the sight ramp—again wiping excess solder away. The solder on both parts should be as thin as possible for greatest strength.

Again, locate the ramp on the top of the barrel, aligning it very carefully, and secure it by means of a small clamp. Heat the assembly (the barrel and the ramp) sufficiently to melt the solder and then let it cool. If the two areas were only *lightly* tinned with solder, the sight will be tight with very little run-out.

With a little practice, such ramps may be installed with little or no exposed solder showing. However, in some cases, there will be a little hairline of solder around the bottom edges of the sight base that you'll probably want to touch-up. Birchwood Casey has two types of solder blacks on the market. One is for tin-lead solders and the other is especially for silver solder. The application of either requires no heat; they react with the solder for a long-lasting finish without damaging the surrounding finish. There is also no after rust or corrosion.

Broken gun parts may be repaired by silver soldering in much the same way as described for installing the ramp. Clean both surfaces of the parts to be joined, but do not try to smooth them. Leave them just as they are; the irregularities will help align them and will add strength to the joint. Clamp the two pieces separately in a vise and apply the flux to the surfaces and carefully heat until the flux melts. Apply the silver solder to each piece and while it is still molten, wipe off the excess with a rag or soldering brush.

When both pieces are cool, clamp them together if possible, or clamp one piece in a vise while holding the other with pliers or tweezers. If the latter method is used, be sure to rest your hand or forearm on something solid so you'll be able to keep the parts perfectly steady and aligned. Apply just enough heat to melt the solder, then remove the torch and let cool. When the part is cool, scrape away any excess solder, clean the joint and finish. The job is done if you did your part. Should the part be out of alignment, reheat the part and reposition the parts for another try—it will only take about 5 minutes.

Under no circumstances should silver soldering or brazing be done on heat-treated parts unless certain precautions are taken and you are equipped to reharden the parts. For example, you should never heat the receiver ring of a bolt-action rifle which has its locking system within this area. Heat that is low enough so that the bluing shows no discoloration is usually considered safe, but anything above this temperature can be dangerous. Even when welding a bolt handle that is a good 4 inches away from the locking lugs, precautions must be taken. One method is to use wet rags to surround the bolt while the heat is being applied to keep the bolt cool. This will confine the heat to the part being welded and will not escape to the critical areas of the bolt; but, be sure to keep the rags wet at all times.

A heat control paste called HEAT STOP is offered by Brownell's that will absorb heat and prevent damage of adjacent parts during welding, brazing, heat-treating and soldering. This chemical acts as an antiflux when soldering, will not harm blued finishes and cleans off easily and completely. Although I've never tried it, the manufacturer claims that when this compound is applied to a steel bar, one end of the bar may be heated red hot while holding the other end in your bare hand! This is some heat control.

Even when silver soldering in less critical areas—like the front sight ramp—certain precautions must be taken. One is to apply the heat evenly over the barrel and not just to one spot. For example, when installing a front sight ramp to the muzzle end of the barrel, the barrel should be heated all around and not just on top where the ramp is to be soldered. If heat is applied only to the

Brownell's Heat Stop acts as a heat sink when applied to metal surfaces.

A set of bolt-bending blocks come in handy when altering bolt handles.

top of the barrel, the barrel could become warped.

Bolt Alterations

If you ever take a notion to install a telescopic sight on some of the older military rifles, chances are the angle of the bolt handle will have to be changed to clear the scope when the action is opened. In some cases, you might even want to alter the bolt handle when using iron sights, just for appearance sake.

There are three basic ways to alter bolt handles. All require extreme heat that cannot be adequately supplied by propane torches. An arc or oxyacetylene welder must be used. Extreme care must be taken so as not to let too much heat reach and soften the critical locking lugs, the cocking sears, and the bolt body itself. As much of the heat as possible must be confined to the area of the bolt handle.

The first method is the use of bending blocks, like the ones shown. These are two-piece casts, hollowed or contoured on the inside to grip the bolt body securely while permitting the bolt handle to protrude from the blocks. These blocks are also designed to shield the bolt body from heat generated during welding. HEAT STOP placed in the block will accomplish this task as well as heat-dissipating aluminum construction of the blocks.

These are the necessary steps for cutting and welding a bolt handle to lower its swing.

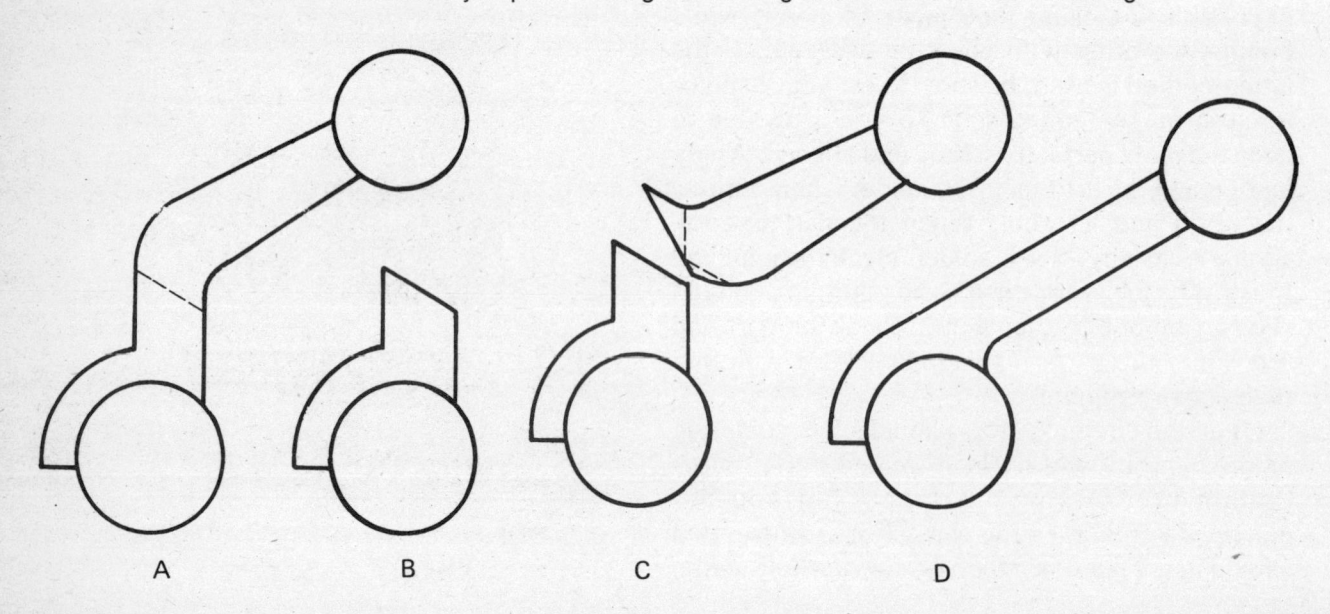

A   B   C   D

128

BOLT WELDING JIG

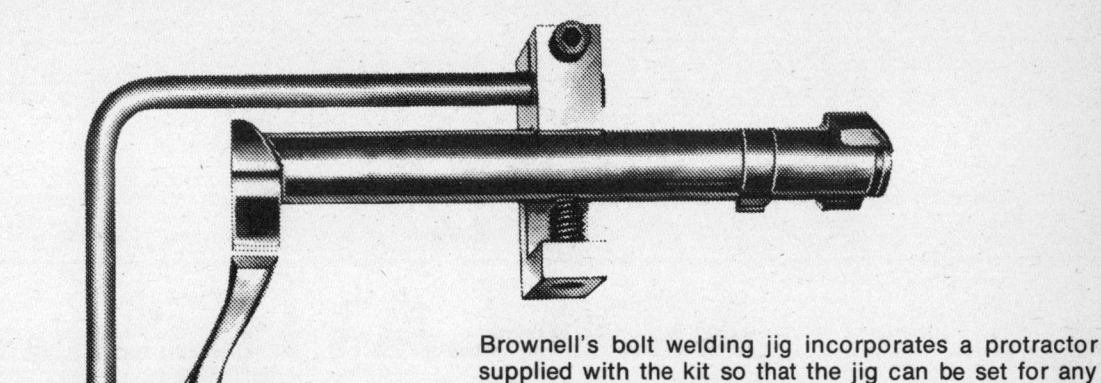

Brownell's bolt welding jig incorporates a protractor supplied with the kit so that the jig can be set for any desired angle or sweepback.

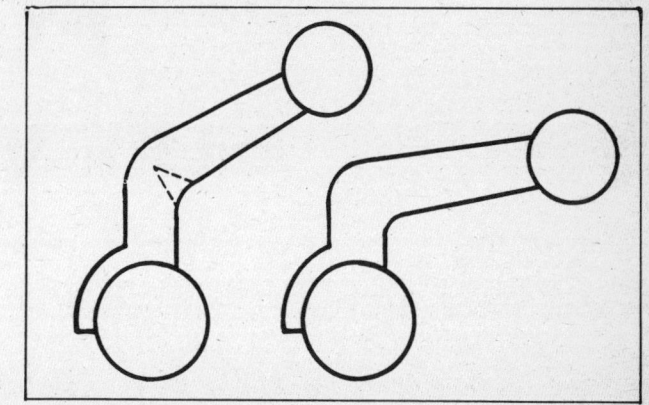

Notching the bolt handle is the simplest of all methods for lowering it to accept a telescopic sight.

To alter the bolt, heat is applied with the welding unit until the exposed handle glows cherry red or about 1400 degrees F. The handle may then be easily hammered or bent into the desired contour with a wrench or lever.

Cutting and welding the bolt is also very popular in gunshops. Before most bolts can be cut, however, they must be annealed by applying moderate heat to the handle only. Again, I recommend using HEAT STOP on the remaining portion of the bolt. Also be sure to remove all parts from the bolt such as safety, firing pin, screws, etc. A dull red or approximately 1000 degrees F. should be sufficient for most bolt handles. Once annealed, the bolt should be allowed to cool slowly; *never quench it in water* as this is likely to make the metal brittle.

As the diagrams show, the bolt is cut off with a hack saw about ¼" from the bolt body. With the bolt handle off, it is now ready for rewelding or a new commercial bolt handle welded to the bolt handle stub. If the existing bolt handle is to be used, grind off portions of the handle as shown.

Aligning the altered bolt handle with the bolt handle stub can be a touchy situation. The best tool to use here is Brownell's bolt welding jig. This jig is unique in that it incorporates a protractor supplied with the kit so that you can set the jig for any desired angle or sweepback. It then locks the bolt handle into position against the stub ready for welding. When welding, again use the same precautions as you did for cutting the handle off; that is, wrap the bolt body with wet rags or else use HEAT STOP during the welding process.

The final method is the simplest of all. All you have to do is notch the bolt handle as shown (after annealing it as discussed earlier), apply HEAT STOP to the bolt body and position the entire bolt in a vise so that the handle may be tapped down and back with a metal hammer. Apply heat over the notch with your torch and when the metal glows bright red, tap the handle into the desired position. Then let it cool slowly.

After any of the above methods have been used, grind and polish the entire handle, devoting special attention to the altered area. The handle may be left bright and shiny or else blued by any of the methods described in Chapter 9.

12
MINI-LATHES FOR GUN WORK

A FULL-SIZE metal lathe costs a lot of money and requires considerable floor space—not to mention the skill required on the part of the operator. Such a lathe does have a place in the gunshop for turning barrels, chambering barrel blanks for a specific cartridge, and threading barrels for installation in actions or receivers. But all of these operations can be "farmed" out until such time as the gunsmith feels such an investment is justified.

On the other hand, a miniature (but mighty) lathe is available and deserves consideration by anyone who does work on firearms. It's called the Unimat 3 and costs considerably less than the full-size models; however, it duplicates all of the more important functions of the larger varieties, except, of course, the capability of working full-length rifle barrels.

The Unimat 3 does have a few features of its own, and with the proper accessories, the gunsmith can perform such work as barrel turning for handguns, boring, threading, sanding and buffing, grinding, etc. It can also be set up as a miniature drill press and milling machine, and it requires little bench space—about 13 x 22 inches. When the time comes that you feel like you need a lathe, the Unimat deserves consideration for your first one. It's easy to learn on, and you'll get the feel of lathe work with only a comparatively small investment. Then, as the need arises, and business picks up, you may want to invest in a full-size lathe with, say, a 14″ swing and 36 inches between centers as described in Chapter 15 on full-size lathes. (Even if you already have a full-size lathe, you'll find many uses for the Unimat 3 on small gun-part work. It makes an excellent second lathe.)

The Unimat 3 and other metal working tools are manufactured in Austria by the Messrs. Maier & Co., but marketed in the U.S. by EMCO-LUX Corp. The Unimat comes ready to use, complete with motor, Jacobs chuck, centers, tool holder, cutting bit and other accessories. For the hobbyist or beginning professional, it is one of the handiest tools you can own, even if you have one of the larger lathes.

Naturally being of this small size, you cannot expect it to take off as much metal per whack as the larger lathes; it will take off as much, but it just takes more passes. Since a large percentage of lathe work in gunshops consists of machining small parts and accessories—such as firing pins, drift pins, etc.—the Unimat will shine in this type of work. Here are the basic specifications:

Distance between centers: 8″
Center height: 1.75″
Swing over bed: 3.6″

Travel of cross slide: 2.1"
Required space: 21.7"
New weight: 15.4 pounds

HEADSTOCK
Hole through spindle: 0.4"
Spindle nose: M 14 x 1
Spindle speeds: 6 (130, 200, 350, 560, 920 40000 rpm)

AUTOMATIC FEED GEAR
Longitudinal feed 0.0008"/rev.

TAILSTOCK
Barrel diameter: 0.7"

Tranverse of barrel: 0.9"
Drill chuck mounting: M 14 x 1

DRIVE UNIT
Ac/Dc motor: 95 watts
Motor speeds: 2100 to 3600 rpm

VERTICAL HEAD
Maximum working height: 5.5"
Drilling stroke: 1.0"
Spindle nose: M 14 x 1

THREADS
Metric: (0.5 - 1.5mm)
Inch: 16 (16 - 56tpi)

The small Unimat lathes have long been popular with gunsmiths. To the left is the new Unimat 3. Below is the Unimat being used to drill a center hole with the stock held in the lathe chuck and a drill secured in the tailstock spindle chuck.

The operations that the Unimat will perform within its limitations are governed only by the skill of the operator and his imagination. The following comments will give you some idea as to some of the uses you'll find for it around the gunshop. Set up as a lathe, the Unimat will machine firing pins, make gun screws, turn drift pins all day and do just about anything desired up to a length of 8", which includes most pistol barrels.

Recently, a customer brought in a Raven .25 auto pistol with a broken firing pin to be repaired. Of course, a factory firing pin is available for nominal cost, but time was of the essence and the customer was willing to pay a premium price to have the gun repaired sooner than it would take to order a firing pin.

A small piece of round stock was found in my "junk" pile, and after measuring and marking the centers of each end, the piece was mounted in the 3-jaw chuck and turned at a speed of 560 rpm. A combination center drill and countersink was used for drilling the center holes with the drill secured in a Jacobs chuck screwed onto the tailstock spindle chuck and a center rest used to support the work.

When drilling center holes, much care should be exercised to prevent breaking off the point. Never crowd the drill and chances are you'll never experience a broken drill. However, if the point should break and become stuck in the work, heat the end of the shaft to a cherry red and allow it to cool slowly so that the drill point will be annealed and can be drilled out.

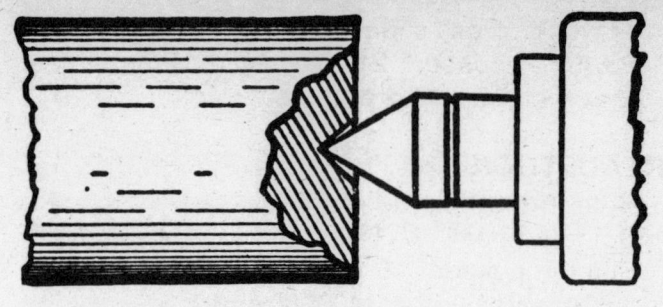

This center hole has been poorly drilled — it's too shallow and at an incorrect angle.

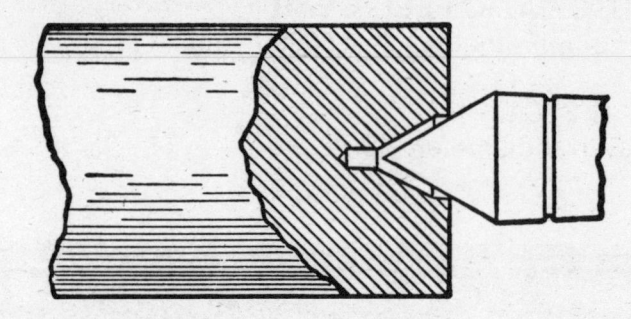

This center hole is also improperly done — it's drilled too deeply to fit the center.

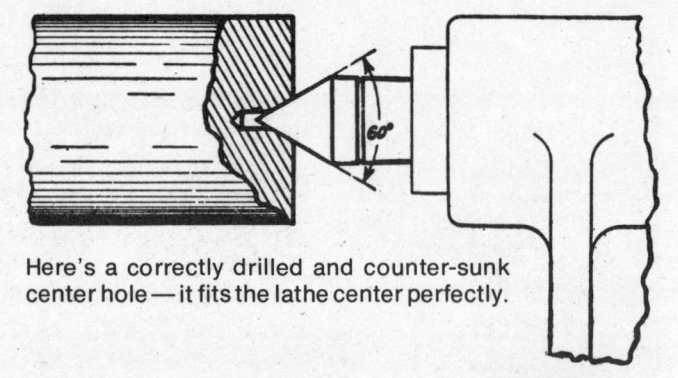

Here's a correctly drilled and counter-sunk center hole — it fits the lathe center perfectly.

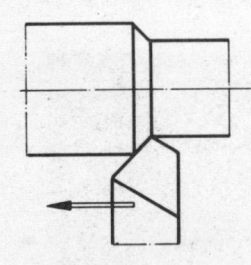

Roughing tools (diagram above) are used to remove large amounts of metal. In the photo to the right, a roughing tool is being used to turn a firing pin to approximate dimensions.

On the firing pin made by the author, the rough shape of the pin itself was marked on the workpiece with an outside thread cutting tool.

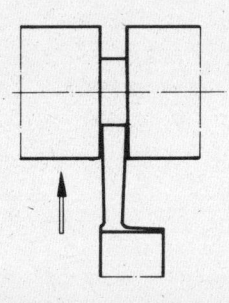

The parting tool shown in the diagram above is used for grooving, or simply parting a piece of metal. To the right is the firing pin — it has been parted at one end of the shaft.

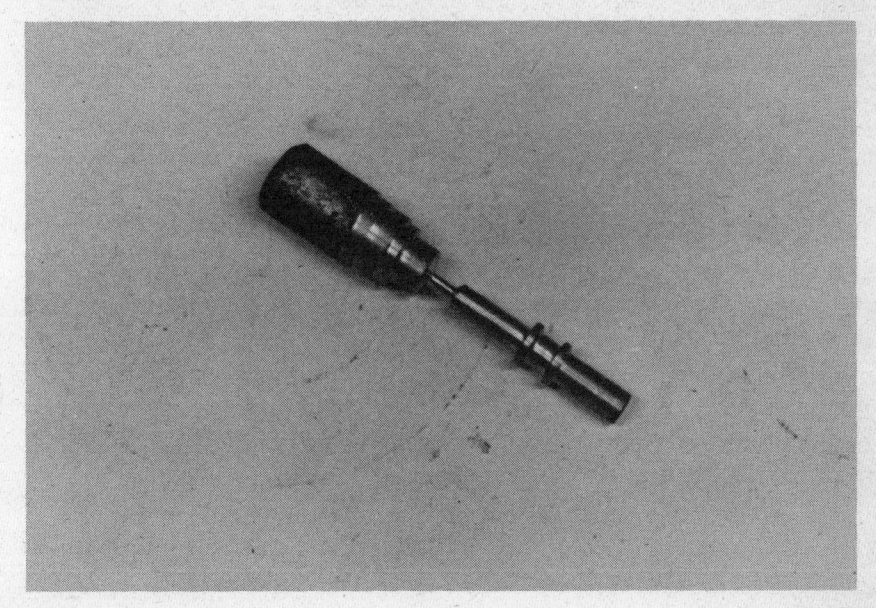

One of the most common causes of poor lathe work is incorrectly drilled center holes. For example the diagram shows a shallow center hole with incorrect angle and no clearance for the tip of the center point. Another diagram shows a center hole that has been drilled too deep, while a third diagram shows a correctly drilled and countersunk hole that fits the lathe center perfectly.

Where the broken firing pin was concerned, the pin itself was used as a guide; that is, measurements were taken to apply to the new work. The pin point was, of course, broken and exact dimensions of this were unknown, but could be guessed at and then fitted perfectly by trial and error. The dimensions and rough shape of the firing pin were marked on the work piece with an outside thread cutting tool and then turned to approximate dimensions with a roughing tool.

At a point in the work where the firing pin began to take shape, a round nosed tool was used to smooth the surface and bring the work to final shape as shown. Then a parting-off tool was used to cut one end of the firing pin away from the shaft. Since the work was getting to the point of having only very thin metal to support the piece, one slight mistake could ruin the entire project. Therefore, the remaining work was then held only by the 3-jaw chuck around a part of the pin that had sufficient metal.

Once the pin was shaped (except for rounding

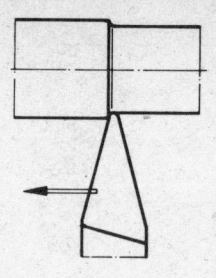

In the diagram above, a round-nose tool can be seen. To the right, that tool is being used to bring the firing pin into final smooth shape.

the firing pin end), the pin was tried in the gun to see if the fit was okay; it fit perfectly. The only remaining work was to shape the firing pin nose and heat treat the part. When heat-treating parts such as these, I hold them with a wire. Pliers should not be used to hold such parts when heat treating as the pliers will conduct heat away from the parts and even heat will not be applied. The part was heated to a cherry red and then dipped (and allowed to cool) in conventional motor oil.

Missing gun screws are always a problem and occur in every gunshop. Many common fillister head screws can be modified or altered to serve in a gun mechanism such as turning the screw head to a smaller diameter, but the finished product does not always look right. The threads often get mashed up from being held in the 3-jaw chuck. The

(Above) When the firing pin was completed, the author tried it in the Raven autoloader to see if the fit was precise.

(Below) If you've got a screw that has the proper threads, but the head is too large, you can turn the head down to proper dimensions in a Unimat.

Once the firing pin was completed, and the fit assured, the author hardened the pin by heat treating.

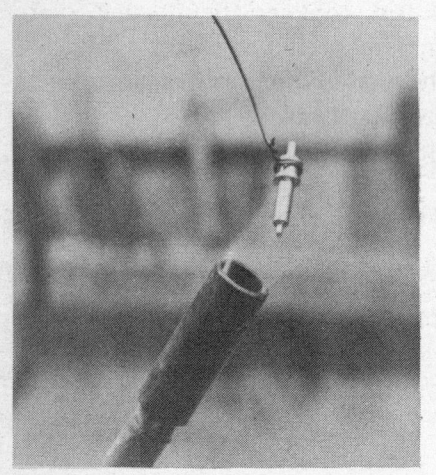

134

best way to replace missing screws (if manufactured replacements are not available) is to make your own on the Unimat 3 from cold-rolled steel.

If an existing screw is not available for reference, Brownell's book, *The Encyclopedia of Modern Firearms Parts and Assembly Vol. I,* contains detailed measurements in chart form of thousands of pins, screws, helical springs, etc., for many different guns. It is also good practice for the gunsmith to make sketches of each different part made and dimensioned for future reference should the part have to be duplicated. Whenever an unusual or rare gun comes into my shop for repair and the gun has to be dismantled, I try to make sketches of all parts and carefully take dimensions should the part ever have to be duplicated.

The procedure for making a screw on the Unimat 3 amounts to taking a piece of cold-rolled steel stock and securing it in the 3-jaw lathe chuck, allowing enough room to work the tool up to, and including, the screw head. Then the head and body are turned, and the end of the screw is chamfered with a 45-degree chamfering tool. Next, thread the screw body with the proper size stock and die. You can do this by hand, or hold the die up to the bolt and run the lathe at its slowest speed (130 rpm). The parting-off tool is then used to cut the screw head away from the steel stock.

At this point, some means of protecting the threads should be provided while rounding, slotting and polishing the screw head. With little difficulty a screw adapter can be turned on the Unimat from tool steel and then drilled and tapped and marked as to what thread it is for. A slot in the adapter comes in handy for removing the smaller screws. It is not absolutely necessary to cut a square end on the adapter, but by doing so, it may be held more positively between the vise jaws when the screw head is slotted.

The screw, fitted in the adapter, is then secured in the lathe chuck and the head rounded and polished. The adapter is then removed, secured in a bench vise, and the head slotted. A screw head slot can be cut with a standard hack saw, but a Starrett screw slotting blade can save much time. They fit any adjustable hack saw frame, eliminating time needed to set up a machine. Several thicknesses of teeth are available and they may also be used for undercutting inside corners and cutting flats on shafts for set screws.

Each blade is hardened throughout for maximum rigidity plus keen cutting edge. Straight milled teeth provide smooth cutting action and nice finish. Each blade tapers in thickness from cutting edge to back to prevent binding and allow quick, easy cutting.

Once the slot is cut, the head is polished again and blued in any conventional manner. If just one screw needs to be blued, the heat-and-oil-dip method described in Chapter 11 is the fastest.

These examples of the Unimat's use does not even skim the surface of those possible. The milling attachment, for example, will allow you to perform many useful milling jobs, some of which are discussed in Chapter 16 on milling machines. Drillings can be performed as discussed in Chapter 13 on the drill press.

Accurate Measurements

When parts are turned or milled on the Unimat 3, certain measurements are necessary to obtain usable finished products. Careful and accurate measurements are also necessary in other areas of the gunsmithing profession and can be acquired only by practice and experience. All measurements should be made with an accurately graduated steel scale or a micrometer. Never use a cheap scale or a wood ruler, as they are likely to be inaccurate and may cause spoiled work.

An experienced gunsmith can take measurements with a steel scale and calipers to a surprising degree of accuracy. This is accomplished by developing a sensitive "caliper feel" and by

Screw slotting hacksaw blades are available in a number of thicknesses. They are also handy for under cutting inside corners and cutting flats on shafts for set screws.

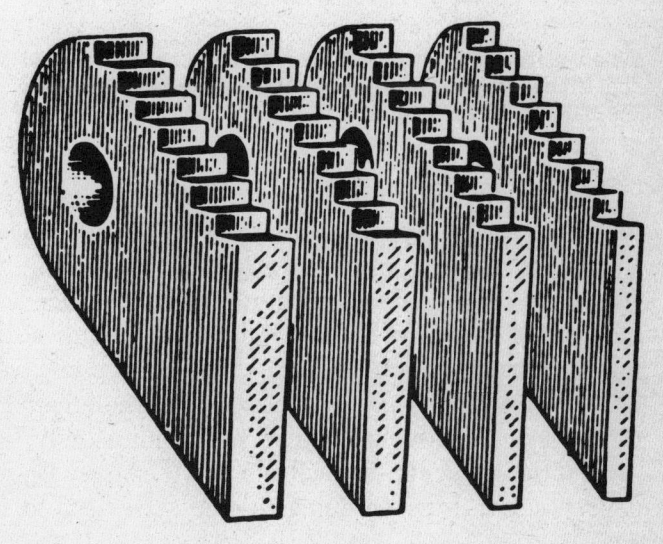

carefully setting the calipers so that they split the line graduated on the scale.

A good method for setting an outside caliper to a steel scale is to hold the scale in the left hand while the caliper is held against the end of the scale and supported by the finger of the left hand—adjustment is made with the thumb and first finger of the right hand.

The proper application of the outside caliper when measuring the diameter of a shaft is to hold the caliper exactly at right angles to the center line of the work and push it gently back and forth across the diameter of the cylinder to be measured. When the caliper is adjusted properly, it should easily slip over the shaft due to its own weight. Never force a caliper or it will deform the instrument and the measurement will not be accurate.

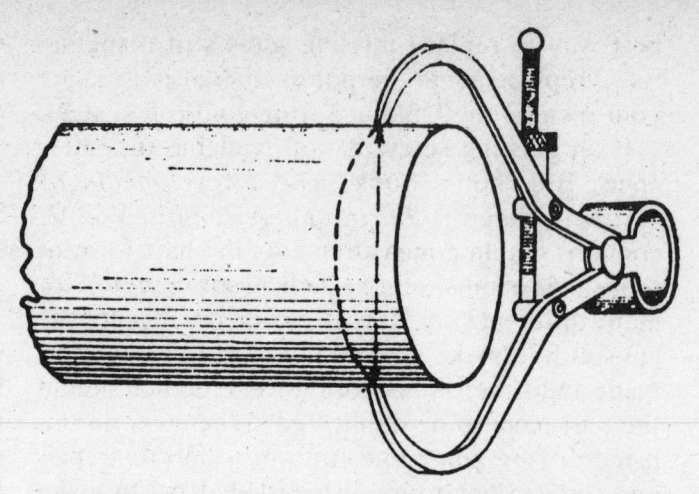

The proper application of the outside caliper when measuring the diameter of a shaft is to hold the caliper exactly at right angles to the center line of the work. Push the caliper back and forth across the diameter of the cylinder to be measured. When adjusted properly, the caliper should easily slip over the shaft. *Never* force the caliper as you might deform it.

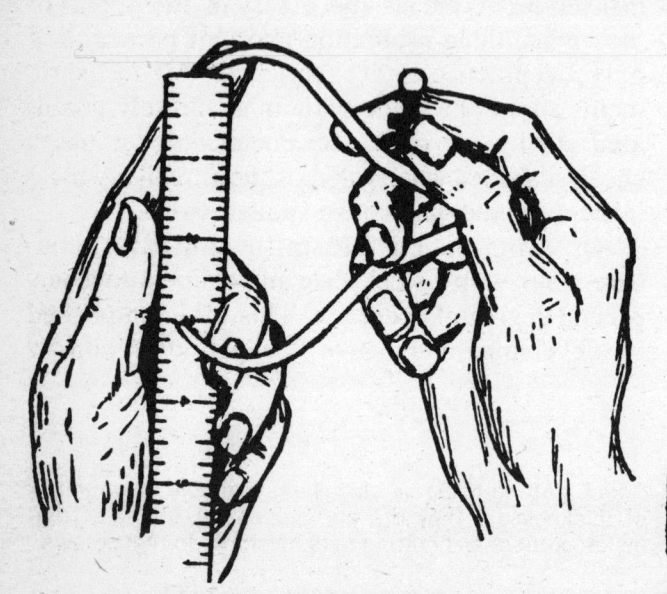

When setting an outside caliper, hold an *accurate* steel rule in the left hand while the right hand holds and adjusts the caliper to the desired measurement.

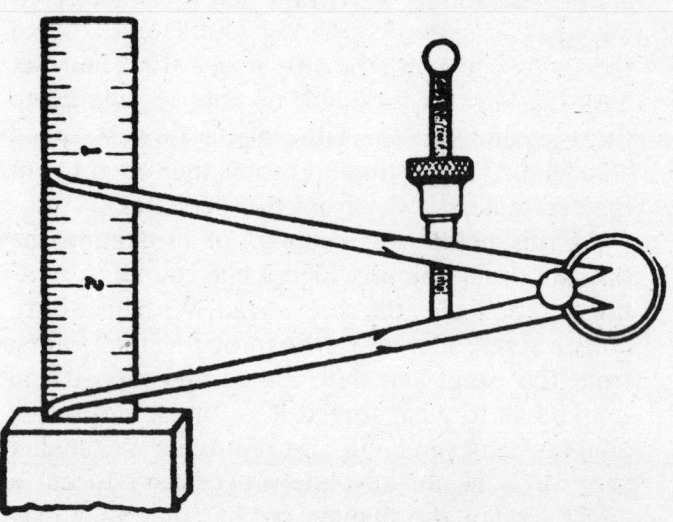

In this diagram, a caliper is being set for a definite dimension by placing the end of the scale against a flat surface while the ends of the caliper are respectively placed at the edge and at the point of the scale desired.

To set an inside caliper for a definite dimension, place the end of the scale against a flat surface and the end of the caliper at the edge and end of the scale. Hold the scale square with the flat surface. Adjust the other end of the caliper to the required dimension.

To measure an inside diameter, place the caliper in the hole as shown and raise your hand slowly. Adjust the caliper until it will slip into the hole with a very slight drag. In doing this be sure to hold the caliper square across the diameter of the hole.

In transferring measurement from an outside caliper to an inside caliper, the point of one leg of the inside caliper rests on a similar point of the outside caliper, as shown. Using this contact point as a pivot, move the inside caliper along the dotted line shown in the illustration, and adjust with the thumb screw until you feel your measurement is right.

To measure the inside diameter of any hollow or recessed object, place the caliper inside as shown and adjust it so it will slip in and out of the hole with a slight amount of drag.

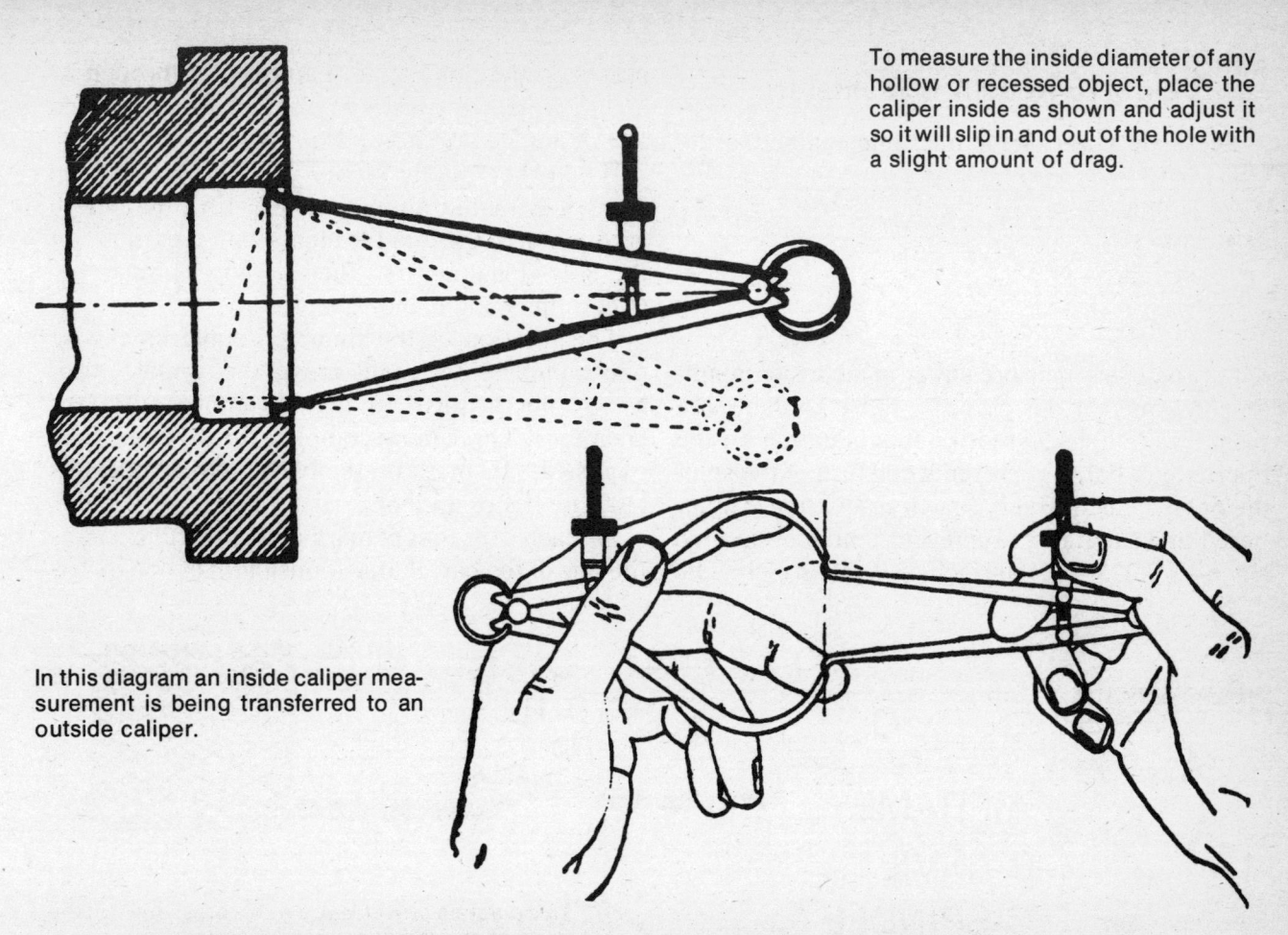

In this diagram an inside caliper measurement is being transferred to an outside caliper.

Dial calipers (top) and a micrometer (bottom) are two measuring devices gunsmiths rely on daily.

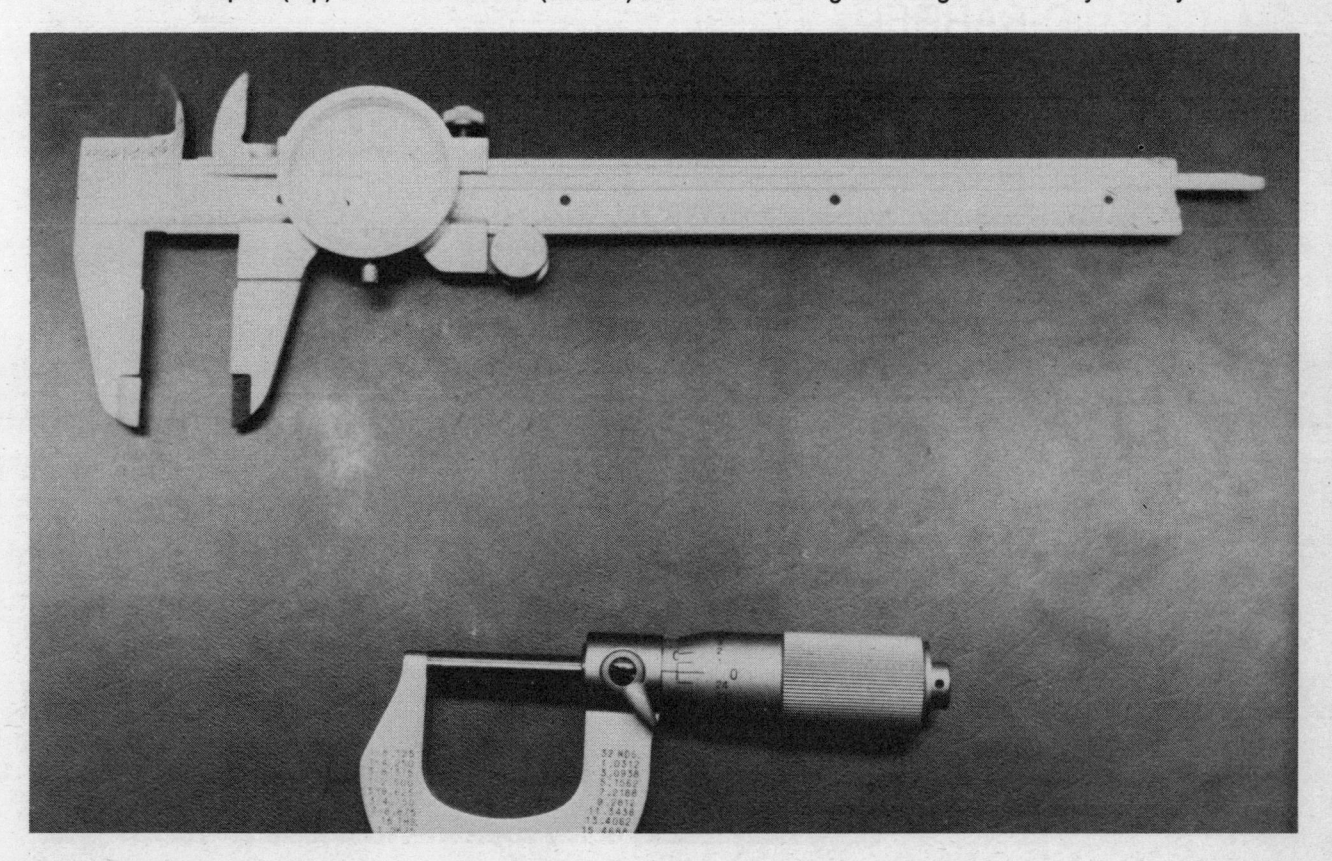

How To Read A Micrometer

The main parts of the micrometer include the following:
- A. Frame
- B. Anvil
- C. Spindle
- D. Hub or barrel
- E. Thimble

Micrometers measure either in inches or in millimeters. but for our purpose, those graduated in inches will be discussed. Each graduation on the micrometer barrel represents one turn of the spindle or 0.025 inch. Every fourth graduation is numbered and the figures represent tenths of an inch since 4 x 0.025 = 0.1000 inch or $^1/_{10}$ of an inch. The marks on the thimble are numbered 1 through 24 and the 25th mark is the return to 0. Usually, 0, 5, 10, 15 and 20 are in larger print.

When the spindle of a 0″-1″ micrometer is in contact with the anvil, you will find that the 0 graduation of the thimble aligns with the 0 mark of the hub—meaning that there is no clearance between the spindle and the anvil.

The rotation of the thimble counterclockwise one complete turn will move the spindle .025″ away from the anvil, giving this amount (.025″) of clearance. Three more complete turns (4 total) will expose a "1" mark on the barrel which indicates .100″ or $^1/_{10}$ of an inch.

As each subsequent mark on the thimble passes the line of the barrel, one thousandth of one inch is added. Therefore, if the thimble is rotated to align the number 10 mark, ten one-thousandths are added to the exposed marks on the barrel. So, if we went to 10 on the thimble beyond .5, our measurement would be .510 as shown in the photograph below.

The fit of the part being measured between the spindle and anvil should be snug—not too tight or

A-FRAME
B-ANVIL
C-SPINDLE
D-BARREL
E-THIMBLE

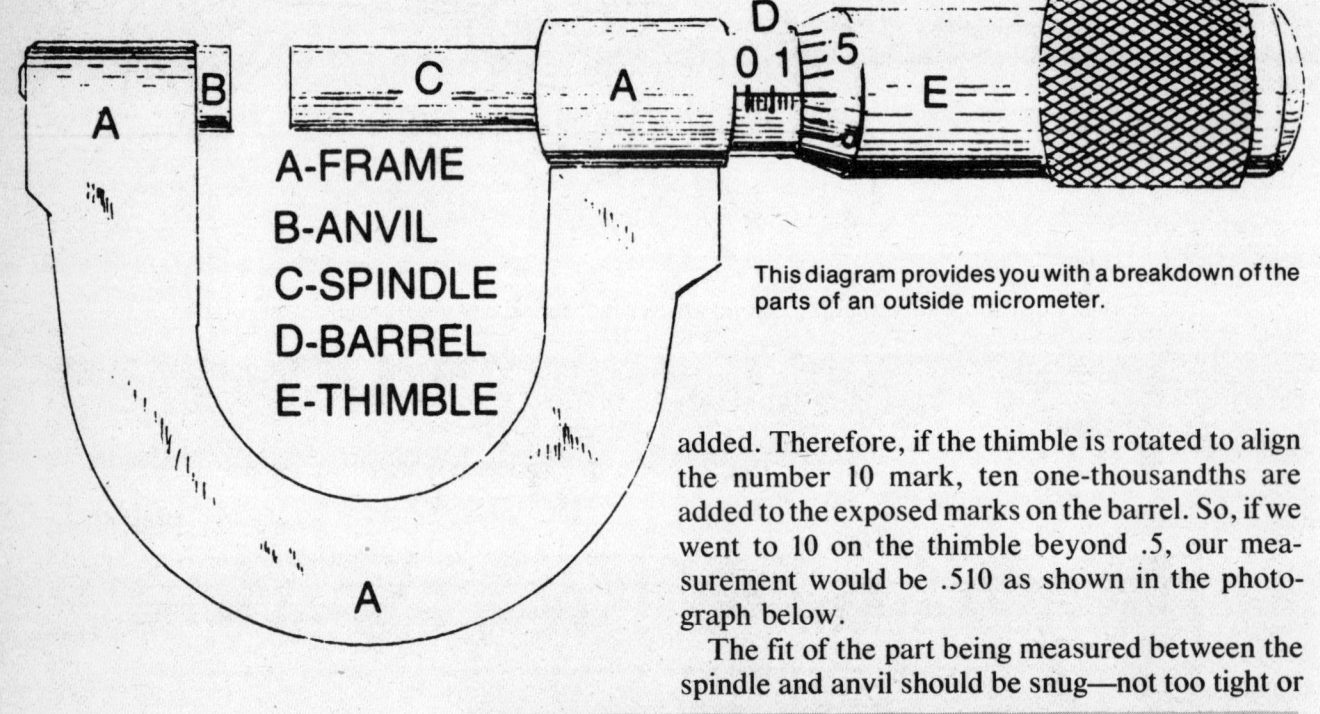

This diagram provides you with a breakdown of the parts of an outside micrometer.

In the setting shown, this micrometer shows a reading of .510″.

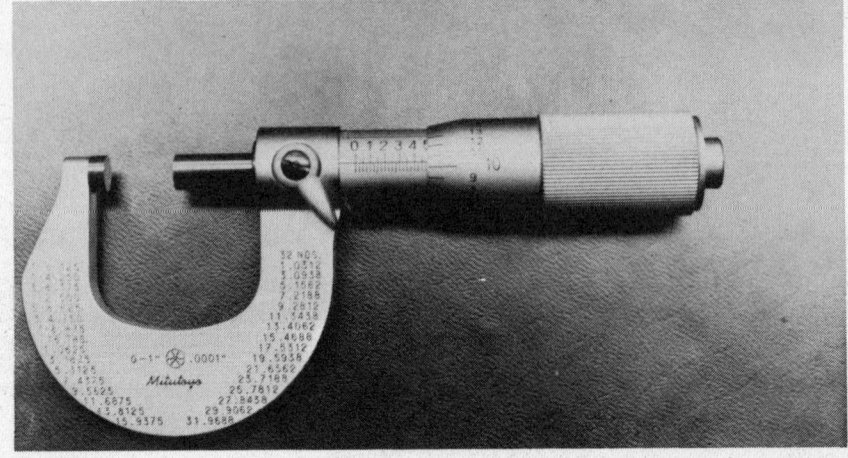

too loose. Most micrometers are equipped with a ratchet stop to provide a measuring force. When applying the measuring force on the workpiece by the ratchet stop—

1. Bring the measuring face of the spindle just in contact with the workpiece resting on the anvil.
2. Stop feeding the spindle.
3. Turn the ratchet stop by 1.5 or 2 turns, which are made in 3 or 4 finger snaps.

The ratchet stop has a spiral spring and two gears engaging each other to provide specified measuring force. The gears may wear and the spring may weaken after long term use, resulting in unconstant or out-of-specified measuring force. Such a ratchet stop must be replaced with a new one.

A device for a constant measuring force other than the ratchet stop is a friction stop (friction thimble). The friction thimble has a device for a constant measuring force inside the thimble. The friction thimble will produce a constant measuring force irrespective of the operator's practice of operation. It is recommended to use the friction thimble to ensure the highest measuring accuracy without human error.

In addition to the marks which denote .025", .10", etc., on the barrel, some micrometers also have ten other lines, numbered 0 to 10 that run the length of the barrel. This is a Vernier scale. These lines measure fractions of one thousandth. To illustrate its use, suppose that you were measuring the diameter of a bullet and the barrel reading was .35 and the thimble read somewhere between 7 and 8. If you wanted to know the exact measurement between 7 and 8, you'd use the Vernier scale.

To use the Vernier scale, look at the lines of the barrel numbered 0 to 10 and find the one line that aligns with one of the one-thousandth marks around the thimble. Only one of the ten lines on the barrel will align exactly with one of the lines on the thimble. The line on the barrel which aligns with a line around the thimble indicates how many tenths of one-thousandths are being measured. Therefore, in our example, if the "7" line on the barrel lined up exactly with one of the lines on the thimble, the bullet diameter would be .3577.

After using a micrometer, care for it as you would any other precision instrument. Clean it and apply anti-corrosives. Apply oil of high quality on the screws when assembling.

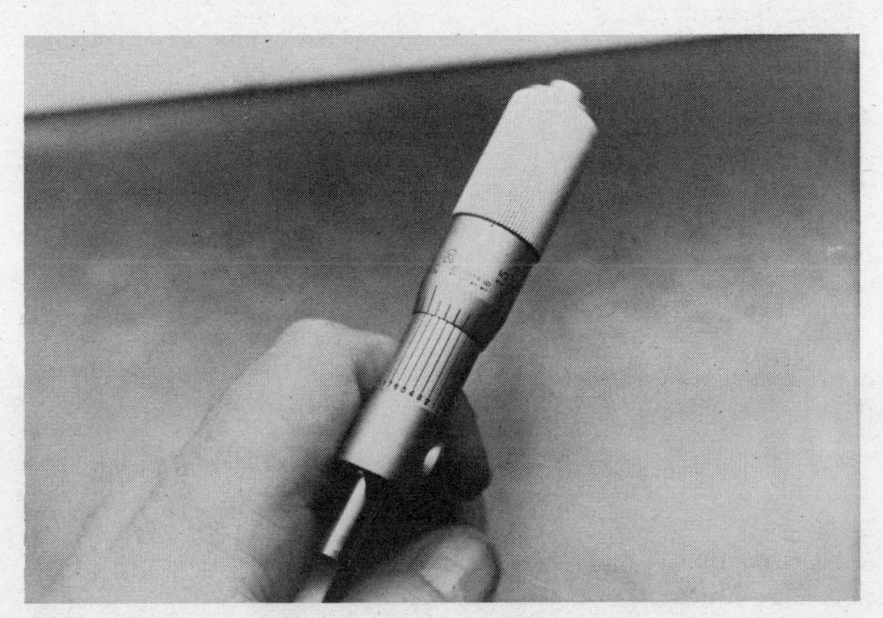

In addition to the marks which denote .025", .10", etc., on the barrel, some micrometers also have ten other lines (numbered 0 to 10) that run the length of the barrel. This is, in fact, a Vernier scale — the lines measure fractions in one thousandths of an inch.

13
THE DRILL PRESS

GUNSMITHS will frequently use drilling tools in their work. The drill may be a small ¼" portable drill motor or a full-size drill press. Regardless of the type used, all have one thing in common—a spiral bit that rotates at a relatively high speed for drilling through wood, metal, plastic, etc.

The heart of a drill press is the spindle which rotates inside a hollow sleeve called the *quill*. A feed handle moves the spindle up and down for drilling. The chuck attached to the spindle is designed to grip a variety of twist drills (usually up to

Rockwell drill press has four speeds for drilling a variety of materials. It's adjustable 8½" x 9" table has slots and side ledges to facilitate work clamping.

½" in diameter) and other accessories.

Drill press tables are designed to be moved up and down on a column to adjust the distance of the chuck from the work. Speeds on most drill presses range from about 700 to 4700 rpm. The lowest speeds are used for drilling metal and large holes in wood while the higher speeds are best for sanding, routing, shaping, etc.

Some drill presses are equipped with a tilting table that permits angle drilling. If the press is not equipped with such a table, a tilting drill press vise

For stationary tables, a tilting drill press vise may be used to tilt the work.

may be used to tilt the work. When drilling on an angle, it is very important that the work be securely clamped to the table, otherwise the work is likely to slide as the bit drills into the material.

The operator should never wear gloves when operating a drilling tool, especially while operating a drill press with the operator holding the object being drilled. Just a slight touch of a gloved hand to the rotating drill bit can entangle the glove material in the drill which can damage the fingers, even cut them completely off!

Another mistake often made when using a drill press is using one known to be defective; that is, one with a faulty switch, an improperly grounded frame, and the like. Here are a few precautions to follow when operating any power drilling tool:

1. Use a clamp or vise when drilling with a drill press. It is much safer than using your hands and it frees both hands to operate the tool.
2. Make sure the electric power cord does not become entangled in the drill bit.
3. Keep drill bits sharp. Dull tools cause rough cuts and excessive slipping.
4. Keep hands, clothing, key chains, etc. clear of all moving parts such as pulleys, belts, bits, and the like.
5. When drilling metal, safety glasses should be worn. Spiraled metal shavings, which can damage the eyes, often fly off from the bit.
6. Always turn the power off when the tool is not in use.
7. Watch the environment. Flammable gases and fumes can be ignited by the arcing electric motor. Never stand in water or on damp surfaces when operating any electric power tool.

Bolt Jeweling

One operation that gunsmiths normally use a drill press for is Damascening metal (often called jeweling or engine turning). This process involves overlapping spot-polish marks on metal that give a hammered effect. To perform this operation, you will need an engine turning chuck. This tool consists of a steel holder with a ⅛" shank and an abrasive charged rubber tip. The specially made abrasive tip gives an even impression on steel and simplifies the work of engine turning and eliminates the danger of cutting deep rings.

Engine turning gives a hammered effect on metal surfaces; it's attractive, and to some degree, helps hold oil.

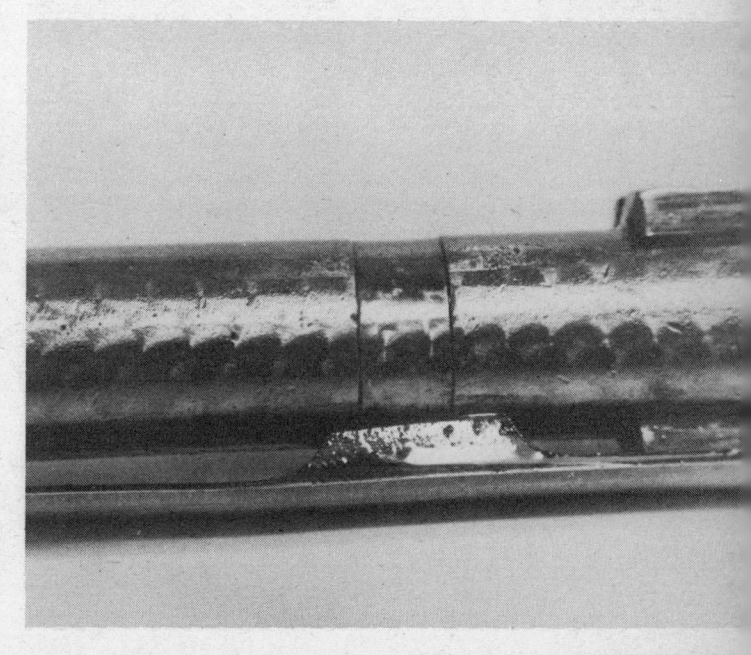

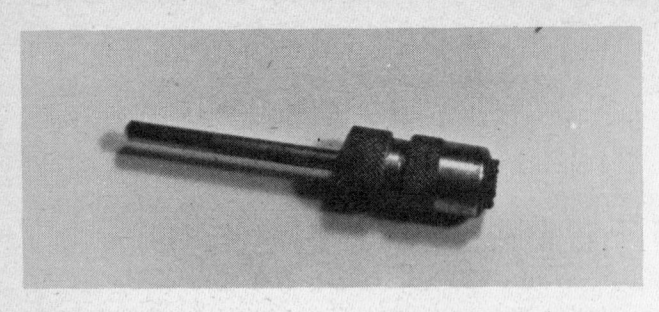

To perform jeweling or engine turning, you will need an engine turning chuck and abrasive tips. (Brownell's can supply both.)

Many shops use engine turning brushes rather than the tips. These brush wires follow the contours of the rounded gun parts better, giving a complete jeweled pattern. They are also reported to be superior on flat surfaces with long tool life. Silicon carbide abrasive and oil are used in conjunction with the wire brush to obtain the pattern. Drill press rpm should be fairly high; above 2000.

When performing engine turning designs on gun bolts, it is recommended that a specially designed fixture be used to hold the bolt (or other object) to be decorated. B-Square's bolt jeweling jig is an excellent tool and holds rifle bolts in position for symmetrically jeweled patterns. The bolt is secured between an arbor inserted into the rear of the bolt and a centering pin in the firing pin hole. The fixture containing the bolt is placed on a drill press table against a straight-edge fence and clamped to the table so that the bolt body is centered under the engine turning tool held in the drill chuck. Coat the bolt with abrasive compound and start the pattern. Start at either end of the bolt, but once started, start from this same end for all rows. Bring the engine turning tip or brush down on the bolt and make the first spot. Then move the fixture along the straight-edge fence approximately one-half the diameter of the spot and bring the brush down again on the bolt to over-lap the first spot.

The B-Square bolt jeweling jig (left) holds rifle bolts in position for symmetrically jeweled patterns. On the right, the jig and bolt have been secured to the drill press table.

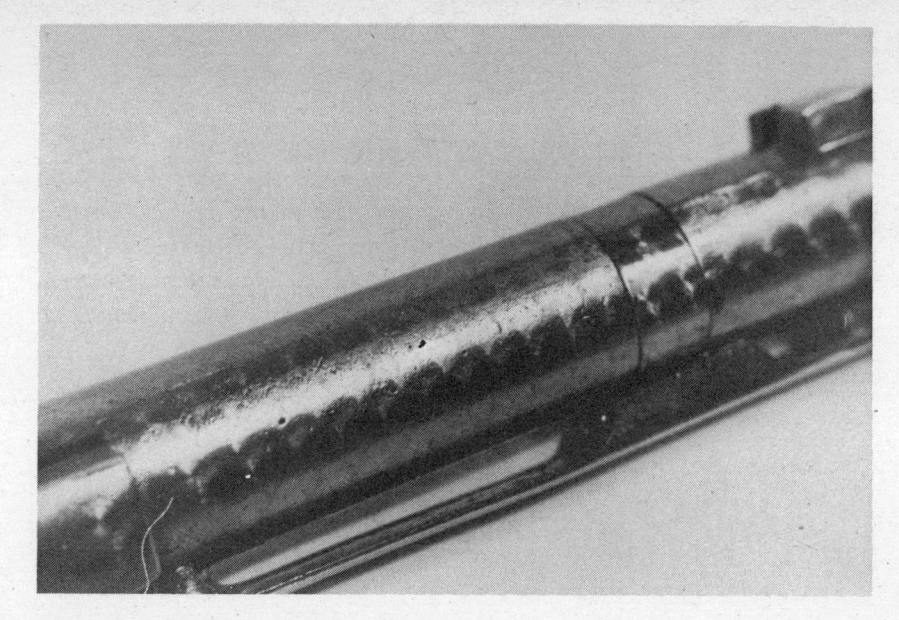

After one row of jeweled spots has been completed, you now turn the bolt approximately ½ spot diameter and repeat the process for another row.

Continue this procedure until one row of spots is completed. Then the bolt is rotated approximately ½ spot diameter and the process repeated for another row. This continues until the entire bolt has been fully jeweled in the areas desired.

The turning knob on the jeweling fixture utilizes an indexed scale to give additional visual checks as the jeweling progresses. The B-Square Jeweling Jig comes complete with one small and one large wire brush, extension holder to clear bolt handle and a small sample can of polishing compound . . . enough to do several jeweling jobs on bolts, hammers, triggers, plates and other gun parts.

Drilling for Scope Mounting

When drilling or tapping an action for scope mounting, a sight jig is a great time-saving device that will greatly simplify the process. One of the best is manufactured by Forster Products of Lanark, Illinois. The use of this device makes drilling and tapping for scope mounts almost foolproof, provided the instructions are followed closely.

This fixture is especially suited for the accurate drilling and tapping of rifle actions and barrels for top mounts and target scope blocks, receiver

The Forster Universal sight mounting fixture is perfect for drilling and tapping barrels and receivers.

143

The barrelled action is positioned in the fixture with the barrel resting on the V-blocks.

Next, raise the rear V-block up to bring the action in contact with the correct size drill bushing.

sights, ramp sights and beads on single-barreled shotguns, as well as side mounts whenever the mounting holes are in line with the centerline of the barrel. The V-blocks align the gun by the barrel so that the drill guide and bushings are exactly centered with the bore. Even if the action is not exactly in line with the barrel, the fixture automatically corrects this error and drills the holes true with the barrel.

The amount of disassembly required to mount the gun in the fixture will depend upon the type of firearm. For example, it is not usually necessary to remove the trigger mechanism on bolt action firearms. The Savage Model 99 requires only the removal of the forearm; the Remington Model 760 requires the removal of the slide bolt as well as the bolt mechanism. Tubular magazine rifles must have the magazine tube removed prior to the drilling operation.

Once the gun is stripped as required, the barrel and action is positioned in the fixture with the barrel resting on the V-blocks; that is, with the action over the end of the fixture having the clearance slot. Whenever possible, the barrel to be drilled should be positioned so that the action is close to the rear V-block, with the cylindrical or straight portion of the barrel supported by the V-block.

Slide the overarm in place over that portion of the action to be drilled and raise the rear V-block

The diameter of the barrel is then measured at the points of contact at the front and rear V-blocks with a micrometer. Next, measure and adjust the front V-block to compensate for the smaller diameter of the barrel. Once level, use aluminum pads under the clamp screws as shown to avoid marring the barrel finish.

On bolt action rifles, raise the flat top support pad on the sight mounting fixture into firm contact with the flat bottom of the action.

up to bring the action in contact with the correct size drill bushing. Next, measure the diameter of the barrel with a micrometer at the points of contact at the front and rear of the V-blocks. As most rifle barrels are tapered it will be necessary to raise the front V-block so that the barreled action is perfectly level. To arrive at this exact difference in height, subtract the small diameter from the larger diameter (found by your micrometer measurements), multiply this value by 0.707 and raise the front V-block that much higher than the rear V-block. This can be done very satisfactorily by measuring the distance with a machinist's rule or, if extreme accuracy is desired, by means of a dial caliper or feeler gauges between the top of the machined boss and the bottom of the V-block. When you have ascertained that the barrel and action is perfectly level, clamp the barrel lightly, using the aluminum pads under the clamp screws to avoid marring the barrel.

On bolt actions, raise the flat top support pad into firm contact with the flat bottom of the action. This squares the action and acts as a support during the drilling operation. The clamp on top of the leveling block is used to hold the action when it is desirable to remove the clamp from the rear V-block so that the overarm may be moved over any part of the action. Now tighten the clamps.

Actions that have no flat bottom surface can be aligned by means of a square from either the top of

145

the overarm or any other machined surface on the fixture. The gun also can be aligned by use of a level, but in this case be sure the fixture is level before lining up the gun.

One method used by many gunsmiths to locate mounts is to place the mount on the action or barrel in the desired position and mark the forward hole on the gun with a scriber or pencil. Next, with the locator pin point down in the front hole of the overarm, slide it over the gun so the point lines up with the mark and lock in place. Drill and tap this hole. Now screw the mount to the gun with one screw. Loosen the overarm and with the tapered point of the locator pin, locate the overarm over the second hole in the mount and lock in place. Lock the spacer block against the overarm. The overarm then can be moved out of the way, the mount removed and the overarm set against the spacer block. The second hole is then drilled and tapped. Other holes in the mount can be located and drilled in the same way. Do not drill the holes with the mount in place as they may prevent drilling the holes on the true center of the action.

When drilling for receiver sights, line up the barrel in the V-blocks in the usual way, but turn the action sideways and square it by means of a small square laid on top of the overarm. Locate the first hole and proceed as previously outlined. The same procedure is then followed when mounting side mounts, but holds true only if all holes are in line with the center line of the barrel.

If the desired holes are not on the center line of the barrel, the fixture can still be used to hold the gun squarely and steadily in the drill press. In this case the overarm is not used.

When drilling and tapping for a ramp sight, the gun is turned around, the muzzle end being at the notched end of the fixture. The V-blocks in this case are raised high enough so the drill bushings will contact the barrel. Allowance must be made for the taper in the barrel as previously explained. In this case, it will be necessary to square the gun with a level. Shotgun beads are mounted by following the same procedure.

Go easy at first and double-check your setups to be sure that you are drilling the holes exactly where you want them. Make sure also that the V-blocks align squarely, by tightening the screws gently at first so that the flat of the screw contacts the flat of the shaft squarely. A twisted V-block will throw you off due to the taper in the barrel, and especially so if the barrel is supported at a point where the taper is abrupt. Extreme care should be used to prevent chips from getting between the finished surfaces of the overarm and the body of the fixture when the overarm is moved. This is equally true of the spacer block. If chips are allowed to lodge between the two surfaces they will impair the inherent accuracy of the fixture. Brush away all chips with a small dry brush before loosening the overarm and spacer block. Also, don't use too much force when tightening the screws holding the overarm and spacer block.

Forster Products also offers a labor-saving auger bit that will bore any arc of a circle leaving a true polished surface. It can be guided in any

When drilling for a ramp front sight, the barrel is positioned so that the muzzle is at the notched end of the fixture.

direction—so necessary in the inletting of gun stocks—without regard to grain of the wood or knots. The bit is guided by its circular rim instead of its center, which is the reason for its special adaptability in hard wood. This bit when used in a drill press will enable the gunsmith to do most of the inletting of stock blanks and save considerable time over the drill and chisel method.

General Procedures for Using the Drill Press

The following are guidelines for using the drill press on all types of work.
1. Select the correct kind of bit or drill and fasten it securely in the chuck.
2. Make sure the proper layout has been made and that the position of the hole is well marked.
3. Check to see if the drill or bit is free to go through the table opening in the drill-press table. Also, when drilling through wood, place an auxiliary piece of scrap wood under the material. This will help prevent splintering when the drill goes through the underside of the work.
4. Adjust the drill press for the correct speed of cutting. The speed should vary with the type of bit, the size, the kind of material and the depth of the hole. In general, the smaller the cutting tool and the softer the material, the higher the speed. Select the approximate speed and then use good judgment when feeding the tool into the material. If the tool smokes, reduce the speed and the feed.
5. Clamp the work securely when necessary, especially when using larger drilling and boring tools, hole cutters, and similar cutting devices. Clamping is a must if the tool has only one cutting edge, such as a hole cutter.

Drill Jigs

B-Square offers several excellent drill jigs for mounting scope sights to various guns. One such jig is for the Winchester Model 94; but one of the most versatile—and probably the most used—is a scope drill jig designed for use on many types of military bolt action rifles.

To use a B-Square scope jig insert the bore aligning arbor into the rifle receiver placing both "V" bushings with their "V" over the arbor

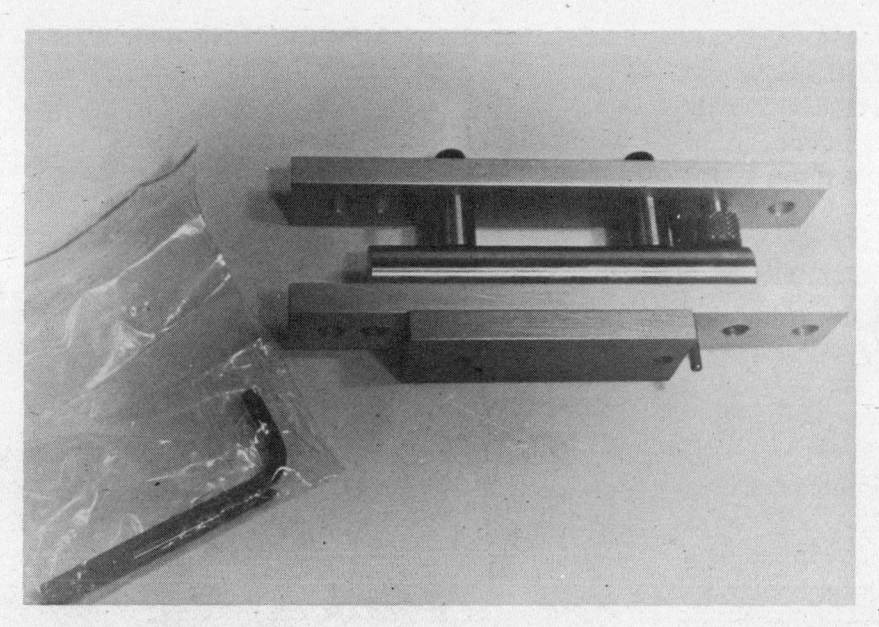

This B-Square scope jig is designed especially for military bolt action rifles.

holes. Place the jig bar recesses (counterbores) on the "V" bushings and also place the base block against the bottom flat of the receiver and insert the allen screws. Before tightening the screws, slide the whole assembly forward until the jig bar stop pin contacts the rear of the front receiver ring. This locates the holes so that the scope mount recoil shoulder will bear against the ring, then place the drill bushing in the hole you want to drill.

The rear hole spacing in both bars will provide .504 (½-inch) spacing for both front and rear Weaver blocks. On some guns the forward Weaver block hole spacing is .860-inch center to center. Use the same hole spacing as for front Redfield holes.

To install Weaver blocks on the rear bridge of

the Springfield A-3 rifle, use the Redfield bar marked "S." This will locate the single hole required through the rifle dovetail. B-Square recommends that the rear hole in the front ring Weaver blocks be located using the Redfield spacing. This will enable Redfield or similar mounts to be installed later if desired by drilling additional rear holes only.

On Mauser type rifles the Weaver block must be filed or ground on its forward end to fit the rear bridge and clear the bolt handle. Clamp the whole unit in a large drill press vise or just hold the barrel and keep the base block flat on the table while drilling. A large base plate can be made to be attached to the base block existing threaded holes.

On all Japanese military rifles, install the base block with the narrowest "hole edge" distance forward. Also, remove triggers when drilling these rifles.

On Springfield A-3 rifles, slide the assembly rearward until the stop pin contacts the edge of the old rear sight dovetail. The scope mounts are located by this dovetail. The rear stop pin in Bar "S" is for this purpose.

On Mexican Mauser rifles check your scope mount before drilling. On most mounts, the recoil shoulder is such that the holes must be drilled .090 ($^3/_{32}$) farther forward than other Mausers. Press or drive the jig bar stop pin up so the bar can go forward the correct amount. (Check the jig location.)

On Argentine Mausers, be careful of a large radius on the rear of the front ring. If a large radius is on the ring of any rifle, press or drive the stop pin up so that it will contact the exact same spot as the mount recoil lug or the mount holes will be located too far to the rear.

On Mauser receivers be sure there is clearance between the "V" bushing and left-hand side of the receiver. On some Mausers, particularly a few small-ring models, it is possible that interference with the "V" bushing will deflect the jig. File or grind the "V" bushing side until it clears. (Be careful not to disturb the arbor contact area of the "V".)

On Springfield 03-A3 rifles the old rear sight dovetail is not centered on the receiver, nor are the serrations on top of the sight dovetail. Also the groove for the bolt, directly under the dovetail bridge, may not be on the vertical bore center line. Your jig should correctly locate the hole(s). Be careful on all holes, that the drill does not deflect and drill off the correct location.

Redfield (and other) recoil shoulders must contact the gun to prevent shearing off the mounting screws when firing heavy loads.

When starting any drilling job, it's a joy to have a good selection of drill bits on hand. When you've finished drilling, return that bit to it's proper place — you won't have to search the next time!

14

THE BENCH GRINDER

A BENCH grinder is essential in most gunshops—it's nice to have and useful for working on both metal and wood. Grinders are used to sharpen tools, drill bits and to maintain the use of several other tools used in gunsmithing work. They will also grind down metal surfaces rapidly and are excellent for such purposes prior to final finishing with a file or buffing wheel.

Safety Precautions

Grinders, like all power tools, are potentially dangerous and certain precautions should always be taken when they are used. To illustrate, not too long ago I was carding down a double barrel shotgun during the hot-water bluing process. I had attached a piece of black stove pipe wire through

The bench grinder seen here is typical of those you'll find in many gunsmith shops. The unit shown is pulling double duty as the wheel on the left is of stitched muslin for polishing while the wheel on the right is for grinding.

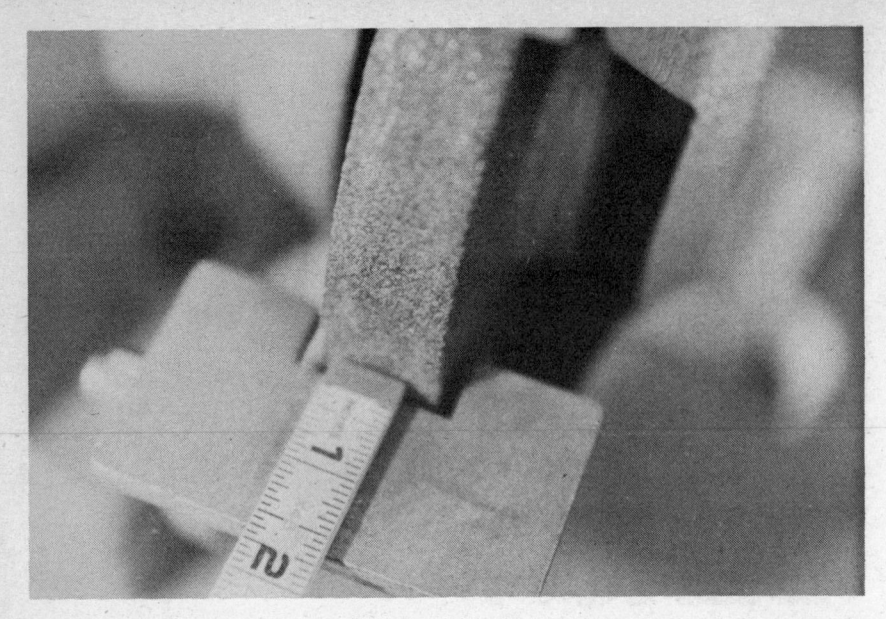

The author suggests adjusting the distance between the grinding wheels and the work rests to maintain 1/8" or less of separation before using.

one of the barrels for dipping them into the tank of boiling water. After applying the acid rusting compound to the metal and letting the rust build up, I would buff or card the rust off with a wire carding wheel attached to my bench grinder. Keeping the wires out of the way of the revolving wheel, I began carding the rust off and I was beginning to get a good blue-black color underneath when a person startled me as he poked his head through my shop door. I turned for an instant to see who he was and the next thing I knew the set of barrels went flying across the room, as I quickly jerked my hand out of the rubber glove that had become entangled in the mess of wires around the carding wheel. My right rubber glove had all four fingers cut off by the stove pipe wire that had wrapped tightly around the grinder shaft. Fortunately, my own fingers were intact—only one was slightly cut.

This incident taught me a very good lesson: never let anything that can become entangled in a revolving power tool come close to it—it's going to cause trouble. Furthermore, when using grinders, first make sure that the grinding wheels are not cracked; replace immediately if a cracked wheel is found. Always use guards and eyeshields on a grinding wheel, and do not over-tighten the wheel nuts. Use only approved flanges, preferably those furnished with the grinder.

Here are some other safety pointers to keep accidents to a minimum when using bench grinders.

1. Remove all adjusting keys and wrenches from the tool prior to use. Form a habit of checking to see that adjusting wrenches are removed from the tools before turning it on.
2. Keep work area clean. Cluttered areas and benches invite accidents.
3 Keep work area well lighted.
4. Don't force a grinder to work. It will do the job better and safer at the rate for which it was designed.
5. Wear proper apparel. Wear protective hair covering to contain long hair.
6. Use safety glasses. Also use face or dust mask if the cutting operation is dusty such as buffing or polishing gun metal.
7. Don't over reach. Keep proper footing and balance at all times.
8. Maintain tools with care. Follow the manufacturer's instructions for lubricating and changing accessories.
9. Always disconnect power tools before servicing.
10. Use proper voltage and connections for power tools and make sure that the tool is properly grounded as discussed later on in this chapter.
11. Keep hands in sight and clear of all moving parts.
12. Never leave power tools unattended. Turn power off just as soon as the job is finished.
13. Watch the environment. *Never stand in water or on damp surfaces when operating an electric power tool.* Be aware that explosive gases can be ignited by arcing electric motor.

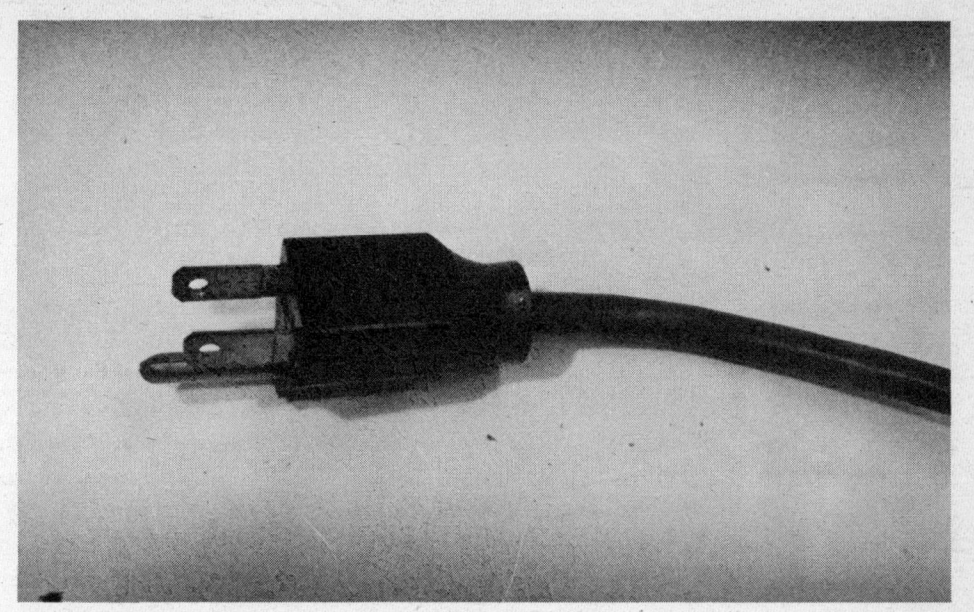

Whenever you're operating electric tools, be sure those tools have a three-prong plug. The third plug serves to ground the tool you work with.

Grounding

All power tools operated by electric current and containing metal housings should be grounded during use to protect the operator from electric shock. Most 120-volt electric power tools are equipped with an Underwriters' Laboratories approved 3-conductor cord with a 3-prong grounding type plug to fit conventional grounding type receptacles. The green-covered wire in the cord should be the grounding wire. Never connect this green wire to a "live" terminal.

Adapters are available for connecting the 3-prong plugs to a 2-prong outlet. When using this type of adapter, the grounding terminal from the adapter must be connected to a permanent ground such as to a properly grounded outlet box. To insure that the outlet box is properly grounded, use a voltage tester, and connect one of the test leads to the "hot" (usually black wire) side of the outlet, and the other test lead to the box or cover screw. The meter should show a reading of between 110 and 120 volts. Repair or replace worn or damaged power cords and/or plugs immediately.

With these preliminary safety precautions out of the way (but not out of your mind) let's see some of the uses the bench grinder has in the gunsmith shop.

Sharpening Chisels and Gouges

Stockmakers know that their chisels and gouges must be kept sharp for them to do their best work. This consists of hand whetting, honing and strop-

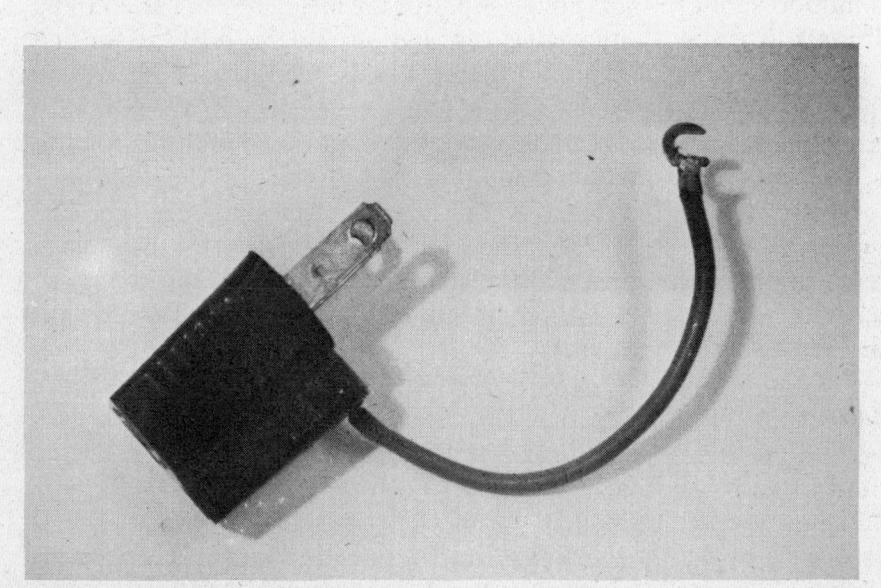

If your power tools don't have a three-prong plug, you can purchase the adapter shown at most any hardware store.

ping the tool for a keen edge. However, prior to these operations, a bench grinder can be used to grind a sharp cutting edge on the tool—saving much hand work. Frank Mittermeier offers a tool holder and stand for sharpening gouges, chisels and V tools on the bench grinder, and enables the operator to get the proper bevel (cutting angle)—12 to 15 degrees—whether they are straight or long spoon or backbend.

To set up the fixture (consisting of stand and tool holder), place it on the workbench with the convex curve of the cross bar approximately ¼" from the grinding surface. A C-clamp may be used to firmly secure the fixture to the bench. Adjust height of the tool holder to about ½" to ¾" below the axis of the grinding wheel. For proper results, it is imperative to adjust the cross bar so that it is square with the grinding surface and level to the bench.

In grinding chisels and skews, the straight edge of the cross bar should face the operator. The tool holder should face the grinding surface from the flat side, and the tool should be placed in the holder as square and centered as possible. In the case of skew chisels, set them in the holder with the cutting edge parallel to the edge of the grinding surface.

When setting up V-tools and gouges, the curved side of the tool holder should face the grinding surface with the convex curve side of the cross bar facing the operator. All tools should be placed as square and centered as much as possible in the tool holder. Tools, depending on their size and shape, should extend approximately 2" from the face of the tool holder to get a cutting bevel from 12 to 15 degrees. Constant back and forth motion should be exercised in the grinding of all tools to avoid over heating and loss of hardness. This movement will also result in a better sharpening job. To further prevent overheating, have a container of water nearby to dip the tools into as the sharpening process progresses. Most bench grinders have a water reservoir built in for this purpose. Curved cutting tools, such as gouges, should be moved over convex surfaces for uniform curves, concentric sharpening and for keeping an even bevel.

The grinding fixture, as shipped from Frank Mittermeier, is set for use on the left wheel of the grinder. Should the fixture be used on the right wheel, unscrew the cross bar and attach the crossbar's other end to the holder. The heavy part of the crossbar's convex curve should be at the lower front side when sharpening gouges.

Whetting, Honing and Stropping

After the proper bevel and sharp cutting edge have been ground on the grinding wheel, the carving tool has to be hand whetted, honed and stropped for a keen edge.

A carving tool should have two cutting bevels—outside and inside. The outside bevel should be ground on the grinder while the inside bevel must be hand whetted or honed. The amount of whetting to be done, depends on the sharpness of the cutting edge after grinding. In other words, if you do a good job on the grinding operation, less work is required during the whetting operation.

Chisels: Whet the 12- to 15-degree bevel in a circular, Figure "8" movement on a flat India oilstone until a fine burr (wire edge) has turned up. The other side of the stone—with the blade almost flat—should be rubbed on the oilstone until a short bevel can be noticed. Follow with honing the chisel by holding the tool in one hand and the Arkansas oilstone in the other hand. Rub the oilstone in an up and down movement with the pressure on the downstroke—against the cutting edge. Hone the large bevel first and then the small bevel. The bevels should be flat and the cutting edges square, so don't round the corners.

Straight Skew Chisel: This type of chisel should have a 12- to 15-degree angle on both sides, as the tool has to cut right and left in sharp corners. Whetting and honing is the same as on the chisel, except that both angles should be equal.

Gouges: The outside bevel can best be whetted by rocking it back and forth on the inside of an India gouge slip. For the inside bevel, use an India round edge slip and stroke the oilstone up and down until the bevel has been formed all around the curve of the tool. On gouges with the No. 9, 10 or 11 sweep, use a round or pointed oilstone to prevent rounding the corners of the tool. For honing, use a hard Arkansas round edge slip. The flat side of the stone should be used for the outside bevel and the rounded edge for the inside bevel. When honing, apply the pressure on the downstroke.

V or Parting Tool: After the outside bevels have been carefully ground to be alike, the bevels should be whetted until they form a burr at the inside of the V. To form the inside bevel use a diamond or knife shaped India oilstone. By grinding and whetting the outside bevel, a sharp edge is

How to Use a Mittermeier Grinding Fixture

The diagrams below show examples of using a Mittermeier grinding fixture. They are as follows:
1. Chisel, on the flat side of the tool holder.
2. Gouge, on the curved side of the tool holder.
3. Spoon chisel, with the cutting edge square to the grinding wheel.
4., 5., 6. A series of gouges in the different positions necessary to get uniform curve and bevel.

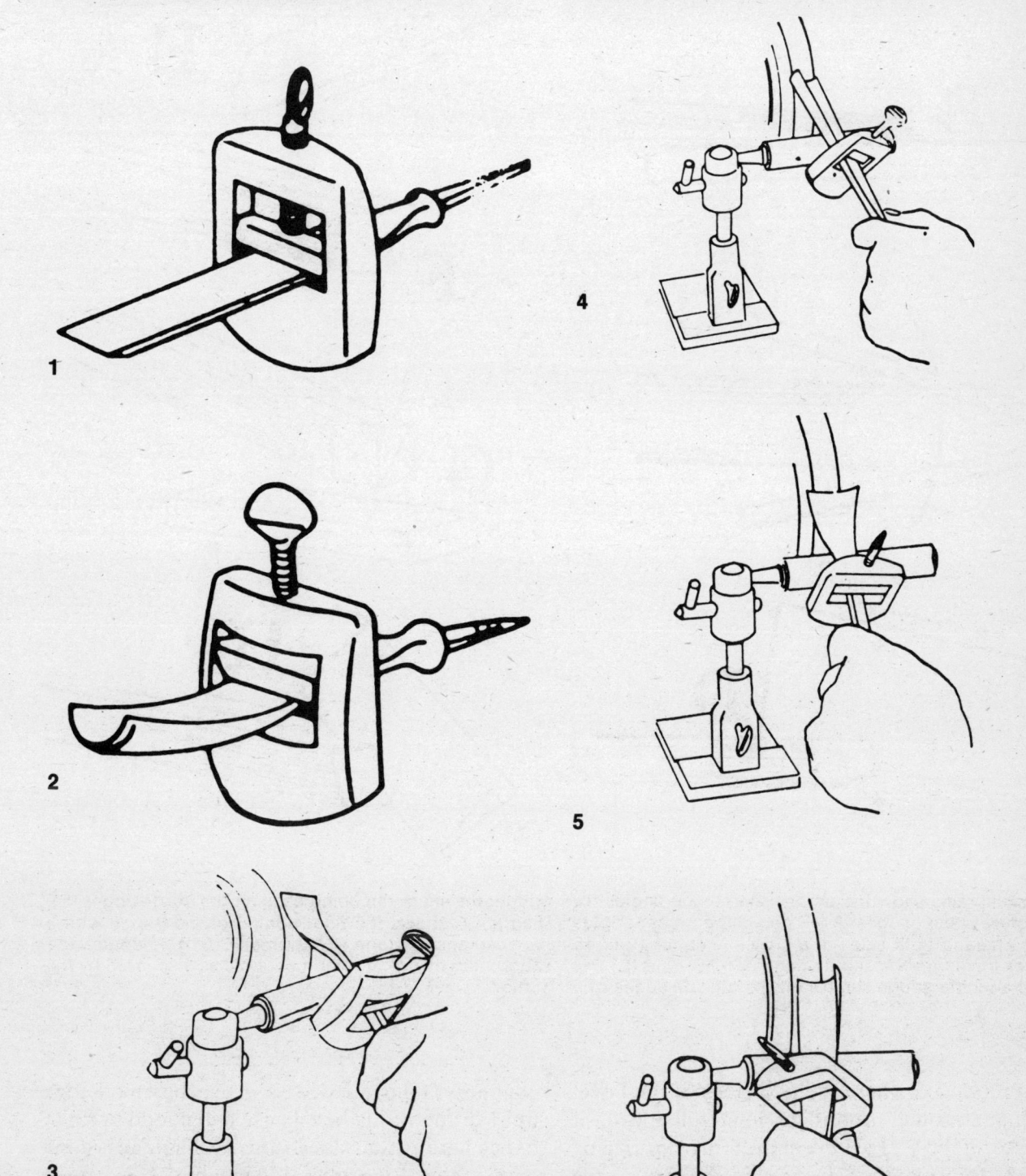

153

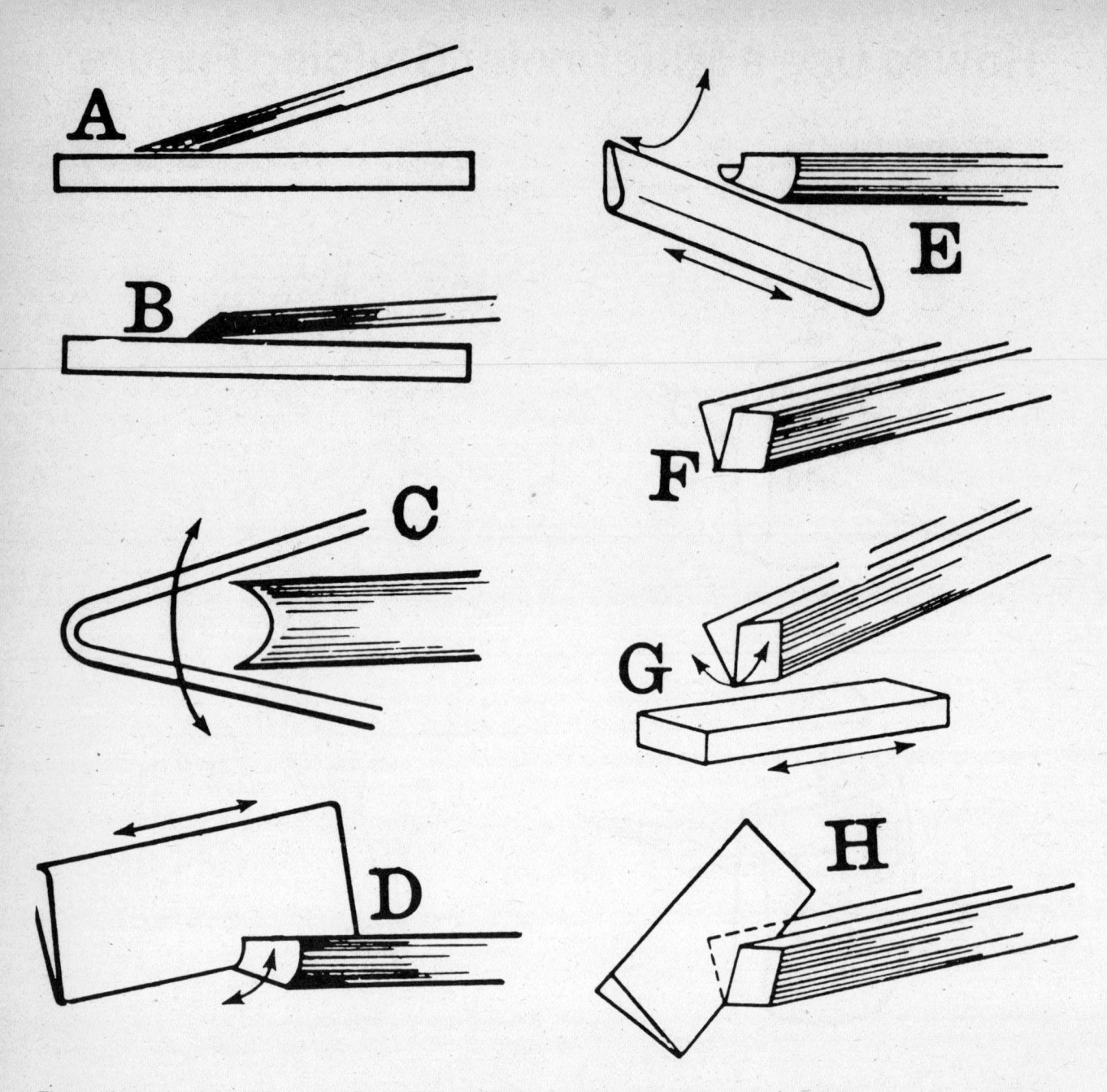

These diagrams show the proper sharpening angles for both chisels and gouges: A & B depict the proper angles for sharpening both sides of a chisel — about 12 to 15 degrees for diagram A, about 4 degrees for B. (C) & (D) The use of an India gouge slip (C) on the outside edges of a gouge; the same slip being used on the inside edges (D). Diagram E shows the final honing of the gouge with a hard Arkansas stone. Diagrams F, G & H depict the sharpening of "V" or "Parting" tools as discussed by the author.

being produced where the two sides of the bevel meet, and a small protruding point will appear at the apex of the V. To prevent the tool from digging in and, for smoother pushing in the wood, the sharp edge should be rounded. The protruding point's outside corner has to be rounded until it conforms with the inner angle. For honing the outside bevels and for removing all traces of roughness at the rounded edge, use the round-edge slip. For the inside bevels use a diamond or knife shaped hard Arkansas oilstone. All honing is done against the cutting edge. When a burr has formed which cannot be easily removed by honing, draw the edge of the tool a few times across the corner of a woodblock or cork; that will remove the burr completely.

To prevent glazing of India and Arkansas oilstones, use a light oil mixed with kerosene. A few extra drops of the oil on the stone is better than letting the stone get dry. Clear the oilstone frequently to avoid accumulation of the black glazing (metal particles). All tools should be stropped before using. The tool is drawn across the strop with the cutting edge trailing to prevent the tool from cutting into the strop.

If you have trouble keeping the proper cutting angle on chisels and gouges during sharpening or honing, make a small box with one sideboard slightly higher to hold a flat oilstone. Lay the beveled side of the tool flat on the oilstone, hold the tool firmly in your hand with the index finger at the outside edge of the higher sideboard. By sliding the tool back and forth, you can keep the bevel at the same angle. Flat chisels, skew chisels and V tools require only straight sliding. Gouges require a pendulum movement, so that the whole sweep of the tool is equally sharpened and honed.

Drill Pointing

Elimination of drill breakage depends to a great extent on the correct point of the drill bit. When the drill is worn down by use, it must be reground or breakage will result. Here is another use for the bench grinder in the gunsmith's shop.

Not only must a drill be reground in time, but it must be properly ground to assure maximum drilling life. It has been estimated that 90% of all drill breakage is caused by incorrect regrinding, and for this reason, too much emphasis cannot be laid on the importance of this operation.

Point-grinding by hand requires great skill and care on the part of the operator, and therefore, a bit grinding attachment is recommended. The grinding attachment locks the drill bit at the proper angle for sharpening and makes the otherwise difficult operation quite simple. Also, if the drill is accidentally allowed to get too hot during the grinding operation, it should never be cooled off in water, but allowed to cool of its own accord. A sudden cooling is almost sure to result in a cracked drill.

When re-pointing a drill, four things must be

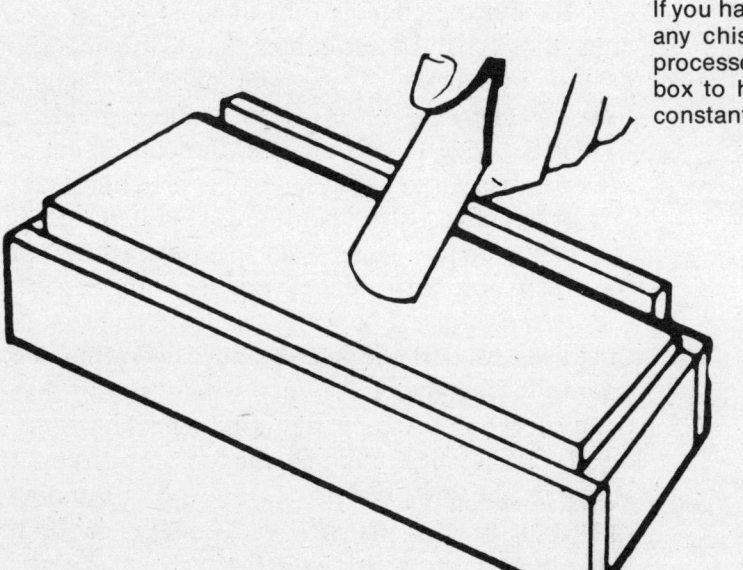

If you have difficulty keeping the correct cutting angle on any chisel or gouge during the sharpening or honing processes, you might want to construct a small wooden box to hold the stone. The high sideboard gives you a constant angle for sharpening.

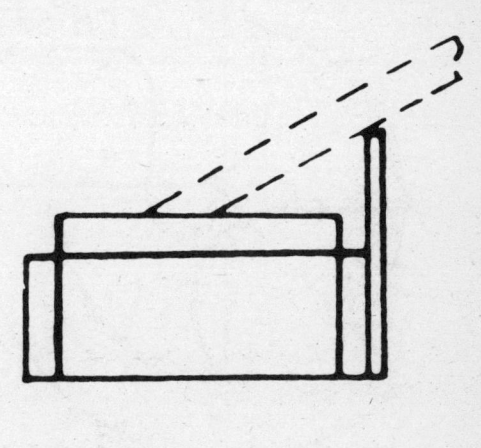

The point angles of this drill bit are ground equally but the chisel point is off center.

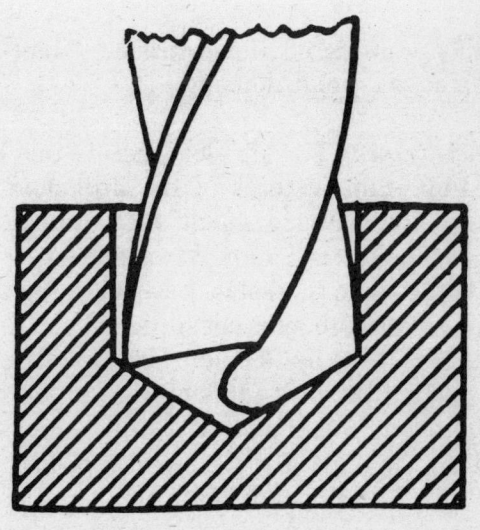

155

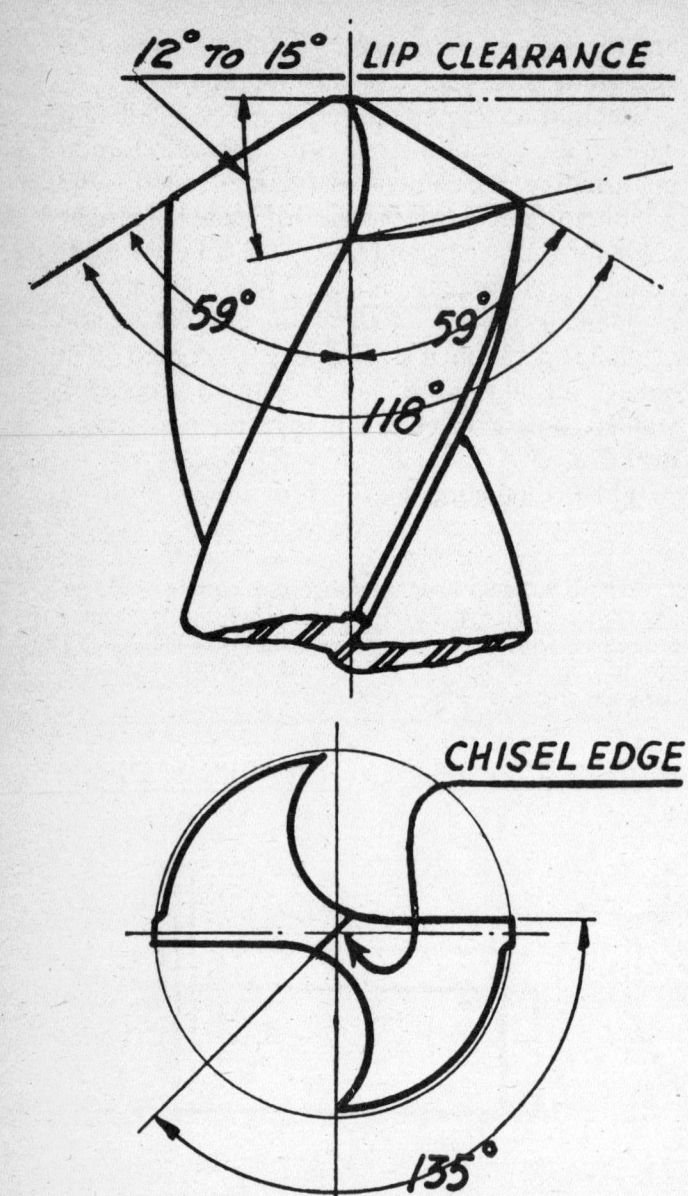

These are the proper angles for drill lip clearance and a chisel edge.

carefully considered: lip-clearance, point-angle, cutting edges, point-thinning.

Lip-clearance: The lip-clearance is one of the most important features of the drill point. The angle of lip-clearance should be within 12 to 15 degrees, measured at the circumference of the drill. If the angle is greater, it weakens the cutting edge; if smaller, there is not sufficient clearance to allow the cutting lip to enter the work. The usual result is that the drill splits up the center.

Point-angle: The angle of a drill point is measured on the axis of the drill. The proper point-angle of a drill depends upon the material being drilled. However, all standard drills are furnished with 59-degree points, as this angle has proven to be the most suitable for the average class of work. In general, the harder the material the greater the point-angle should be. For example, a point-angle of 75 degrees is recommended for manganese steel, while for wood, fiber and similar materials, a point-angle of 30 degrees is recommended.

Cutting Edges: The two cutting edges of a drill must make exactly the same angle with the center line of the drill; that is, while the 59-degree angle may vary a little one way or the other, the variation must be uniform in both cutting edges. A difference in angle will cause one edge to cut differently from the other, causing an unequal strain on the two edges.

If the cutting edges are of unequal length, the chisel-point will be off-center and will cause the drill to cut oversize. If the point-angle is changed from 59 degrees, as originally made, it will be found that, due to this change, the cutting edges are no longer straight but have become either convex or concave. If the point-angle is changed appreciably, it may be necessary to grind the flutes of the drill in order to produce straight cutting edges.

Point-Thinning: The web of a drill increases in thickness toward the shank and a web-thinning operation becomes necessary when the drill has been shortened by repeated grindings. This operation is essential to minimize the pressure required to make the drill penetrate. The point-thinning operation must be carried out equally on both sides of the web, otherwise the web will be off-center and the drill will produce an oversize hole. Care must also be taken to see that the thinning operation is not carried too far up the web, thus weakening the point of approximately 1/8 of the drill diameter.

Grinding Wheels

A soft, medium grain wheel, approximately 8"x2", should be used for sharpening drills. Drills should be ground on the face and not on the side of the wheels, although this is sometimes practiced in gunshops. The face of the wheel should be trued by proper dressing before drills are ground, otherwise correct results cannot be obtained. A grinding wheel dresser is the simplest, surest and most practical way to restore a true flat face on a grinding wheel. This tool will even level out gouges and grooves and also clean out loading from grinding soft metals.

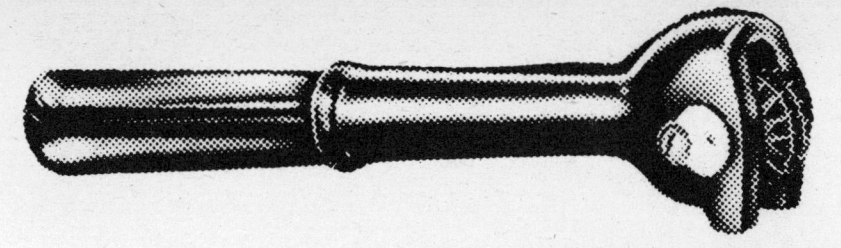

A grinding wheel dresser is the simplest way to restore a true flat surface to a grinding wheel.

When regrinding a drill bit (above), it should be held at an *approximate* angle of 45 degrees to the vertical (Right) All point grinding must be dry. If the drill gets too hot during grinding, set it aside and let it cool on its own.

The drill should be held at an approximate angle of 45 degrees to the vertical and all point grinding must be dry. If during the grinding, the drill is accidentally allowed to get too hot, allow it to cool of its own accord. If the drill has been repointed, it should be examined to make sure that the margin shows no sign of wear, particularly at the extreme corners of the drill point.

Cut-Off Wheels

Cut-off wheels may be secured in a bench grinder and are useful in gunshops for fast and easy completion of all sorts of cutting jobs. Most are manufactured in sizes from 2″ to 6″ diameter. The part being cut, however, must not be clamped rigidly for the cut. Rather, the part should be hand-held. Such a tool is useful for cutting such items as drift pins from a single rod and similar applications. High tensile strength man-made textiles reinforce these wheels to resist breakage under twisting pressures and impact. Obtain Brownells catalog for description and prices.

15
LATHES FOR METAL WORK

THE SCREW cutting engine lathe is the oldest and most important of machine tools and, from it, practically all other machine tools have been developed. They vary in size from the small jeweler's lathes for making very fine, miniature parts to the large gap-bed lathes and special-purpose lathes used in high-production work. In between these extremes are many models of varying lengths and capacities. You must select the size that best suits your needs. The maximum size of work that can be handled by the lathe is used to designate the size of the lathe; that is, the diameter and length of the work. For example, a 10" x 36" lathe is one having a swing over the bed sufficient to take work up to 10 inches in diameter and having a bed length or distance between centers of 36 inches.

When selecting a lathe for gunsmithing work, the most important point to consider is the size and amount of work that you anticipate doing. The lathe should be large enough to accommodate the various classes of work that will be handled. This is determined by the greatest diameter and length of work that will be machined in the lathe. Ideally, the lathe selected should have a swing capacity and distance between centers at least 10% greater than the largest job that will be handled.

There are, of course, further considerations that everyone should take into account before purchasing a lathe. For example, if you lack experience at operating a lathe and you don't anticipate very many conversion jobs, then you could probably get by very nicely with the Unimat 3. The small parts such as firing pins, drift pins, screws and the like can be easily turned on the small, inexpensive Unimat.

On the other hand, if you are an experienced machinist and plan to do a lot of conversion work which requires barrel turning, bolt facing, chambering and threading of barrels, then you will need a larger lathe like the Jet Model 1236p bench lathe. This lathe is manufactured by JET Equipment & Tools and is an excellent choice for the average gunsmith doing conversion work and other gunshop machine work. The only change that I would like to see on this lathe is a slightly larger hole in the headstock spindle to insure that rough barrel blanks and shotgun barrels can be held close to the chuck face for chambering, sleeving and the like.

Each type of lathe has its advantages and disadvantages, and the final decision to purchase one should be made only after the gunsmith has thoroughly and truthfully analyzed his abilities, anticipated specialty, and most probably future desires. Then he should write for and study all the lathe manufacturer catalogs available or, better

The lathe is the oldest of the machine tools, and they vary in size. Only the gunsmith can determine the type and size of lathe best suited for his needs.

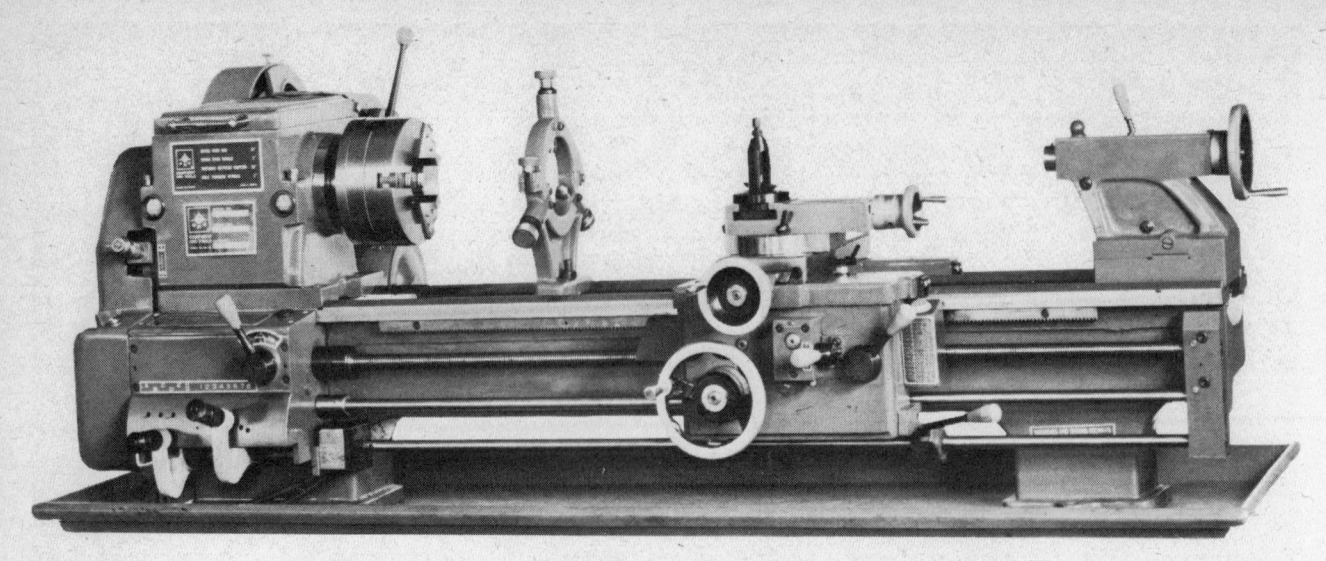

Depending upon your experience and needs, one of the smaller lathes, like the Unimat, might serve your needs adequately. However, if you are an experienced machinist and plan on doing barrel turning, chambering, etc., the Jet Model 1236p shown would serve you better.

yet, visit some dealers close by. Then, and only then, would I recommend buying a lathe. When you shell out thousands of dollars for a lathe these days, you certainly want one that will best suit your current and future needs.

Parts of a Lathe

A lathe is made up of many parts. The principle parts include: bed, headstock, tailstock, carriage, feed mechanism, thread-cutting mechanism.

Bed: The lathe bed is the foundation on which the lathe is built, so it must be substantially constructed and scientifically designed. Prismatic V-ways have been found to be the most accurate and serviceable type of ways for lathe beds and have been adopted by most of the leading machine-tool manufacturers. The two outer V-ways guide the lathe carriage, while the inner V-ways and flat way align the headstock and tailstock.

Headstock: The headstock is the most important unit of the lathe and should be back-geared. The back gears provide a means of controlling the spindle speed. A back gear lever engages the back gear for slow spindle speeds (75 to 280 rpm) or disengages back gear for high spindle speeds (295 to 1100 rpm).

Tailstock: The tailstock assembly is movable on the bed ways, and carries the tailstock spindle. The tailstock spindle has a standard Morse taper at the front end to receive a dead center. The tailstock handwheel is at the other end to give longitudinal movement when mounting the workpiece between centers.

Carriage: The lathe carriage includes the apron, saddle, compound rest and tool post. Since the carriage supports the cutting tool and controls its action, it is one of the most important units of the lathe.

Feed Mechanism: Quick change gear lathes are preferred in gunshops where frequent changes of threads and feeds are required. On most lathes, the quick-change gear box is located directly below the headstock on the front of the lathe bed. A wide range of feeds and threads per inch may be selected by positioning the gears. The index plate is an index to the lever settings required to position the gears for the different feeds and numbers of threads per inch. The distance, in thousandths of an inch, that the carriage will move per revolution of the spindle is given in each block for the corresponding gear setting.

The reversing lever is used to reverse the direction of rotation of the screw for chasing right- or left-hand threads, and for reversing the direction of feed of the carriage assembly. Levers on the quick-change gear box should never be forced into position.

Installation

One of the most important ways to ensure maximum performance from your new lathe is to

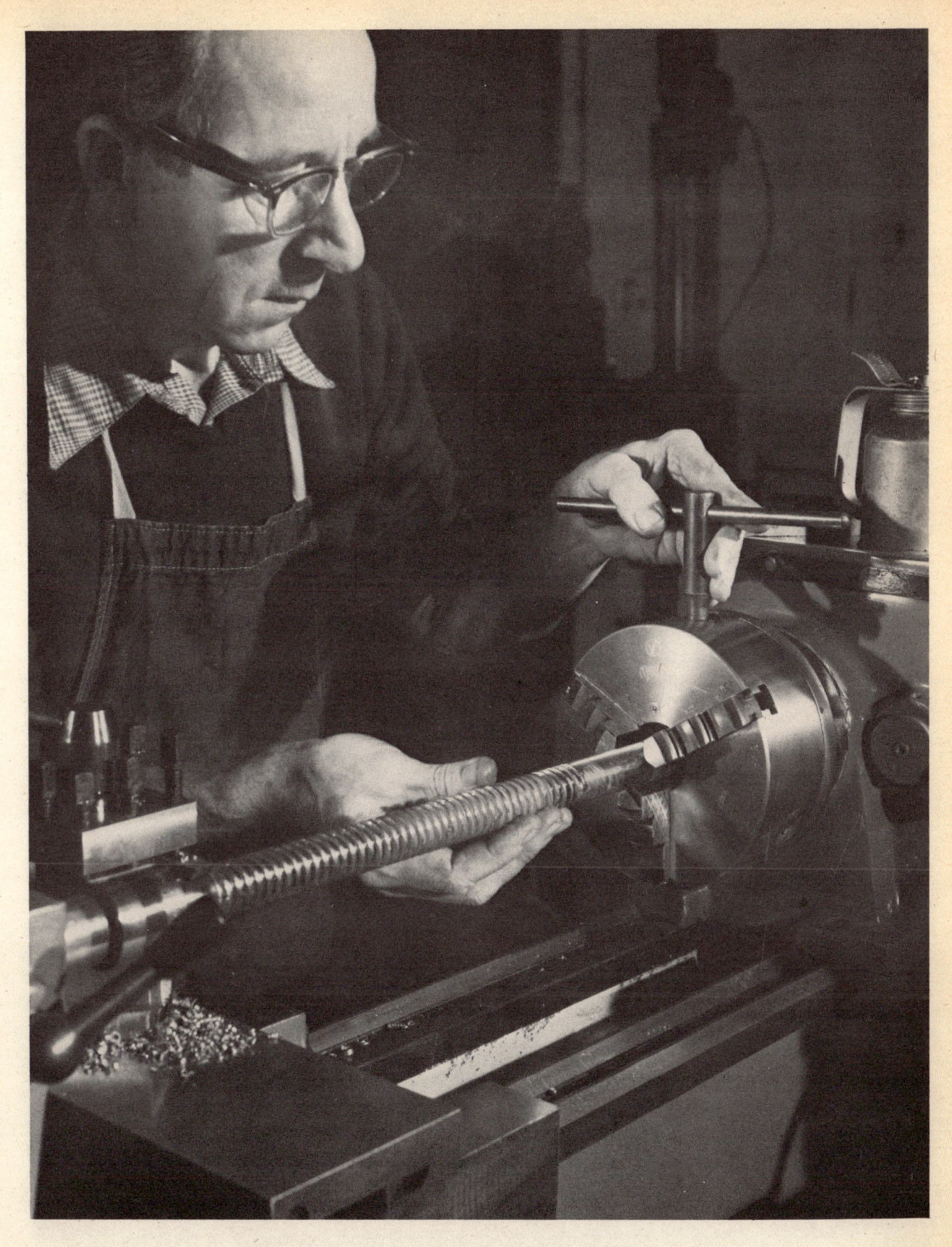

The machinist is adjusting the *headstock* on this lathe — the *tailstock* is to the left. The *workpiece* is in the machinist's right hand.

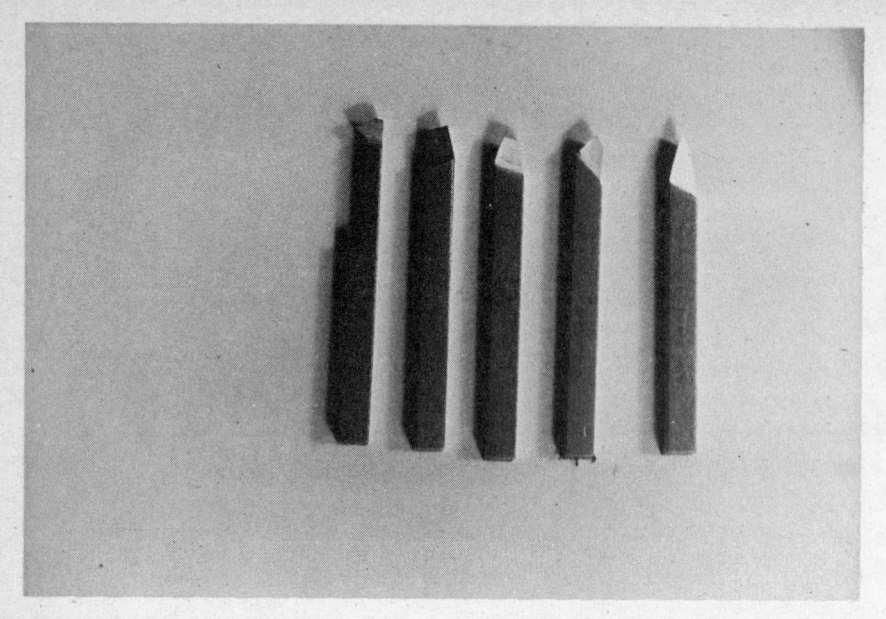

These are some of the common cutting tools used on a lathe. From left: cutter bit for rough turning; side tool; planing tool; parting-off tool and thread-cutting tool.

ensure that it is properly cleaned and accurately installed before use. Before starting a new lathe, the operator should carefully study the action of the various parts and become thoroughly familiar with the operation of all control levers and knobs.

Do not operate the lathe under power until it is properly set up and leveled. Also make sure that all bearings have been oiled and that the belt tension, between the motor and the lathe pulley, is correct. Always give the lathe pulley a twist by hand to make sure the lathe runs freely before starting a lathe under power.

In order to machine metal accurately and efficiently, it is necessary to have the correct type of lathe tool with a sharp, well-supported cutting edge (ground for the particular kind of metal being machined) and set at the correct height. High-speed steel cutter bits mounted in forged steel holders are the most popular type of lathe tools.

The cutting tools shown are the most common in use. Each has a specific purpose and the descriptions to follow give the application of each.

Cutter Bit for Rough Turning: Used for removing a large amount of material in a short time.

Side Tools: Used for longitudinal and transverse turning and for turning acute corners.

Planing Tool: Used to obtain a smooth transverse surface.

Parting-Off-Tool: Used for grooving and parting-off workpieces. In using this type of bit, the tool bit point must be mounted to the exact center height and the slowest speeds must be used. Also use lubrication.

Thread-Cutting Tool: Used for cutting screw threads. When using this type of cutter bit to cut screw threads, always keep the work flooded with oil in order to obtain a smooth thread. Machine oil may be used, but lard oil is better.

Inside Boring Tool (not shown): Used for turning inside work.

Knurling is a metal-displacement process normally applied to metal with the lathe. The *pattern* of the knurl is the same on all three examples shown; however, the *grade* of the knurl is not. From left: coarse, medium and fine knurling.

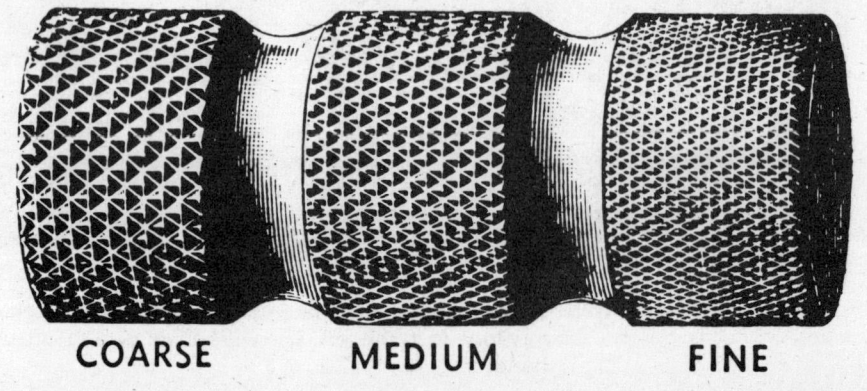

COARSE   MEDIUM   FINE

Special Lathe Work and Tools

There are also classes of work involved in gunsmithing that require special tools, the most important of which are described below.

Knurling

Knurling is the process of embossing the surface of a piece of work in the lathe with a knurling tool secured in the tool post of the lathe. The pattern of the knurl is the same as in the examples shown, but is of different grades—coarse, medium and fine.

For all knurling operations, the lathe should be arranged for the slowest back-geared speed. After starting the lathe, force the knurling tool slowly into the work at the right end until the knurl reaches a depth of about 1/64 of an inch. Then engage the longitudinal feed of the carriage and let the knurling tool feed across the face of the work. Plenty of oil should be used on the work during this operation.

When the left end of the knurl roller has reached the end of the work, reverse the lathe spindle and let the knurling tool feed back to the starting point. Do not remove the knurling tool from the impression but force it into the work another 1/64 of an inch, and let it feed back across the face of the work. Repeat this operation until the knurling is finished.

Filing and Polishing

All tool marks can be removed from metal gun parts, such as rifle barrels, and a smooth, bright finish obtained on the surface by filing and polishing. Use a fine mill file and file with the lathe running at a speed so that the work will make two or three revolutions for each stroke of the file. File just enough to obtain a smooth surface. If too much filing is done, the work will be uneven and inaccurate.

Keep the left elbow high and the sleeves tightly rolled up so there will be no danger from being dragged into the headstock or workpiece as it revolves. Also keep the file clean and free from chips; use a file card frequently.

Once the filing has been completed, a very smooth, bright finish may be obtained by polishing the work with several grades of emery cloth. Use oil on the emery cloth and run the lathe at high speed. Be careful not to let the emery cloth wrap around the revolving work.

Lapping

Certain hardened gun parts are often finished in the lathe by lapping. Emery cloth, emery dust and oil, diamond dust and other abrasives are used. Usually the lathe spindle is operated at high speed.

The lap may be very simple—consisting of a strip of emery cloth attached to a shaft—or it may be elaborately constructed of lead, copper, etc. Some very fine and precise work may be accomplished by careful lapping.

Spring Winding

Coil springs of all kinds may be wound on the lathe. Special mandrels are used for irregularly shaped springs. The lead screw and half nuts of the lathe are usually used to obtain a uniform lead so that the coils are all equally spaced.

The Use of the Center Rest

The center rest is used for turning long shafts like gun barrels and for boring and threading spindles. To mount work in the center rest, first place the center rest on the lathe, then place the work between centers, slide the center rest to its proper position, and adjust the jaws upon the work. Careful adjustment is required because the work must revolve in these jaws. When the jaws are

This is an end view of a lathe's center rest; it's used to center and hold long shafts of metal (gun barrels) or boring or threading spindles.

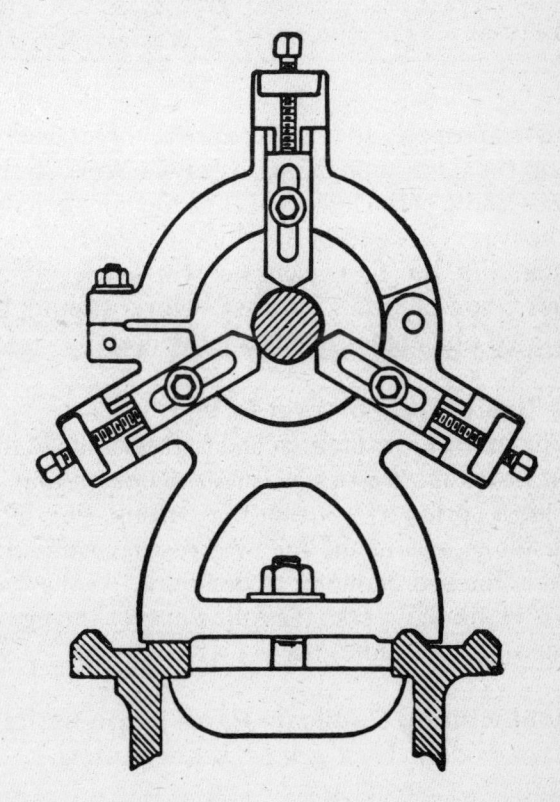

UNIVERSAL 3-JAW SCROLL CHUCK

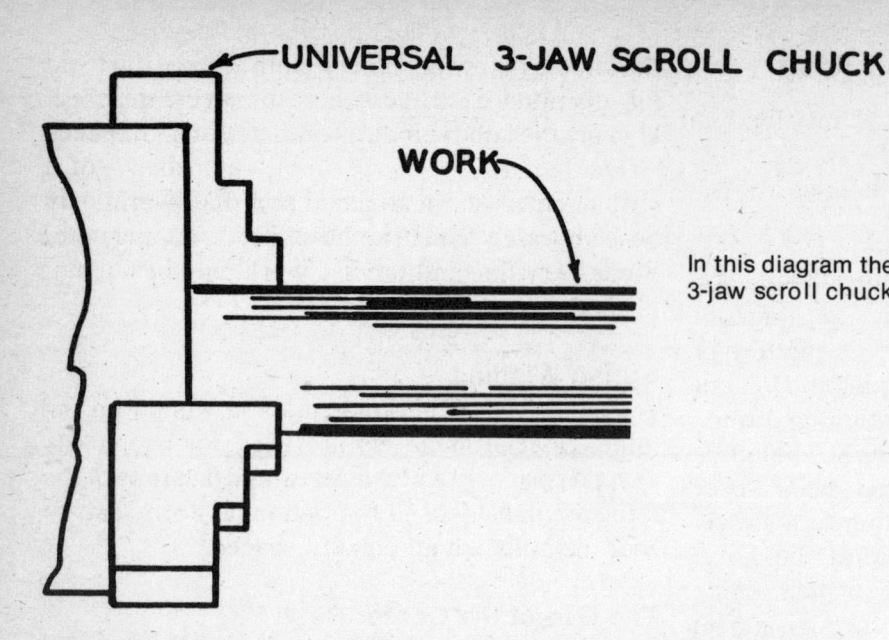

WORK

In this diagram the workpiece is being held in place by a 3-jaw scroll chuck secured to the headstock.

This is an example of a workpiece mounted on its centers using a "lathe dog" and a wet leather thong. The face of the head spindle plate is unscrewed from the shoulder about three or four turns and the work tied securely to the face plate with several heavy, wet leather thongs. The face plate is then screwed onto the spindle which tightens the lacing and holds the workpiece firmly.

adjusted properly so that the work revolves freely, clamp the jaws in position, fasten the work to the head spindle of the lathe and slide the tailstock out of the way. One end of the work may be held in a chuck, but for fine accurate work, the chuck should not be used. Rather, work should be mounted on centers, using a lathe dog.

The Use of the Follower Rest

The follower rest is attached to the saddle of the lathe to support work of small diameter that is liable to spring away from the cutting tool. The adjustable jaws of the follower rest bear directly on the finished diameter of the work. As the tool feeds along the work, the follower rest (being attached to the saddle) travels with the tool.

Manufacturing Duplicate Parts in the Lathe

The modern back-geared screw cutting lathe can be fitted with rapid production attachments and used to advantage on many manufacturing operations. The accuracy of the lathe combined with the efficiency of the special attachments make it ideal for production work requiring special accuracy.

When the lathe is equipped with special tools, it serves as a special machine. Then when the job is finished, the special tools can be removed and the lathe used for regular work. I'd recommend writing to the larger lathe manufacturers stating your specific needs. They will be able to tell you of the availability of such special attachments and also make a cost quotation.

Milling in the Lathe

A milling and keyway cutting attachment will take care of a great deal of milling in the gunshop that does not have enough work to warrant the installation of a milling machine. The cut is controlled by the hand wheel of the lathe carriage, with the cross feed screw of the lathe and the vertical adjusting screw at the top of the milling attachment. All milling cuts should generally be taken with the rotation of the cutter against the direction of the feed.

The Lathe in the Gunshop

The back-geared, screw cutting lathe is fre-

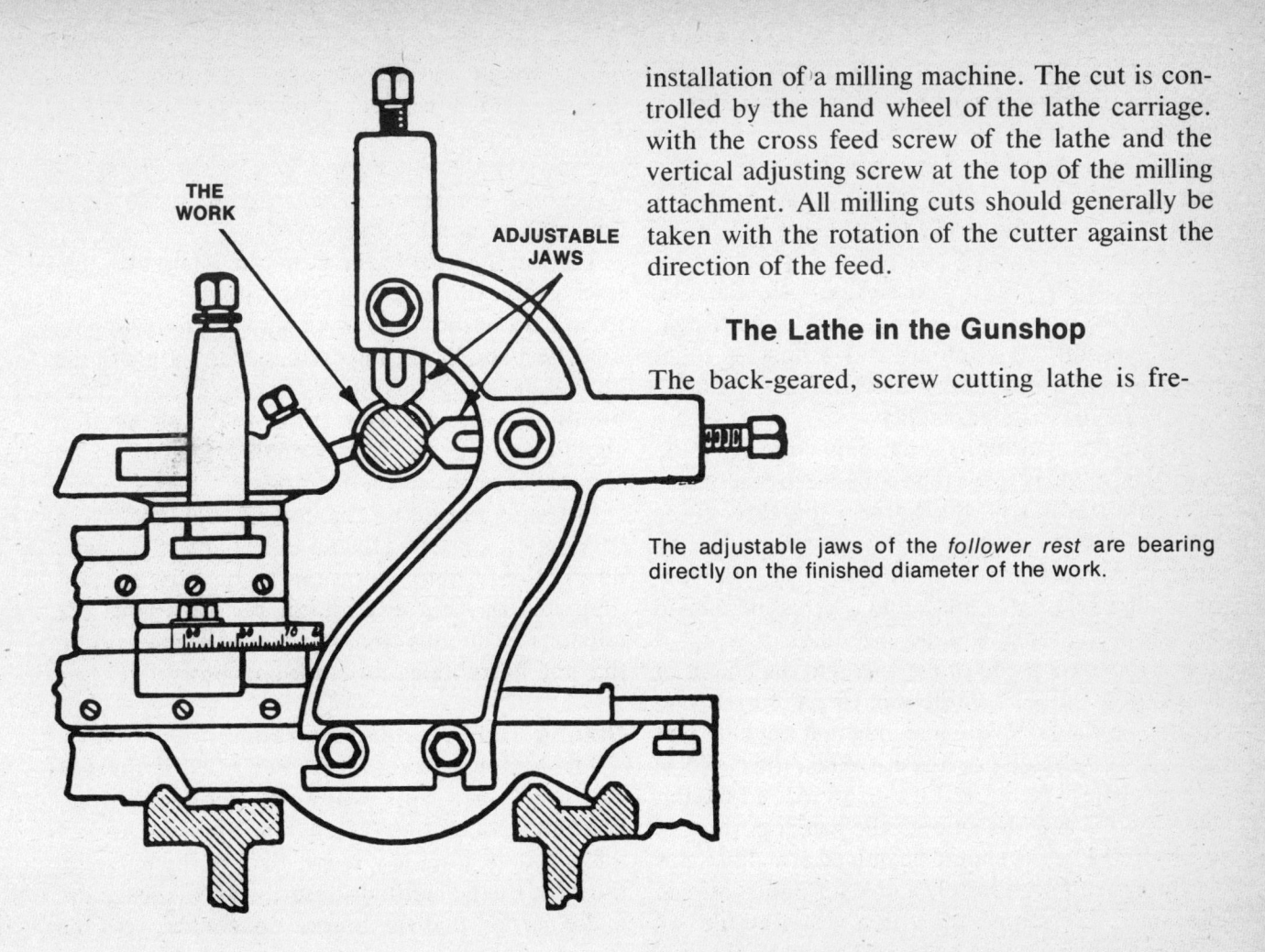

The adjustable jaws of the *follower rest* are bearing directly on the finished diameter of the work.

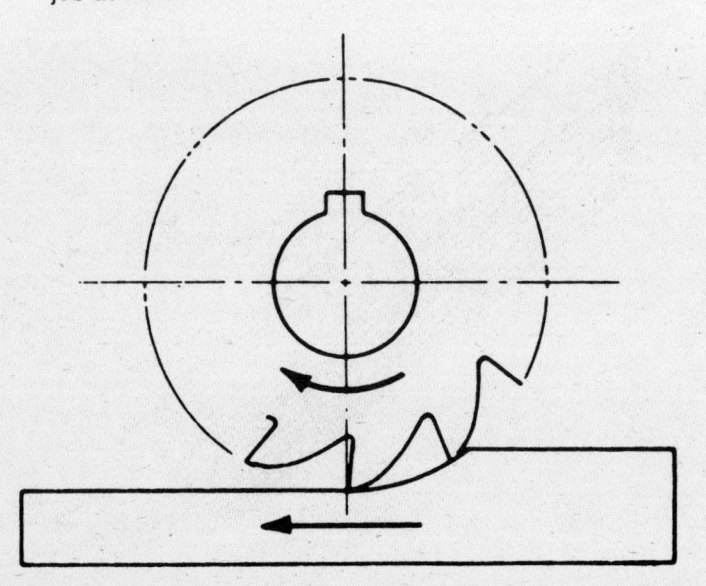

The milling and keyway cutting attachment will take care of a great deal of milling in the gunshop that does not have enough work to warrant the installation of a milling machine.

Generally, milling cuts should be taken with rotation of the cutter running *against* the direction of the feed. However, when removing large amounts of metal — rough cutting — the feed and direction of the cutter are, perhaps, best set up identically as shown here. Cutter type, direction of rotation and speed are all dependent upon the job at hand.

165

quently called the "universal tool," and this applies in gun repair work as well as in the industry in general. Most of the parts used in firearm mechanisms, and especially the barrel, bolt, etc., were originally made on lathes or in special machines which are adaptations of the lathe.

A lathe with 9" or 11" swing is very practical for handling such jobs as threading rifle barrels; chambering barrel blanks for a specific cartridge; turning barrels to contour, and a host of other operations. Special attachments used on the lathe greatly increase its versatility.

One of the operations commonly done in a lathe is turning down rifle barrels. This is especially true of certain military rifle barrels that are going through the process of being sporterized. The original barrels are often rough, ugly, uneven. Such a barrel may be placed in a lathe and turned smooth if the work is done carefully.

Put the breech end of the barrel in the chuck or live center, attach a lathe dog to the barrel, and tighten up the faceplate with dog and rawhide belt lacing as discussed previously. When the barrel is running true in the lathe, turn, use a second-cut flat file or a mill file and smooth the rough portion of the barrel. The file should be moved at right angles to the axis of the barrel, and with light uniform pressure. Then finish up with a very fine file.

When a barrel must be turned down to obtain a lighter-weight barrel, warping sometimes occurs as the strains are released during the removal of metal. This is especially true of old military rifle barrels. On the other hand, modern steel barrels have little tendency to warp even when large amounts of metal are removed.

To turn a barrel in the lathe, make certain that the barrel is turned concentric with the bore if it is to be held in the three-jaw chuck. A muzzle plug must be made for the tailstock, which should fit the bore at the muzzle as closely as possible—without binding. A round-nose (finishing) cutting tool should be used, and only a small amount of metal should be removed on each pass.

Pressure caused by the cutting tool, heat from friction, etc., is going to cause the barrel to expand during the turning operation, so be sure to compensate for this expansion by adjusting the tailstock frequently; that is, relieve the pressure so that the barrel does not spring or bow.

Cutting and Crowning Barrels

The best way to cut and crown rifle barrels is to use the lathe. This way, you reduce a time-consuming operation (when done by hand) to only a few minutes of easy work. Secure the barrel in the lathe by the methods described previously and make certain that the bore is concentric with the outside of the barrel. Then using a cut-off tool, and

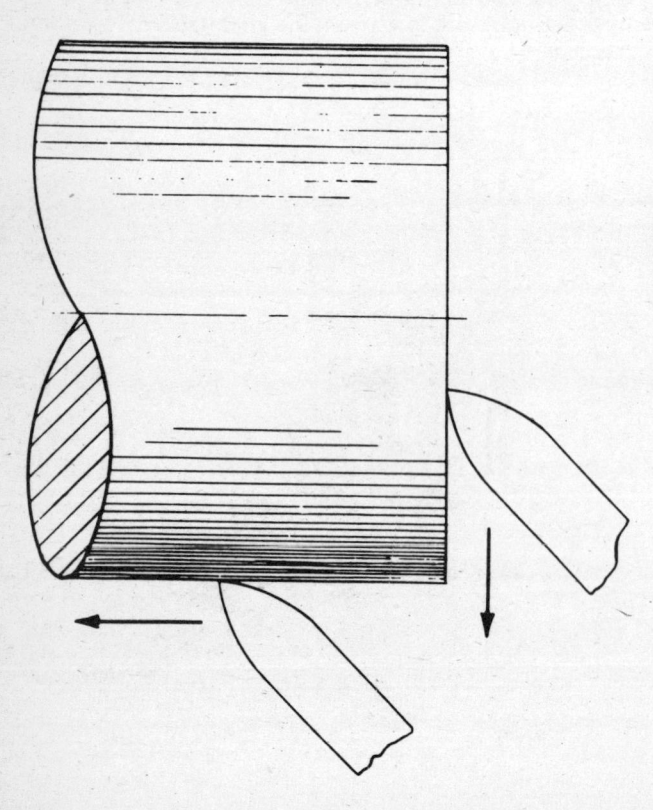

When crowning a barrel, the muzzle (left) is trued up — cut square — and then, using a right-hand side tool, the muzzle is trued by feeding the tool outward from the center as shown. Once the barrel is cut and trued, a special crowning bit (below) — available from Brownells — may be used in the tool holder to form the correct curvature on the muzzle.

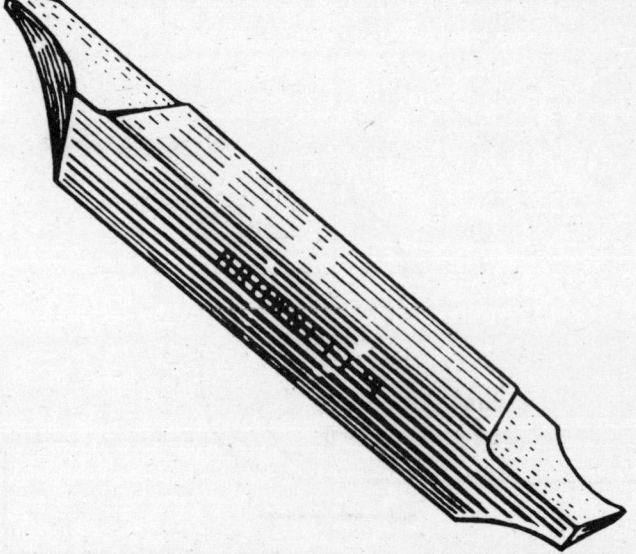

After the curvature has been properly formed on the muzzle, a round brass ball is coated with abrasive powder and oil — Clover Brand compound works perfectly for this job — and worked against the muzzle with a hand grinding tool. This puts the finishing touches on a proper crowning job.

the lathe running at low speed, cut the barrel at the desired location. (Be sure to use plenty of cutting oil during this process.) Once cut, the barrel may then be trued with the right-hand side tool, feeding it outward from the center. The tool, of course, must be sharp and ground to an angle of 58 degrees to prevent interference with the tailstock center. You should be careful not to bump the end of the tool against the lathe center, as this will break off the point.

Once the barrel is cut and trued, a special crowning bit may be used in the tool holder to form the correct curvature on the muzzle. A barrel crowning lathe bit may be purchased from Brownell's. They are professionally ground to give maximum cutter strength and proper clearance as the cutter tip enters the bore and the shank approaches the barrel. By taking careful cuts and moving the table back and forth, any degree of crown shape can be cut. The cutter should be placed in the tool holder and drawn straight toward the barrel to cut the rounded profile desired. Then a round brass ball may be used in a hand grinding tool to add the finishing touches. (The ball should be coated with abrasive powder and oil such as Clover abrasive compound.)

Chambering Rifle Barrels

Chambering rifle barrel blanks for a specific cartridge or rechambering a barrel for a new cartridge goes hand in hand with barrel threading and headspace, and all three operations will be discussed here.

In general, chambering consists of reaming out the breech of a barrel with chambering reamers forming the exact chamber dimensions into which the cartridge fits. The body of the reamer is sharpened by grinding and honing the face of the flutes. Repeated grinding, however, will eventually cause the reamer to become undersize, but a lot of metal can be cut before this happens if care is exercised in storing, grinding and using the reamers.

A roughing reamer is used only to rough out chambers, and therefore, no attempt is made with these reamers to carry out the exact form of the chamber. They have a solid pilot and are usually made with four flutes. The leads are backed up with plenty of metal to give strength so that they can really hog out metal during the chambering operation. Reamers may be used by hand with extension handles, but are usually used in lathes for convenience and speed. When using the lathe, the barrel is secured in the lathe chuck and the reamer is forced into the bore, being held in the tailstock. Therefore, the barrel turns and the reamer remains stationary. It is kept from moving by using a lathe dog when held by the tailstock center, or the Jacobs chuck when held in this manner.

Starting with the roughing reamer, it is run into the barrel bore up to its stop. Stops consist of collars or merely grease pencil marks on the reamer. Light cutting oil should be used during this operation. Then the finishing reamer is used, again using light cutting oil and cleaning out all metal chips frequently. At this point the chamber is

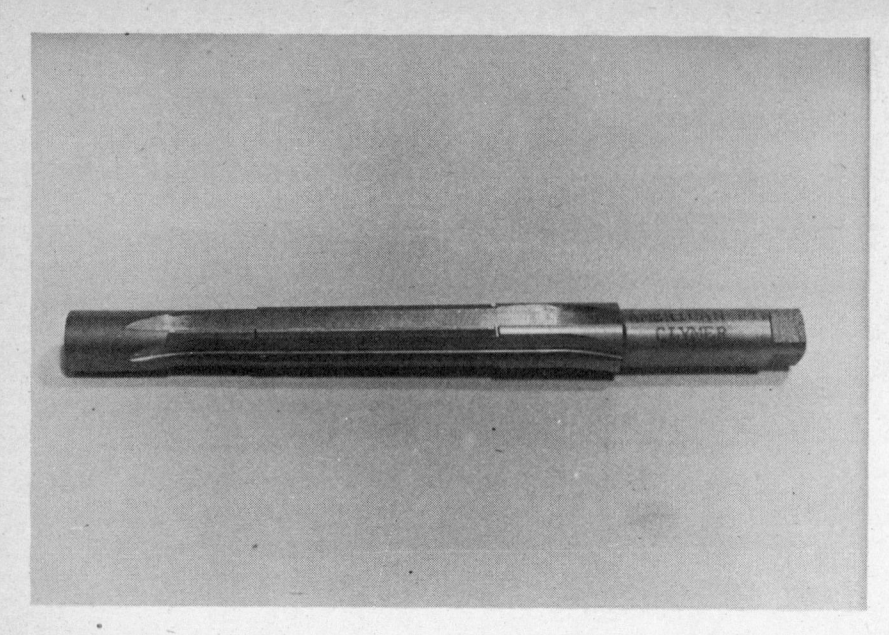

This particular Clymer chambering reamer is for the big .458 American.

checked by headspace gauges in the usual manner, and the chamber deepened by cut-and-try methods until the desired headspace is achieved.

Threading rifle barrels is definitely a job for the lathe. To set up the lathe for cutting a barrel thread, first determine the number of threads per inch to be cut, and adjust the lathe accordingly. Secure the barrel in the lathe and use a center or thread gauge to set the threading tool point at an exact right angle to the work.

Before starting the actual cutting of a right-hand thread, be sure that the change gear train is assembled properly and that the reverse lever is in the correct position to feed the carriage toward the headstock. Adjust the lathe for the lowest possible speed. Use a compound rest and advance the tool with the rest so that the first cut will be about .003".

Start the lathe and engage the half-nut lever on the carriage. The angle of the compound rest should allow the back of the tool to take a fine chasing cut on the finished side of the thread while the cutting edge does the work of forming the thread. Apply plenty of lubricant to the work. When the point of the tool reaches the groove at the end of the thread, raise the half-nut lever on the carriage, back out the cross feed a turn or two, and return the carriage by hand to the starting point. Advance the cross feed to its original position then advance the compound rest for the desired depth of cut, and engage the half-nut lever for the second cut. Follow the same routine on all succeeding cuts.

The first few cuts should be approximately .005" advance of the compound feed and the following cuts gradually reduced until the last few cuts taken are only about .001". A final pass through the thread with no advance whatever will usually clean up any remaining high spots.

16
MILLING MACHINES

A MILLING machine can certainly be a worthwhile tool in any gunshop, but unless the shop specializes in making a lot of gun parts from patterns or duplicates, a milling machine is certainly not absolutely necessary to carry out general gun repair. By today's standards, a milling machine is really not too expensive if there is enough work for it. But the machine itself is only part of the story. If a lot of different cutters are needed, we're talking about quite an investment.

In general, a milling machine is a power-driven machine that cuts metal by means of a multitooth rotating cutter. The machine is constructed in such a manner that the workpiece is fed to a rotary cutter—instead of revolving as on a lathe, or reciprocating as on a planer.

A variety of gunsmithing operations can be performed on the JET-15 machine which is ideal for the professional gunshop. First of all, you have a complete drill press and all of the operations described in Chapter 13 can be performed on this machine. Furthermore, many kinds of workpieces can be machined on this unit: hammers, trigger guards, almost any small gun part you can name—including receivers!

The multitooth milling cutters used with a milling machine remain sharp much longer than a single cutting tool and the cutting action of a milling machine is continuous, as compared to the intermittent cutting when using a hand file or even a shaper or planer. The milling machine has a power-driven spindle, and an arbor for holding multitooth cutters fits into this spindle. The cutting edges or teeth of revolving circular cutters remove a controlled amount of metal at each revolution of the cutter. The workpiece is mounted on a movable table, and is fed against the cutter. The table can be moved either by hand feed or by power feed. When several cutters are mounted on the arbor, several surfaces can be machined in one operation.

The milling machine was originally developed for manufacturing the small and irregularly-shaped parts used in the construction of firearms, and the milling process is still employed very extensively in the production of similar work, especially when intricate profiles are required and the parts must be interchangeable. Obviously, this same machine can produce replacement parts for firearms and can even be used to make complete firearms.

Operators of milling machines should again be aware of certain safety precautions. The following suggestions should be noted and remembered:

1. Do not move an operating lever without knowing in advance the action that is going to

Either of the two milling machines shown—the Jet 15 (left) and the Jet 16 (right)—would find good use in the gunshop. Obviously, the unit on the left is somewhat abridged compared to the unit on the right. The size of unit eventually selected will depend upon the type of work currently being done—or anticipated—in your own shop.

In general, a milling machine is a power machine that cuts metal by means of a multi-toothed cutter. The cutter shown is called a "convex" cutter—the cutter itself is on the left, the type of cut it makes is on the right.

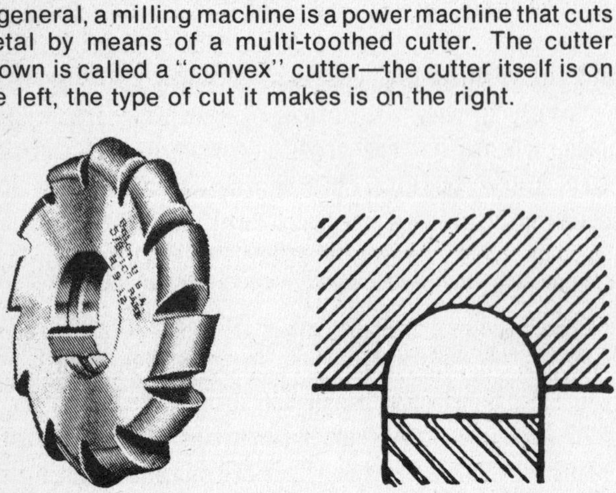

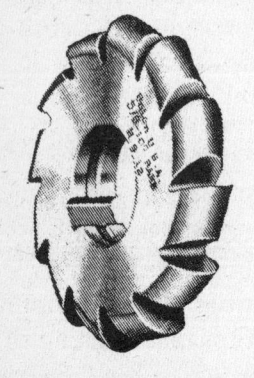

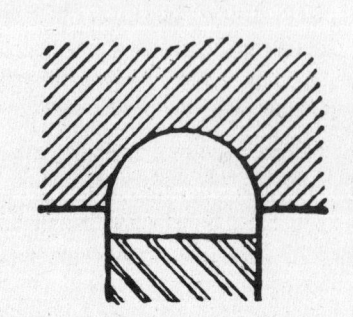

take place.

2. Never play with the control levers or carelessly turn the handles of the milling machine while it is stopped.

3. Do not lean against, or rest the hands on a moving table; if it is necessary to touch a moving member, make sure of the direction it is moving.

4. Do not attempt a cut without being sure that the work is held securely in the vise or fixture and that the holding member is fastened to the machine table.

5. Remove chips with a brush or other suitable means—never with the fingers or hands.

6. Before operating a milling machine, study it thoroughly; then, if an emergency should arise, the machine can be stopped immediately.

7. Stay clear of the milling cutters; never touch a cutter.

8. Keep your milling machine cleaned and properly oiled at all times.

Workpieces must be mounted properly and securely. Clamping devices, such as T-bolts, toe dogs, screw pins and the like are used to hold milling machine workpieces. Always keep cutters clean and sharp as dull cutters wear more rapidly than sharp ones, and do not last as long as cutters kept in proper condition.

Proper speed and feed rates are governed by

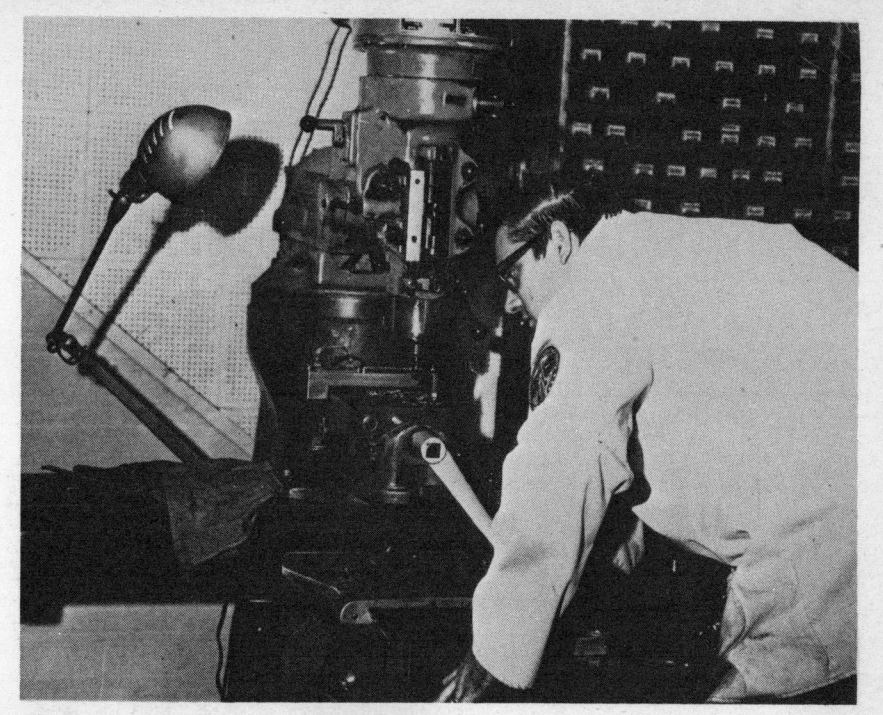

One of the beauties of a milling machine is the fact that the machine does the work, not your hands. It's just a matter of plugging in the right information, a degree of patience and some metal-working experience.

In this instance (left), a custom 1-piece trigger guard is being turned out on a milling machine. The cutter being used is an end-mill cutter—it's used for general purpose end-milling operations in all types of materials. A close-up of the cutters can be seen below.

several factors which include material, cutter width, depth of cut, surface finish, power and speed available, and cutting fluid. The amount of material to be removed per minute and the relationship between depth of cut and feed influence cutter speed. The feed rate is the rate at which the work advances past the cutter, which is commonly referred to as "inches per minute."

Practical Applications

A course on milling machine operation would

take many volumes which is much more space than we have available in this book. Then again, experience is the best teacher of all, and working under an expert machinist is probably the best way to learn the use of a milling machine. Therefore, the remaining pages in this chapter will be devoted to the many attachments available for the milling machines and how they are put to practical use in the modern gunshop.

Double-angle cutter: Double-angle cutters are used for such operations as fluting taps, reamers, and the like. The teeth on one side have an inclination of 48 degrees and on the other, 12 degrees—giving an included angle of 60 degrees for the tooth spaces. This is the preferred cutter for milling helical teeth as the 12-degree side will clear the radial faces of the teeth and produce a smooth surface.

End mill: An end mill cutter is used for general purpose end-milling operations on all types of materials, and is suited for surface milling, profiling, slotting, etc. It is made for either right-hand or left-hand rotation.

Several types of cutting ends for end mills are available which make them adaptable to a variety of uses such as profiling, end milling, slotting, surface milling, and many other milling-machine operations. Some different types of end mills are as follows:

1. Two flute
2. Shell end
3. Multiple flute
4. Carbide-tipped
5. Single end
6. Double end
7. Ball end
8. Hollow

Fly cutter: Can be used to mill intricate shapes that do not warrant the expense of formed cutters.

Formed cutters: These cutters are specially made to meet various milling requirements such as for cutting curved or irregular surfaces. One type of formed cutter is the *convex cutter* which is used to mill half-circles in all types of materials. A *concave cutter* is used to mill convex half-circles while *corner-rounding cutters* are used to mill convex quarter-circles.

Half side cutter: These cutters are plain milling cutters of cylindrical form that have teeth around the periphery on one or both sides. Side mills are used for side milling, for slotting, and for straddle milling work. If the cutter has teeth on only one side, it is a *half side milling cutter*.

Helical cutter: This type of cutter is especially adapted for milling thin work or intermittent cuts where the amount of slack to be removed varies.

Slotting cutter: Used to mill shallow slots, such as screw-head slots. Thin, straight-toothed, plain milling cutters are generally called slitting saws. A

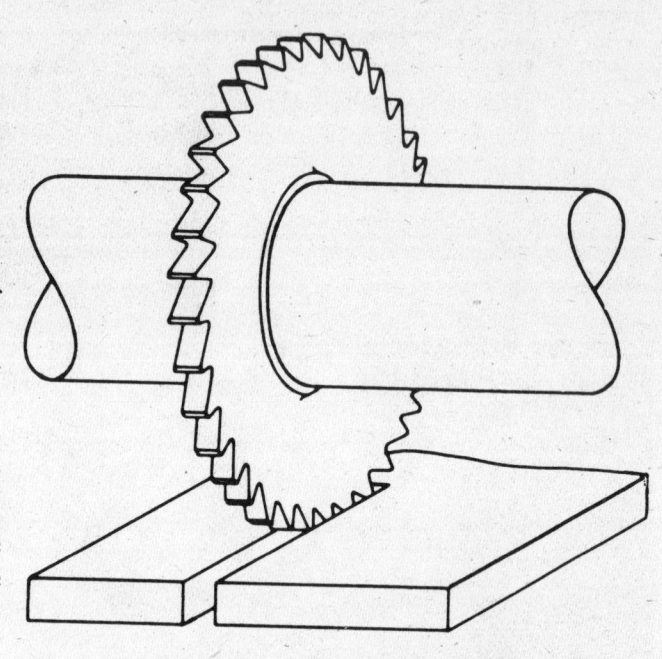

The "slotting cutter"—often called a slitting saw—is used for general purpose slotting or cutting-off chores.

plain metal-slitting saw is used for general-purpose slotting, parting, or cutting-off operations of moderate depth in both ferrous and non-ferrous materials.

The staggered-tooth metal-slitting saw is made with alternate helical teeth for shear cutting action and chip clearance between the side teeth. They are used for heavy-duty slotting in all types of materials. This type of saw can make deeper cuts under coarser feeds than other types of saws.

The screw-slotting cutter shown is ground with side clearance and is used for slotting screw heads made of all materials. They are used only for making short, shallow slots.

Woodruff cutters: The Woodruff cutter is used for cutting Woodruff keyseats, slots and grooves in all types of materials.

Screw-slotting cutters like the one shown are ground with side clearance. It's made to cut screw slots in all materials.

A "Woodruff" cutter is used to cut keyseats, slots and grooves in most materials.

The selection of the type of milling cutter used is also influenced by the following factors:

1. Milling cutters with comparatively few widely spaced teeth can remove more metal in a given time without stressing the cutter or overloading the machine than cutters with a comparatively large number of teeth.

2. Fine-tooth cutters are inferior to coarse-tooth cutters, so far as their relative tendency to "chatter" is concerned.

3. The free cutting action of coarse-tooth cutters is due chiefly to the fact that less cutting action is required to remove a given amount of metal; that is, each tooth takes a larger, deeper cut.

4. Wide spaces between the teeth allow the cutting edges to be backed up as needed, which is not always possible with teeth that are closely spaced.

5. Moderate rake angles reduce power consumption, and are desirable on cutters that are used on mild steel. Large rake angles are undesirable because of the tendency to chatter.

6. The helical angle has little effect on power consumption. However, a large helical angle is desirable because it requires few cutter teeth, gives smoother cutter action, and reduces the tendency to chatter.

7. With few exceptions, coarse-tooth cutters are superior to fine-tooth cutters for production work.

Indexing

The index head on the milling machine is used to rotate a piece of work through given angles—usually equal divisions of a circle. An indexing head, in combination with the longitudinal feeding movement of the table, is used to impart a rotary motion to a workpiece for helical milling action, such as in milling the helical flutes of a cutter.

To operate the index head, the spindle is rotated through a desired angle by turning the index crank which controls the interposed gearing. In most dividing or indexing heads, 40 revolutions of the index crank are required for one revolution of a spindle. The dividing head can be used for several different methods of indexing and index tables are provided by the machine manufacturers to aid in obtaining angular spacings and divisions.

The simplest method is called *direct* or *rapid indexing* in which the spindle is turned through a given angle without interposition of gearing. Plain indexing is an operation in which the spindle is turned through a given angle with the interposition of gearing between the index crank and the spin-

Dividing heads can be used for several different methods of indexing. Proper index tables are provided by the milling machine maker and aid in obtaining angular spacings and divisions. The dividing head shown is for a Unimat-SL miniature machine tool.

dle. This gearing usually consists of a worm on the index crankshaft which meshes with a worm wheel on the spindle.

Compound indexing is performed by first turning the index crank to a definite setting as in plain indexing, and then turning the index plate itself to locate the crank in the correct position. Compound indexing can be used to obtain divisions that are required for gun work and goes beyond the range of plain indexing.

Differential indexing is a method of indexing where the spindle is turned through a desired division by manipulating the index crank; the index plate is rotated, in turn, by proper gearing that connects it to the spindle. As the crank is rotated, the index plate also rotates a definite amount, depending on the gears that are used. The result is a differential action of the index plate, which can be either in the same direction or in the opposite direction in relationship to the direction of crank movement, depending on the gear setup. As motion is a relative matter, the actual motion of the crank at each indexing is either greater or less than its motion relative to the index plate.

In compound indexing, the index plate is rotated manually, with a possiblity of error in counting the holes. This is avoided in differential indexing; therefore, chances for error are greatly reduced. In the differential indexing operation, the index crank is moved relative to the index plate in the same circular row of holes in a manner that is similar to plain indexing. As the spindle and index plate are connected by interposed gearing, the index plate stop pin on the rear of the plate must be disengaged before the plate can be rotated.

Angular indexing is the operation of rotating the spindle through a definite angle (in degrees) by turning the crank. Sometimes, instead of specifying the number of divisions or sides required for the work to be milled, a given angle, such as 20 degrees, 45 degrees, etc., may be specified for indexing. The number of turns of the index crank required to rotate the spindle one degree must first be established to provide a basis for rotating the spindle through a given angle. Usually, 40 turns of the index crank are required to rotate the spindle one complete revolution (360 degrees). Thus, one turn of the crank equals 360÷40=9 degrees; or one ninths turn of the crank rotates the spindle one degree. Accordingly, to index one degree, the crank must be moved as follows:

1. On a 9-hole index plate, 1 hole.
2. On an 18-hole index plate, 2 holes.
3. On a 27-inch index plate, 3 holes.

Block indexing (sometimes called multiple indexing) is adapted to gear cutting. In this operation, the gear teeth are cut in groups separated by spaces; the work is rotated several revolutions by the spindle while the gear teeth are being cut.

The chief advantage of block indexing is that the heat generated by the cutter (especially when cutting cast-iron gears with coarse pitch) is distributed more evenly around the rim of the gear; thus, distortion due to local heating is avoided, and higher speeds and feeds can be used.

For small milling jobs, don't overlook the Unimat. This Unimat has been set up for just that purpose.

Milling on the Unimat 3 Machine

For hobbyists or gunshops without sufficient work to keep a full-scale milling machine in operation, the Unimat 3 (as discussed in Chapter 12) can be set up for many practical milling operations at relatively low cost. A few of the practical applications follow.

Scope Mounts for Lee-Enfield

Obtaining a low, tight-fitting scope mount for the .303 Lee-Enfield rifle has always been a challenge since the only rear support on the action is the charger guide bridge, and the top of this bridge is quite a bit higher than the front receiver rings. The Unimat 3 can be used to adapt two regular scope mounts for this rifle.

A Weaver No. 53 top mount is used as a starting basis. The rear of this mount is carefully marked so that it can be cut and squared to fit inside the recess of the charger guide bridge. The Unimat 3 is then set up for milling by transferring the power drive from the headstock to the drilling and milling attachment, securing the milling table to the cross feed base, and clamping the scope base to the milling table. During the milling operation, the workpiece must be held tightly. In this case, the scope mount is clamped to the milling table with T-nut screws and flat clamps. This setup gives sufficient tightness to avoid excessive vibrations during the milling operation and also to keep the work from moving.

This Weaver No. 53 sight base has been milled and squared to fit snugly into the charger-guide recess on the bridge of a .303 Lee-Enfield. With the mount placed in the receiver bridge as shown, note the mount ring screw slot. It's too close to the guide for use; this slot will have to be recut about ½" further forward before a proper fit is obtained.

At this point (above), the rear end of the Weaver base has been secured in the charger slot via two screws through the sides of the charger bridge—now the two main screw holes on the receiver ring can be located, drilled and the base installed and the scope mounted (below).

An end mill cutter is used in the Jacob's chuck for removing the required metal from the rear of the base so it will butt tightly inside the charger guide bridge recess. At this point, you'll notice that the mounting screw guide slot in the base is located too close to the charger guide for proper mounting, so this slot will have to be recut about ½" toward the front of the sight from its original location. This operation may be performed with a taper pin router chucked in the milling attachment. These cutters take the place of routing cutters and drills, as they will start without first drilling. They also cut freely without build up, and are easily guided along the pattern.

Drill and tap two small holes for screws through the charger guides to anchor the rear end of the mount. Then locate the two main screw holes on the front receiver ring and drill and tap these as required. These four holes will hold the scope tightly during firing providing you properly located the two rear holes (through the charger guides). Those holes must be perfectly centered into the sides of the scope base, as you don't have too much metal to play with.

Dovetailing Rifle Barrels

Universal sight base cutters are made for factory sights with a 60-degree shoulder and ⅜" base. They are available from most gunsmith suppliers, and if you have a milling/drilling attachment for your mini-lathe, you can perform this operation with the precision of a more expensive full-size milling machine. Here's how I used the Unimat 3 to dovetail a front sight slot on a 24" rifle barrel.

The tailstock on the lathe bed is removed, as well as the tool holder on the cross slide. Then a milling and fixture table is secured to the cross slide and the vertical drill and milling attachment along with the drive unit is positioned in place for milling.

To cut out a front dovetail slot in a barrel using a Unimat, make sure the action is properly leveled and cut a ¼" slot about .085" deep across the barrel as shown.

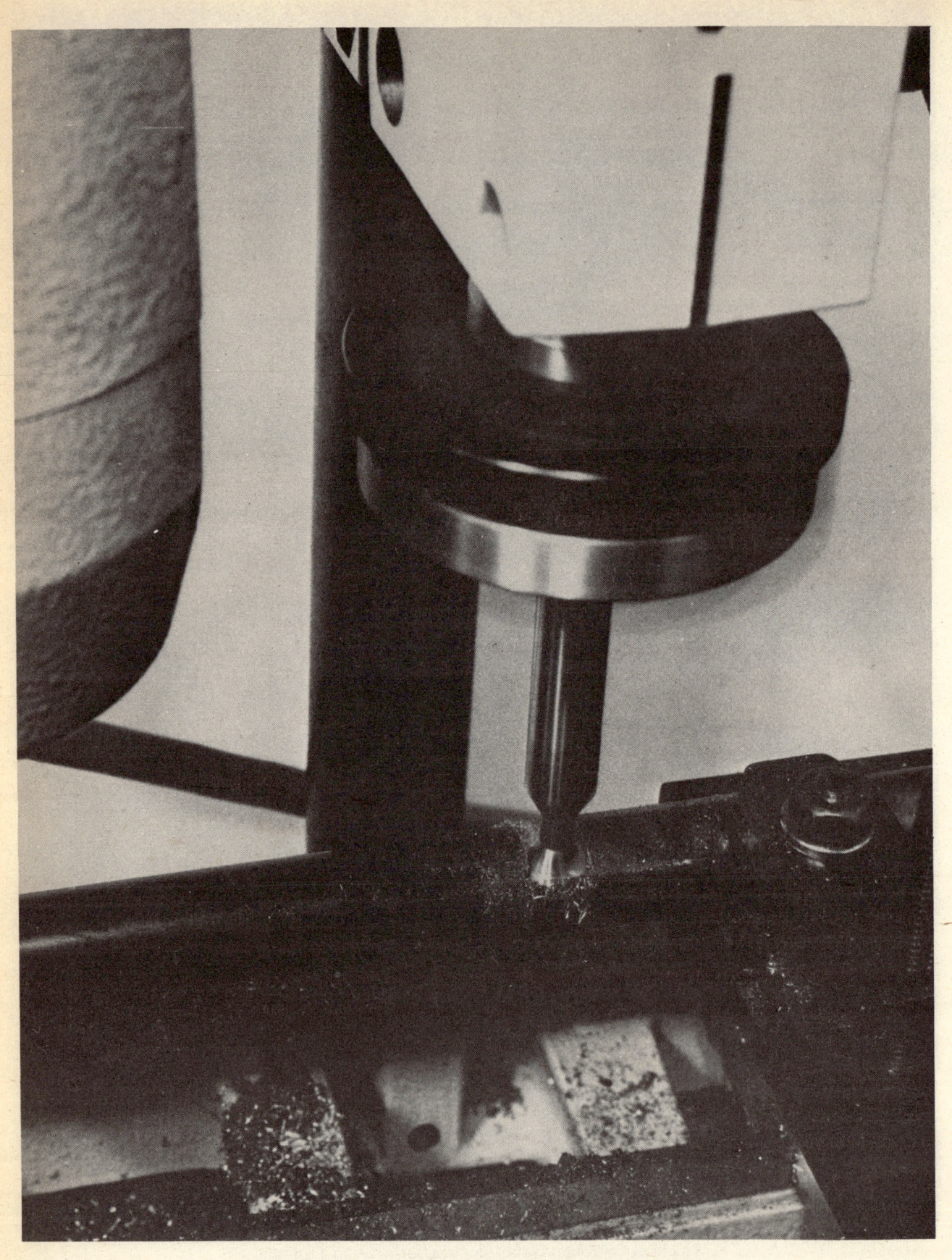

You next run a wider end-mill cutter (about 5/16") through the same slot and finish up with a standard 3/8" dovetail cutter.

The rifle is leveled horizontally and held in place by T-nuts and clamps on the milling table so that the barrel is parallel to the lathe bed. If the lathe is solidly mounted to a bench, the milling table and clamps will support the barrel and action securely without further supports. However, for long barrels and heavy actions, you'll probably want to support the action end also, but make sure this end is free to move back and forth (about 1") when the cross feed is used during the milling operation.

Leveling the rifle is done with a level placed against a flat surface on the rifle. If you cannot find a flat place from which to orient the rifle, you can use a spud or an expandable arbor from a bore sighter. Merely insert the arbor into the bore without the bore sighter attached, and use the flat surface on this arbor to place a small level. When a barrel is to be shortened, mark the barrel and the slot for the new sight position before cutting off the barrel.

With the rifle leveled and the new slot position placed directly under the vertical drill/milling attachment spindle, use a ¼" end mill cutter to cut a straight slot across the barrel to a depth of about .085". A second pass is made with a wider end mill cutter (about 5/16") to cut the slot as wide as the top part of the dovetail sight. Then the slot is checked for accuracy and cut to full depth of the dovetail involved. All passes are made with the cross feed on the lathe bed.

The standard four-fluted 3/8" dovetail cutter will not fit in the Jacob's chuck that comes with the Unimat 3, but the universal 3-jaw lathe chuck may be screwed onto the spindle and used to hold the cutter. Most of these sight base cutters are made .010" undersize with a plus or minus .005" tolerance so that the slot can be precision-cut to the exact size on the second cut.

You'll find that the initial cutting with the end-mill cutters is extremely slow on the Unimat 3, so be patient and take it easy so as not to bind the machine. The sight-base cutter, however, will go through the slot like a hot knife cutting butter.

The procedure just described is for cutting dovetail slots for front sights only. We haven't found a practical way to use the Unimat 3 for cutting rear sight slots as yet. You could obtain an extra cross feed attachment and secure the barrel to the milling table mounted on one of the cross feeds (with the barrel perpendicular to the lathe bed) and the vertical drill and milling attachment secured to the other cross feed, but the setup time involved would make it more profitable to cut the slot by hand.

17

MISCELLANEOUS GUNSMITHING TOOLS

THERE IS a class of tools that may be classified as a luxury; that is, while not essential to general gunsmithing work, these tools are mighty nice to have around. In compiling this list, it was noted that a luxury item in one person's shop may be a very essential tool in another's—depending upon the type of work normally done. Such tools will include power hacksaws, band saws, testing facilities, heat-treating furnaces and the like.

Power Hacksaw

Power hacksaws are designed to make sawing of metal a mechanical rather than a hand operation. One type of power hacksaw commonly found in some of the larger gunsmithing shops has a drive shaft that's connected by a V-belt and gears to the electric motor mounted on the machine. The work table is equipped with a vise that can be mounted either straight or at an angle to the blade. The mechanism raises the hacksaw blade on the return stroke so as to prevent dulling of the blade by dragging it over the work as the blade is returned to the starting position. Another important feature on this power hacksaw is a blade safety switch that automatically stops the machine if the blade should break during operation of the saw. This feature prevents any damage that could result if the machine continued operation with a broken blade.

Small power hacksaws can be used on square or round stock up to 3 or more inches—quite sufficient for any gun barrel that will be encountered. High speed tungsten steel and high speed molybdenum steel are the most commonly used materials in power hacksaw blades. The common tooth types are described as follows:

Regular tooth blades are for cutting and contouring most ferrous and hard non-ferrous metals used in the shop. Straight-faced teeth continuously rake chips out of the saw cut.

Hook tooth blades have a 10-degree positive rake angle, making fast cutting rates possible at reduced feed pressures. For non-ferrous metals, non-metallics and tough alloys of 3" section and larger. Rounded gullets allow fast chip removal.

Skip tooth blades have a 0-degree rake angle. Widely spaced teeth provide extra chip clearance. Shallow gullets increase band strength. It is recommended for cutting large sections.

There are also different tooth sets for various cutting jobs. In general, there are two types: the raker set and the wavy set. Both have a right and left positioning of teeth to provide clearance for the back of the blade and prevent binding in the saw cut. These tooth sets are described as follows:

Raker Set: Teeth are set alternately right and

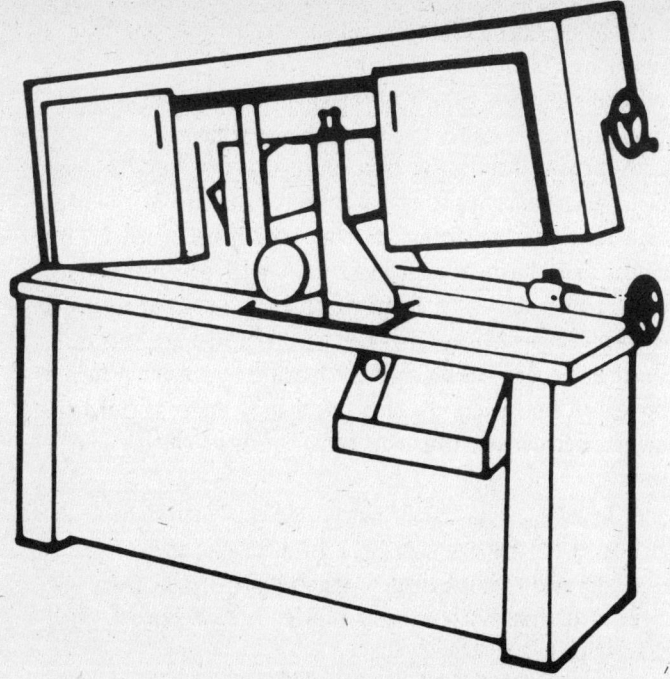

Power hacksaws are designed to make the sawing of metal a "power" process, not a hand operation. The power hacksaw shown is typical of those found in some of the larger gunsmithing shops.

These hacksaw blades represent the more common tooth varieties. From top to bottom: regular; hook; skip. Each has its own particular use around the gunshop.

Tooth Types

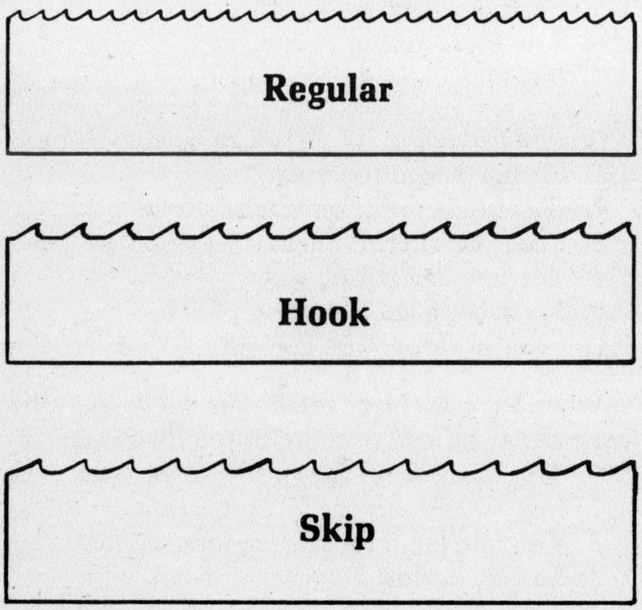

Regular

Hook

Skip

left, followed by a straight raker tooth to remove chips (and load) and improve cutting action.

Wavy Set: Groups of teeth are set in the shape of a curve alternating right and left to distribute the chip load over many teeth.

To operate the power hacksaw, secure the work in the vise so that the blade will saw at the desired place. The blade is then lowered on to the work carefully to start the cut. Never allow the blade to strike the work as this will damage or break the teeth. The machine should be adjusted so that the blade lifts about 1/8" on the return stroke. Otherwise the blade will be damaged if allowed to be

Hacksaw blades come in two types of "tooth sets" — raker set or wavy set. The raker teeth are set alternately right and left, followed by a straight raker tooth to remove the chip and load and improve cutting action. The wavy set has groups of teeth set in the shape of a curve alternating right and left to distribute the chip load over many teeth.

Tooth Set

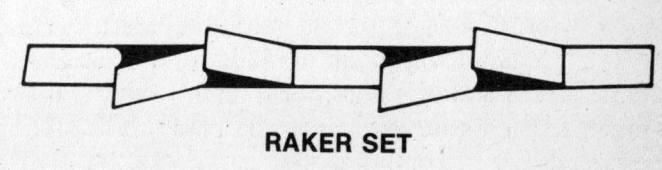

RAKER SET

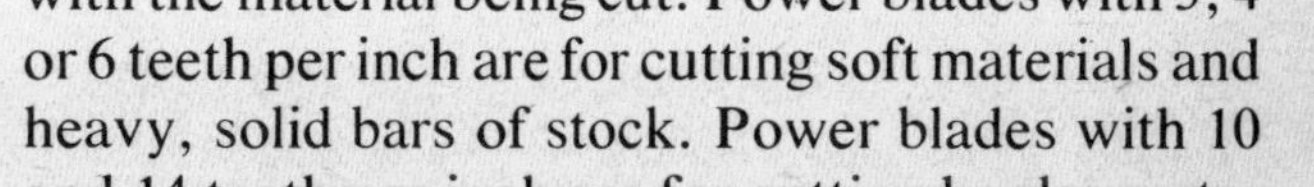

WAVY SET

dragged back across the work.

The cutting speed of a power hacksaw varies with the material being cut. Power blades with 3, 4 or 6 teeth per inch are for cutting soft materials and heavy, solid bars of stock. Power blades with 10 and 14 teeth per inch are for cutting harder materials and stock of smaller size. Selection of teeth per inch based on saw contact area can be made from the following table:

No. of Teeth Per Inch	Saw Contact Area
3	4" to 12"
4	2" to 6"
6	3/8" to 4"
10	1/4" to 1/2"
14	Less than 1/4"

Data on selecting speed and feed is given below:

Material	Speed, Strokes Per Minute	Feed, Sq. Inches Per Minute
Aluminum	120 to 150	2.0 to 4.5
Brass	120 to 150	1.5 to 3.5
Bronze	90 to 120	0.5 to 1.5
High Density Alloys (Udimet, Waspaloy, Inconel, etc.)	30 to 60	0.2 to 0.7
Cast Iron	90 to 120	1.5 to 3.0
High Nickel Alloys	60 to 90	0.8 to 1.5
Low to Medium Carbon Steel	120 to 150	2.0 to 3.0
Tool Steel	60 to 90	0.5 to 2.0
High Speed Steel	60 to 90	0.5 to 1.0
Stainless Steel	60 to 90	0.5 to 1.5
Structurals	120 to 150	—

Without proper mounting tension, a power hacksaw blade cannot deliver the cutting efficiency built into it by its manufacturer. Not enough tension will result in blade runout, accelerated wear and/or a poor finish on the work. Too much tension can also cause the blade to break, especially at the pinholes.

Use the chart below to tension power blades

Blade Width	Redstripe and Bluestripe High Speed	Greenstripe High Speed
Direct Pull Recommended Torque Wrench Readings (Approx.)		
1"	125 ft./lbs.	150 ft./lbs.
1-1/4"	175 ft./lbs.	200 ft./lbs.
1-1/2"	200 ft./lbs.	225 ft./lbs.
1-3/4"	225 ft./lbs.	250 ft./lbs.
2"	250 ft./lbs.	275 ft./lbs.
2-1/2"	275 ft./lbs.	300 ft./lbs.
Direct Pull Recommended Fixed Tension Device Readings (Approx.)		
1"	1000 in./lbs.	1200 in./lbs.
1-1/4"	1800 in./lbs.	2000 in./lbs.
1-1/2"	2000 in./lbs.	2250 in./lbs.
1-3/4"	2250 in./lbs.	2500 in./lbs.
2"	2500 in./lbs.	2750 in./lbs.
2-1/2"	2750 in./lbs.	3000 in./lbs.

correctly. Check your reading after one or two cuts and increase the tension slightly as the blade becomes stabilized in position. With machines where the saw blade is tensioned by lever action, use approximately 50% of these readings.

A power hacksaw blade cannot deliver its best cut-off performance on a machine in poor mechanical condition, so the machine should be maintained on a regular basis with emphasis on such items as yoke alignment, blade tensioning, fit of pins in pinholes, dirt between blade and holder, feed pressure, belts and hydraulic system. When a blade is installed on the machine, care should be exercised to see that the right amount of tension is used.

Some of the reasons for blade *breakage* are:
1. Blade contacting work before in motion
2. Cutting with a new blade in slot cut by dull blade
3. Not enough blade tension
4. Feed pressure too heavy when cutting thin section
5. Using a dull blade
6. Material loose in machine vise
7. Blade too thin or too narrow for feed and material

Some of the reasons for power hacksaw blades *not cutting straight* are:
1. Not enough blade tension
2. Dull blade
3. Hard spot in material forcing blade out of path
4. Feed pressure too heavy
5. Feed mechanisms not functioning
6. Saw frame out of alignment
7. Machine capacity inadequate

Premature dulling of teeth can be caused by:
1. Cutting speed too great
2. Blade fails to lift on return stroke
3. Feed pressure too heavy
4. Teeth facing wrong way
5. Incorrect blade selection
6. Lack of (or wrong) coolant

When hacksaw blade teeth start *ripping out*, the reason may be one or more of the following:
1. Too many teeth for cutting large work section
2. Too few teeth for cutting thin section
3. Sawing against a corner or sharp edge

4. Sawing a large cross section of soft material with too fine teeth at too heavy a feed or too slow a speed

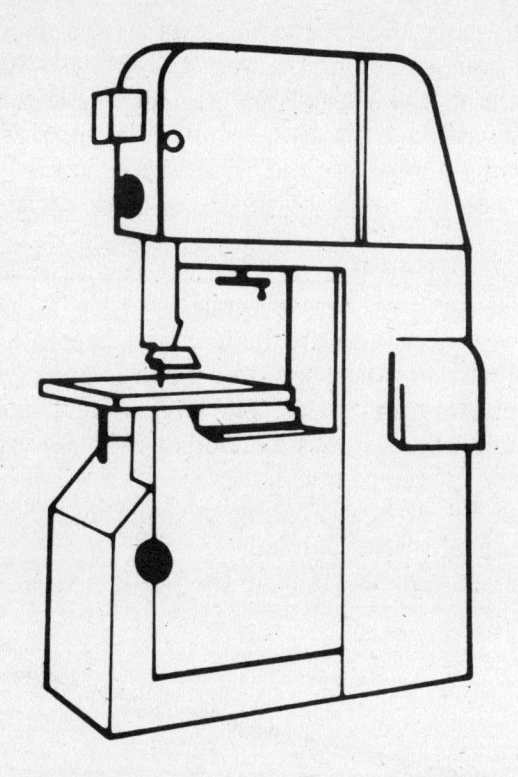

Bandsaws

Like power hacksaws, power bandsaws are designed to make the sawing of metal a mechanical operation. Rather than having a single blade secured in a frame, the bandsaw utilizes a flexible, thin, narrow ribbon of steel which forms a loop to ride on two wheels. One of these wheels is powered by an electric motor mounted on the machine. They are used for heavy-duty sawing of metals.

One of the most important factors in operating a bandsaw is a proper cutting speed. If the machine is operated at too fast a speed, the teeth are not allowed sufficient time to cut into the material. As a result, they merely rub over the surface of the work creating friction that rapidly dulls the cutting edge and wears out the blade.

Many variations of power bandsaws are available, but all of them can be grouped into three classifications; that is, horizontal machines for cut-off sawing, vertical machines for straight and profile sawing at conventional speeds, plus vertical machines for non-ferrous and friction cutting.

Shapers

The gunsmith who does a lot of specializing

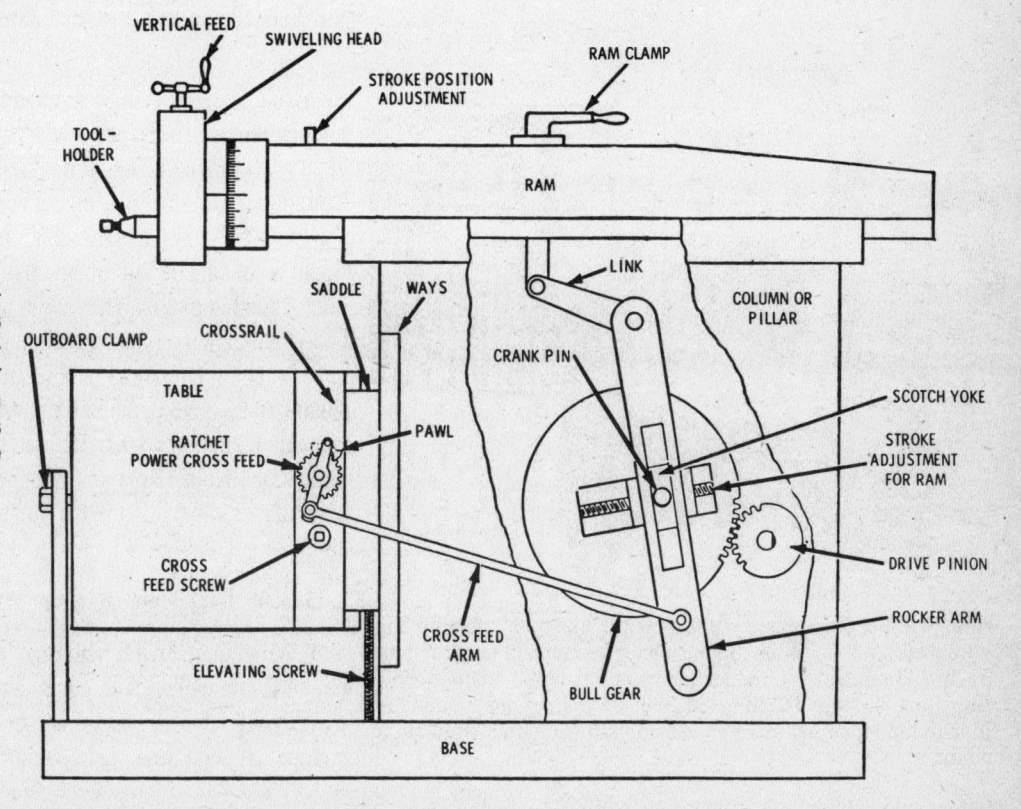

This power bandsaw is typical of those suitable for gunsmithing chores. Before buying one, be sure to consider the type and amount of work you'll be doing that would require a power tool such as this.

A shaper is used for turning out such gun parts as hammers, triggers, trigger guards and other such items. The gunsmith who specializes in this sort of work will find the shaper a necessity.

183

might find it necessary to purchase a shaper for turning out parts such as hammers, triggers and the like. The cutting tool is moved in a horizontal plane by a drive shaft having a reciprocating motion, and it cuts only on the forward stroke. The work is usually held in a vise bolted to a table that can be moved either vertically or horizontally. Any device that can be attached to a work table for holding and positioning the work piece is considered to be a fixture. Numerous fixtures can be used to set up castings having odd shapes for machining.

When a gun part is to be cut out, the operator must decide on the number of cuts necessary. However, usually one or two roughing cuts and one or two finishing cuts are all that's required—depending on the shape of the work and finish desired.

Gunsmiths' Furnaces

The gunsmith who makes a lot of his own tools and parts will find a heat-treating furnace very useful. Several types are available ranging in price from a few hundred dollars to over $1,000. The Huppert electric heat-treating furnace is designed specifically for precision heat-treating in gunshops. It is simple to operate and service.

In the gunshop, pins, sears, reamers, springs, hammers and many other parts and tools require proper hardening. Many gunsmiths are able to accomplish this hardening with a gas flame, but the process can not be controlled this way. The odds against one obtaining the correct hardness every time are high. The investment in an electric heat-treating furnace insures complete control over hardening, tempering and annealing. Complete instructions are normally furnished with each furnace.

Most heat-treating furnaces are not very large because they will be used mainly for small parts. One with a capacity to handle parts up to 8" in length and 4" wide should be quite adequate for most gunsmithing needs. The largest one listed in Brownell's catalog has a chamber 5½" high by 5" wide by 13" deep, but its cost is high—requiring quite a lot of heat-treating business to make it economically worthwhile.

For removing parts from the hot furnaces, one

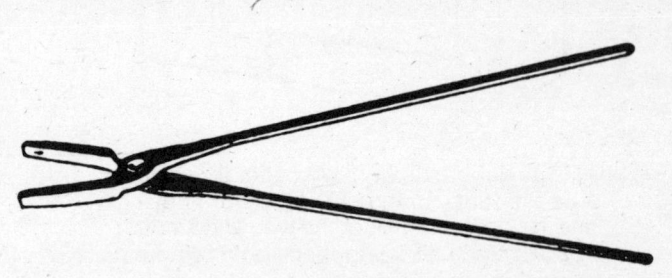

When handling small parts that are being heat treated in a furnace, tongs like these are necessary.

or more sets of tongs are necessary. Special tongs, available from Frank Mittermeier, Inc., are specially designed for small parts being handled in heat-treating furnaces. They are made from ¼" stock and are about 16" long. They provide a means of insuring a positive grip on various objects and permit the operator to exert leverage from such a distance that his hands will not be affected by the heat of the object being held. Many gunsmiths seem to get by with a pair of pliers, but when used to handle hot objects, pliers will quickly loose their temper and consequently their usefulness—much the same as many gunsmiths themselves!

Shooting Facilities and Chronographs

Every gunsmith should have shooting facilities to test various firearms and loads. Ideally, the gunsmith should have a bench rest and a 100-yard range for testing, sighting-in, chronographing, etc.

Heat-treating furnaces will be found handy by gunsmiths who make a lot of their own tools, or reharden certain gun parts. The cost of these furnaces ranges from a few hundred dollars to over $1,000. The furnace shown is made by Huppert and is designed for precision heat treating.

PLANS FOR A SHOOTING BENCH

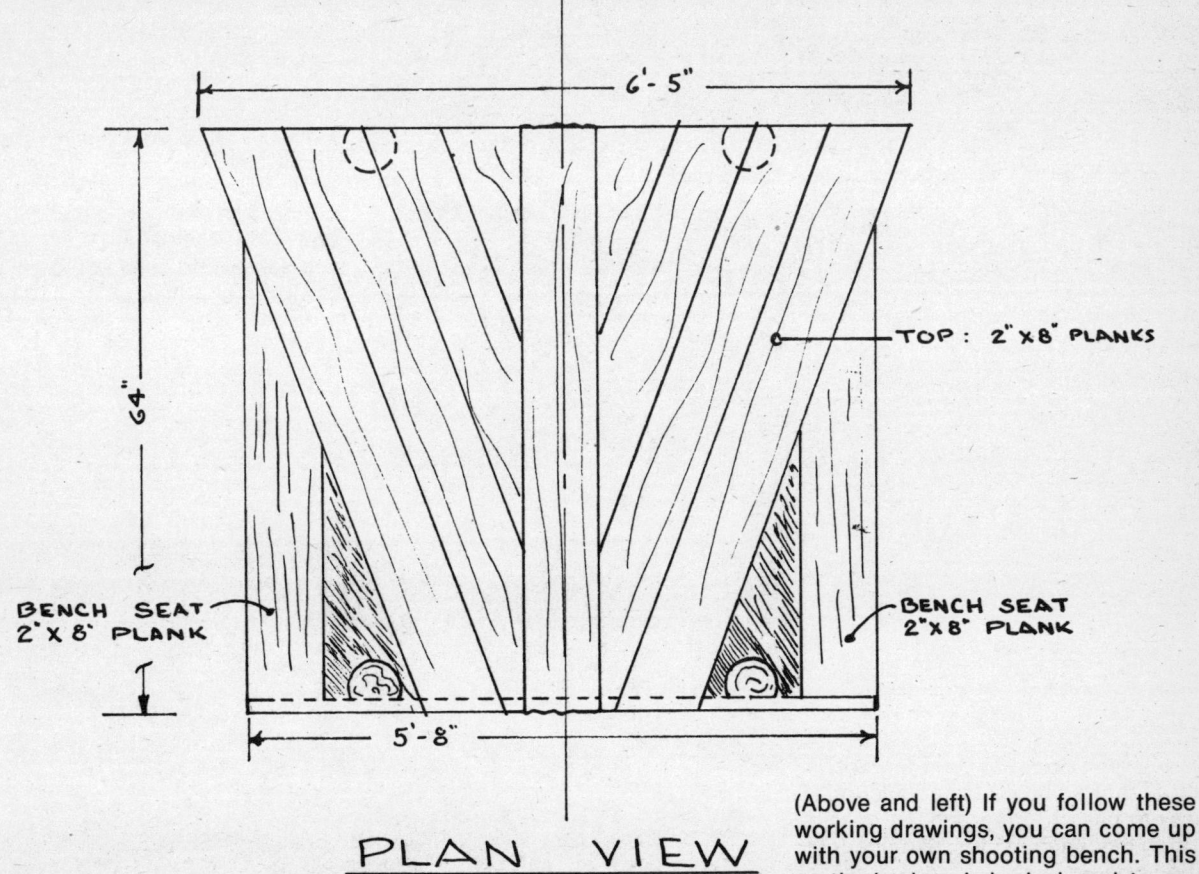

Plan view labels: 6'-5", 64", TOP: 2"x8" PLANKS, BENCH SEAT 2"x8" PLANK, BENCH SEAT 2"x8" PLANK, 5'-8"

PLAN VIEW

Front view labels: 2"x8", 2"x8", 6" ⌀ POSTS

FRONT VIEW

(Above and left) If you follow these working drawings, you can come up with your own shooting bench. This particular bench is designed to accommodate the needs of both left- and right-handed shooters.

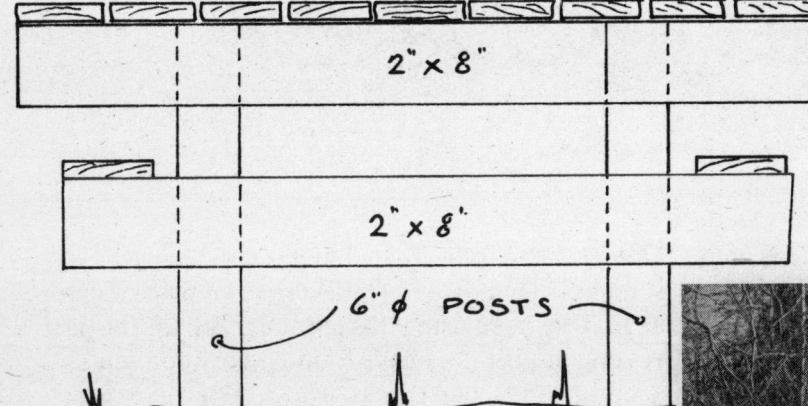

Here is the finished shooting bench. It is designed for right-handed shooters. Made from a design supplied by gun writer Jim Carmichel, it's well suited for sighting-in chores.

One of the handiest items you can have for the above purposes is a shooting bench. My own shooting bench was built from a design supplied from Jim Carmichel. This bench is only for right-hand shooters; however, plans for a right- and left-handed bench are shown here.

This particular bench was built from plans similar to the author's; and, while it is decidely in need of repair, it should be mentioned that this bench pretty well withstood the elements, and served the needs of many shooters for over 30 years!

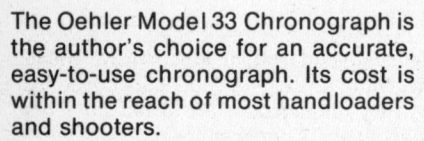

The Oehler Model 33 Chronograph is the author's choice for an accurate, easy-to-use chronograph. Its cost is within the reach of most handloaders and shooters.

Another item of interest—especially for gunsmiths who handload—is an electronic chronograph. At one time these instruments were very expensive and only factories or other professional outfits could justify the expense of purchasing such equipment. However, recent miniaturization of electronic components has brought the chronograph within the budget of many serious shooters.

In general, chronographing is the determination of the speed of a projectile, usually expressed in feet per second (fps). This is accomplished by recording the time the bullet takes to pass from one point to another—the "start-stop" points being screens of either paper, plastic or simply light activated. One of the better chronographs, and the easiest to use, is the Model 33 manufactured by Oehler Research. It includes new-design "Skyscreens" that cost very little each to replace if damaged. I've been using this chronograph for the past several months and have found it very convenient, accurate and a pleasure to use. It reports recorded velocity immediately after each shot is fired plus the number, in sequence, of the shot. The hooded readout is easy to see, and the instrument can be set (internally) for a variety of screen spacings. At the end of a test session, pushing the "Summary" button successively gives: lowest velocity, highest velocity, extreme spread, standard deviation and average velocity.

In the Oehler Model 33, time is measured by counting the ticks of a very accurate electronic clock. The clock ticks at the rate of one million pulses per second. As the bullet passes over the first skyscreen, a signal is sent to the chronotach telling it to start counting the pulses. When the bullet passes over the second skyscreen, a signal is sent telling the chronotach to stop counting the pulses and to then display the time or convert the distance and time to velocity for the display. All this takes less than one-tenth of a second after the shot is fired. Not only does the Model 33 compute velocity from time and distance, but it automatically examines the data from each round recorded and computes the essential statistics for velocity at the end of a test lot. While this may seem radical for a handloader's chronograph, the best industrial units used this technology for years before it was extended to the handloader's market.

To use the Model 33 chronograph, remove the cover by first removing the two screws on each side. The distance switch is at the center of the electronic circuit board and is usually set at 10 feet when the unit is shipped from the factory. The distance shows in little windows as you look at the switch from the rear and can be readily changed by rotating the switch elements using the knurled grip showing just above the numbers. Set the numbers for your spacing in feet.

While the cover is off, install six size "D" flashlight batteries. Alkaline batteries are suggested for best performance and long-range economy, but ordinary zinc-carbon batteries will normally work well for a few hours. Install three batteries in each tube. The positive tips of the batteries fit into the red insulating washers on the battery holders. If the total battery voltage drops below 6.6 volts, the decimal point in the lower right corner of the display will appear. This is a positive indication that the batteries are low and the system will soon fail to work properly. If you see no digits displayed when the unit is turned on, it's time for fresh batteries.

The initial setting-up of the skyscreens is a little troublesome, but once in place, actual chronographing is very simple. The bases of the skyscreens should be mounted so that they are 3 to 5 inches below the bore line and between the gun and the downrange target; therefore, any shot that comes close to hitting the target will *not* hit the skyscreens.

Connect the cables from the skyscreens to the input jacks of the chronograph so that the screen nearest the muzzle is connected to the start input. (Make sure that the plugs are pushed all the way into the jacks.)

Turn the chronograph on and the unit will immediately display 0 for velocity and 00 for round number. Shoot over the screens and the display will immediately show the velocity at the left side with round number 01 at the right side of the window. Six-tenths of a second after the velocity is displayed, the system is reset and ready for the next round even though the display continues.

After firing a test lot of ammo, the chronograph will display the summary. The summary is started by pushing the *summary* button. You can request a summary at any time. The first number displayed after pushing the display button is the lowest velocity encountered in the lot and will be identified

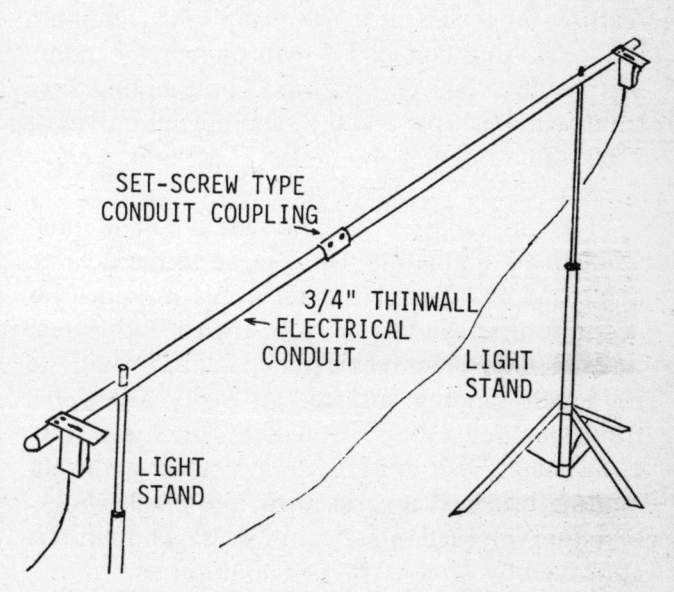

When mounting your chronograph's sky screens, you might want to consider this set up — it's easy to erect, take down and transport.

by "LO" in the display window. After observing and recording the low figure, push the button again and the display will show the high denoted by "HI." Push the button again to display the velocity range or extreme spread denoted by "ES." Push the button again to display the average velocity denoted by an "A." Push the button again to display the standard deviation denoted by "SD."

If you push the button one more time, the display will show a velocity of zero and the number of valid rounds included in the summary. At this point you can either fire more rounds to be included in a composite summary or cycle through the summary display again. The system will not recognize signals from the skyscreens during the display of the summary until you reach the point where the round number and zero velocity is displayed. Turning the unit off will clear all the statistical information and it will be ready for a new lot when you turn it back on.

Band Sanders

A new motorized table top disc/belt sander has been recently offered by Dremel which should be ideal for sanding, shaping, polishing, cleaning, sharpening and many other uses around the gunshop. The new Dremel Model 730 is only 15-inches high by 10-inches wide by 11-inches deep and features a 1-inch wide by 30-inches long aluminum oxide sanding belt and 5-inch diameter sanding disc with adhesive backing. The sanding disc rotates at 4400 rpm and the sanding belt moves at 2700 square feet per minute. The unit weighs approximately 11 pounds.

The work table for the disc sander can be tilted 45 degrees to align the work piece to the desired angle and an adjustable miter gauge provides for accurate disc sanding at most angles. Other features include a removable platen which provides a rigid belt sanding surface, an easily accessible front/mounted ON/OFF switch, Universal 110-120V, 60 Hz belt driven 2.2 amp motor with self-limiting brushes, and an attractive black shock-resistant molded plastic housing. The unit is approved by Underwriters Laboratories.

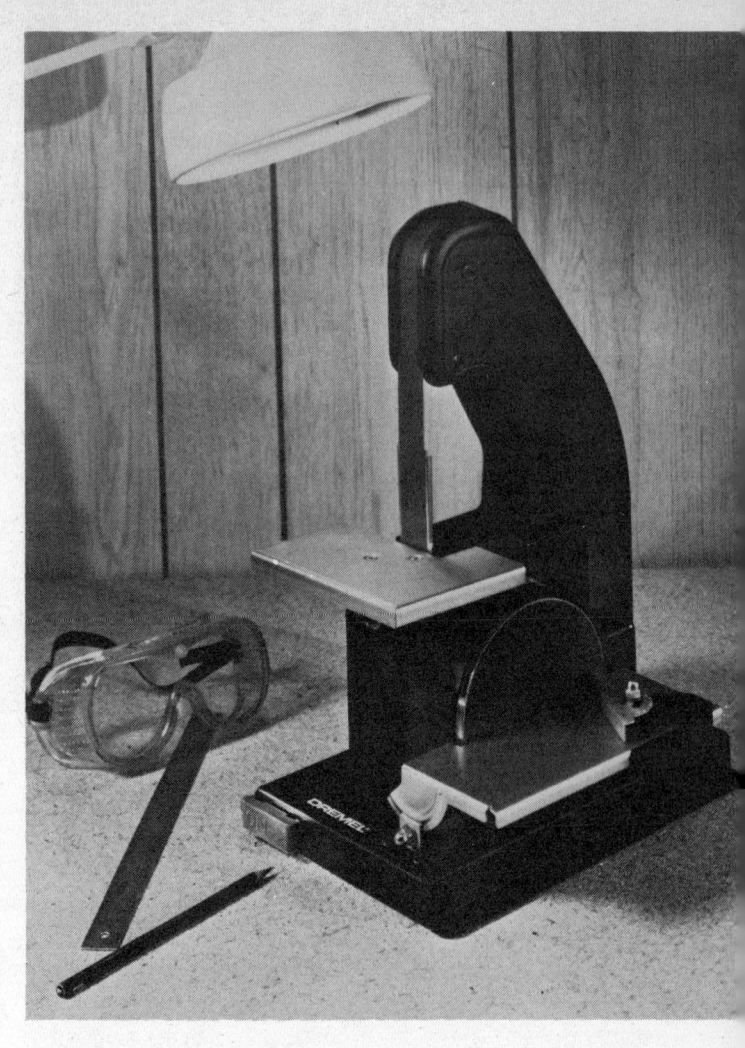

Dremel's combination disc/belt sander is a handy, small unit that's only 15 inches high. It fits on just about any workbench and handles chores ranging from sanding to polishing and sharpening.

For small welding jobs around the shop, the "Superwelder" comes in handy. The entire Superwelder kit (below) comes with everything you'll need except a 12-volt battery. To the right, the Superwelder has been hooked up and is ready to start welding.

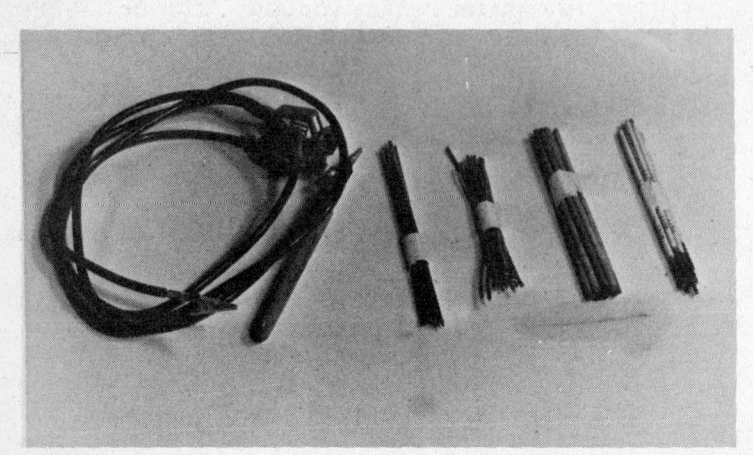

Superwelder

There is little doubt that an arc welder in any shop that works with metal is handy, if not indispensible, depending upon the type of work done—and how much. Few shops, however, have enough welding jobs to warrant the purchase of an outfit. They'd do better to take their few jobs to a professional welding shop and let them do it.

For small welding jobs around the gunshop, such as building up hammer sears, there's a little outfit called the Superwelder. For your investment you'll receive an electrode holder, two lead wires with battery and work clips, and an assortment of carbon, brass, and copper electrodes along with several pieces of solder. Although small, this outfit is not a toy. The same precautions must be taken as you would with one of the larger outfits; that is, you'll be working with molten steel and fire. Wear heavy gloves and a long sleeved shirt or jacket to protect your hands and arms. You'll want a welder's helmet for eye and face protection, or if you work behind a shield, at least wear safety goggles. Always work in a well ventilated area and do not breathe the fumes.

All you need to put this outfit in operation is a regular 12-volt auto storage battery. One of the wire leads is connected to the negative terminal of the battery and to the work. The lead to which the electrode holder is connected is secured to the positive battery terminal. You're now ready to use the arc torch for spot welding, cutting, heating, marking and soldering. As with any other job, practice is needed to do satisfactory work, so use plenty of tin cans and other scrap metal to practice on before you attempt to repair a broken gun part.

One of the best ways to learn cutting and welding with this outfit is with carbon electrodes. Connect the positive lead clip to the carbon electrode and your work to the negative lead clip. With your eye protection in place, slowly draw the carbon electrode across a tin can's surface, not touching the surface, but keeping the electrode near enough to maintain an arc. You will find that the arc will cut through the metal just like a hot knife cuts butter. At first you'll probably have an uneven cut, but after some practice at maintaining an arc, you'll find the cuts will be smoother and easier.

To spot weld with the carbon arc torch, place the two work pieces together and join them tightly with a C-clamp. Connect the negative wire to the work and quickly touch the carbon torch end to the work itself. You will find that you'll have joined the two pieces permanently. When spot welding, always be certain that the surfaces to be joined are clean and dry. Failure to weld and fuse together are usually due to dirt, water or insufficient contact between the metals to be joined. It is necessary to just touch the carbon to the work—don't hold it there for any length of time. However, if you don't maintain contact enough, the work will not join; too much contact will melt or burn the work.

This carbon torch may also be used for marking metals—even hardened steel. Merely connect the leads as described previously and write across the surface of the metal and the surface will be marked. When necessary, you can sharpen the carbon tip with a file to provide a better tip for finer marking. Again, battery life will be much longer between charges if you maintain an arc and do not make direct contact between the carbon and the work.

To solder with this outfit, first make certain that the surfaces to be joined are clean and dry. Then, using the carbon tip, heat the work so the solder flows. (Both soft and silver solder may be used with this outfit.) The carbon arc torch may also be used to heat any metal to soften it so it can be worked better, marked or annealed.

For your first practice welding jobs with this outfit, the manufacturer recommends that you use copper or brass. These electrodes will be used in the same way you welded, cut or marked with the carbon arc torch. Metal electrodes will take much more practice than the arc torch and requires a well-charged battery. Flux can be sprinkled on the work but you must be careful that only enough is used. If too much flux is used, contact is lost between the work and the electrode.

Striking and maintaining an arc is very similar to striking a match and requires a lot of practice for some individuals, while others get the hang of it more quickly. Practice will enable you to do much or even all of your own welding.

As mentioned previously, this Superwelder will not handle large welding jobs as will the more expensive models. However, with practice, you will find yourself using it to repair broken gun parts and for building up surfaces on metal parts. Even if you use this as an instructional device—and later go to the larger models for your actual work—it's still worth the money. There are several good books on the market that will help you become a

Brownell's Acraglas (above) is not only used for glass-bedding jobs, it's one of the best "tools" you can use for mending broken stocks or grips. The little Winchester Model 60A (right), came into the author's shop with its stock broken into two pieces — the repair was made with Brownell's Acraglas.

better welder. One is *Welding Technology* published by Howard W. Sams, Inc. You'll probably find it at your local library.

Brownell's Acraglas

You may be wondering why we are mentioning a material such as Acraglas in a book on gunsmithing tools. We are doing so because Acraglas has become a "tool" in nearly every professional gunshop in the country. Besides glass bedding for a 100% wood-to-metal contact for improving accuracy, Acraglas is one of the best "tools" I know of for making stock repairs.

A few months ago, a customer brought in a Winchester Model 60A, .22 caliber rim fire single shot rifle with a broken stock. The stock had been broken completely in two when the owner ran between two trees with the rifle in his hands. The butt stopped abruptly on the tree to the left while the barrel did the same on the tree to the right; the result was a completely broken stock at the forward end of the pistol grip. The owner then tried gluing it, but after being subjected to a little dampness, the stock again separated.

This little rifle had been given to the owner by his favorite uncle, and he wanted it preserved (as near as possible) in its original condition. A replacement stock was not readily available, and he didn't want to go to the expense of making a new one from a walnut blank. This is where Brownells

Acraglas kit came in.

I re-broke the stock where it had been broken previously and then removed all of the old finish with G96 Finish Remover. Dents were raised with a soldering gun and a damp cloth while scratches were removed with abrasive paper and the sharp edge of a piece of broken glass. The rough edges of the break were cleaned with a toothbrush dipped in AWA 1-1-1; next came the mixing of the Acraglas components.

The mixing ratio of Acraglas is 4:1; that is, pour 1-oz. of Acraglas resin into the graduated cup that comes with the kit. Stop pouring, however, just before the 1-oz. mark is reached and allow the resin to level in the cup. Then slowly pour the balance needed to the 1-oz. mark on the cup. Add one-quarter ounce of Acraglas hardner, using the same pouring procedure as before. Be sure the cup is level so you'll obtain an accurate reading, and don't add more than ½-oz. as too much hardner prevents proper hardening.

Acraglas in itself is glass-clear, but a tube of special duPont dye is furnished with each kit. With this you can color the Acraglas mix to blend with the color of the individual stock. It is better, however, when repairing stocks to have the Acraglas a little lighter rather than darker than the wood.

Open the small pack of dye and pour a sufficient amount into the mix to obtain the color desired. Stir the mixture gently, smoothing out the lumps of stain against the side of the cup with the paddle furnished with the kit. (At this point, add more stain if needed.) After two minutes (timed) stirring, add one-half of the packet of "Floc" to the mix if you're using the mixture for bedding. (In this case of a stock repair, no Floc was used.) The mixture was then applied to the broken gunstock and the two parts were carefully joined—aligning the jagged edges of each piece precisely. Then the entire assembly was clamped tightly in a padded vise. Excess solution that emerged from the crack during compression was wiped off the outside of the stock before letting it set and harden further.

A couple of hours after the application, the stock was removed from the vise, and surplus exposed Acraglas was removed with a dull knife, being careful not to scratch the wood in the process. The stock was finished in the normal way. Although a hair line is visible where the break was (if you look closely), the stock is as strong—if not stronger—than it was originally.

When used in conjunction with inletting, allow 1/16" to 1/8" clearance in the barrel channel and behind the recoil lug. The wood in the barrel channel should be left rough rather than sanded smoothly to add strength to the wood itself by creating more exposed wood surface and therefore realizing the full advantages of Acraglas' strength-giving qualities. Be sure to use sufficient release agent on all metal surfaces which might come in contact with the Acraglas solution. Shake vigorously while in the jar and then apply to the metal surfaces.

One of my customers recently purchased an Acraglas kit from me to bed his Winchester Model 70. The next day, he came back to the shop with the barrel permanently attached to the wood. He had not read the first page of the instructions accompanying the kit and had failed to use the release agent. By saturating the area with Acetone, and striking the barrel with a rubber hammer, we were finally able to break the barrel loose from the stock.

For bedding, mix Acraglas as described before; use the Floc and stir the mixture two minutes longer to assure that this mixes thoroughly with the solution. Then with the paddle, spread the prepared Acraglas in a ridge down the center of the barrel channel to prevent air from being trapped when the barrel is seated. Also fill the recoil lug recess sufficiently to completely fill the recess when fitted. Firmly press in the release-agent coated barrel and action to the desired depth.

When Acraglas shows signs of hardening after an hour or two, remove all surplus exposed solution with a dull knife or spatula, being careful not to scratch the gun's metal or wood finish. Leave a small bead of Acraglas above wood between the stock and metal to be sanded to contours of stock after final curing.

Under normal conditions, the barrel and action can be removed from the stock within 24 to 36 hours. In cases of extremely tight fits, the careful use of a soft rubber mallet will help in getting the metal and wood separated. Should you find bubbles or the like between the metal and Acraglas, these can be filled by applying fresh mixed Acraglas in minute quantities and re-bedding the barrel and action. Bonding will be complete and as strong as if the void had not existed. Be sure that all voids to be filled are completely free of the release agent before filling.

Locating Top Dead Center of Gun Barrels

Every gunsmith is called upon from time to time

The T.D.C. center-finding device (above) is used to find the exact dead center of round stock (barrels) as can be seen to the right. It's precise, and it allows you to accurately locate front sight screws or sight holes.

to install sights on shotgun and rifle gun barrels, and there's always the problem of finding the exact top dead center of the barrel. The T.D.C. Company of Portland, Oregon offers a handy device that is designed to determine the exact top dead center on secured round stock such as gun barrels, providing the barrel and action are level. This can be checked using the T.D.C. tool as a level.

The device is placed on the barrel as shown. The hook is designed to determine the exact distance from the muzzle to the front sight. When the centering bubble is precisely aligned between the reference lines, the hole in the top of the device is exactly top dead center of the barrel. Then, using the "dimpler punch", *lightly* tap that spot with a hammer to mark the barrel. The level in the T.D.C. is extremely sensitive—again, just a *slight* tap with the hammer or you might dislodge the T.D.C. setting. A standard center punch may then be used to enlarge the "dimple" if necessary.

The imaginative gunsmith will find many uses for the T.D.C. centering device. For instance, it can be used for layouts on extractor slots or as a common level in "free" setups, etc. If you can't find this device locally, they can be ordered from Frank Mittermeier.

18
PLATING FIREARMS

NICKEL PLATING has long been a favorite finish for many handguns. It provides decorative effects; protection against rust and corrosion, and a wear-resisting surface. Although nickel has been the traditional favorite, other metals have included chromium, gold, silver, brass and copper. Chromium, for example, when applied to metal gun parts provides a surface harder than the hardest steel, which protects the base metal, reduces wear, lessens friction and, at the same time, provides an attractive appearance.

Most metal plating is accomplished by a process called "electroplating" which uses an electric current to deposit the plating over the base metal. In general, the object to be plated becomes the cathode (negative plate) in an electrolyte cell that contains (in some chemical compound) the type of metal which is to be plated onto the base material. Anodes are used on all sides of the object so that electricity may flow from all directions to the article being plated and cause an even deposit of the plated metal.

The exact chemicals, currents, voltages, temperatures and general procedure will vary with the kind of metal being plated and the type of method being used. For example, nickel plating often is done with an electrolyte containing nickel sulphate or nickel ammonium sulphate, to which is added ammonium sulphate to increase the conductivity; some acid to help keep the anode rough; and something like glue or glucose to make the plating extra bright.

The anodes may be of some material, such as carbon, which is not affected by the electrolytic action. When using this method, all the plated metal must come from the electrolyte and chemicals containing this metal must be added to the liquid at various intervals. In other plating methods, the anode is made of the plating metal. As an example, in plating with brass, the anode is of brass. Then brass dissolves from the anode into the electrolyte which is deposited from the electrolyte onto the cathode or object to be plated. The object of this method is to get metal dissolved into the bath (electrolyte) as quickly as it plates out. As the anode metal dissolves, it generates a voltage just as dissolving a metal generates a voltage in a conventional storage battery. Under ideal conditions, this generated voltage would equal the voltage consumed in depositing metal on the cathode, so the external source would need to provide only enough voltage to overcome the resistance in the cell and the connections.

Before we get into the plating process, it should be observed that you may not want certain areas of a gun plated. A good example would be the sear

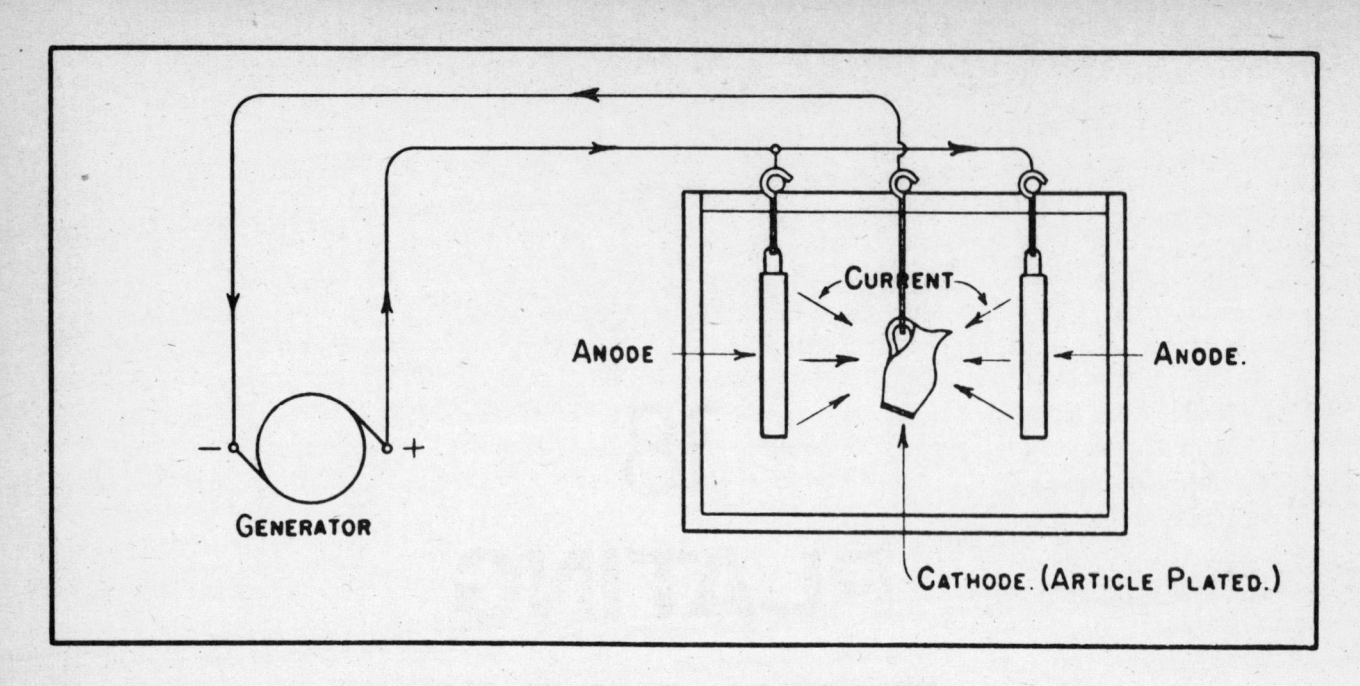

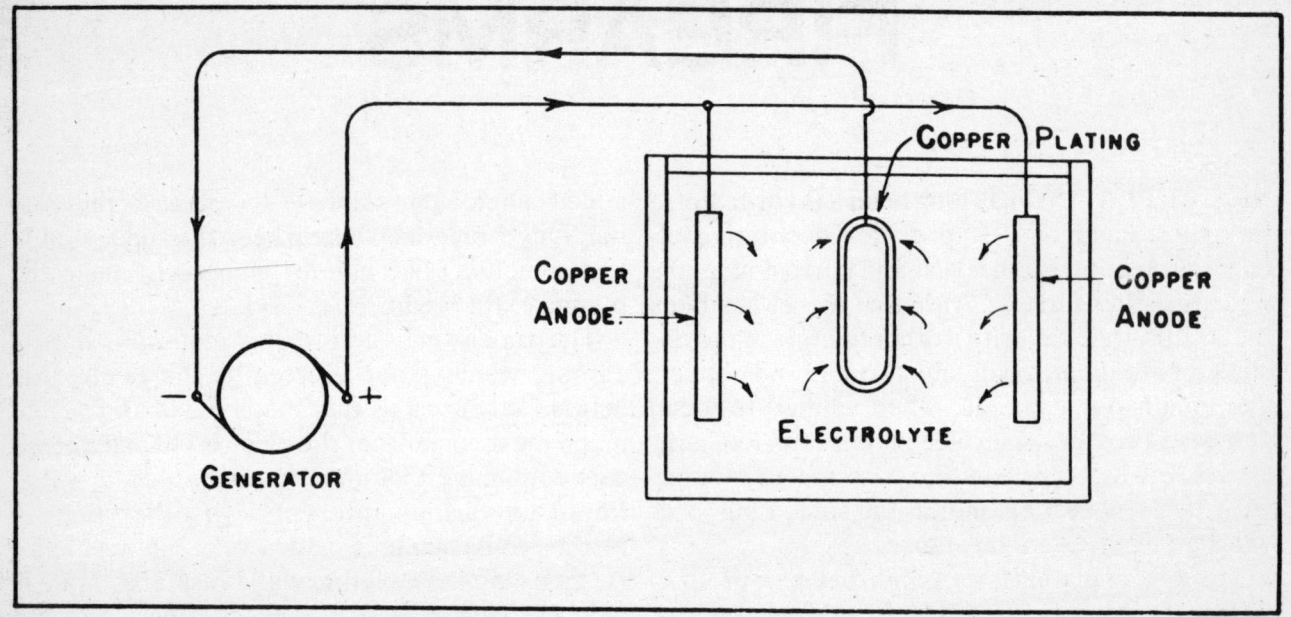

(Top) When plating, anodes are used on all sides of the object being plated so that the electricity may flow from all directions, to that object, so that an even deposit of plating metal results. In this case, the electrolyte solution contains the plating material. (Above) In other plating methods, the anode is made of the plating metal. In this case, the anodes are of copper and dissolve into the electrolyte which in turn deposits the copper plate on object.

engagement areas on a handgun hammer and trigger. Until recently, you had to plate those parts and then redress them to work as perfectly as they did prior to plating. Brownell's now offers what they call their Stop-Off Lacquer. You simply apply the lacquer to the portion of any part you don't want plated and plate the entire part normally.

When the plating process is done, take some Brownell's Stop-Off Stripper and wipe it on to the area lacquered prior to plating—that lacquer and any build up of plating comes right off. Believe me, it's a super system for keeping the trigger pull "just the way you had it."

Stripping

Stripping is used to remove old plating, and to brighten up oxidized surfaces and also to clean inaccessible places. In general, there are four ways to take nickel plating off a gun. First, the finish may be removed electrically; that is, the object to be stripped becomes the anode, and a piece of metal such as brass or stainless steel is used as a cathode. Secondly, you can polish it off in much the same way as you would in polishing off old blue on firearms.

Pure nitric acid will also strip nickel from iron or steel without attacking the base metal as long as it is pure. However, such conditions as humidity in the air changes the purity of the acid, and then it can literally dissolve a gun in a very few minutes. Nitric acid is also very dangerous to handle.

The fourth stripping system uses chemicals for the process. It's a companion system to the electroless nickel plating system offered by Brownell's. It will not pit or etch steel. It has excellent stability and a long, active solution life. Because of an easy replenishment system, solution life can be further extended which cuts the operating costs. The components contain no cyanide so they can be shipped easily via UPS. The solution operates at a slower rate of stripping than most other systems which give complete control, and it will remove most nickel plating on firearms.

To strip, the gun should be disassembled and heavy emphasis placed on cleaning. This thorough cleaning prior to beginning the stripping sequence removes all gunk, gun oils and so on. The cleaning must be thorough to allow the stripping operation to work efficiently. The stripping steps are as follows; detailed steps follow the general outline below:

(1) *Pre-clean:* Use trichloroethane on cotton swabs and brushes to remove as much foreign matter, powder residue, gun oils, etc., as possible. Do not use a petroleum based cleaner such as gas, kerosene, mineral spirits, or gun cleaners; they will leave a residue on the part.

(2) *Flowing Water:* (Use same tank as used for plating process.) Submerge parts for ten seconds and agitate to float away loosened residue.

(3) *Acid-Cleaning Tank:* Submerge parts for three seconds and agitate. This further cleans parts and removes foreign residue, especially oil.

(4) *Flowing Water:* Submerge parts for five seconds to flush acid cleaner from surface of metal.

(5) *Nickel-Stripping Tank:* Submerge parts in stripping tank until all nickel is removed from the bright steel base metals. The stripping solution must operate at 200-210 degrees Fahrenheit. Water lost by evaporation should be replaced during the stripping cycle in order to maintain the original volume of solution. Parts will have to be removed from the stripping tank to be thoroughly checked to see that they are completely clean of the nickel plating.

(6) *Flowing-Water Tank:* Submerge parts for two minutes to flush away all of the stripping solution. Allow stripped parts to air dry normally, or use compressed air to speed dry. The gun can now be polished or put back through the plating cycle. If you are not going to polish or plate immediately, be sure to oil gun surfaces with water displacing oil (nye oil, "HOLD," Brownell's No. 2 or some other basic rust preventative which does not contain *any* of the exotic penetrants which could contaminate future bluing or plating of the gun).

Two tanks are required for the stripping operation, and must be different ones from those used for plating to avoid cross-over contamination. Be sure to mark them plainly "FOR STRIPPING ONLY," and preferably keep them in a different storage area (or on a different shelf). The stripping tanks can be fairly small in size since you will rarely strip more than one gun at a time. The tank can be stainless steel (Grades 304 or 316 only),

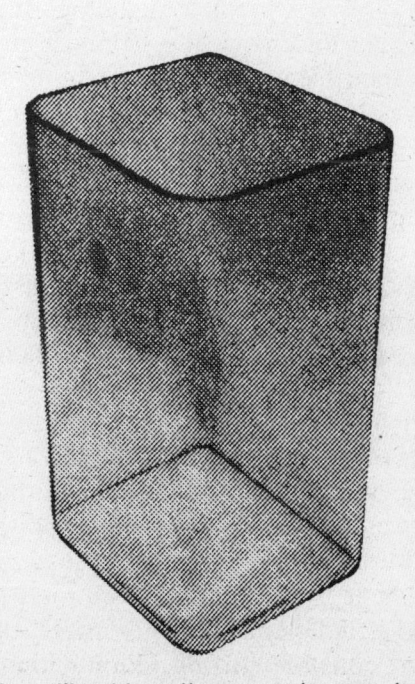

Plating jars, like this gallon pyrex jar, can be obtained from Brownells. Works for either electroless or electrolytic plating and is large enough to contain most pistol frames, barrels or rifle actions or trigger guards.

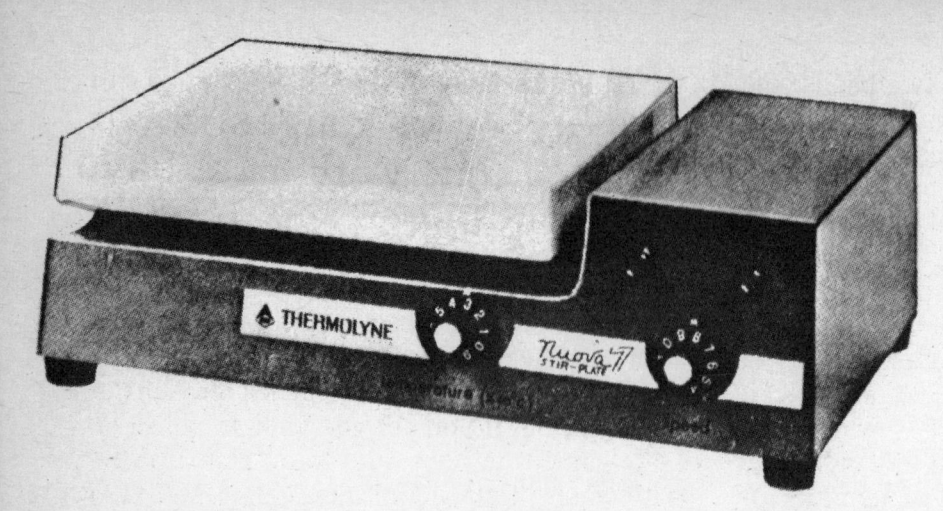

If you anticipate doing much plating, you might want to consider getting one of Brownell's Nouva-7 electric stir/hot plates. The unit gives you a constant source of heat and controlled agitation. It's also designed for chemically stripping gun parts.

ceramic, pyrex, quartz or other suitable materials that can withstand the 200-degree Fahrenheit operating temperature. Because of their convenience and availability, pyrex/laboratory tanks in both round and square styles may be used and are available from Brownell's.

If a direct gas flame is used for the heat source, the pyrex tank must be protected from thermal shock. (Special instructions are included with each pyrex tank ordered from Brownell's and explain in detail how to make a "sand bath" to protect the tank and keep it from breaking.) If you anticipate much plating, however, it is recommended that you purchase the Electric Stir/Hot Plate, also available from Brownell's. This unit provides a reliable source of constant, even heat plus thoroughly controllable agitation. It is specially designed for chemically stripping gun parts as well as their electroless nickel plating system.

The large 7⅛" square, heavy cast aluminum top has embedded heating elements and is machined flat for optimum heat transfer and uniform top plate temperatures. A "demand" thermostat maintains close temperature control and compensates for room temperature or line voltage fluctuations, holding surface temperatures within ± 3 degrees C. Heat indicator light tells when top is heating.

The stirring part of the unit features an extremely strong stirring torque from 60 to 1000 rpm. The Alnico V-drive magnet is located close to the top plate to assure strong magnetic coupling and to prevent jitterbugging. A solid state speed control gives excellent slow speed control, high starting torque and is independent from voltage changes, maintaining constant stirring action. Controls for the Electric Stir/Hot Plate are up front, easy to use and isolated from the heat of the top plate to assure long trouble-free life. When heating a one gallon jar of solution, the unit is capable of raising the temperature of the solution approximately 1 degree per minute. The unit is fully guaranteed to give excellent service. When using this heating unit, the pyrex tank can be placed directly on the heating plate.

The purpose of the acid cleaning tank is to clean only, and the solution should consist of 50% hydrochloric acid and 50% pure (distilled) water. The tank must be covered when not in use again, and, must be marked "STRIPPING ONLY" to prevent any mix-up with the plating tanks. To mix one gallon of solution for the acid cleaning tank, measure 2 quarts (64 fluid ounces) of clean water and pour into the tank. Measure 2 quarts (64 fluid ounces) of hydrochloric acid and pour very slowly into the water already in the tank. Remember, *always add the acid to the water and not vice versa*. When mixing this solution, *always* wear goggles and rubber gloves.

To mix one gallon of stripping solution, first wash the stripping tank with clean water to remove any residue or possible contaminate. Pre-measure 1 gallon of clean water in the tank, and make note of its depth by measuring it with a dip stick. Measure 51 fluid ounces of clean water (hot or cold) and pour into the stripping tank. Measure 32 fluid ounces of Brownell's Concentrate 778, and pour slowly into the water already in the tank. Immediately begin mechanical agitation of the solution at a moderate rate. Begin heating the solution, and bring it up 120 degrees F.

Continue by measuring 1.25 pounds (dry weight) of Concentrate 778-R. Slowly add this concentrate to the solution allowing the heat and agitation to dissolve the powder. It will probably take about 10 minutes before the powder is completely dissolved and the bath changes to a clear light-yellow color. Now add sufficient clean water to bring the total solution volume up to one gallon, and then bring the solution up to the operating temperature of 200 to 210 degrees F. Do not, however, exceed the 210-degree maximum. Check the thermometer several times to be sure that the heat setting is holding the temperature constant. When it is, the stripping solution is ready for use.

During use, the stripping solution will darken noticeably and, after 2 to 3 hours of use, it will become the color of deep mahogany, or very strong tea. This is normal and doesn't seem to affect anything. Parts should be suspended on iron wire, just as in the plating process as discussed later. Do not use any other kinds of wire. Once parts are submerged in the stripping solution, they should not be removed until stripping is complete to avoid contamination.

As water is evaporated out of the stripping tank, it should be replaced. Use the dip stick method, or make a mark on the side of the pyrex tank. Do not allow parts to stick above the solution level as the fumes from the stripping solution cause very rapid rusting and pitting—which does not happen to parts that are left submerged. The rate of stripping will vary greatly depending upon the type and thickness of plate that is being removed along with other factors. Most will fully strip between 45 minutes and 1½ hours. If parts do not strip in 2 to 2½ hours, the solution is too weak and must be replenished. On some guns the nickel plate is deposited on top of a copper plate which was put on the metal first as an undercoat for the nickel. These pieces will strip slowly, and the solution will turn the copper dark in color. However, as the copper is stripped away, the dark surface will disappear and all the plating will be removed down to the bare steel surface.

Agitation of the solution is important and is done at the same rate as for plating. If the solution is not agitated, stripping will be much slower because the stripping solution (remaining close to the metal) becomes saturated with removed nickel and slows down in removing more. Fresh solution must flow by the metal surfaces at all times to distribute the dissolved nickel throughout the full gallon of stripping solution. One gallon of fresh stripping solution will remove the nickel plating from about four Colt .45 semi-automatic pistols. After this, the solution normally must be replenished. To replenish the stripping solution, first make certain that no guns or parts are in the stripping tank. Then be sure the agitation system is working and the solution is being agitated thoroughly. Also, be sure the temperature is between 200 and 210 degrees F. Add 2 ounces (by dry weight) of Concentrate 778-R to the stripping solution and continue agitation until all the concentrate 778-R is dissolved.

This replenishment will normally allow the stripping of approximately the same amount of nickel as did the original fresh solution. However, after six replenishments of the stripping solution with Concentrate 778-R, the solution will become super-saturated with dissolved nickel and will fail to strip any more. Dump the solution, wash the tank thoroughly with clean water and mix up a fresh batch.

After stripping is completed, turn off the heat, leave the solution in the pyrex tank and allow both to cool to normal room temperature while still sitting on the source of heat. If you take the pyrex tank off the hot plate and set it on a cold bench or counter top, it's possible that the thermal shock will break the tank. Once cooled, do not store the stripping solution in the stripping tank. Pour it into a clean brown plastic chemical jug. Be sure to mark the jug "STRIPPER" and "POISON." Also, label that jug as to how many times the solution has been replenished. To reuse, simply pour back into the thoroughly clean stripping tank, bring up to heat with agitation to correct operating temperature and begin the cycle.

Stripping is a slow process and, of all the sequences involved with nickel plating, it's the most worrisome, so don't expect instant results. It must work slowly so as not to pit or etch the steel.

Plating Operation

Twelve steps are required to properly plate a gun. These are outlined below and in the flow chart provided on page 199. Do not take any shortcuts. Do each in turn, as given, for the time specified. Then go on to the next step. Layout of the plating room is completely optional, but do try to set up your tanks so a logical progression from tank to tank can be done handily. (The steps to follow are for Brownell's Electroless Nickel Plating; however, further information may be obtained from Brownell's directly.)

Polishing: Polish and prepare the metal exactly as for bluing. As in bluing a firearm, plating will not hide or fill scratches or pitting. A high gloss nickel finish requires metal preparation equal to "master-grade" bluing preparation; that is, polishing right on down to No. 555 grit. A satin nickel finish can be achieved by using glass beading (very fine sand blasting), or a coarse wire scratch wheel with light pressure on the gun.

Pre-Clean: While this step is not an absolute must, it is highly recommended for best plating results. Use AWA 1-1-1 and saturated cotton swabs to thoroughly clean all surfaces areas including holes, crevices, and the like. This removes any old grease and accumulated crud, silicone oils and other gun oils plus polishing residue; especially residue left by wax- or grease-based polishing compounds. Do not use petroleum based solutions like gas, kerosene, mineral spirits or gun cleaners. If at all possible thoroughly blow all parts clean with a medium to high pressure air gun to help clean off loosened gunk.

Flowing-Water Rinse: Submerge parts in the flowing-water tank for about 10 seconds to help float away any particles of foreign matter loosened by the pre-clean step.

Pickling Tank: Submerge parts for 3 seconds. The parts will start to "gas" (similar to Alka Seltzer tablets) and this further removes any foreign contamination.

Flowing-Water Tank: Submerge in tank for 3 seconds and agitate to flush pickling solution from surface of metal.

Hot Cleaner Bath: Submerge parts in tank for 10 to 15 minutes with operating temperature at 180 degrees F. Agitate occasionally to ensure good surface cleaning.

Flowing-Water Tank: Submerge for 5 seconds and agitate to flush cleaning solution from surface of metal.

Pickling Tank: Submerge for 5 seconds to "activate" the surface of metal for plating. Parts will start to "gas" indicating surface is activated. This step, in addition to cleaning, will make the nickel "strike" the metal surface quickly assuring a good initial bonding to the surface.

Flowing-Water Tank: Submerge for 3 seconds and agitate to flush pickling solution from surface of metal.

Nickel Plate Tank: First determine thickness of the plate you wish to apply. For optimum results, 3/8-mil plating depth is considered to be the best for guns. This thickness will require 45 minutes of submersion in the plating solution. Start the agitation system and submerge the parts to be plated into the plating solution. (Make sure they do not touch each other or the sides of the tank.) Be sure that agitation is thorough, and that whirlpooling does not develop. The solution must operate between 190 and 195 degrees F. optimum. Once the pieces are in the plating solution, do not remove them until the desired length of time has elapsed. If you do, even for an instant, you will ruin the plating job and have to start over. When the predetermined time has elapsed to plate the thickness desired, remove the parts from the plating solution.

Flowing-Water Tank: Submerge the parts for a minimum of 2 minutes and agitate to flush the nickel solution from the metal surface. There is no maximum time limit in this tank as the nickel plating process has been completed. Remove the parts from tank and allow them to dry normally or use compressed air for faster drying.

Inspection: Check all parts and components carefully to assure an even plate of all desired surfaces prior to assembly of the gun. However, if a part or component is not nickel plated as desired, it cannot be put back into the nickel tank. The part must be stripped of all nickel and reprocessed from bare metal! If all parts and components are satisfactory, wipe all parts clean and dry with a soft cloth to remove water spotting or lingering wet areas in holes, etc. If a high-gloss finish is desired, you can buff the parts *lightly* on a loose muslin wheel to bring up the luster, or use a Professional Nickel Final Polishing Cloth. If the buffing wheel is used, use only No. 555 white Polish-O-Ray and *very light pressure* as any form of polishing will remove metal, and you will be removing the nickel plate you just put on. Simichrome polish can also be used to increase the luster of a high gloss finish. Reassembly of the gun is the final step.

The complete plating procedure consists of two phases, both equally important. First is a preparation of the metal to enter the plating solution and second, the actual plating of the metal. Any attempt at short cuts in the procedure usually results in a poor plating job, wasted time and material. At first the process will seem lengthy, especially the cleaning steps prior to putting the piece into the plating tank. However, with a little practice you can complete the plating process in about the same amount of time required for a good blue job.

The preparation phase is a step-by-step sequence in getting the metal absolutely clean of all foreign residue and down to the bare metal. When metal is stripped of all protective coating, it absorbs oxygen and oxidizes very quickly when in the open air. Oxidation on the metal surface pre-

ELECTROLESS NICKEL PLATING STEPS

| 1 POLISH | → 5 seconds | 2 PRE-CLEANER | → 10 seconds | 3 FLOWING WATER TANK | → 3 seconds | 4 PICKLING TANK | → 3 seconds | 5 FLOWING WATER TANK | → 10-15 minutes 180° | 6 HOT CLEANER BATH |

| 7 FLOWING WATER TANK | → 5 seconds | 8 PICKLING TANK | → 3 seconds | 9 FLOWING WATER TANK | → 45 Min. for 3/8-mil 195° | 10 NICKEL PLATING TANK | → 3 seconds | 11 FLOWING WATER TANK | → 2 minutes | 12 INSPECTION |

NICKEL STRIPPING STEPS

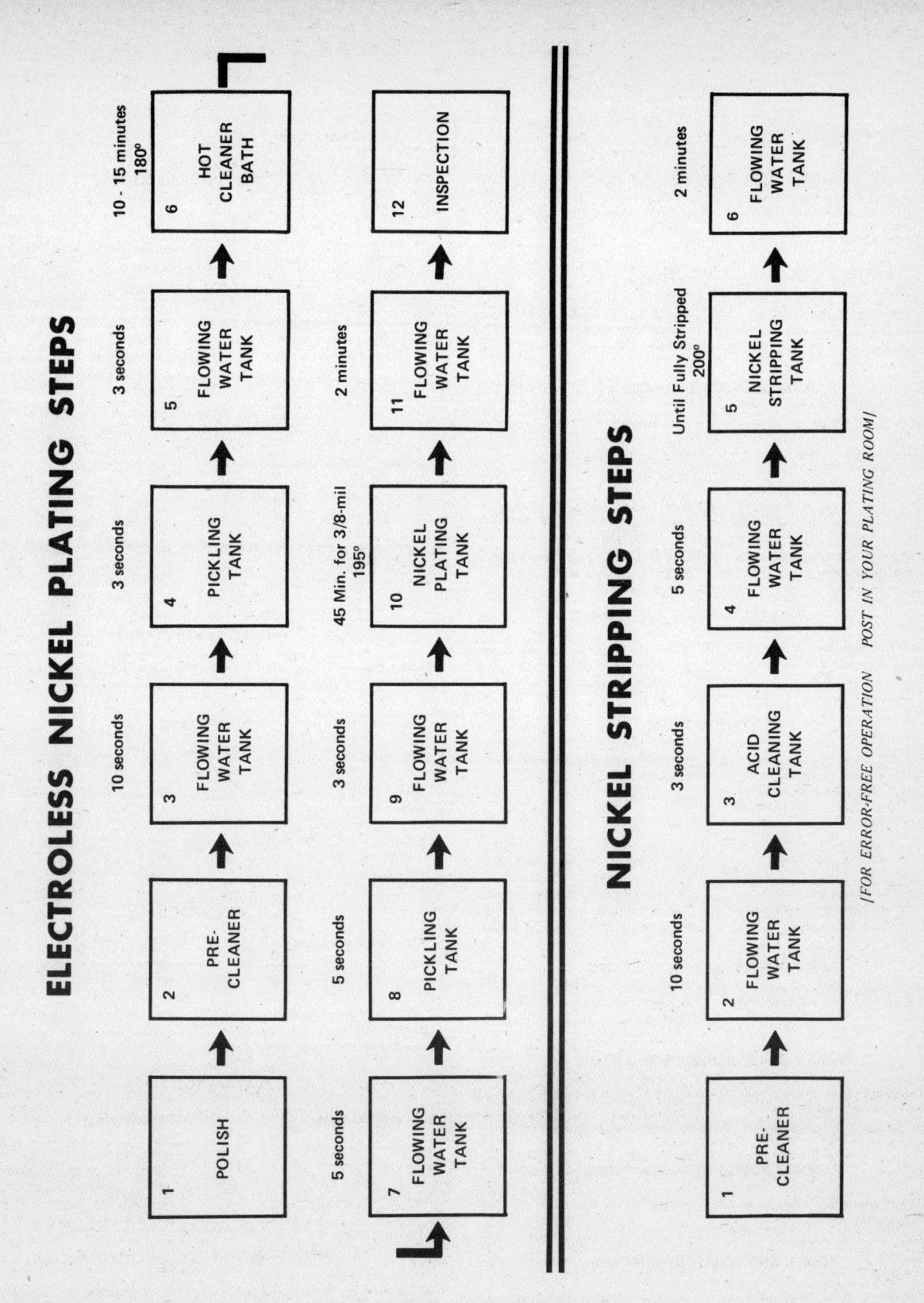

| 1 PRE-CLEANER | → 10 seconds | 2 FLOWING WATER TANK | → 3 seconds | 3 ACID CLEANING TANK | → 5 seconds | 4 FLOWING WATER TANK | → Until Fully Stripped 200° | 5 NICKEL STRIPPING TANK | → 2 minutes | 6 FLOWING WATER TANK |

[FOR ERROR-FREE OPERATION POST IN YOUR PLATING ROOM]

vents good initial bonding of nickel to metal. Therefore, the time between each step should be as short as possible. Work quickly but at a steady pace between each step. Timing in the tanks, in seconds, does not require a stop watch. If you say the words, "One thousand and one" it takes one second. Hence "one thousand and one, one thousand and two, one thousand and three," will take three seconds. Try it, it works.

Equally important is the flushing step between each tank. It prevents the carrying or "drag out" of chemicals from one tank to another tank with

199

TROUBLESHOOTING CHART

MALFUNCTION

Probable Cause — **Remedy**

NEW BATH DOES NOT PLATE

1. Improper make-up. — Bring bath into specs if can determine mistake. If not, discard bath.

2. Incorrect bath volume. — Adjust bath if can do so correctly. If not, discard.

3. Temperature too low. — Check Thermometer; heat source. Must operate between 190 - 200°F with 195°F optimum.

POOR SURFACE ACTIVATION

1. Acid too old or too weak. — If so, remake.

2. Oil contamination in tanks. — Find source, clean up, then remake all baths.

3. Poor rinsing between cleaning steps. — Increase agitation or water flow.

4. No nickel strike on stainless steel or hardened steels. — See special note on "Wood's Nickel Strike" to activate surface.

"SMUT" FORMS ON SURFACE AFTER PICKLING

Result of over-activation of surfaces by pickling solution. — Wipe off parts with cloth and repickle for shorter time and/or reduce strength of pickling solution.

CONTAMINATIONS

1. Check for galvanized, aluminum, copper or brass in tanks, racks, hanging wires, stir rods. Check for leaded steel, heavily soldered or brazed parts. — Discard contaminating metals & remake baths.

2. Residual acid left from stripping. — Generally will have to discard bath.

3. Containers, mixing cups, stir rods, etc. mixed between plate bath, cleaning bath, pickle bath. — Generally have to discard solutions. Always use separate mixing/measuring cups and label for which bath used.

RAPID DEPLETION OF A-1, B-1, 778

Poor chemical reaction: result of storage below 50° F. — Return to solution as described below. Ideal storage is 60° - 90° F.

WORKING LIFE DEPLETES TOO SOON

Plating solutions stored in tanks, open containers, and not light proof containers. — MUST ALWAYS be kept in dark brown chemical jugs when not actually in use to preserve working life.

SURFACE ROUGH WITH SCRATCHES

Probably not polished to fine enough grit before plating. — Plating will not hide anything!

ROUGH AND SCRATCHY SURFACE

Dirt on surface of metal entrapped under plating. — Strip, really clean this time and replate.

"PEBBLEY" SURFACE

Plating solution agitation too slow. — Increase speed to just before cavitation or whirlpooling starts. Surface can be cleaned up with 555 White polish on loose muslin wheel and very light pressure.

MALFUNCTION

Probable Cause — **Remedy**

"CRATERED" SURFACE

Plating solution agitation too fast. — Slow down agitator with speed control. Part must be stripped and replated. Will not polish out.

"SANDY" SURFACE

Took part out of plating bath and put back in during plating cycle. — Do Not Remove Parts Once Put into Plating Tank. You will get a "false plate" which must be stripped and replated if careful polishing does not remove.

DISCOLORATION ON SURFACE

1. Shaded "grey" streaks caused by parts touching, hanging loops too tight, too large a part in too small a tank. — Use larger tank; run more than one batch. Use "O" shaped hanging loops.

2. Adding water during time part is in plating tank. — Water to top-off volume can be done only when no parts are in plating tank; then temperature must be restabilized to 195°F.

SMEARS, STREAKING

Surface not clean. — Remember, Clean - Clean - Clean and Clean again. Strip and replate.

PLATING CAME OFF

1. Surface not clean. — Strip, reclean and plate.

2. Tried to plate Stainless Steel or hardened steels. — See special note on "Wood's Nickel Strike" to activate surface.

3. You took it out of the plating bath to look at it and put it back in for some more plating. — You cannot do this for it will "false plate" and may come off. Strip and replate.

PLATING TOO THIN

1. Tried to plate with depleted solution. — Check mil-usage record on storage jug. Make new solution then strip and replate.

2. Check surface area-to-volume of plating bath ratio. 1 gallon does only 114 square inches ½-mil thick. — May require larger container and more solution volume.

PLATING TOO THICK

Too long in plating bath. — Reduce time in plating bath. 1 hour gives ½-mil; 45 minutes gives ⅜-mil; ½ hour gives ¼-mil. Generally thick plating can be polished off with 555 White on loose muslin wheel adjusting pressure and checking fit often. Be sure not to cut thru plating.

CASE HARDENED/CAST STEEL PLATES UNEVENLY

1. Many Case hardened surfaces do not activate as well as unhardened steels. — Leave in pickle tank longer than normal until good gassing occurs.

2. High silicone content of some cast steels may inhibit plating. — Pre-clean to the point of "over-kill" with Trichloroethane to remove silicone.

3. Cast parts will usually not polish well enough for "Bright" Nickel Plating. — Suggest sandblasting cast surfaces before plating for a deluxe "Satin" Nickel Finish.

200

resulting chemical contamination of the second tank.

If you can blue guns, you can plate guns. It's only a matter of familiarization and practical experience. The major difference is that plating requires extreme measure to assure parts are clean prior to entering the plating solution. As with all types of metal finishes, it is best to make a test run by using scrap parts until you become familiar with the process instead of making the first plating job on a new gun. According to Brownell's, the most common cause of poor plating jobs can be directly traced to lack of cleaning or contamination of solutions.

It is possible to plate one or two parts for two hours and give them a one-mil plate build-up if desired. This can occasionally be done to tighten up loose fitting screws, pins and other slightly worn parts. Plating past this one-mil thickness is not practical. And, be sure to remember that every surface will receive the same amount of plate and increase by the same thickness. So, while you may tighten up threads of a screw, you may also keep the head from fitting flush, or fitting the counterbore at all.

Agitation of the plating solution is critical for too great an agitation will result in whirlpooling, which draws air into the plating solution. This extra air will "crater" the nickel plating being put on the metal surface and you will have to strip the piece and start over because the poor plating cannot be saved. Too little agitation will result in "pebbling" of the plated surface (little humps and random bumps). This is more easily remedied, for the part need only be polished carefully with 555 white Polish-O-Ray on a loose muslin wheel to remove the "pebbles."

Sand blasting of parts prior to plating is one of the most universally appealing finishes you can give your guns. Especially consider decorative use of sand blasting; for instance, sand blast the entire cylinder, then polish just the outside back up to bright, leaving the flutes sand blasted. Once plated, the contrast between bright and satin is very handsome.

Polishing prior to plating is more important than you can realize as you read this chapter. Every scratch, rough spot, wobble or nick is highlighted by the plating; it will hide absolutely nothing, not even those things bluing will sometimes hide. So, consider the satin finish if you don't want to go to the trouble of doing the high degree of polishing required for a mirror-bright finish.

Do not mix and add more fresh plating solution to a partially used batch. This is a tempting idea, but don't do it, for you then lose track of the plating capacity of the total solution.

Solution heat-up in the pyrex tanks can be greatly hurried by making a "tank jacket" from fiberglass furnace duct insulating panels. Cut those panels to fit like an open-ended box and seal the corners with duct tape. Make a lid from a pyrex glass sheet or hi-temp plastic, and be sure to use that lid on any enamel tanks. It will cut evaporation and shorten heat-up time.

Because of the acids used, parts not directly under the surface of the plating bath will rust badly—worse than in the bluing room. The small amount of water that condenses on hanger rods and falls back into the plating bath is of no consequence. But, do take precautions by keeping all easily rustable equipment and items out of the plating room.

If you are working on a rusty gun that you want to put through a rust or bluing remover solution, you must do so before you polish the gun. Most removers contain phosphoric acid which acts as a "passifier" to steel, and will prevent it from plating. Polishing will remove this passified surface, so you must polish thoroughly and completely. Then the pre-cleaning, pickling and cleaning steps in the plating sequence should properly "activate" the steel surface. If you notice that the part does not "gas" in the pickling tank immediately, you may have to leave it in for a few more seconds to be sure that the surface is sufficiently activated for the nickel plating to "strike" the surface and adhere correctly.

The troubleshooting chart provided in this chapter will help you to correct problems that may arise when using Brownell's Electroless Plating Method. When the chart advises to "strip and plate," it does not mean run the part through the stripper and then directly back into the plating tank. It means to take the part through the stripping sequence, then through the entire 12 steps of the plating sequence! If you skip a step and put a dirty part back into the plating tank, it will not plate correctly that time either. *You cannot skip any step of any sequence*.

Most of the material in this chapter came from Brownell's instructions for plating firearms which were compiled by Ralph Walker and the crew at Brownell's. We are, indeed, indebted to them.

19

GUNSMITHING: CONTINUING EDUCATION

GUN REPAIR isn't something you can learn quickly by simply buying a few tools, studying a couple of gunsmithing books, and then start tearing your favorite pride-and-joy apart. Not that it isn't possible to teach yourself this way, but you'll save a lot of time—not to mention spoiled work from trial and error—if you start with some professional instruction.

Ideally, the best way to learn gun repair is to attend one of the bona fide gunsmithing schools. Some of them include:

Colorado School of Trades
1545 Hoyt
Lakewood, CO 80215

Lassen Community College
P.O. Box 3000
Susanville, CA 96130

Montgomery Technical Institute
P.O. Drawer 487
Troy, NC 27371

Murray State College
Tishomingo, OK 73460

Oregon Institute of Technology
Small Arms Dept.
Klamath Falls, OR 97601

Pennsylvania Gunsmith School
812 Ohio River Blvd.
Avalon, Pittsburgh, PA 15202

Trinidad State Junior College
Trinidad, CO 81082

For some of you, attending one of these colleges or schools may not always be possible. You have to earn a living and therefore, full-time instruction is out of the question. In this case, you may find that one of the home study schools can solve the problem; location, working hours, age, and educational background provide no barriers for the serious, motivated home study student. Furthermore, a person taking a home study course can progress at his own pace—as fast as he or she can master the lessons or as slowly and irregularly (within reason) as necessary. Two gunsmithing correspondence schools are:

Modern Gun Repair School
4225 North Brown Avenue
Scottsdale, AZ 85251

North American School of Firearms
4500 Campus Drive
Newport Beach, CA 92663

Another way to learn the profession is to work as an apprentice under a professional gunsmith, but most firms are not too eager to hire a person as an apprentice unless he knows a little basic gun repair already; that is, they should be able to start earning the firm money at the beginning.

Any person who finishes any of these courses and obtains a comprehensive reference library (and knows how to use it) should have the basic knowledge required to start in gun repair work. What follows is a look at the curriculums of two on-campus gunsmithing schools and a review of the courses offered by two correspondence schools. As a gunsmith, I'm constantly asked about the courses these schools offer; the following will, indeed, give you an in-depth look at a few solid gunsmith training programs.

Montgomery Technical Institute

Montgomery Technical Institute is located in Montgomery County in the Piedmont section of North Carolina. Montgomery (a rural area) is in the hunting and fishing center of the Uwharrie Reservation. Approximately 75% of the county's 488 square miles is forest. (The Uwharrie National Forest encompasses over 46,000 acres.) Montgomery is the home of at least 21 hunt clubs and three bass fishing clubs.

Troy, the county seat, is less than 100 miles from the major cities of Charlotte, Durham and Winston-Salem. Montgomery Technical Institute is accredited by the Southern Association of Colleges and Schools and the North Carolina State Board of Education. The school provides day or night classes, financial aid and is approved for veterans.

The gunsmithing curriculum at MTI provides the student with instruction in metal machine operation, metallurgy, finishing, and woodwork. Specific instruction focuses on the use of hand and machine tools in metalwork: lathes, milling machines, bench grinders and surface grinders. Additionally, the gunsmithing student learns the principles of buffing, polishing and bluing; inlays, checkering and finishing stocks; barrel fitting and chambering. Repair work, consisting of diagnosis and correction of problems, is greatly stressed since this work is a substantial source of income for the gunsmith. Once these gunsmithing skills are learned, instruction focuses on the methods of manufacturing rifle, handgun and shotgun ammunition.

The gunsmithing curriculum consists of 24 months of study, divided into eight quarters of eleven weeks each. Classes meet 27 hours per week. At the conclusion of study, the student will not be a master gunsmith, but he will be a very advanced apprentice prepared to work with a master or establish his own shop.

First Quarter
GSM 1001 (Gunsmithing I)
Introduction: The introductory period will familiarize the student with the use of hand tools as he begins metal work. With metal files and hacksaws, each student will make a center gauge, drill gauge,

The "art" of hot bluing is taught at all of the gunsmithing schools.

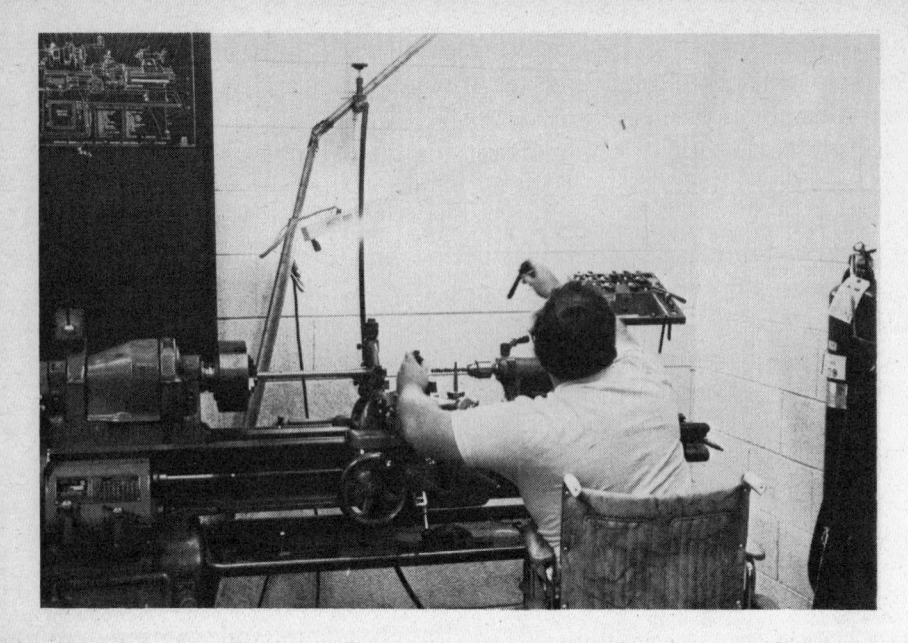

Lathe operation is also part of what the gunsmithing student will learn at one of the professional schools.

butt plate templates and pistol grip templates for future use. As he works, he will be taught blueprint reading and layout and will become proficient in transferring dimensions from blueprint to metal.

Since patience and precision are two of the most important qualities of a gunsmith, this period will give the instructor the opportunity to appraise the student's abilities. Depending on the ability of the individual, this phase should require about 54 hours of classwork.

Introduction to Machine Tools: Students will learn the basic skills involved in operating lathes, milling machines, bench grinders, surface grinders and the drill press. They will be taught the principles of operation and set-up of each machine. Safety measures will be stressed at every step of operation. As the student learns to properly use the machine tools, he will learn to correctly sharpen tool bits and drill bits.

Second Quarter
GSM 1002 (Gunsmithing II)
Machine Tools: Machine tool operation will continue and become more specialized as the students participate in the selection and manufacture of basic hand tools. Jigs and fixtures common to the trade. They will be given blueprints to read and interpret to make jigs, fixtures (holding devices), and specialized tools for use during the learning process and in future employment. The following projects will be required:

Bolt forging blocks
Bolt welding blocks
Barrel vise
Bushings
Action wrench and bolts for action wrench (2)
Bolt forging inserts
Adapter for action wrench for Remington, Savage, and Jap
Rear guard screw drilling jig
Buttstock clamp for shotgun inletting
Burnishing reamer, .22 Rim Fire
L.C. Smith mainspring compressor
Spanner wrench for pump shotgun fore-ends
Spring-winding fixture
Colt ratchet wrenches
Soldering clamp for front ramps
Colt crane extractor bushing wrenches (3)
Swivel counterbores (2 sets)
Revolver frame wrenches (5)
Reamer extensions for Clymer reamers (2)
Reamer wrench for chambering
Barrel centering tool for crowning
Barrel spinner
Action mandrels for barrel spinner (2)
Front guard screw bushing counterbore
Mauser guard screw counterbore
Turning rings for rifle barrel shanks (6)
Checkering cradle
Drift pin block
Shotgun magazine tube dent remover
Bushing Wrench, .45 auto

Oxyacetelyne welding, soldering, brazing, hardening and tempering of metal will be taught in conjunction with completing the projects. This

Heat treating of certain gun parts is something the professional gunsmith *must* learn; either at the elbow of a master, or, at one of the professional schools.

segment begins with lectures on nomenclature and safety procedures and continues through individual instruction in using the oxyacetelyne torch. Successful completion of projects in butt joint, lap, fillet, built-up and bolt welding, soft soldering, silver soldering and brazing are required.

Heat treating of steel, including hardening and tempering, will be taught. Students will use the electric furnace to heat-treat under controlled temperature and the oxacetelyne torch and forge for visual heat-treat by watching the color of the steel.

Third Quarter
GSM 1003 (Gunsmithing III)

Bluing of 10 firearms will be required. Students should obtain firearms that are in good operating condition as repair work will not be permitted in this phase of the course. These should consist of two-bolt action high power rifles, two pump shotguns, two semi-automatic shotguns or rifles, and two handguns. In addition, two double barrel shotguns will be included to teach the rust bluing method.

Buffing instruction will involve the use of the four-wheel method and the belt sander. In addition to buffing, polishing, and bluing procedure and formulae, this unit will include the operations, construction and maintenance of modern firearms in the commercial field. Various actions and their principles will be explained as students disassemble and reassemble firearms. Two methods of bluing, *Baker* and *Immersion,* and the formula and procedure for each, will also be taught.

Fourth Quarter
GSM 1004 (Gunsmithing IV)

Stocks: Students will begin by learning about the types of wood suitable for stocks and the reasons for their suitability. The choice of wood will be determined by individual preference.

Students will construct two sporting rifles custom made from stock blanks and one sporting rifle custom made from a semi-inletted stock. Construction of these three rifles is required. During the process, they will be taught the correct procedures for inletting by the use of hand chisels and rasps for the first rifle. Use of the router will be introduced in the construction of the second rifle. Using different colors and varieties of wood, students inlay designs of their choice in rifle stocks.

Checkering is an important step in stock construction. Students will learn to lay out checkering patterns and to transfer these patterns to the wood with proper checkering tools, using both hand tools and a power checkering head. This unit includes refinishing old stocks as well as finishing new ones. Students will learn to correctly remove old finish, sand, and apply new finish. They will sand, seal and hand rub to bring out the natural color of the wood. Oil, lacquer, and varnish finishing methods will be taught.

Fifth Quarter
GSM 1005 (Gunsmithing V)

Stocks: Students will use the procedures learned

in constructing rifle stocks and will construct one each of the three basic types of shotguns: stock bolt, box lock, and side lock stocks. As shotgun stocks are in two pieces, students will construct butt stocks and forearms. Forearm construction will include standard type and beavertail.

Custom handgun grips for revolvers and semi-automatic handguns will be made. The student will also learn to install contrasting wood, fore-end tips, and pistol grip caps. Finishing will be done according to procedures learned the previous quarter. Installation of recoil pads is also taught.

Sixth Quarter
GSM 1006 (Gunsmithing VI)
Barrel Fitting and Chambering: Students will learn to thread barrels, chamber, and set proper head space for military and commercial actions, and to adjust head space on rifles that need head space corrections. They will learn to correctly crown rifle barrels in the standard crowns and target crowns. This unit will also include taper turning to change the diameter of barrels, and contouring to replace old barrels with new barrels having the exact dimensions.

Students will be taught to install poly-chokes and to modify existing chokes on shotguns. Installation of poly-choke ribs will also be included. Depending on individual ability, this unit should require about one month of class work to complete.

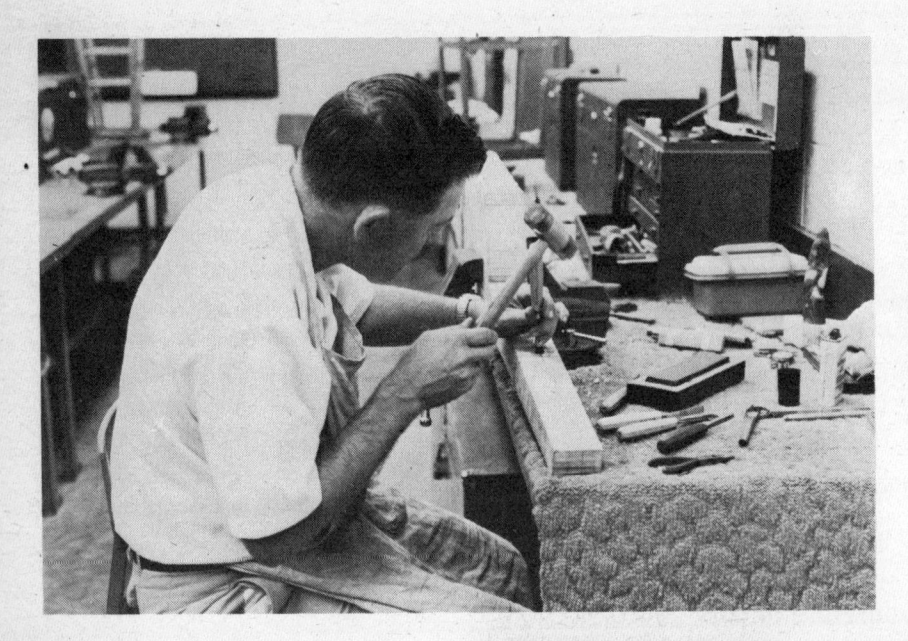

Stock making and inletting are vital parts of learning the gunsmith's trade. This student is inletting a trigger guard in a stock blank. Note the carpet-padded bench.

This student is setting up a lathe for a chambering job.

Sight Mounting: Approximately two weeks of class will be spent on installation of scope mounts. This will include two-piece mounts, one-piece mounts, side mounts, and target mounts. Students will learn to install receiver sights and open sights, and must be able to cut dovetails in the barrel for the installation of sights on rifles and handguns. They will also be taught how to boresight in the shop and how to install shotgun beads.

Introduction to Repair Work: Since repair work is the gunsmith's major source of income, emphasis will be on diagnosis and correction of malfunction problems, manufacture of parts and the installation of factory parts. For the remainder of this quarter, students will begin to repair firearms. The instructor will verify each diagnosis and procedure for repair before any work is done. All repair work will then be double checked by the instructor and must be done to his satisfaction.

Seventh Quarter
GSM 1007 (Gunsmithing VII)

Students will continue to diagnose and correct malfunction problems under the direct supervision of the instructor. They will be given progressively more advanced problems to solve and more complicated parts to manufacture.

Students will be instructed in accurate record keeping of time and expense involved, particularly concerning the manufacture of parts in the shop. The instructor will continue to verify malfunctions, diagnoses, and procedure for repair, and double check to be sure the work is properly done.

Eighth Quarter
GSM 1008 (Gunsmithing VIII)

Students should have enough experience and training to quickly recognize common malfunction problems and should be able to work with a minimum of supervision.

The instructor will continue to verify malfunctions, diagnoses, and procedures for repair and double check to see that the work is properly done. The more time students spend in practice and repetition of repairs, the more proficient and skilled gunsmiths they will become.

Gunsmiths are required to have a Federal Firearms License. There will be class lectures and instructions on procedures for applying for this license and the necessary record keeping involved to satisfy the requirements of the Bureau of Alcohol, Tobacco, and Firearms. In anticipation of opening his own shop, the student will be instructed on applying for and obtaining various city, county, and state licenses required, and the federal, state, and local laws governing the establishment of a gunsmith shop and the sale of firearms. On file in the classroom will be copies of firearms legislation from each state.

Reloading: Approximately one week of the final quarter will be spent learning to assemble reloading components into rifle, handgun, and shotgun ammunition. Students will also review ballistics, bullet weights and powder charges.

Special Note on Related Courses

Gunsmithing students will be required to take communication skills, human relations, and one elective before they are eligible for graduation. Also, they may be required to take a course in the fundamentals of mathematics if such a need is determined. Additionally, students in gunsmithing may take courses in beginning typing, small business operations, business law, small business taxes, the metric system, and any other course that is taught in the individualized instruction center in which they might have an interest. The students may take these courses at their convenience.

The student will be required to obtain the following tools during the periods indicated.

Introduction:
1. Tool box (such as Kennedy Machinists Chest 526)
2. 6" steel rule
3. Scribe
4. Hacksaw (18 teeth per inch)
5. Flat file 6"
6. Flat file 8"
7. Flat file 10"
8. Half round file 10"
9. Triangular file 4"
10. Triangular file 6"
11. Needle file set
12. File card (file cleaning brush)
13. Machine tools textbook

Bluing:
1. Ball peen hammer 8 oz.
2. Plastic tip hammer 6 oz.
3. Pin punch set (4 piece)

4. Brownell's screwdriver and tips, #81 solid handle
5. Pin vise
6. Safety glasses

Stock Tools:
1. Wood chisel set
2. Surform round
3. Surform half-round
4. Surform blase—flat
5. Cabinet rasps 8"
6. Cabinet rasps 10"
7. Cabinet rasps 12"
8. Half-round bastard cut 8"
9. Half-round bastard cut 12"
10. Round file 6"
11. Round file 8"
12. Stock wood—2 blanks
13. Semi-inlet stock (1)
14. Tip wood (3)
15. Actions (3)
16. Barrels (3)
17. Shotgun blanks (3)
18. Block hand sander
19. Sights
20. Recoil pads
21. Sling swivels

Machine Tools (optional):
1. 0-1 micrometer
2. Lathe centergauge
3. V-thread gauge

Colorado School of Trades

The Colorado School of Trades was founded in Denver, Colorado, on July 15, 1947. The school has given students interested in guns the opportunity to learn "gunsmithing" in a reasonable amount of time. To learn gunsmithing would take many years of apprentice training. The Colorado School of Trades has grown and expanded over the years and is considered by leaders in the firearms industry to be one of the finest schools of gunsmithing in the country.

At the present time the school is situated in Lakewood, a suburb of Denver. The area is in the heart of a business district which affords students the opportunity to seek employment while attending school. The Institution is situated in a 18,500 square foot building; approximately 15,000 square feet is devoted to shop area. The building has fluorescent lighting throughout the shop, classrooms and office areas. The building is heated by natural gas and ample doors and windows provide adequate ventilation.

Included in the school's equipment is a 42 unit power machine shop, bluing department, 164 metal student work benches, a handloading room that is equipped with up-to-date equipment for teaching handloading of ammunition and a student library. Welding benches are provided for teaching eight students at a time, with complete oxyacetylene welding equipment. For heat treatment, a 3.4, kw electric furnace is provided for

At all of the gunsmithing schools, the students have a full opportunity to discuss the progress being made on a particular project with their instructors.

In this instance the instructor is discussing the merits of a student's repair job on a Winchester pump action rimfire.

heat treating carbon steel. The work bench facilities and equipment accommodate 164 students per session; however, there are additional benches for miscellaneous purposes. Classrooms, which accommodate 40 students at a time, are available for class lectures and course theory.

An annex building is provided that contains 4,200 square feet of shop space and an air-conditioned classroom. Included are 100 steel work benches, eight power machines and gun bluing equipment, all lighted by fluorescent lights. The annex can accommodate 100 students at a time. The Colorado School of Trades' philosophy is: "To teach the design, function and use of different types of small sporting arms, their repair, making of parts, proper shop procedure and techniques to prepare students to conduct their own business or as employees in the gunsmithing trade."

The Colorado School of Trades' curriculum is as follows:

Related Subjects
(Class Room 1 hour per 9 hours of shop time)

1.	Orientation and General Safety	4 hours
2.	Hand Tools	5 hours
3.	Mathematics	6 hours
4.	Blueprint Reading	10 hours
5.	Drills, Taps and Sharpening	10 hours
6.	Grinding, Sanding, and Polishing	10 hours
7.	Gun Bluing and Browning	10 hours
8.	Stockmaking	18 hours
9.	Ballistics and Handloading	15 hours
10.	Use of Firearms Theory	5 hours
11.	Gun Sights	7 hours
12.	Welding	12 hours
13.	Heat Treatment	10 hours
14.	Engine Lathe	20 hours
15.	Milling Machine	5 hours
16.	Universal Grinder	5 hours
17.	Design and Function	65 hours
18.	Trigger Assemblies	5 hours
19.	Conversion	20 hours
20.	Business Training	20 hours
21.	Special Hand Tools	5 hours

Related Subjects
Total Hours (approximately) 267

Shop Operations *(7 hours per day)*

22.	Bench	300 hours
23.	Drill Press	25 hours
24.	Grinding, Sanding Polishing	24 hours
25.	Gun Blue and Brown	225 hours
26.	Stockmaking	500 hours
27.	Handloading	12 hours
28.	Welding	100 hours
29.	Heat Treatment	25 hours
30.	Use of Firearms Practice	30 hours
31.	Engine Lathe	185 hours
32.	Milling Machine	24 hours
33.	Universal Grinder	8 hours
34.	Barrel Fitting and Headspacing	35 hours
35.	Gunsight and Mounts	15 hours
36.	Chokes	10 hours

37. Bolt Action Guns	100 hours
38. Single Shot Guns	30 hours
39. Lever Action Guns	60 hours
40. Pump Guns	170 hours
41. Auto loader Guns	200 hours
42. Double Barrel Guns	150 hours
43. Black Powder Guns	30 hours
44. Revolvers	100 hours
45. Auto Pistols	100 hours
46. Trigger Assemblies	20 hours
47. Conversions	25 hours
Shop Operations	
Total Hours (approximately)	2493
Total estimated hours for the course (approximately)	2760

Correspondence Gunsmithing Schools

The only two gunsmithing correspondence schools that I know of at the present time are Modern Gun Repair and North American School of Firearms. Of course, there are scores of correspondence courses offered by colleges and universities throughout the country that fit in very nicely with the gunsmithing profession: welding, lathe operation, machine shop courses and blueprint reading are just a few. Most of these earn the student credit toward a degree. But let's concentrate on the two schools offering courses solely in gunsmithing.

In examining sample lessons supplied by Modern Gun Repair School and North American School of Firearms, each showed strong and weak points which were balanced out by similar variations in the other. Both schools are approved by the Veterans Administration for GI training, and both have a staff of well-known professional consultants—P.O. Ackley, Ralph Walker, etc. Also, time-payment plans are available at each.

Courses for both schools are surprisingly complete, well thought out and well written, but neither of the schools' courses are capable of turning out a finished gunsmith any more than any college or university. What these courses do offer is an educational background in gun repair and ballistics, confidence and judgment as to what jobs the students are capable of performing. Who could ask for more?

Modern Gun Repair School

Modern Gun Repair School is now operated by Mr. and Mrs. John C. Kadon in Scottsdale, Arizona. The total course consists of 40 lessons covering everything from setting up shop, stock finishing, checkering and carving and lathe lore to bluing, jeweling and polishing—even bookkeeping and advertising. A consulting service is provided for students on any gun repair problem at no additional cost.

Modern Gun Repair School has some excellent lessons on firearm disassembly and the remaining lessons were adequate to give the student a background in the subjects covered. The main drawback in the lessons I examined was the lack of suitable illustrations. Lesson 36A, for example—on inletting, fitting and shaping of stocks—was well written and accurate, but the lack of illustra-

Assembly and disassembly of firearms is an important part of any gunsmithing student's course of study.

tions made some of the points hazy. I doubt that a student who had never inletted a stock previously could complete a stock just by reading the lesson. However, I understand that the school has recently hired Ms. Kathy Desmond to illustrate all the lessons, and if the quality of these illustrations compares with the quality of the present text, this course is going to be hard to beat by anyone.

Tests are completed after each lesson and mailed to the school where they are graded by instructors Lour Kaar and Jack Burger. I would have preferred to have seen a little more comprehensive exam, but like their brochure says: "The knowledge gained by this course is more important than the grade you get."

North American School of Firearms

When Leonard Valore, Director of Educational Services at North American School of Firearms, shipped a package of sample lessons to me, opening it was a pleasant surprise. There was Brownell's Catalog, information on how to obtain a Federal Firearms License, and loads of other goodies. The lessons were well written, factual and extremely well illustrated—leaving little doubt as to what the lessons were trying to get across.

Right off the bat, Unit 1 goes into gun bluing and the explanation of "hot water" bluing is the best I've seen anywhere. The same unit continues with detailed information (drawings and text) on building a suitable work bench for gun repair work. The lessons to follow cover ballistics, troubleshooting handguns, shoulder arms, and black powder firearms; converting military weapons to sporting arms; firearms design, checkering, stock finishing and business administration.

All of the material examined was very easy to read and understand and the many illustrations created interest throughout. NASF also provides the student with a basic set of tools, a subscription to *Shotgun News,* and a lifetime consultation service.

Any person who finishes either of these courses and who obtains a complete reference library (and knows how to use it) should have the basic knowledge to make any gunsmithing firm a good employee. Some of the students may even step right into a business of their own.

20
INTRODUCTION TO PRO GUNSMITHING

THIS CHAPTER is directed mainly toward the prospective gunsmith. However, the problems of sufficient cash and credit, tools and equipment, shop location, layout and costs, as well as obtaining required training would no doubt be of great interest to the existing professional also.

Prerequisites of a Gunsmith

Gunsmithing can be a profitable business, but before entering into such a venture, one must be familiar with all the essentials for successful operation. There are many hazards of getting started—many more than most people realize—and the sooner the potential gunsmith realizes this, the sooner he will be able to operate the business with reasonable smoothness and impunity.

A person who is considering entering the gunsmithing business must first take a long hard look at himself to determine if he is in fact qualified to handle such a business. If he is not satisfying his current employer, chances are he won't satisfy his future customers in the gunsmithing business. On the other hand, a person who doesn't mind long hours and hard work and who has proven that he has a good knowledge of firearms and repair techniques, is familiar with modern shop practices and is able to get along with people, at least has one foot in the door.

Still, just because a person may be proficient in the operating principles and repair techniques of firearms doesn't mean that he is guaranteed success in the gunsmithing business. Too often, people emphasize their strong points and fail to recognize their weak ones. For example, a person may be an excellent machinist, a stickler for detail, and have a good knowledge of troubleshooting and repair of all types of firearms but, owing to lack of sufficient financing, executive ability, or general knowledge of the business, he is not qualified to operate a gunsmithing firm.

The requirements of a person entering the business are many but, aside from a knowledge of firearm repair, refinishing and maintenance techniques, *confidence* and *enthusiasm* are probably two of the most important traits a potential gunsmith can have. With confidence in himself and enthusiasm to conquer obstacles and make the business run on a profitable basis, most level-headed, well-trained gunsmiths will have a chance.

The prospective gunsmith should further have a good knowledge of firearm regulations (federal, state and local), a relatively good knowledge of firearm design, reasonable mathematical ability, the ability to accomplish goals through men (not by men), the willingness to make sacrifices, a knowledge of cost estimating and a good knowledge of business fundamentals. Any prospective gunsmith who lacks any of the above-mentioned requirements should take steps to acquire them.

Learning the Basic Fundamentals

Gun repair isn't something you can learn quickly by simply buying a few tools, studying a couple of gunsmithing books, and then start tearing your favorite pride-and-joy apart. Not that it isn't possible to teach yourself this way, but you'll save a lot of time—not to mention spoiled work from trial and error—if you start with some professional instruction. Ideally, the best way to learn gun repair is to attend one of the bonafide gunsmithing schools.*

For some of you, attending one of these colleges or schools may not be possible. You have to earn a living and therefore, full-time instruction is out of the question. In this case, you may find that one of the home study schools can solve the problem; location, working hours, age and educational background provide no barriers for the serious, motivated home study student. Furthermore, a person taking a home study course can progress at his own pace—as fast as he or she can master the lessons or as slowly and irregularly (within reason) as necessary.

Another way to learn the profession is to work as an apprentice under a professional gunsmith, but most firms are not too eager to hire a person as an apprentice unless he knows a little basic gun repair already; that is, they should be able to start earning the firm money at the beginning. Any person who finishes any of these courses and who obtains a comprehensive reference library (and knows how to use it) should have the basic knowledge required to start in gun repair work.

Proper Direction of Personnel

Most gunsmithing firms start out as a one-man operation, and this is how it should be. Expenses are kept to a minimum until the business starts to gain momentum. Eventually, however, a shop that does good work is going to be swamped with work and a decision will have to be made whether to start turning down work or hire additional personnel. Both ways have their advantages and disadvantages. The person who chooses to remain a one-man operation and turn down excessive work will continue to keep operating expenses down and probably have less worries and financial difficulties; but, if and when he decides to take a vacation, the business and work will have to stop. Furthermore, if he continues to turn down work, ill feelings may result and the local people take their business elsewhere. Eventually, his work may become slack, and he won't have enough to support even his one-man operation.

The person who decides to hire additional personnel will have more freedom (if he hires the *right* people) to take care of the business end of the operation; take a day off occasionally to fish for that lunker bass in a nearby stream, and to be the "front" man for the firm. He will also be able to get the work out faster, providing better relationships with his customers. But the financial burden is going to be greater. His employees have bills to pay and will have to be paid regularly and on time. If work gets slack for a few weeks, the employees payroll will have to go towards overhead if no profits are made.

Since a large gunsmithing operation entails getting a gun repair or refinishing project completed in the shortest possible time, in a workmanlike manner, and with the least possible expense, it follows that the man leading such an organization must be a rather highly qualified person. What are some of the qualifications of a gunsmith in regard to directing personnel? First, the gunsmith must be a leader. Not one who merely gives orders, but one capable of stimulating job interest and have his men turn out a good job not necessarily because they have to, but because they want to.

Ideally, the gunsmith should have the ability to do almost any gun repair job as well as, if not better than, the men under his supervision. There are some exceptions. A firm may hire an expert engraver to boost the services offered by the firm. Since gun engraving is an art in itself, the owner of the shop would not be expected to perform work as well as the master, although the master is being paid by the owner. The gunsmith should further be an organizer with the ability to organize his men, equipment and materials in an orderly manner that will produce maximum efficiency. His judgment should inspire confidence and his character should be above reproach. There are also other factors like education, physical and emotional stability, interest in the morale and welfare of his men—all of which encourage the men to respect the

---

*See Chapter 19 for a list of gunsmithing schools.

gunsmith, enabling him to properly direct them better.

Knowledge of Cost Estimating

In general, estimating the cost of gun work is the determination of a sound cost and proper price for a given project in advance of performing the work. While no estimate can be absolutely correct to the penny (except by accident), most can be surprisingly close to the actual cost of the project. The procedures necessary in making an estimate of a gun repair consist of calculating the necessary materials, parts, etc., and then adding labor and direct job expenses to arrive at an estimated cost. To this, overhead and profit are added to arrive at a bid price.

Those who perform gunsmithing estimates must also be aware of the many job factors that will vary from job to job. For example, a badly pitted barrel on a Winchester Model 70 in for rebluing is going to take more time than the same model gun that has no pits. The gunsmith must also take into consideration the depreciation and consumption of tools, purchasing expenses, interest on borrowed money, and so on.

Sufficient Cash and Credit

Many gunsmiths, especially those starting out in their homes, have been able to get started on less than $1,000 cash. However, for a business of any size, $10,000 to $25,000 cash should be considered the absolute minimum. There are many who have tried starting a business in gun trading and repair on less than this amount, using credit almost entirely, but many of them are still trying to get started.

Besides the cash mentioned previously, the gunsmith should also have a line of credit equal to three months' operating expenses. Therefore, if the average monthly operating expenses is $4,000, the gunsmith should have a line of credit equal to about $12,000. This is usually going to take security, and often means mortgaging one's home and other assets to obtain such credit. In any event, the prospective gunsmith should investigate the sources of his anticipated finances, and then make certain that the funds or a line of credit will be available at the time he needs them. A letter of confirmation from a bank and suppliers should be obtained.

How would you feel if you happen to sell, say, 40 new guns to customers in one weekend? You didn't have the guns in stock, but each customer gave you a deposit of $25 towards the total purchase price of, say $200, to be paid when the guns came in. The total amount paid by your customers equals $1,000, but where are you going to get the remaining money, of say $5000, to purchase the "ordered" guns? If you already have a line of credit with a supplier for this amount, you're in business. If not, you may have to forego the sales.

Shop Location

The ideal gunshop location, in my opinion, is in a rural area (with outside shooting-range facilities) that is within a 45-minute drive from a large city. Every shop that I know of in a location like this is busy seven days a week with a backlog of work running from one to two years! Of course, there are other factors involved. You have to provide good service and turn out top-quality work. But there *are* other locations.

My own shop is located in a rural area that is 12 miles from a town of only 7500 population. Yet, I get much work from the area—due to the good hunting and a high rate of gun enthusiasts—as well as much work from Washington, D.C., which is over 75-miles away. I would dare say that a good gunsmith who runs an honest operation will do well regardless of his location—even if most of his work comes from mail order.

In most cases, the best place to start out is in your own home. This keeps your initial investment and overhead down until you get on your feet, and you won't have an umpteen-year lease over your head if you decide to close shop after a few months (as would probably be the case if you leased a shop building).

Regardless of the shop's location, the physical arrangement of the shop is an important factor in providing for efficient servicing of the work. In some instances, because of the limitations of the type of building, floor area, type of building access, relation to streets, yard area, and so on, it may not always be possible to provide an ideal physical arrangement of facilities; however, intelligent planning can usually provide for the maximum efficiency under the given conditions.

Tools and Equipment

The type and amount of tools that a gunsmith will need to begin operation will naturally vary depending upon the type and volume of business that will be done. A one-man operation doing general repair work and some refinishing projects can get by on a surprisingly small amount of tools.

The basic gunsmithing tools listed below are found on the work bench of practically all professional gunsmiths. This tool list covers the minimum essential tools needed to do good work on the usual kind of firearm in need of repair. They are the rock on which to build or expand your professional assortment of fine tools and instruments. They should be the best quality that you can afford and should include:

- Workbench
- Large bench vise
- Gunsmith's screwdrivers
- Pliers
- Hammer
- Bench knife
- Spring vise
- Sight-base file
- Pillar file
- Scribe hook
- Cleaning brushes
- Wood rasp
- India stones
- Allen wrench set
- Woodworking chisels
- Checkering tools
- Checkering cradle
- Drill press
- Dremel Moto-tool with attachments
- Bench buffer/grinder
- Bluing tanks and source of heat
- Drift punches

A professional gunsmith can do a surprisingly large amount of gun repair work with only the above tools, but chances are you're going to need some additional items on your very first job. Don't let this worry you. Your first customer has probably been used to waiting from three to six months on gun repairs; and, the week or ten days it takes to get an additional tool or so should not make that much difference. From this point on, buy tools only as you need them. The above list of tools, although meager, will cost you, but all of them will be used frequently and will quickly pay for themselves. Others might not do so well, so go easy.

Parts and Materials

The subject of obtaining gun parts is covered in Chapter 20, Miscellaneous Gunsmith Tools. Materials, like gun parts and tools, are dependent upon the type of work the gunsmith plans to do and many other factors. In general, the beginning professional should obtain the following items and then add to the list as the need arises.

- Cleaning materials for shotguns, rifles and handguns
- Touch-up bluing solution
- Bluing salts
- Buffing compounds
- Stock refinishing supplies
- Silver solder and flux
- Case hardening compound such as Brownell's Hard 'n Tuff
- Supply of WD-40
- Cutting and tapping oil
- Aluminum blackening solution
- Cleaning pads
- Shop swabs
- Steel wool
- De-greasing compound such as Dicro-Clean 909
- Rust and Blue remover

Summary of the 1968 Gun Control Act

The Gun Control Act of 1968 covers the licensing of persons engaged in the firearms business and regulates the sales, manufacture, transfer, importation and exportation of all firearms and ammunition. All firearms including gun actions, receivers and frames, all ammunition and all reloading components except pellets and nonmetallic shotgun cases without primers are covered by this act. Certain specified antiques and muzzleloading guns do not come under restrictions. Any person or business involved in the sale or transfer of guns or in the repair of guns or any other gunsmithing activity needs a license. This includes anything you do to a gun that belongs to someone else.

The Gun Control Act contains Federal licensing standards for firearms-related businesses. An example of such standards is: The applicant must have a business premises (which can be a part of his home). This business premises must be open to his clientele during the hours specified in the application.

The application shall be approved if: The applicant is 21 years or more of age; is not prohibited from shipping or receiving firearms or ammunition in interstate commerce; has not willfully violated the GCA or its regulations; has not willfully failed to disclose required material information or willfully made false statements concerning material facts in connection with application; and has premises for conducting business or collecting.

The cost for the various firearm licenses are as follows:

Firearms (other than destructive devices):
Manufacturer $50
Importer 50
Pawnbroker-Dealer 25
Dealer 10
Gunsmith 10
Collector (only for curios
and relic firearms) 10

Destructive devices and destructive device ammunition:
Manufacturer $1,000
Importer 1,000
Dealer 1,000

All ammunition except that for destructive devices:
Manufacturer $10
Dealer 10

All gun sales must be recorded on standard government forms plus any state or local forms as required in your area. You must maintain records showing from whom you received each gun, when you got it, to whom you sold or transferred it and when. Any gun received for repair, alteration, etc. must also be entered in your record books. Ammunition sales must also be recorded.

Following is a brief summary of the major provisions of the Federal Firearms Control Act of 1968 and the recent opinions that affect it. You should have a thorough understanding of this prior to getting your license and after getting your license, you must have an equal understanding of the entire law. A copy of the complete law will be included with your license.

1. If you work on guns for others in your home of place of business you must be licensed under the Act. It is the government's position that you are responsible for the guns while in your possession. Also, if a customer refuses to pay for services you rendered, you will take possession of the gun in lieu of payment, sell the gun to cover these charges and thus come under the Act. Or, if the guns are stolen while in your possession, there are no records if you are not licensed. This applies to all phases of work: bluing, finishing, stocking, cleaning, repairing, scope mounting—anything, except the antique, replica and muzzleloading industry as specified and enumerated under the law.

2. The guns brought to you must be entered in your firearms record in chronological order. This will be the same book in which you will keep records of new or used guns bought for re-sale. When the customer picks up his gun, it should be so noted in the "disposition" side of the record. (Actually, this is nothing more than good business procedure anyhow!) Record books for both firearms and ammunition are available at very reasonable prices from Brownells and other major suppliers to the trade.

3. If you build rifles, i.e., chamber and attach barrels to actions and then build the complete gun, you need only the Dealer's License. You are not considered "manufacturing," because you are only assembling parts made by other manufacturers. If, however, you actually make the action from scratch from a piece of steel, then you are manufacturing, and must purchase a Manufacturer of Firearms license and comply with the special marking procedures. Also, as a manufacturer, you can be shipped all items covered by the law just as though you had a standard dealer's license.

4. If you reload for anyone other than yourself you must have a Manufacturer of Ammunition license. This applies even if the customer brings you the brass, powder, primers, bullets and even lends you his tools, you are still loading for someone else and must have a license. If you use new brass cases, never fired, you must also collect and pay excise tax. With a Manufacturer of Ammunition license, you can only sell, be sold and receive ammo and ammo components covered by the law. You cannot sell or receive firearms or parts covered by the Act. To do so, you must also have a Dealer's license.

5. Military Personnel: Licenses cannot be issued to individuals living within the military compound. Those "living on the state-side economy" can be issued licenses if they meet all other requirements of the Act.

After reading the above, it all probably sounds a bit involved and complicated. Actually, this is not the case, except for the record keeping requirements for ammunition sales. This does require a bit of unnecessary time. Otherwise, if you are legitimate and your intentions are legitimate, you will experience absolutely no difficulty.

About the License: First, write to the Department of the Treasury, Bureau of Alcohol, Tobacco and Firearms at the same address where you pay your Federal Income Taxes. Ask for: "Application for License under U.S.C. Chapter 44 Firearms." Do not send money at this time. The license fee of $10 goes in with your filled-out license application.

When you get the application, study it thoroughly before starting to fill in the X's. There are a couple of questions which might throw you a little and a few others about which you might be uncertain as to what is wanted. The following are the ones the men in the trade have asked about most often:

Question 9: This asks the location of the building in which you intend to operate. Home, commercial building, or "other." Be exact on this. If you use a small building close to your home, *so specify*. Or if it is to be in your home, *say so*.

Question 11: Line number 8 covers activities of average gunsmith/dealer operations. Check the box or boxes that pertain to your business. ("NFA" stands for *National Firearms Act*, which covers such firearms as full automatics, sawed-off shotguns and rifles, silencers and machine guns, including DEWATs*.)

If you reload ammo for other than your own personal use, a Manufacturer's License (Line No. 5) is required.

Question 13: Very important. Give those hours when you will actually be doing gun work, have open shop hours, or if at home as a side-line, give the afternoon and evening hours when you intend to, or are actually working on guns. This applies to Saturdays and Sundays as well. If there are days when you are open certain hours by "appointment only" and open to the public the other days, put this in the chart. Some gunsmiths operate by appointment only and are never open to the public. This is perfectly legal—so long as you keep it that way or advise the ATF of the change.

Read very carefully the quotation from ATF, Ruling 73-13, published August 6, 1973, in ATF Bulletin No. 1973-8. Note particularly the last two paragraphs, and the requirement that if a gunsmith applicant begins buying and selling firearms, he then must comply with the "open to the public" and "regular business hours" regulations as does a regular dealer.

---

*Deactivated War Trophies.

21
GUN PARTS

ANYONE who is involved in the repair of firearms—whether hobbyist or professional—will eventually need to obtain replacement parts. While replacement parts usually present few problems for modern firearms (most are obtainable from the manufacturer), obsolete firearms are a different story. However, in this latter case, a thorough knowledge of dealers dealing in obsolete gun parts will lessen the burden tremendously.

The first step in "tooling up" for gun parts is to write all of the firearm manufacturers and request their catalog of gun parts. Their addresses may be found in the "Directory of the Arms Trade" in the *Gun Digest* (DBI Books, Inc., Northfield, IL 60093). You'll receive their current parts list along with prices. In most cases, there will be an exploded view of the firearm with all parts numbered and then a reference list or schedule giving the name of the part. Besides the information you'll need to order gun parts, these catalogs are also valuable references for assembly and disassembly of firearms.

For both modern and obsolete arms, the following reference books will be of value: *The Gun Digest Book of Exploded Firearm Drawings*, *Brownell's Encyclopedia of Modern Firearms* and DBI Books new series entitled *The Gun Digest Book of Firearms Assembly/Disassembly*. This

There is hardly a day that goes by that at least one of these four books is not used in the author's gunshop. Those involved in gun repair will find any reference book invaluable.

218

RUGER NEW MODEL SINGLE-SIX® REVOLVER

An exploded drawing of firearms not only helps in identifying parts but is also a great aid for the assembly and disassembly of firearms.

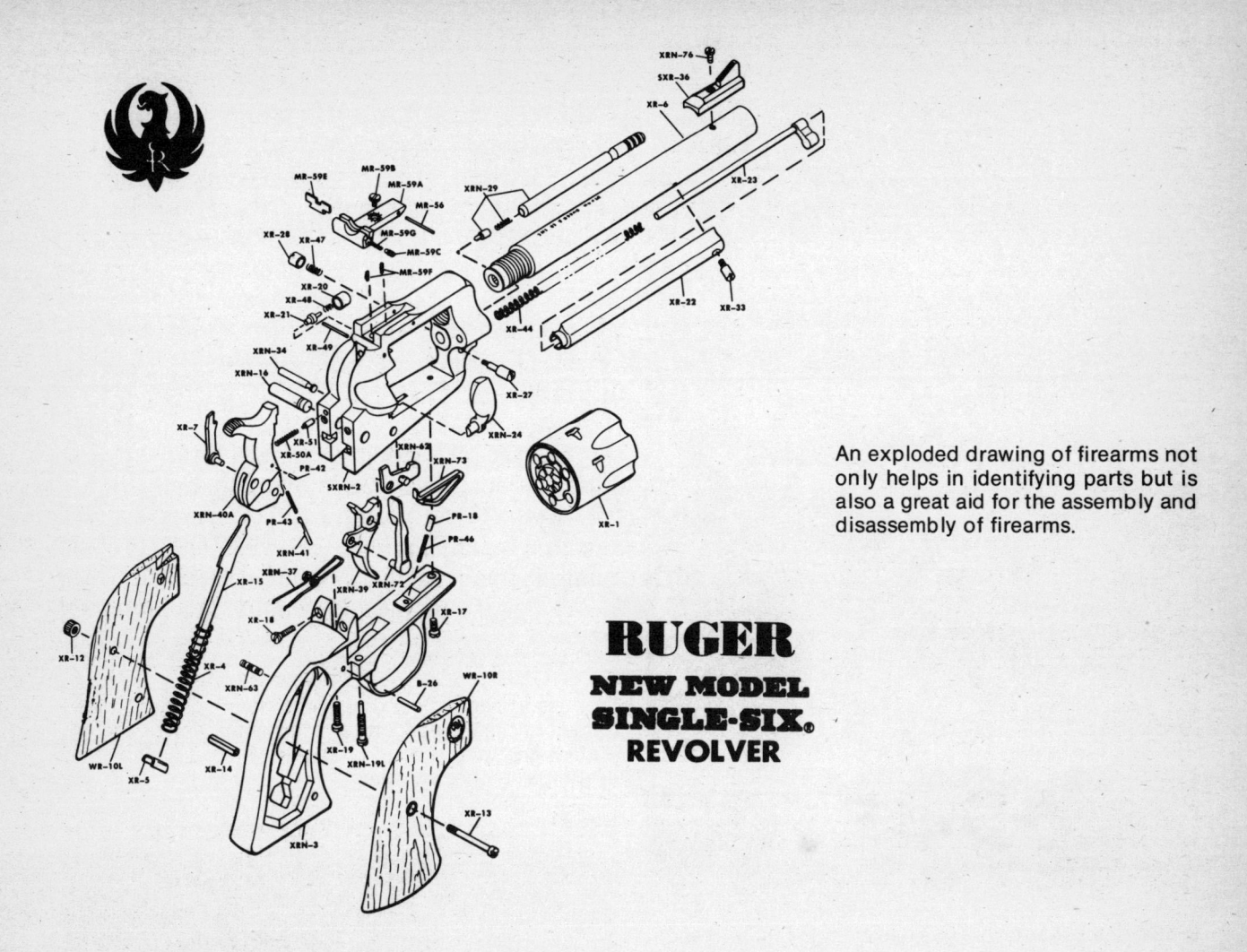

5-book series tells you how to do it all; perhaps the most complete series of assembly/disassembly books ever published. All of these books have detailed drawings or photos of both modern and antique firearms. Should you be working on a particular gun with a broken part, and you aren't sure just what it is, one of these books should tell you. However, if you still cannot find it, make a sketch of the part (or take a *good* close-up photo) and send it to one of the antique gun parts dealers, giving all of the details you know about the gun in question; that is, model, serial number, etc. Chances are one of their experts will know what the part is and will be able to either furnish it or tell you the best source to obtain it.

A few of the major suppliers of obsolete gun parts include:

Antique Gun Parts, Inc.
1118 S. Braddock Ave.
Pittsburgh, PA 15218

Bob's Place
Box 283J
Clinton, IA 52732

Dixie Gun Works
Hwy. 51, South
Union City, TN 38261

Numrich Arms Co.
West Hurley, NY 12491

Sarco, Inc.
323 Union St.
Stirling, NY 07980

Walter Lovewick (Winchester Parts)
2816 N.E. Halsey St.
Portland, OR 97232

Stoeger Industries
55 Ruta Court
So. Hackensack, NJ 07606

British Lee-Enfield rifle obtained from local pawn shop; chamber is welded shut but there were still many parts that could be salvaged.

the hunks of metal or perhaps toss the whole batch of cut-up parts in a nearby river.

If you have a Federal Firearms License, you may be able to work out a deal with your local police department whereby you would be allowed to disassemble the guns for the minor parts (screws, cylinders, springs, etc.) and then you would be responsible for cutting up the frames and barrels and disposing of them—under the supervision of the local courts. In other words, you'd be offering to dispose of the firearms in exchange for the minor parts.

Always be on the lookout for all junk guns that can be used for spare parts. You'll find a few with missing bolts, no stocks, ruptured barrels, etc.—all of which can be used for the parts that are intact. Recently I purchased an old Western Field pump shotgun that had a ruptured barrel for which no replacement part is readily available. Of

This assortment of handgun parts was legally obtained from confiscated weapons at a law enforcement agency. Frames and barrels had to be destroyed by law, but many useful parts were salvaged.

I've had relatively good luck obtaining obsolete spare parts by purchasing old junk guns for a very low price and then salvaging the parts. For example, I recently purchased a British Lee-Enfield rifle in .303 caliber from a local pawn shop that had its barrel and chamber welded shut. I believe I paid $10 for the gun. A short time afterwards, the brass butt plate was sold for $5; the rear sling swivel for $3; the magazine for $5 and the extractor for $2. I've already made $5 profit on the deal and I still have the stock and other parts that can be used in the future.

Another source of gun parts is your local police department. Law enforcement agencies are continually confiscating firearms (mostly handguns) from criminals to be used as evidence and other reasons. Every so often, these weapons have to be disposed of—usually by hiring a local welder to cut the weapons up with a cutting torch and then bury

This Western-Field pump shotgun had a ruptured barrel which was removed — the remaining parts will be used for replacements on other guns.

course, another barrel could be fitted, but the cost of the operation would prohibit doing so on such an inexpensive shotgun. The owner wanted the barrel cut off below the ruptured area and rechoked, but I explained that this could not be done since the barrel length would then be under the minimum prescribed by law. So the owner wound up trading the "junk" gun in on another. The ruptured barrel was removed and disposed of and now I've got complete parts for this shotgun should one come into the shop for repair.

You might try advertising in local newspapers for junk guns. There are thousands of damaged and abused firearms in attics, closets and basements all over the country that the owners might want to part with, but due to the condition of those guns, the owners think that no market is out there. A short ad in a newspaper may bring to light the fact that you want the guns regardless of their condition. Numrich Arms has, for instance, obtained many parts in just this way. Also check the newspapers for estate sales or public auctions. I've seen a bunch of damaged guns thrown in a box which brought only a dollar . . . and the auctioneer had to toss fifty cents out of his own pocket to get this!

Experience has proven that those dealers who are able to furnish replacement parts the quickest seem to get the most business. From this it would seem that all a dealer has to do is to buy umpteen dollars worth of gun parts, sit back and watch the cash and the customers flow in. But this is not the way it usually happens. Chances are if you would buy, say, $10,000 worth of gun parts at random, you wouldn't sell $10 worth of parts in three months from the selection you purchased. The secret is to be *selective*. The key is knowing what guns are used the most in your area and what parts on these guns are subject to the most wear or breakage.

For example, the Savage/Stevens Models 80 and 87A .22 rim fire semi-automatic rifles are very popular in my area (and I'm sure all over the country). Hardly a week goes by that one of these does not come into the shop with feeding problems. In almost every case, the trouble could be traced to either a worn cartridge lifter or a weak magazine spring or both. After ordering these parts for about a dozen rifles that took anywhere from three to four weeks each, and noticing the unhappy expressions on my customer's faces (when they would come in weekly to inquire about their gun), I finally decided to order a dozen or so lifters and springs for these rifles. Now I can repair the rifles, in most cases, while the customer waits. Needless to say, customer/dealer relations have been improved tremendously.

Another common replacement part is a firing pin for singleshot, break-open shotguns. There are thousands (make that millions) of Iver Johnson Champion, Stevens, H&R, Western-Field single barrel shotguns in use throughout the country. All of these will eventually need a replacement firing pin. A kit is available from Brownells that contains 25 shotgun firing pins and this kit will take care of most needs. It costs very little and you can make

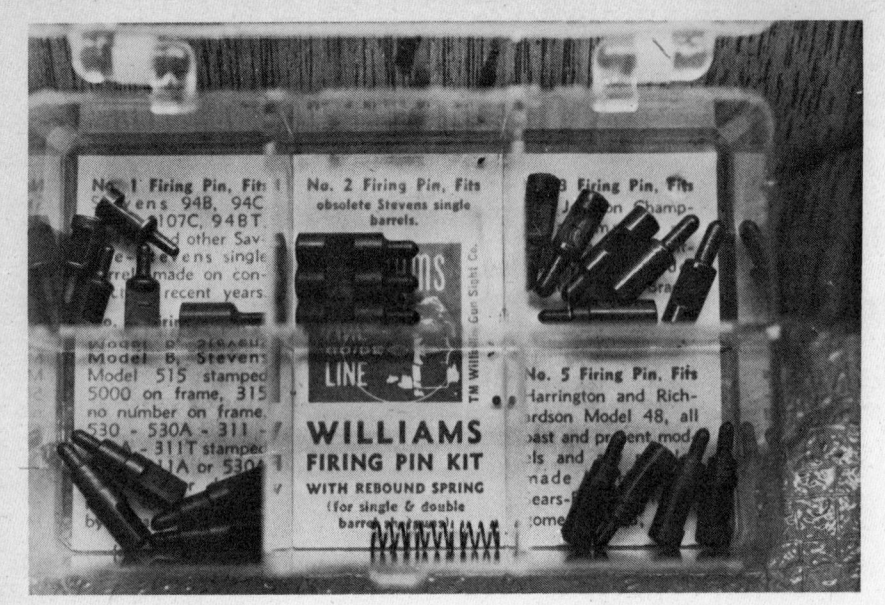

A good assortment of firing pins for single-barrel shotguns is a necessity. Replacement of this sort of part is usually fast, and inexpensive.

over 100% profit if you're in the gun-repair business; it's a good investment for any gunsmith. I went one step further. After having several old single and double barrel shotguns come in for repair for which no replacement parts were available, I purchased a Unimat 3 Miniature Machine Lathe. Now I can turn out drift pins, firing pins and other simple parts for almost any firearm that comes in for repair.

You should note that when an unusual firearm comes in your shop for repair (one on which little or no reference material is available) you should take notes of the disassembly procedure as you learn it (probably by trial and error) and also list dimensions of the parts that are subject to the most wear. These notes will come in handy should another gun of this type come in later. But be sure to file the information where you can put your hands on it. Keep a separate file drawer for gun-part information only; then file the information in alphabetical order by manufacturer's name, and then by model number.

A person just starting out in the gun repair business—either working out of his home or from a commercial shop—may be somewhat at a loss as to what spare parts should be purchased initially. If I were starting from "scratch," here's a list of gun parts that I would purchase. They can be obtained from the manufacturers or one of the gunsmith supply houses.

Weaver scope parts kit
Universal rear sight elevator kit
Shotgun sight kit
Weaver top and side mount base assortment
Fillister head screw kit
Sight base screw kit
Roll-pin kit
Firing-pin kit
Spring kits
5 Cartridge lifters for Stevens 87-A Rifle
5 Remington .22 pump fore-end supports
1 Winchester Model 12 safety

To this list may be added other parts as you see a need for them.

Making Your Own Parts

In most cases, you can purchase parts from manufacturers much cheaper than you can make your own. Factories turn out thousands of each part and for a particular item that you'd pay, say, $1 for, this same part may cost you $20 or more in time. However, there are certain situations where the making of a part yourself is warranted. For example, when no factory parts are available; when the customer needs the gun repaired quickly and does not have the time to wait for a factory replacement; or perhaps when the customer wants a modification of the factory part.

With a little tinkering and patience many parts can be made right in your own home shop, and without the expense of a lot of power tools. For example, such items as hammers for handguns and shotguns can be made from flat scrap iron. Choose a piece of the correct thickness and proceed to layout the part to be made—either by tracing the original part or by careful measuring. The part may be rough shaped by drilling along the border of the part with a drill press. Then final shaping can be done with an assortment of files.

Of all the parts used in firearms, you will most likely be called upon to make more gun springs than any other. Fortunately there is a good supply of spring stock assortments available that makes the making of springs much easier. For example, Brownells offers no less than six different gunsmith spring-stock assortments and are described as follows:

Assortment No. 69 consists of compression service springs with a soft action that are mainly designed for locks, sporting equipment and the softer acting gun and camera springs.

Assortment No. 71 consists of twelve assorted compression springs of medium to hard action. This assortment is made especially, for servicing guns and will handle ninety percent of the shop needs.

Assortment No. 150 contains small spring wire (diameters from .020" to .062") that may be used to make gun and miscellaneous small springs.

Assortment No. 152 contains round, oil tempered spring stock in diameters from .062" to .120". These can be annealed and re-tempered.

Assortment No. 151 contains small flat spring stock of widths $1/16"$ to $3/8"$ and thicknesses from .015" to .045". These are ideal for making small flat springs for guns, locks, cameras, tackle, etc. Hand-bendable, they can be annealed and retempered.

Assortment No. 149 is for large flat guns and lock springs and consists of 12 assorted pieces of flat spring stock cut into 18" lengths #1070 carbon steel, annealed and spheroidized (put into a very soft state). They will forge and temper into gun-quality spring requirements.

The Unimat 3 and other small lathes are relatively inexpensive and can be put to work making all sorts of gun parts, especially when the milling attachments are purchased for the machine. Firing pins, sight bases, drift pins, and the like are just a few of the many items that may be turned out on this machine. So long as you take your time, and don't try too large a job, this little machine will perform just like the more expensive models. In fact, for very small jobs, such as firing pins and drift pins, the Unimat 3 is usually easier to set and will perform the job better than the large lathes. With the thread-cutting attachment, you can turn out gun screws and trigger guard bolts all day and never tire the machine out. For larger parts, or where productivity is important, you should go to one of the larger lathes and milling machines. The work that can be performed on these machines is limited only by the capabilities of the operator.

A Unimat 3 miniature lathe can be used to turn out firing pins or other small parts when original parts are unavailable.

22

GUNNING CALCULATIONS

GUNSMITHS, ballisticians, serious hobbyists, and others involved with gunning mathematics in the past have rated the slide rule as one of their most important instruments, since it helped reduce long minutes of paper-and-pencil calculations to a few simple manipulations of the "slipstick" and "runner." While the slide rule has proved indispensable since its invention in the 1850s, there is now something faster, more versatile, more compact, more accurate, and better able to solve today's gunning problems involving mathematical calculations. It's the electronic pocket calculator.

There is no need to explain the fundamentals of electronic calculator operation, since this information may readily be obtained from the handbook accompanying these devices, and since practically anyone can master the operations of an electronic calculator in a single evening. The paragraphs that follow will explain how to make specific basic gunning calculations. Actual directions will be given for pressing the required keys in each case.

A selected number of examples have been chosen. These are basic; by no means do they attempt to cover all of the possible uses of the calculator. Other examples solvable by the same processes will readily occur to the reader.

We find that the type of electronic calculator possessed by most gunsmiths and ballisticians is an inexpensive device costing less than $100. This discussion will be limited to that type. However, any calculator capable of adding, subtracting, multiplying and dividing may be employed, except for problems involving reciprocals, square root and similar functions.

Bullet Energy

To find the striking energy of a bullet when the velocity at impact and the weight of the bullet in grains is known:

A. Key in velocity value
B. Press the multiplication key
C. Key in the velocity value again (to square)
D. Press multiplication key
E. Key in bullet weight in grains
F. Press division key
G. Key in the number 450240 and press = key.
H. Read answer displayed as the striking energy in foot pounds.

Example: Let's find the striking energy of a 405-grain bullet with a velocity of 1930 feet per second. All figures are at the muzzle:

Solution:

		See Displayed
A.	Key in velocity value 1930	1930
B.	Press the multiplication key "×"	1930
C.	Key in velocity value again 1930	1930
D.	Press multiplication key "×"	3724900
E.	Key in weight of bullet 405	405
F.	Press division key ÷	1508584500
G.	Key in number 450240	450240
H.	Press "equals" key (=) and read	3350

Therefore, the energy of the 405-grain bullet at a velocity of 1930 fps is 3350 foot pounds.

Sectional Density

Sectional density is the weight of a bullet in relation to its diameter. This figure is used as a gauge for determining flight characteristics. To determine sectional density:

A. Key in weight of bullet in grains
B. Press division key
C. Key in the number 7000 (to convert grains to pounds)
D. Press division key
E. Key in bullet diameter
F. Press division key
G. Key in bullet diameter again
H. Press equals key and read answer on panel

Example:
Find the sectional density of a 180-grain bullet with a diameter of .308".

Solution:

		See Displayed
A.	Key in weight of bullet in grains 180	180
B.	Press division key	180
C.	Key in number 7000	0.0257
D.	Press division key ÷	0.0257
E.	Key in bullet diameter .308	0.308
F.	Press division key ÷	0.0835
G.	Key in bullet diameter .308	0.308
H.	Press equals key and read answer on panel	0.271

The bullet in question has a sectional density of .271.

Telescopic Sight Adjustments

To determine the number of clicks on the scope adjustment to move a bullet on a target a certain distance:

A. Key in the distance the bullet should move in inches.
B. Press the division key.
C. Key in the number of inches that one click moves the bullet.
D. Read answer on panel as the number of clicks required.

Example:
In sighting in a .243 Winchester at 100 yards, using a Lyman 4x scope which has a ¾" click value at 100 yards, the first two shots are placed on the target 4½" to the left of the point of aim.

Solution

		See Displayed
A.	Key in distance the bullet should move 4.5	4.5
B.	Press division key ÷	4.5
C.	Key in .75	0.75
D.	Press equals key and read	6

Therefore, 6 counterclockwise clicks of the windage adjustment knob should put the bullet dead center at 100 yards.

Correcting Factory Velocity Tables

Factory-published velocities of a given load are usually based on a barrel length of 26 inches (there are some exceptions). To find the *actual* velocity in your rifle, the following velocity correction table may be used.

Barrel Length	Multiplication Factor
26"	1.000
25"	0.993
24"	0.985
23"	0.979
22"	0.969
21"	0.964
20"	0.954
19"	0.944
18"	0.939

To use this table, merely multiply the published factory velocity of the multiplication factor opposite the barrel length in question.

Example:

The factory-published velocity of a 139-grain bullet in 6.5 x 54mm is 2580. What is the velocity in an 18-inch barrel carbine?

Solution:

		See Displayed
A.	Key in factory velocity	2580
B.	Press multiplication key ×	2580
C.	Key in factor opposite 18″	0.939
D.	Press equals key (=) and read	2422

Therefore, the actual velocity in an 18-inch barrel is 2422 fps.

Calculating Bullet Drop

When a bullet leaves the muzzle of a rifle it begins to drop, just as it would if you held a bullet in your hand and then let it go. However, certain aerodynamic forces, acting upon the bullet when it is fired, keep that projectile from falling quite as fast as it would if merely dropped from one's hand. One of the more convenient devices for determining bullet drop is the Powley High-Velocity Chart. Homer Powley, former chief ballistician at Colt, introduced this chart in the mid-50s. To use this chart to calculate the drop of a particular bullet, three factors must be known:

1. The actual velocity of the bullet in the rifle in which it is fired; *not* the published velocity.
2. The ballistics coefficient of that bullet.
3. The height of the line of sight above the bore.

The ballistic coefficient of a bullet determines its ability to resist air drag, maintain velocity and energy as it travels to the target, and shoot flat. Two methods are commonly used to determine the ballistic coefficient of a bullet. The more popular one was introduced in the '30s by Wallace H. Coe and Edgar Beugless, ballistics engineers at du Pont. This method compares an actual bullet to a point-shape chart, and when the closest possible match is made, the chart provides a point-shape factor—a number which is then divided into the bullet sectional density to give the ballistic coefficient.

The other method is direct measurement by means of firing tests. The test range must be instrumented so that both muzzle velocity and time of flight over a known range are measured for each shot fired. A digital computer program then derives the ballistic coefficient of each test bullet from these measurements.

For the average shooter, the best and easiest way to obtain the ballistic coefficient of a given bullet is from the bullet's manufacturer. Tables are available that give the sectional density, ballistic coefficient, etc., from nearly every bullet manufacturer.

The third factor—line of sight above the bore—can vary from gun to gun, but for open sights assume ½″; for conventional scope mounted rifles, assume 1½″, and for scopes with see-thru mounts, figure 2″.

Let's assume that we want to find the bullet drop of a .243, 75-grain Sierra hollow point bullet fired in a .243 Winchester rifle at an actual velocity of 3100 fps. Conventional scope mounts are used. The ballistic coefficient from Sierra's Reloading Manual is .265 for this bullet. With this data, we can now figure the bullet drop using Powley's chart.

The Powley chart should be affixed to the wall

The Powley Chart should be affixed to the wall with tape or thumb tacks so that it's at a convenient height.

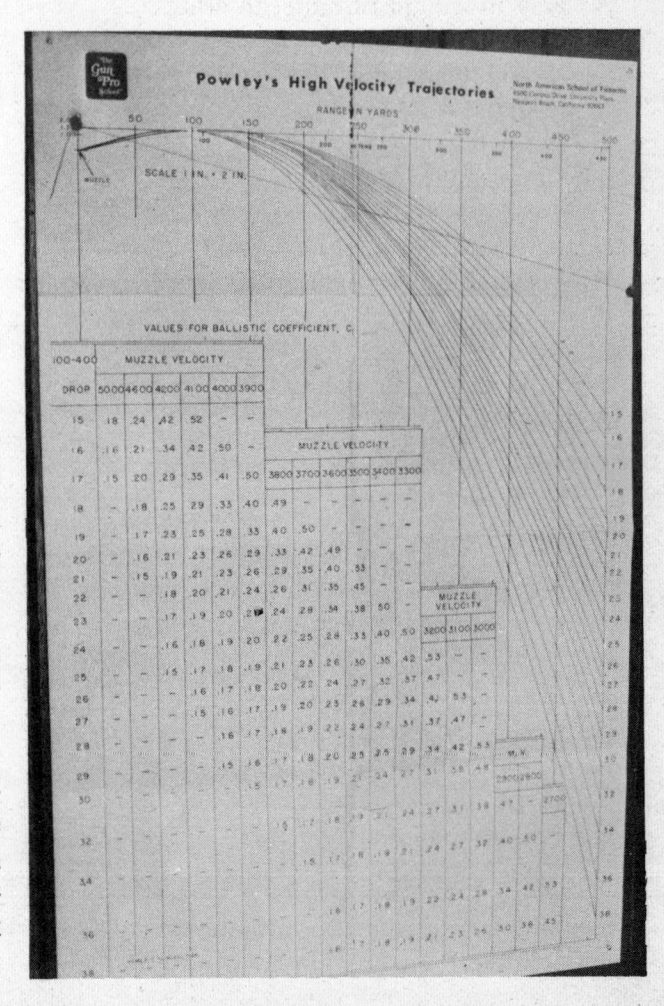

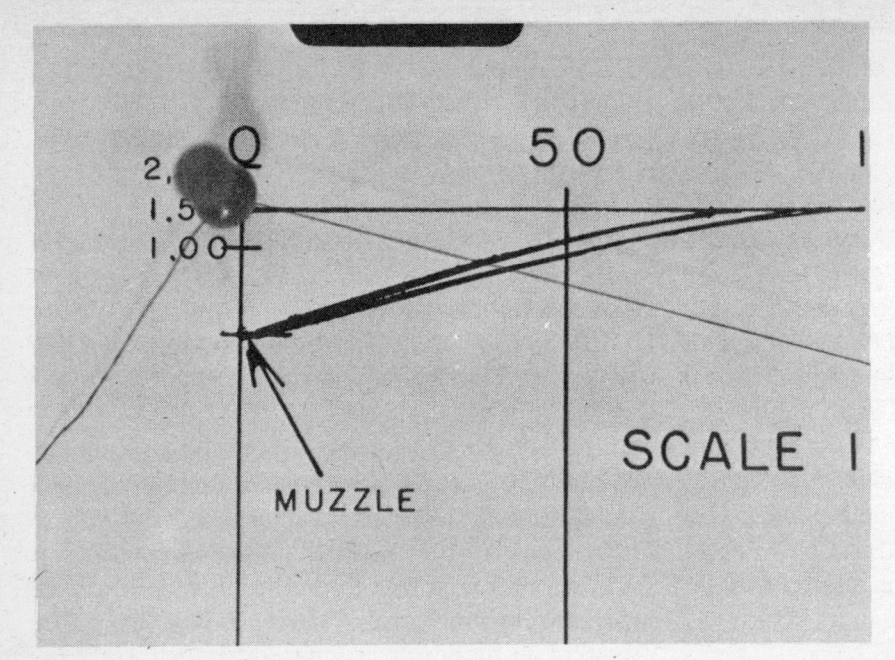

Place a tack (with the thread attached) at the 1.5 inch mark on the chart.

with tape or thumb tacks so that it's at a convenient height; that is, so that it can be easily reached as you're using it. Now you'll need a piece of heavy black thread about 40 inches long. Tie a thumb tack at each end of this thread.

In our example, we are using a rifle with a conventional scope, so we'll place one of the tacks (with the thread attached) at the 1.5" mark on the chart as shown in the accompanying illustration. We are now ready to calculate the trajectory of the 75-grain .243 bullet from muzzle to 500 yards.

The corrected (actual) velocity of our example bullet is 3100 fps, so find the vertical column headed "MV" on the chart; 3100 will be located at the lower right section of the chart. You'll also find the ballistic coefficient numbers—minus the third decimal. So trace an imaginary line from the ballistic coefficient of this bullet (.265) straight across to the extreme right vertical line which will end at curve 38. Place a thumb tack here.

Let's assume that we wish to use a 200-yard zero, meaning the bullet will strike dead on at this distance from the muzzle. Follow curve 38 from the bottom reference mark until it intersects the

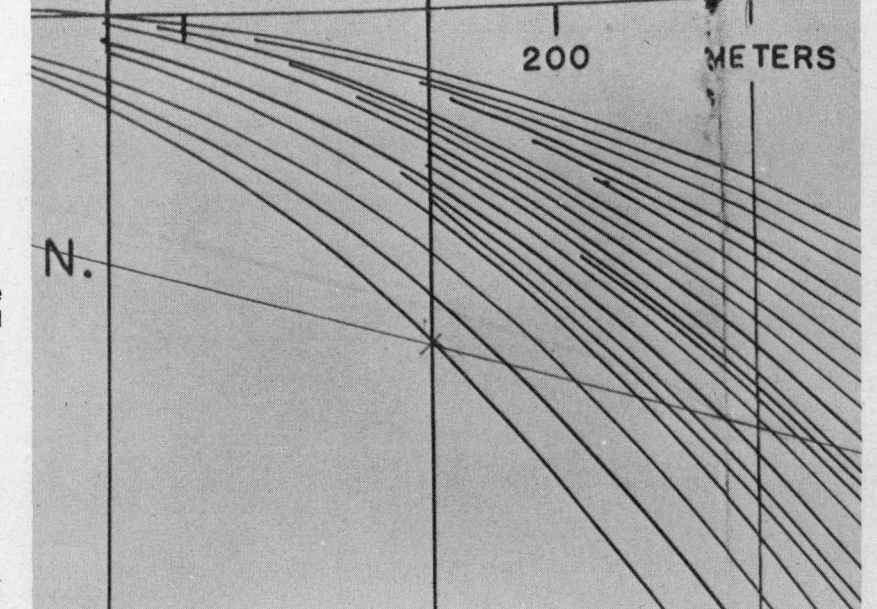

Make a light pencil mark where curve 38 intersects the vertical line headed 200 on the chart.

vertical line headed 200 on the chart. Make a light pencil mark at this intersection point.

Pick up the loose tack at the other end of the thread and stretch it to the right so that it crosses directly over the 200-yard zero point that you just marked with an "X." Secure the tack to the wall, to right of the chart. This thread represents the line of sight relative to 200-yard zero.

Now let's calculate the bullet drop at 250 yards, 300 yards and 400 yards. Follow curve 38 to where it intersects the vertical line marked 250. Make a light pencil mark at this point. Use an engineer's scale that is calibrated in tenths of an inch and measure the distance, against the 250-yard vertical line, between the thread and the pencil mark you just made. The figure is 1.85", but since the chart scale is 1" = 2" (half-scale), this figure will be doubled.

Solution:

See Displayed

A. Key in 1.85   1.85
B. Press Multiplication key ×   1.85
C. Key in 2   2
D. Press equals key = and read   3.7

Therefore, the drop of our bullet at 250 yards will be 3.7" below the line of sight.

The distance (measured with the engineer's scale) from the thread to curve 38 where it intersects the 300-yard vertical line is 4.4". This, doubled, would be an 8.8" drop at 300 yards. At 400 yards the measured distance is 12.5" actual drop if this figure were doubled.

Now let's check the Sierra Reloading Manual to see how close our figures are compared to their calculations. Sierra had no figures for 250 yards, but at 300 yards they show that this bullet will drop 7.87" as compared to 8.8" on our chart. Nearly an inch off! At 400 yards, Sierra shows the bullet drops 24.33 inches as compared to our 25 inches. About ⅔" off. Personally, I doubt if a groundhog at either of these ranges would know the difference if the crosshairs were held dead center of his chest.

23
GUNSMITH'S LIBRARY

The following list of titles represents a good selection of books for both the hobbyist and professional. If your geographic location is remote, or if you just don't happen to have a book store in your immediate locale, we would suggest you contact Ray Riling Arms Book Company, 114 Greenwood Ave., Box 135, Wyncote, PA 19095. Riling's has a solid reputation for providing the hunter, shooter or gunsmith with the books he needs—even rare, or simply out-of-print books.

Advanced Gunsmithing by W.F. Vickery, Small-Arms Technical Pub. Co., Onslow Cty., N.C. As the name implies, this is a book for the professional. It gives principles and instructions on barrel making, boring, reaming, rifling and chambering—all done by means of small power tools or entirely by hand on a hand-rifling bench using rifling heads, barrel and chamber reamers which can be made in the gunshop. It further tells about headspacing, barrel changing, action alterations and barrel lining, together with some highly applicable chapters on the reboring and chambering of rusted or shot-out barrels and obsolete rifles. Extensive treatment is given the popular .22 rimfire and its peculiar problems. There is a full chapter on shotguns and their repairs or alterations.

This book is now out-of-print, but the professional will probably want to acquire this one because it takes up where the others leave off. You'll probably be able to obtain a copy from Ray Riling, but you're going to pay dearly for it.

Black Powder Gunsmithing, by Ralph T. Walker, DBI Books, Inc., Northfield, IL. Covers everything from replica building to restoration. Also includes directory of suppliers.

Checkering and Carving of Gunstocks, by Monty Kennedy, Stackpole Books, Harrisburg, PA. This is an extensive and specialized work that covers its subject fully from both utilitarian and decorative standpoints. The full-size patterns range from easy ones to some that will take many jobs and much experience before one should attempt them.

Complete Guide to Gunsmithing, by C.E. Chapel, Barnes & Co., NY, NY. A thorough treatment of the care, repair, alteration and decoration of rifles, pistols, revolvers and shotguns. Starting with the selection of hand and power tools it moves right into checkering of stocks and engraving of metal parts and continues to range over the entire field of firearms.

Elementary Gunsmithing, by Perry D. Frazer, Small-Arms Technical Pub. Co., Onslow Cty., NC. Another out-of-print book that is intended solely as a guide to the beginner in guncraftsmanship. It is the ideal book for the boy or adult who has just become interested in firearms. (A recently published book with the same goals is *Basic Gunsmithing* by John Traister, published by TAB Book, Blue Ridge Summit, PA.)

Firearm Bluing and Browning, by R.H. Angier, Stackpole Books, Harrisburg, PA. While this is a qualified, practical and complete treatise covering the art of gun bluing, I've found little use for it in my own shop. It is interesting reading, but most of the techniques described are dated.

Gun Digest Books of Firearms Assembly/Disassembly, by J.B. Wood, DBI Books, Inc., Northfield, IL. At this printing, DBI Books plans a 5-part series: Part I Automatic Pistols; Part II Revolvers; Part III Rim Fires; Part IV Center Fires; Part V Shotguns. As you read this, the first four books should be available with the shotgun book (Part V) becoming available in the fall of 1980. This is, perhaps, the most comprehensive assembly/disassembly series ever undertaken. Field stripping as well as detail-stripping of most popular firearms is covered. Invaluable.

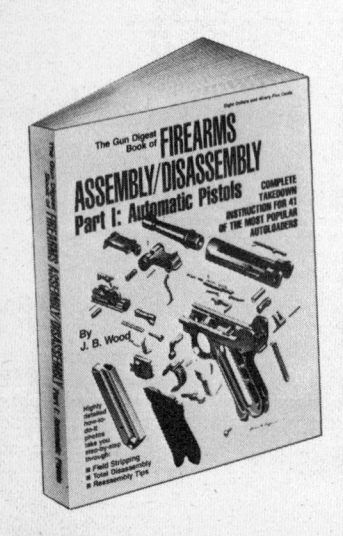

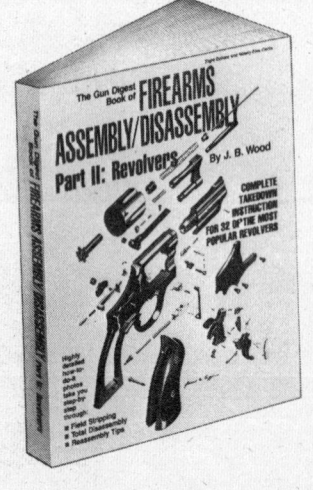

Gun Owner's Book of Care, Repair & Improvement, by Roy Dunlap with photos by Jim Carmichel, Outdoor Life—Harper & Row, NY. A good book for the beginner. Exceptional step-by-step photos of each job makes the going easier.

Gunsmith Kinks, compiled by Bob Brownell, F. Brownell & Sons, Montezuma, IA. I've read this book through three times already. It's an endless fountain of knowledge covering the care, service, repair and building of firearms. The book contains techniques, trade secrets, etc., of the country's leading full- and part-time gunsmiths. It's geared for the professional, hobbyist, hunter and the target shooter.

Gunsmithing, by Roy F. Dunlap, Stackpole Books, Harrisburg, PA. This book covers a lot of technical information and instruction on practically every phase of the gunsmithing trade. It may be a little too advanced for the raw beginner, but you'll eventually find it invaluable once you get started on gun repair work and refinishing firearms.

Gunsmithing Simplified, by Harold E. MacFarland, A.S. Barnes, NY, NY. This book has been out of print for a few years, but A.S. Barnes & Co. (the publisher) informed me that it is now being reprinted and should be available when you read this. This book presents a lot of technical information in a manner easily understood by the layman. Many professional secrets are revealed that can save you hours of work, produce better guns, and leave you with money to spare. Some of the topics include, modernizing sporting rifles, converting military rifles, handguns, shotguns, chambering, carving, stockmaking, trigger adjustment, how to make tools and small parts.

Gunsmith's Manual, by Stelle & Harrison,

Rutgers Book Center, Highland Park, NJ. This is a reprint of a book originally published in 1882 and deals mainly with the fabrication, finishing and repair of flint and caplocks—although some information is given on the early breechloaders of the day. This is an excellent text for those doing work on muzzleloaders.

Gunstock Finishing and Care, by A. Donald Newell, Stackpole, Harrisburg, PA. A thorough and advanced book of more than 100 formulae for the compounding of finishes the gunstocker can make and apply correctly. All early and modern finishes pertaining to gunstocks are covered in detail.

Hobby Gunsmithing, by Ralph Walker, DBI Books, Inc., Northfield, IL. This is one of the better up-to-date works on gun repair written by a veteran gunsmith. Written in a breezy, lucid style, and profusely illustrated with step-by-step photos and drawings. Emphasis is placed on working with few tools to get a lot of projects completed. If you're willing to try, this book will tell you how.

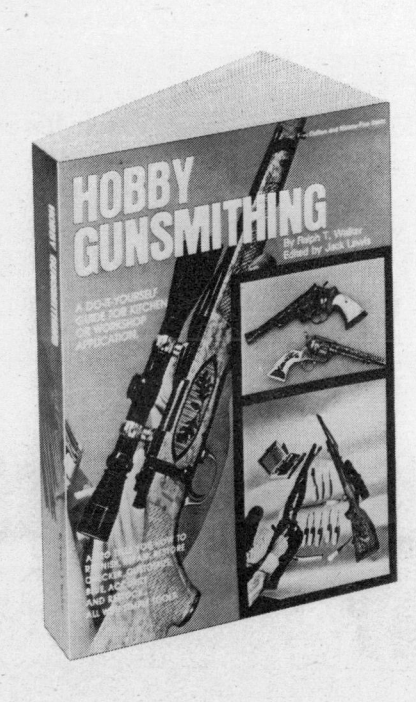

Home Gunsmithing Digest, 2nd ed., by Robert A. Steindler, DBI Books, Inc., Northfield, IL. Here's another "must" for the beginner and profesional alike. Covers complete what, how-to and why information on such items as checkering, silver soldering, heat-treating, bolt jewelling, touch-up bluing, etc.

Modern Gunsmithing, by Clyde Baker, Standard Publishing, Huntington, W. VA. Although out of print at this writing, this is still one of the best books on gunsmithing ever written for the shooting man. It's written for the ordinary guncrank for use with the tools and facilities of the average home, farm or ranch; so you won't need access to an elaborate machine shop to carry out the many ideas and suggestions.

NRA Gunsmithing Guide, National Rifle Association, Washington, D.C. This useful guide contains many of the American Rifleman articles on gunsmithing. It's packed with information for both the amateur and professional. Metal working details are given on rebarreling, reamer making, welding, etc. Woodworking is also covered.

Pistolsmithing, by George C. Nonte, Jr., Stackpole Books, Harrisburg, PA. A comprehensive, basic book on the art of pistolsmithing. Troubleshooting the pistol, as well as maintaining the pistol are just some of the subjects that are thoroughly covered. It's a must for any gunsmith doing handgun work.

Professional Gunsmithing, by Walter J. Howe, Stackpole Books, Harrisburg, PA. The author takes up the subject of professional gunsmithing in a broad and comprehensive manner—approaching it from the angle of basic principles and logical reasoning. While some of the information is dated, Howe treats in detail the specific jobs and types of repair work which, from experience, have shown to be most frequently encountered in the gunshop.

The Amateur Guncraftsman, by James V. Howe, Funk & Wagnalls, NY, NY. This was my first book on gunsmithing and I still enjoy reading through it from time to time. It's out of print, but you may be able to find a copy in one of the used book stores or from Ray Riling. This is a thoroughly practical handbook for the beginner.

The Modern Gunsmith, by James V. Howe, Funk & Wagnalls, NY, NY. Another excellent text by James V. Howe and also out-of-print. Two volumes are required to contain all of the information given on gun repairing, refinishing and other techniques. It's a little dated in some cases, but every gunsmith will want a set of these, if only for the many bluing formulas found in the books.

24
GLOSSARY OF FIREARM TERMS

ACTION: The breech mechanism of a firearm through which it is loaded. The action also secures the cartridge or shell in the chamber to prevent discharge to the rear.

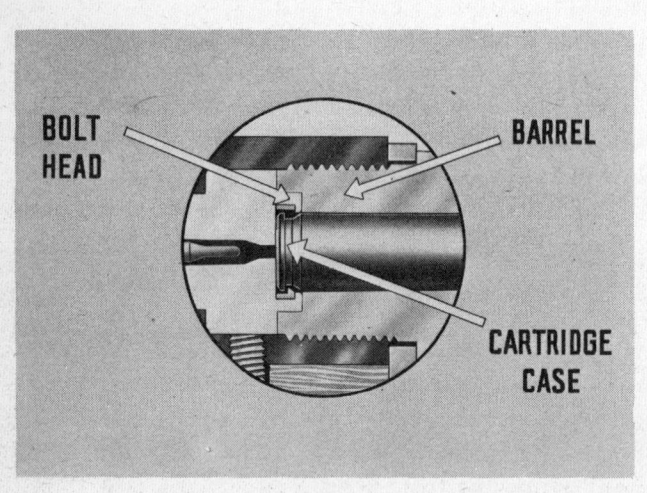

ACTION, BOLT: Cylindrical-shaped breech action that contains a bolt, firing pin, spring, etc., which is opened and closed, and otherwise operated by a handle.

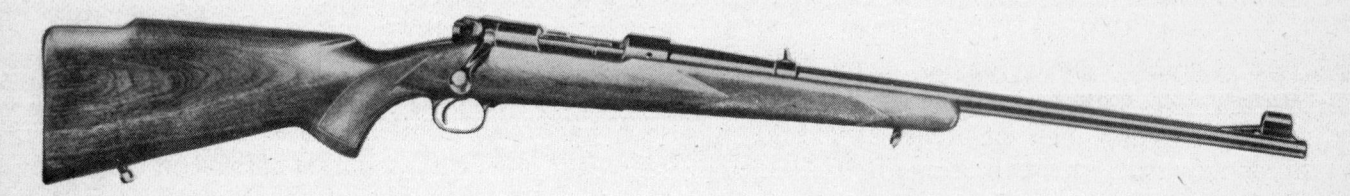

ACTION, LEVER: A breech action that is opened, closed and operated by means of a lever, usually formed as a rearward extension of the trigger guard.

ACTION, PUMP: A breech action which is opened, closed, and operated by means of a sliding fore-end which is formed into a convenient handle for this purpose. Also termed *trombone* or *slide-action*.

AMMUNITION: Cartridges, shotgun shells or both that contain powder, bullet or shot and a cap to ignite the powder.

ANNEAL: To render metals soft by heating to a red color and allowing it to cool.

ANVIL: A small multi-legged piece of brass inserted in a primer that acts to allow the priming composition to be crushed against it, causing a spark to ignite the main powder charge.

AUTOMATIC: A term commonly used for a self-loading firearm. A better term is "semi-automatic" for these weapons since a firearm is truly automatic only when it continues to fire as long as the trigger is held back.

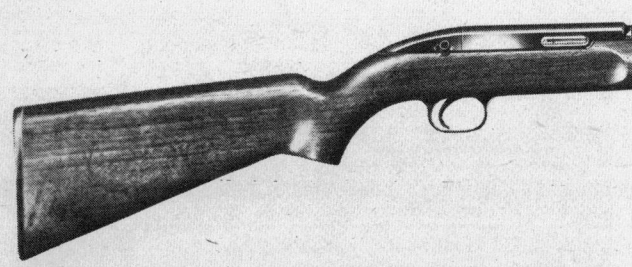

BARREL: The part of a firearm through which the bullet or shot is driven by the powder. It directs the projectile toward its target and allows (usually) the powder to burn completely before the projectile is on its own in flight through the air.

BORE: The hole through the barrel of a firearm measured from land to land. In rifled barrels, the groove diameter is the distance between opposite grooves.

BREECH: The rear end of the bore of a firearm where the cartridge is inserted into the chamber.

BREECH BOLT: Part of the action which closes the breech, and sustains the head of the cartridge when the gun is fired.

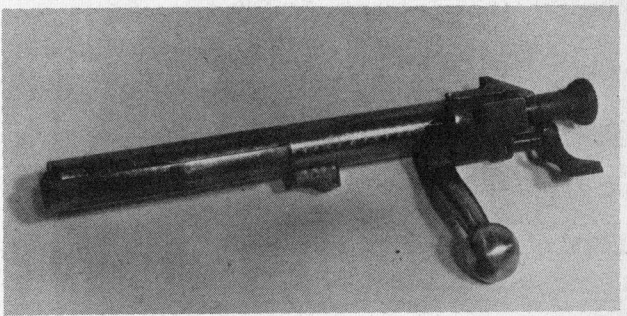

BULLET: The projectile fired from a rifle or pistol.

BUTT: Part of the gun stock which comes in contact with the shoulder of the shooter.

BUTT PLATE: The plate of hard rubber, steel, aluminum or synthetic material which is attached to and, protects the rear end of, the buttstock. Butt pads are also used to soften the feel of recoil from shotguns and rifles*.

CALIBER: Principally the bore (or land-to-land) diameter of a barrel; *not* actual bullet diameter in modern usage. Also used to refer to the actual designation of a cartridge such as, "caliber .308 Winchester." Also used as a unit measure to describe bullet nose shape, i.e. "4-caliber ogive" or seating depth, "1-caliber seating depth," and in big-gun terms, barrel length in units of bore diameter. A 50-caliber 6-inch gun has a barrel 50X6" or 300 inches (25 feet) long.

CANT: Leaning of a rifle to one side or the other so that the sights are not in a truly vertical plane. This results in the bullet striking the target on the side of the cant and slightly low.

---

*See Recoil Pad.

233

CAP: A percussion cap for use with cap-and-ball guns; also the cup and priming-compound pellet of a conventional shotshell primer. Also sometimes used in place of the word "primer."

CARBINE: A short-barreled rifle like the Winchester Model 94 or the Marlin 336.

CARRIER: The mechanism in a magazine or repeating firearm which carries the cartridge or shotgun shell from the magazine into a position to be pushed into the chamber.

CAST-OFF: A slant in a gun stock *away* from the face of a right-handed shooter.

CAST-ON: A slant in a gun stock *toward* the face of a right-handed shooter.

CENTERFIRE: Term used to identify a cartridge having its primer inserted in the center of the head of the shell or case.

CENTER PUNCH: Punch with a short sharp point for marking metal, usually before drilling with bit.

CHAMBER: The enlarged portion of the bore, at the breech in which the cartridge rests when in a position to be fired.

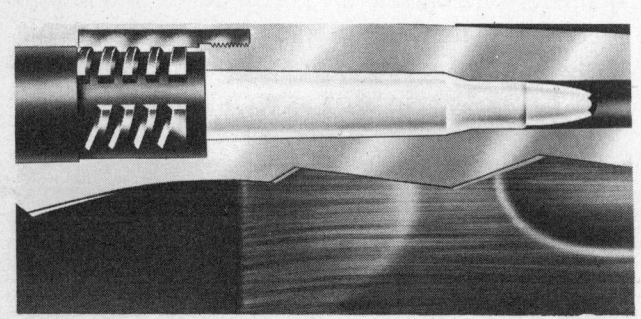

CHECKERING: Applies to diamond-shaped patterns cut in wood or metal parts for the purposes of minimizing slippage, and for decoration.

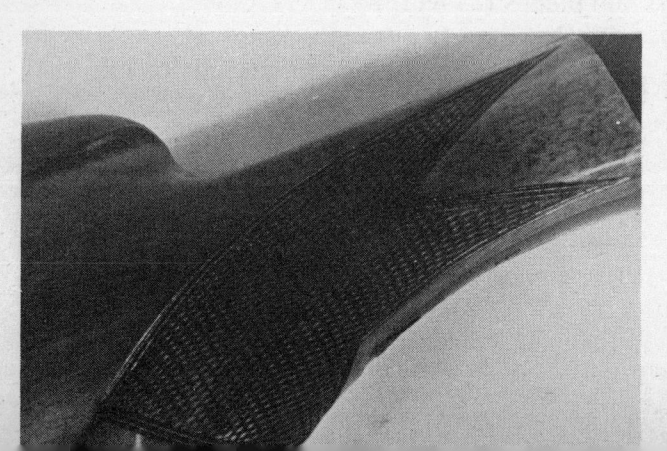

CHEEK PIECE: A raised, carved portion of the butt stock on one side of the comb against which the shooter rests his cheek when aiming.

CHOKE: The constriction in the muzzle end of a shotgun barrel to control the shot pattern. Degree of choke is measured by the approximate percentage of shot pellets in a shot charge which hit within a 30-inch circle at 40 yards.

COCK: To ready the hammer or firing pin of a gun so that it is in a position to fire.

COMB: Top of the butt stock or part of the stock which extends from the heel to a point just back of the hand as the stock is grasped. A proper comb guides the face to a position where the eye falls quickly into the line of aim.

CONE: The slope of the forward end of the chamber of a rifle or shotgun which decreases the chamber diameter to bore diameter. Sometimes called the forcing cone.

CROSSBOLT: Transverse bolt used to lock the standing breech and barrels of a side-by-side or over-under shotgun.

CYLINDER: The part of a revolver which contains the cartridge chambers and revolves so that each cartridge lines up in turn with the barrel so that it can be fired.

DAMASCUS BARRELS: Barrels made by a special process of welding alternate strips of iron and steel together in sort of a twisting fashion. Also referred to as "twist" barrels.

DRIFT: The deviation of the projectile from the plane of departure due to rotation. The degree of drift can be affected by certain wind conditions.

DROP: The distance a projectile falls due to the force of gravity. Drop must be corrected by means of sight adjustment for the difference between the line of sight and the line of departure. Drop also refers to the height between the line of sight and the top of the stock comb or heel.

DUMMY CARTRIDGE: A cartridge case and bullet—but *without* powder or primer—used for testing the feed, extraction and ejection of actions.

EAR PROTECTOR: Plugs, acoustical muffs, or similar devices that help eliminate the sound of gun shots.

EJECT: The action of throwing a cartridge from the breech after extraction. This is often accomplished by spring action.

EJECTOR: A mechanism on firearms that ejects the fired or unfired shell clear of the gun.

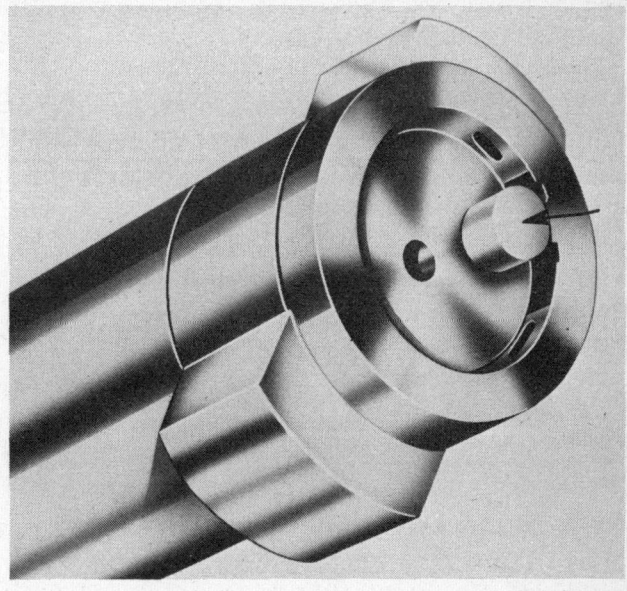

ELEVATION: The vertical sight adjustment to bring the point of aim to the proper elevation to compensate for bullet drop.

ENGINE TURNING: The process of polishing circular spots on metal (usually rifle bolts) with a spinning abrasive rod.

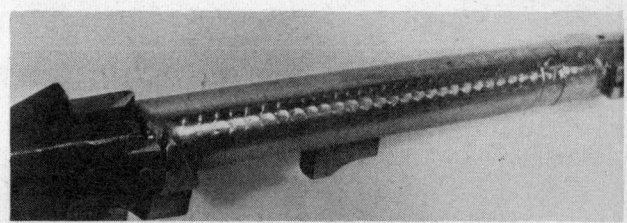

ENGRAVING: The art of cutting patterns or designs into the metal parts of a firearm to improve its appearance and to increase its value.

EXTRACT: The process of removing a cartridge case from the chamber of the action.

EXTRACTOR: The hooked device which withdraws the cartridge out of the chamber when the breech mechanism is opened.

EYE RELIEF: The optimum distance the eye must be held from the ocular lens of a telescopic sight to obtain a full field of view through the scope.

FEED: The action of transferring cartridges from the magazine of a repeating or semi-auto gun into the chamber of the barrel.

FIRING PIN: The pointed nose of the hammer of a firearm—or the separate pin or plunger—that dents the primer of a cartridge or shell to fire the round.

FOREARM: The forward portion of a stock under the barrel which serves as the fore grip on the arm. Frequently called "fore-end."

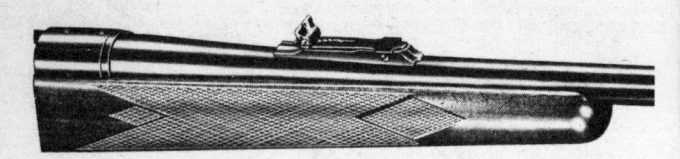

FRAME: The framework of a firearm to which the barrel and stock are fastened and in which the breech, lock and reloading mechanisms are located.

FREEBORE: The unrifled portion of the barrel between the rifling and the end of the chamber.

GALLERY: The term usually applied to an indoor rifle or handgun range.

GAS-CUTTING: The escaping of propellant gas between a bullet and the bore of the barrel—usually caused by the bullet being undersized for the bore.

GAS OPERATION: A system used in semi- or fully-automatic firearms where some of the propellant gases are vented out of the bore through a small port to operate the action.

GAUGE: The measurement of the bore diameter of a shotgun. The gauge is the number of lead balls, of the diameter of the gun bore, that make a pound of lead. Therefore, 20 balls which fit the bore of a 20-gauge shotgun would weigh one pound.

GLASS BEDDING: The reinforcing of a wooden gunstock by adding a fiberglass/epoxy compound to strengthen the stock and improve accuracy and consistency of point of bullet impact. The compound is also useful for repairing broken stocks.

GRIP: The small part of the stock—often called the "wrist"—to the rear of, or just below, the action where the hand of the shooter grasps the firearm for shooting.

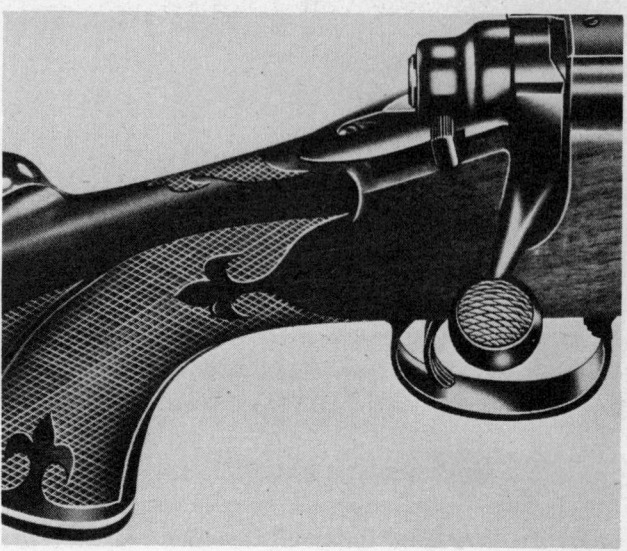

GROUP: A number of consecutive shots, usually five or ten, fired at a target with constant aim and sight adjustment; their bullet holes making a group on the target.

GUARD SCREW: The screws that hold the action and trigger guard to the stock.

HAMMER: That part of a firearm which strikes either the cartridge rim or primer or strikes the firing pin, driving the latter forward so that it indents the primer or rim of the cartridge, causing it to discharge. The hammer is actuated by a mainspring and controlled by the trigger.

HAMMERLESS: Firearms having the hammer concealed within the breech mechanism, or, a firearm that literally has no hammer and is striker fired, i.e., a spring activated firing mechanism.

HEAD SPACE: That dimension in a firearm which determines whether the cartridge is tightly breeched up in the chamber when the breech, breech block or breech bolt is shut. When head space is too little, the breech will not close on the cartridge. When there is too much, misfires begin to occur, and the safety factor is lowered. Excessive headspace is dangerous and may result in serious injury. Headspace may be checked with headspace gauges available from gunsmith supply houses.

HINGE: The joint in a break-down, breech-loading rifle or shotgun connecting the barrel or barrels with the frame.

LANDS: That portion of the original bore surface of a rifle barrel which lies between the grooves.

LEADING: Deposits of lead left in the bore of a rifle, handgun or shotgun.

LENGTH OF STOCK: The distance in a straight line from the center of the trigger to a point midway between the heel and toe of the butt plate, on the surface of the plate. Required stock length depends upon the physical conformation of the shooter; men of short stature or short arms requiring shorter stocks.

LINE OF SIGHT: The straight line passing from the eye through the sights to the target.

LOCK: The combination of hammer, firing pin, sear, mainspring and trigger which serves to discharge the cartridge when the trigger is pulled.

LOCK SPEED: The time consumed between the releasing of the firing mechanism and the explosion of the cartridge.

LOCKING BOLT: The bolt used in a break-down, breech-loading gun to lock the breech in its closed position.

LUG: In a break-down, breech-loading shotgun or rifle a lug on the barrel which secures the barrel to the frame. Lugs on the front of a bolt or breech block which rotate into slots to lock the action for firing are termed locking lugs.

MAGAZINE: A box or tube on or in a repeating firearm, in which the cartridges are carried in a position to be fed into the chamber by means of the reloading mechanism.

MAGAZINE, BOX: One in which the cartridges are horizontally stacked.

MAGAZINE, FULL: A tubular magazine reaching the full length of the barrel.

MAGAZINE, HALF: A tubular magazine reaching half the length of the barrel.

MAGAZINE, TUBULAR: One in which the cartridges are carried end-to-end in a tube located either beneath the barrel or within the stock.

MAINSPRING: The spring, either flat or coiled, which provides the energy to carry the hammer or firing pin forward to strike the primer.

MATTED RIB: A raised, solid rib along the top length of (generally) a shotgun barrel to cut reflection and improve sighting.

METAL FOULING: A deposit of bullet-jacket metal left in the bore of a rifle.

MOUNTS: Metal bases and rings used to secure a telescopic sight to the barrel or receiver of a firearm.

OVER AND UNDER: Term used to describe a double barrel shotgun or rifle with one barrel superimposed over the other.

PISTOL: A handgun in which the cartridge is loaded into a chamber which is in the barrel. Pistols may be single shot, repeating or semiautomatic. When the cartridges are loaded in and fired from a revolving cylinder, the pistol is termed a revolver*.

PITCH OF BUTT: The angle of the butt or butt plate with relation to the gun's barrel. If, for example, the butt of a gun is rested on a flat surface on the floor with the barrel in a vertical position, and the barrel muzzle inclines at two inches from perpendicular, the butt is said to have a pitch of two inches.

POWDER: The finely divided chemical mixture that supplies the power used in shotgun and metallic ammunition. Originally, all propellent powder was black powder, which was formed in grains of varying size, the size of the grain determining the rate of burning and suitability for various cartridges in black powder arms. Modern powders are smokeless and their base is either nitroglycerine or nitrocellulose, or a combination of the two.

*See Revolver.

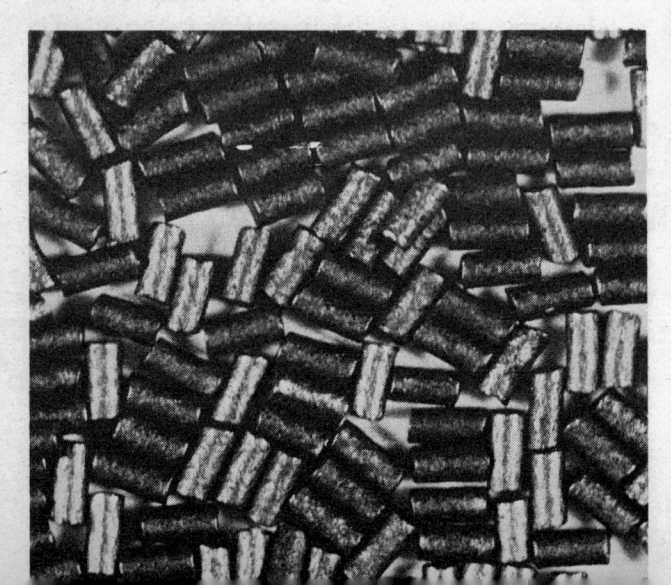

PRIMER: The small cup, or cap, seated in the center of the base of a centerfire cartridge or shot shell and containing the igniting compound. When the primer is indented by the firing pin, the priming compound is crushed, and detonates, thus igniting the charge of powder. Rimfire cartridges contain the priming compound within the folded rim of the case, where it is crushed in the same manner.

PROJECTILE: A ball, shot or bullet fired from a firearm.

PUMP GUN: Common name for a slide action, repeating firearm.

RECEIVER: The frame consisting of breech, locking and reloading mechanisms of shotguns or rifles.

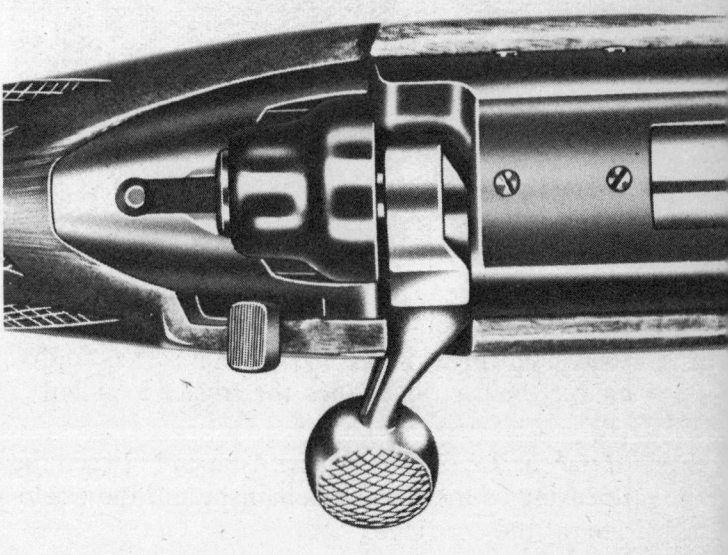

RECOIL: The backward movement or "kick" of the firearm caused by the discharge of the cartridge.

RECOIL PAD: A soft rubber pad which replaces the usual butt plate on a shotgun or a high power rifle. Used to ease or soften the recoil on a shooter's shoulder.

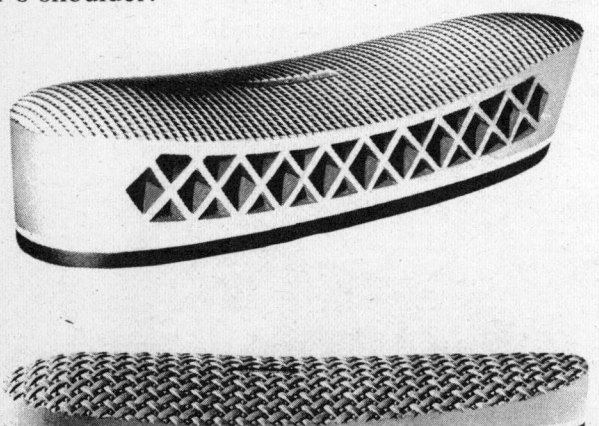

REPEATING FIREARM: Any rifle, shotgun or pistol, other than a revolver, having a magazine in which a reserve supply of cartridges is carried, and a repeating mechanism which, when operated, ejects the fired cartridge case and replaces it with a loaded cartridge, ready to fire.

REVOLVER: A pistol in which the cartridges, usually six or more, are placed in firing position by a revolving cylinder.

RIB: The raised bar, usually slightly concave on its upper surface, and usually matted, which forms the sighting plane extending from breech to muzzle of a gun.

RIFLE: A shoulder-mounted firearm with the bore of its barrel cut or rifled with spiral grooves; the object of which is to cause the projectile to rotate on its axis when fired, thus increasing its range and accuracy.

RIFLING: The spiral grooves cut in the bore of a rifle or pistol barrel. The object of these grooves is to rotate the elongated projectile so that it will fly point-on to the target.

SAFETY: The mechanism, lever or other device which mechanically locks a firearm against the possibility of discharge.

SEAR: The device in the lock of a firearm which holds the hammer or firing pin in its cocked position. When the trigger is pulled to the rear it disengages the sear, which in turn releases the hammer or firing pin.

SELF-LOADING: A type of firearm which, by pulling the trigger, utilizes the energy of recoil or the powder gases, together with a heavy counterbalanced bolt and strong bolt spring, to eject the fired case, load a fresh cartridge from the magazine into the chamber, and close the breech ready to fire another round. The trigger must be pulled for each shot. Also termed autoloading or semi-automatic.

SHOTGUN: A smooth bore firearm which shoots a large number of small shot rather than a single large projectile.

SIDE BY SIDE: A double barrel shotgun or rifle with the barrels horizontally alongside of each other.

SIGHT RADIUS: The distance between the front and rear sights. The longer this distance, the greater the accuracy attainable.

SMOOTH BORE: A firearm without rifling.

STANDING BREECH: The face of the frame of a double barrel shotgun which closes the barrels at the breech.

STOCK: The wooden part of a shotgun or rifle, or the grip panels on the handle of a pistol or revolver.

STOCK, BUTT: The butt section of a firearm in which the forearm is separate from the butt stock.

STOCK, ONE-PIECE: The stock of a rifle in which the butt stock and fore-end are all in one piece.

TAKE-DOWN GUN OR RIFLE: A firearm in which the barrel and adjacent parts can be readily separated from the receiver or action—permitting the arm to be packed in a short container.

TANG: One of the two arms or shanks of the frame or receiver of a gun, extending to the rear, and inletted into the grip of the stock.

THROAT: The forward portion of the chamber where it tapers to meet the diameter of the bore proper.

TRIGGER: The small lever within the trigger guard. When pulled to the rear, it releases the hammer or firing pin, which discharges the cartridge in the chamber.

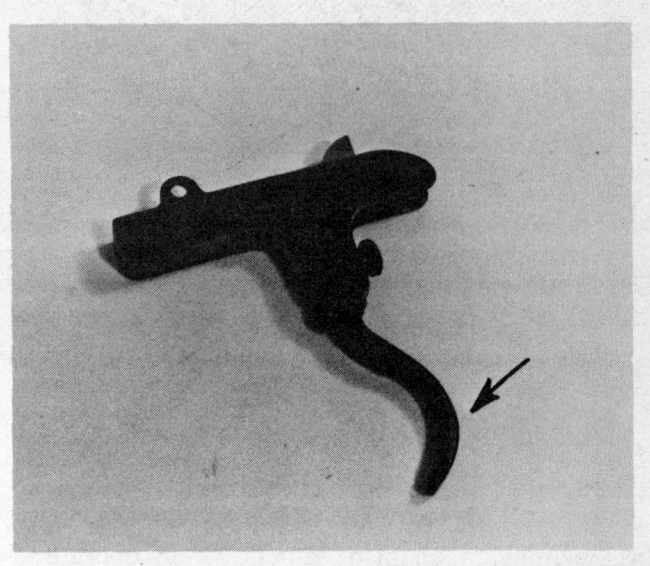

TRIGGER, SET: A type of trigger that can be set so that it will release the sear with a much lighter pull than the normal trigger.

TRIGGER GUARD: A guard surrounding the trigger (or triggers) of a firearm for general protection and safety purposes.

VELOCITY: The speed of the bullet or shot charge, measured in feet per second at or near the muzzle.

VENTILATED RIB: A raised sighting plane affixed to a shotgun barrel by posts, allowing the passage of air to disperse the mirage rising from a hot barrel which distorts the shooter's view of the target. Very useful on trap guns.

WATER TABLE: This is the flat space on the under side of the barrels of a break-down, double barrel gun at the breech, which bed on or form flat surfaces of the frame.

ZERO: The range in yards at which the sights of a rifle have been adjusted to center a group of shots at the point of aim at the same distance.

25
DIRECTORY OF TRADE SOURCES

Cleaning and Refinishing Supplies

A'n A Co.
Box 571
King of Prussia, PA 19406

Armite Labs.
1845 Randolph St.
Los Angeles, CA 90001

Armoloy Co. of Ft. Worth
204 E. Daggett St.
Ft. Worth, TX 76104

Birchwood-Casey
7900 Fuller Rd.
Eden Prairie, MN 55344

Bisonite Co., Inc.
P.O. Box 84
Kenmore Station, Buffalo, NY 14217

Blue and Gray Prods., Inc.
817 E. Main St.
Bradford, PA 16701

Jim Brobst
299 Poplar St.
Hamburg, PA 19526

GB Prods. Dept., H & R, Inc.
Industrial Rowe
Gardner, MA 01440

Browning Arms
Rt. 4, Box 624-B
Arnold, MO 63010

J.M. Bucheimer Co.
Airport Rd.
Frederick, MD 21701

Burnishine Prod. Co.
8140 N. Ridgeway
Skokie, IL 60076

Caddie Products Corp.
Div. of Jet-Aer
Paterson, NJ 07524

Chem-Pak Inc.
Winchester, VA 22601

Chopie Mfg. Inc.
531 Copeland
La Crosse, WI 54601

Clenzoil Co.
Box 1226, Sta. C
Canton, OH 44708

Clover Mfg. Co.
139 Woodward Ave.
Norwalk, CT 06856

Dri-Slide, Inc.
Industrial Park
1210 Locust St.
Fremont, MI 49412

Durango U.S.A.
P.O. Box 1029
Durango, CO 81301

Forty-Five Ranch Enterpr.
119 S. Main St.
Miami, OK 74354

Gun-All Products
Box 244
Dowagiac, MI 49047

Frank C. Hoppe Div.
P.O. Box 97
Parkesburg, PA 19365

J & G Rifle Ranch
Box S 80
Turner, MT 59542

Jet-Aer Corp.
100 Sixth Ave.
Paterson, NJ 07524

Kellog's Professional Prod., Inc.
P.O. Box 1201
Sandusky, OH 44870

K.W. Kleinendorst
48 Taylortown Rd.
Montville, NJ 07045

LPS Res. Labs., Inc.
2050 Cotner Ave.
Los Angeles, CA 90025

LEM Gun Spec.
Box 31
College Park, GA 30337

Liquid Wrench
Box 10628
Charlotte, NC 28201

Loner Products, Inc.
P.O. Box 219
Yorktown Heights, NY 10598

Lynx Line Gun Prods. Div.
Protective Coatings, Inc.
20620 Fenkel Ave.
Detroit, MI 48223

Marble Arms Co.
420 Industrial Park
Gladstone, MI 49837

Micro Sight Co.
242 Harbor Blvd.
Belmont, CA 94002

Mill Run Prod.
1360 W. 9th St.
Cleveland, OH 44113

Mirror-Lube
P.O. Box 693
San Juan Capistrano, CA 92675

New Method Mfg. Co.
Box 175
Bradford, PA 16701

Northern Instruments, Inc.
6680 North Highway 49
Lino Lake, MN 55014

Numrich Arms Co.
West Hurley, NY 12491

Outers Laboratories
Box 37
Onalaska, WI 54650

Radiator Spec. Co.
1400 Independence Blvd.
Charlotte, NC 28201

Realist Inc.
N. 93 W. 16288 Megal Dr.
Menomonee Falls, WI 53051

Reardon Prod.
103 W. Market St.
Morrison, IL 61270

Rice Gun Coatings
1521-43 St.
West Palm Beach, FL 33407

Rig Products Co.
21320 Deering Ct.
Canoga Park, CA 91304

Rusteprufe Labs
Sparta, WI 54656

Saunders Sptg. Gds.
338 Somerset
No. Plainfield, NJ 07060

Schultea's Gun String
67 Burress
Houston, TX 77022

Service Armament
689 Bergen Blvd.
Ridgefield, NJ 07657

Silicote Corp.
Box 359
Oshkosh, WI 54901

Silver Dollar Guns
P.O. Box 475
Franklin, NH 03235

Sportsmen's Labs, Inc.
Box 732
Anoka, MN 55303

Taylor & Robbins
Box 164
Rixford, PA 16745

Testing Systems, Inc.
#5 Tenakill Pk.
Cresskill, NJ 07626

Texas Platers Supply Co.
2453 W. Five Mile Pkwy.
Dallas, TX 75233

Totally Dependable Prod., Inc.
P.O. Box 277
Zieglerville, PA 19492

C.S. Van Gorden
120 Tenth Ave.
Eau Claire, WI 54701

WD-40 Co.
1061 Cudahy Pl.
San Diego, CA 92110

West Coast Secoa
3915 US Hwy. 98S
Lakeland, FL 33801

Williams Gun Sight
7389 Lapeer Rd.
Davison, MI 48423

Winslow Arms Inc.
P.O. Box 783
Camden, SC 29020

Wisconsin Platers Supply Co.
see: Texas Platers Supply

Woodstream Corp.
P.O. Box 327
Lititz, PA 17543

Zip Aerosol Prods.
21320 Deering Court
Canoga Park, CA 91304

Custom Gunsmiths

Dietrich Apel
see: Paul Jaeger, Inc.

Atkinson Gun Co.
P.O. Box 512
Prescott, AZ 86301

E. von Atzigen
The Custom Shop
890 Cochrane Crescent
Peterborough, Ont.
K94 5N3 Canada

Bain and Davis Sptg. Gds.
599 W. Las Tunas Dr.
San Gabriel, CA 41776

Joe J. Balickie
Rt. 2 Box 56-G
Apex, NC 27502

Al Biesen
W. 2039 Sinto Ave.
Spokane, WA 99201

Roger Biesen
W. 2039 Sinto Ave.
Spokane, WA 99201

John Bivins, Jr.
200 Wicklow Rd.
Winston-Salem, NC 27106

Lenard M. Brownell
Box 25
Wyarno, WY 82845

Jim Clark
Custom Gun Shop
5367 S. 1950 West
Roy, UT 84067

Homer L. Dangler
Box 254
Addison, MI 49220

Bill Dowtin
P.O. Box 72
Celina, TX 75009

Bill English
4411 S.W. 100th
Seattle, WA 98146

Ken Eyster
Heritage Gunsmiths Inc.
6641 Bishop Rd.
Centerburg, OH 43011

N.B. Fashingbauer
Box 366
Lac Du Flambeau, WI 54538

Jerry Fisher
1244 4th Ave. West
Kalispell, MT 59901

Larry L. Forster
Box 212
Gwinner, ND 58040

Dale Goens
Box 224
Cedar Crest, NM 87008

Griffin & Howe
589 Broadway
New York, NY 10012

Martin Hagn
Herzogstandstandweg 41
8113 Kochel a. See
W. Germany

Iver Henriksen
1211 S. 2nd St. W.
Missoula, MT 59801

Hoenig-Rodman
6521 Morton Dr.
Boise, ID 83705

Paul Jaeger
211 Leedom St.
P.O. Box 67
Jenkintown, PA 19046

John Kaufield Small Arms Eng.
7698 Garden Prairie Rd.
Garden Prairie, IL 61038

Monte Kennedy
P.O. Box 214
Kalispell, MT 59901

Kennon's Custom Rifles
5408 Biffle
Stone Mtn., GA 30083

LeFever Arms Co.
R.D. 1
Lee Center Stroke
Lee Center, NY 13363

Al Lind
7821 76th Ave.
Tacoma, WA 98498

Phillip Pilkington
P.O. Box 2284
University Station
Enid, OK 73701

C.H. Weisz
Box 311
Arligton, VA 22210

W.H. Wescomb
P.O. Box 488
Glencoe, CA 95232

Gun Parts, U.S. and Foreign

Badger Shooter's Supply
Box 397
Owen, WI 54460

Behlert Custom Guns, Inc.
725 Lehigh Ave.
Union, NJ 07083

Philip R. Crouthamel
513 E. Baltimore
E. Lansdowne, PA 19050

Charles E. Duffy
Williams Lane
West Hurley, NY 12491

Federal Ordnance Inc.
9634 Alpaca St.
So. El Monte, CA 91733

Fenwick's Gun Annex
P.O. Box 38
Weisberg Rd.
Whitehall, MD 21161

Jack First, The Gunshop Inc.
44633 Sierra Highway
Lancaster, CA 93534

Greg's Winchester Parts
P.O. Box 8125
W. Palm Beach, FL 33407

Hunter's Haven
Zero Prince St.
Alexandria, VA 22314

Walter H. Lodewick
2816 N.E. Halsey
Portland, OR 97232

Numrich Arms Co.
West Hurley, NY 12491

Pacific Intl. Merch. Corp.
2215 J St.
Sacramento, CA 95816

Potomac Arms Corp.
Zero Prince St.
Alexandria, VA 22314

Martin B. Retting, Inc.
11029 Washington
Culver City, CA 90230

Sarco, Inc.
323 Union St.
Stirling, NJ 07980

Sherwood Dist. Inc.
18714 Parthenia St.
Northridge, CA 91324

Simms
2801 J St.
Sacramento, CA 95816

Clifford L. Smires
R.D. Box 39
Columbus, NJ 08022

N.F. Strebe Gunworks
4926 Marlboro Pike, S.E.
Washington, D.C. 20027

Triple-K Mfg. Co.
568 6th Ave.
San Diego, CA 92101

**Gunsmith Supplies,
Tools, Services**

Albright Prod. Co.
P.O. Box 1144
Portola, CA 96122

Alley Supply Co.
Carson Valley Industrial Pk.
Gardnerville, NV 89410

Ames Precision Machine Works
5270 Geedes Rd.
Ann Arbor, MI 48501

Anderson Mfg. Co.
P.O. Box 3120
Yakima, WA 98903

Armite Labs
1845 Randolph St.
Los Angeles, CA 90001

B-Square Co.
Box 11281
Ft. Worth, TX 76110

Jim Baiar
490 Halfmoon Rd.
Columbia Falls, MT 59912

Behlert Custom Guns, Inc.
725 Lehigh Ave.
Union, NJ 07083

Al Biesen
W. 2039 Sinto Ave.
Spokane, WA 99201

Bonanza Sports Mfg. Co.
412 Western Ave.
Faribault, MN 55021

Brookstone Co.
125 Vose Farm Rd.
Peterborough, NH 03458

Bob Brownell's
Main & Third
Montezuma, IA 50171

W.E. Brownell
1852 Alessandro Trail
Vista, CA 92083

Maynard P. Buehler, Inc.
17 Orinda Hwy.
Orinda, CA 94563

Burgess Vibrocrafters, Inc.
Rt. 83
Grayslake, IL 60030

M.H. Canjar
500 E. 45th
Denver, CO 80216

Chapman Mfg. Co.
Rt. 17 at Saw Mill Rd.
Durham, CT 06422

Chase Chemical Corp.
3527 Smallman St.
Pittsburgh, PA 15201

Chicago Wheel & Mfg. Co.
1101 W. Monroe St.
Chicago, IL 60607

Christy Gun Works
875-57th St.
Sacramento, CA 95819

Clover Mfg. Co.
139 Woodward Ave.
Norwalk, CT 06856

Clymer Mfg. Co.
14241 W. 11 Mile Rd.
Oak Park, MI 48237

Colbert Industries
10107 Adella
South Gate, CA 90280

A. Constantine & Son, Inc.
2050 Eastchester Rd.
Bronx, NY 10461

Dave Cook
720 Hancock Ave.
Hancock, MI 49930

Cougar & Hunter
G 6398 W. Pierson Rd.
Flushing, MI 48433

Alvin L. Davidson Prods.
1215 Branson
Las Cruces, NM 88001

Dayton-Traister Co.
P.O. Box 593
Oak Harbor, WA 98277

Dem-Bart Checkering Tool, Inc.
6807 Hiway #2
Snohomish, WA 98290

Dremel Mfg. Co.
4915-21st St.
Racine, WI 53406

Chas. E. Duffy
Williams Lane
West Hurley, NY 12491

Peter Dyson Ltd.
29-31 Church St.
Honley, Huddersfield,
Yorksh. HD72AH England

E-Z Tool Co.
P.O. Box 3186
25 N.W. 44th Ave.
Des Moines, IA 50313

Edmund Scientific Co.
101 E. Glouster Pike
Barrington, NJ 08007

F.K. Elliott
Box 785
Ramona, CA 92065

Forster Prods., Inc.
82 E. Lanark Ave.
Lanark, IL 61046

Keith Francis, Inc.
Rte. 4, Box 146
Coos Bay, OR 97420

G.R.S. Corp.
P. O. Box 1153
Emporia, KS 66801

Gager Gage & Tool Co.
27509 Industrial Blvd.
Hayward, CA 94545

Gilmore Pattern Works
P.O. Box 50231
Tulsa, OK 74150

Gold Lode, Inc.
181 Gary Ave.
Wheaton, IL 60187

Gopher Shooter's Supply
Box 278
Faribault, MN 55021

Grace Metal Prod.
115 Ames St.
Elk Rapids, MI 49629

Gunline Tools, Inc.
719 No. East St.
Anaheim, CA 92805

H.&M.
24062 Orchard Lake Rd.
Box 258
Farmington, MI 48024

Half Moon Rifle Shop
490 Halfmoon Rd.
Columbia Falls, MT 59912

Hartford Reamer Co.
Box 134
Lathrup Village, MI 48070

Paul Jaeger Inc.
211 Leedom St.
Jenkintown, PA 19046

Jeffredo Gunsight Co.
1629 Via Monserate
Fallbrook, CA 92028

Jerrow's Inletting Serv.
452 5th Ave. E.N.
Kalispell, MT 59901

K&D Grinding Co.
Box 1766
Alexandria, LA 71301

Kasenite Co., Inc.
3 King St.
Mahwah, NJ 07430

J. Korzinek
RD #2, Box R
Canton, PA 17724

LanDav Custom Guns
7213 Lee Highway
Falls Church, VA 22046

John G. Lawson
1802 E. Columbia Ave.
Tacoma, WA 98404

Lea Mfg. Co.
237 E. Aurora St.
Waterbury, CT 06720

Lightwood & Son Ltd.
Britannia Rd.
Banbury, Oxfordsh.
OX1 68TD, England

Lock's Phila. Gun Exch.
6700 Rowland Ave.
Philadelphia, PA 19149

Marker Machine Co.
Box 426
Charleston, IL 61920

Michaels of Oregon Co.
P.O. Box 13010
Portland, OR 97213

Viggo Miller
P.O. Box 4181
Omaha, NE 68104

Miller Single Trigger Mfg. Co.
R.D. on Rt. 209
Millersburg, PA 17061

243

Fran Mittermeier
3577 E. Tremont
New York, NY 10465

Moderntools Corp.
Box 407, Dept. GD
Woodside, NY 11377

N&J Sales
Lime Kiln Rd.
Northford, CT 06472

Karl A. Neise, Inc.
5602 Roosevelt Ave.
Woodside, NY 11377

Palmgren Prods.
Chicago Tool & Eng. Co.
8383 South Chicago Ave.
Chicago, IL 60167

Panavise Prods., Inc.
2850 29th St.
Long Beach, CA 90806

C.R. Pedersen & Son
Ludington, MI 49431

Richland Arms Co.
321 W. Adrian St.
Blissfield, MI 49228

Riley's Supply Co.
121 N. Main St.
Alvilla, IN 46710

Ruhr-American Corp.
S Hwy. #5
Glenwood, MN 56334

A.G. Russell
1705 Hiway 71N
Springdale, AR 72764

Schaffner Mfg. Co.
Emsworth
Pittsburgh, PA 15202

Schuetzen Gun Works (SGW)
624 Old Pacific Hwy. S.E.
Olympia, WA 98503

Shaw's
Rt. 4, Box 407-L
Escondido, CA 92025

L.S. Starrett Co.
Athol, 01331

Texas Platers Supply Co.
2453 W. Five Mile Pkwy.
Dallas, TX 75233

Timney Mfg. Co.
2847 E. Siesta Lane
Phoenix, AZ 85024

Stan de Treville
Box 33021
San Diego, CA 92103

Twin City Steel Treating Co.
1114 S. 3rd
Minneapolis, MN 55415

Will-Burt Co.
169 S. Main
Orrville, OH 44667

Williams Gun Sight Co.
7389 Lapeer Rd.
Davison, MI 48423

Wilson Arms Co.
63 Leetes Island Rd.
Branford, CT 06405

Wisconsin Platers Supply Co.
See: Texas Platers Supply Co.

W.C. Wolff Co.
Box 232
Ardmore, PA 19003

Woodcraft Supply Corp.
313 Montvale
Woburn, MA 01801

Handgun Accessories

A.R. Sales Co.
P.O. Box 3192
South El Monte, CA 91733

Baramie Corp.
6250 E. 7 Mile Rd.
Detroit, MI 48234

Bar-Sto Precision Mach.
633 S. Victory Blvd.
Burbank, CA 91502

Behlert Custom Guns, Inc.
725 Lehigh Ave.
Union, NJ 07083

Belt Slide, Inc.
1114 N. Lamar, P.O. Box 15303
Austin, TX 78761

Bingham Ltd.
1775-C Wilwat Dr.
Norcross, GA 30093

C'Arco
P.O. Box 308
Highland, CA 92346

Case Master
4675 E. 10 Ave.
Miami, FL 33013

Central Specialties Co.
6030 Northwest Hwy.
Chicago, IL 60631

D&E Magazines Mfg.
P.O. Box 4579
Downey, CA 90242

Laka Tool Co.
62 Kinkel St.
Westbury, L.I. NY 11590

Lee Precision Inc.
4275 Hwy. U
Hartford, WI 53027

Los Gatos Grip & Specialty Co.
P.O. Box 1850
Los Gatos, CA 95030

Matich Loader
10439 Rush St.
South El Monte, CA 91733

Mellmark Mfg. Co.
P. O. Box 139
Turlock, CA 95380

W.A. Miller Co., Inc.
Mingo Loop
Oguossoc, ME 04964

No-Sho Mfg. Co.
10727 Glenfield Ct.
Houston, TX 77096

Pachmayr
1220 S. Grand
Los Angeles, CA 90015

Pacific Intl. Mchdsg. Corp.
2215 "J" St.
Sacramento, CA 95818

Pistolsafe
Dr. L.
N. Chili, NY 14514

Platt Luggage, Inc.
2301 S. Prairie
Chicago, IL 60616

Sile Distributors
7 Centre Market Pl.
New York, NY 10013

Sportsmen's Equip. Co.
415 W. Washington
San Diego, CA 92103

Bill Dyer
503 Midwest Bldg.
Oklahoma City, OK 73102

Essex Arms
Box 345
Phaerring St.
Island Pond, VT 05846

R.D. Frielich
396 Broome St.
New York, NY 10013

M. Tyler
1326 W. Britton
Oklahoma City, OK 73114

Whitney Sales, Inc.
P.O. Box 875
Reseda, CA 91335

Dave Woodruff
Box 5
Bear, DE 19701

Handgun Grips

Crest Carving Co.
8091 Bolsa Ave.
Midway City, CA 92655

Fitz
653 N. Hagar St.
San Fernando, CA 91340

Gateway Shooter's Supply, Inc.
10145-103rd St.
Jacksonville, FL 32210

Herrett's
Box 741
Twin Falls, ID 83301

Mershon Co., Inc.
1230 S. Grand Ave.
Los Angeles, CA 90015

Mustang Custom Pistol Grips
28715 Via Montezuma
Temecula, CA 92390

Robert H. Newell
55 Coyote
Los Alamos, NM 87544

Rogers Grips
Gateway Shooters Supply
10145-103rd St.
Jacksonville, FL 32210

Safety Grip Corp.
Box 456
Riverside St.
Miami, FL 33135

Jean St. Henri
6525 Dume Dr.
Malibu, CA 90265

Schiemeier
Box 704
Twin Falls, ID 83301

Sile Dist.
7 Centre Market Pl.
New York, NY 10013

Southern Gun Exchange, Inc.
4311 Northeast Expressway
Atlanta, GA 30340

Sports, Inc.
P.O. Box 683
Park Ridge, IL 60068

Muzzle-Loading Guns, Barrels or Equipment

A & K Mfg. Co., Inc.
1651 N. Nancy Rose Ave.
Tucson, AZ 85712

Luther Adkins
Box 281
Shelbyville, IN 47176

American Heritage Arms, Inc.
Rt. 44 P.O. Box 95
West Willington, CT 06279

Anderson Mfg. Co.
P.O. Box 3120
Yakima, WA 98903

Armoury, Inc.
Rt. 202
New Preston, CT 06777

Beaver Lodge
9245 16th Ave.
Seattle, WA 98106

John Bivins, Jr.
200 Wicklow Rd.
Winston-Salem, NC 27106

Blue & Gray Prods, Inc.
817 E. Main St.
Bradford, PA 16701

G.S. Bunch
7735 Garrison
Hyattsville, MD 20784

Butler Creek Corp.
Box GG
Jackson, WY 83001

Conversion Arms, Inc.
P.O. Box 449
Yuba City, CA 95991

Cache La Poudre Rifleworks
168 N. College
Ft. Collins, CO 80521

Challanger Mfg. Co.
118 Pearl St.
Mt. Vernon, NY 10550

R. MacDonald Champlin
P.O. Box 74
Wentworth, NH 03282

Chopie Mfg. Co.
531 Copeland Ave.
LaCrosse, WI 53601

Classic Arms Intl., Inc.
20 Wilbraham St.
Palmer, MA 01069

Connecticut Valley Arms Co.
Saybrook Rd.
Haddam, CT 06438

Earl T. Cureton
Rt. 2 Box 388
Willoughby Rd.
Bulls Gap, TN 37711

DJ Inc.
1310 S. Park Rd.
Fairdale, KY 40118

Leonard Day & Co.
316 Burt Pits Rd.
Northampton, MA 10160

Dixie Gun Works, Inc.
P.O. Box 130
Union City, TN 38261

EMF Co., Inc.
Box 1248
Studio City, CA 91604

Eagle Arms Co.
Riverview Dr.
Mt. Washington, KY 40047

Euroarms of America, Inc.
14 W. Monmouth St.
Winchester, VA 22601

The Eutaw Co.
Box 608
U.S. Hwy. 176W
Holly Hill, SC 29059

Ted Fellowes
Beaver Lodge
9245 16th Ave. S.W.
Seattle, WA 98106

Firearms Imp. & Exp. Corp.
2470 N.W. 21st St.
Miami, FL 33142

Marshall F. Fish
Rt. 22N
Westport, NY 12993

Clark K. Frazier/Matchmate
RFD 1
Rawson, OH 45881

C.R. & D.E. Getz
Box 88
Beavertown, PA 17813

Golden Age Arms Co.
14 W. Winter St.
Delaware, OH 43015

A.R. Goode
Rt. 3 Box 139
Catoctin Furnace
Thurmont, MD 21788

Green River Forge, Ltd.
P.O. Box 885
Springfield, OR 97477

Harper's Ferry Arms Co.
256 E. Broadway
Hopewell, VA 23860

Hopkins & Allen Arms
#1 Melnick Rd.
Monsey, NY 10952

International Arms
23239 Doremus Ave.
St. Clair Shores, MI 48080

JJJJ Ranch, Wm. Large
Rt. 1
Ironton, OH 45638

Art LeFeuvre
1003 Hazel Ave.
Deerfield, IL 60015

Les' Gun Shop
Box 511
Kalispell, MT 59901

Lever Arms Serv. Ltd.
771 Dunsmuir
Vancouver 1, B.C. Canada

Log Cabin Sport Shop
8010 Lafayette Rd.
Lodi, OH 44254

Lyman Products Corp.
Rt. 147
Middlefield, CT 06455

McKeown's Guns
R.R.1
Pekin, IL 61554

Judson E. Mariotti
Beauty Hill Rd.
Barrington, NH 03825

Maurer Arms
2366 Frederick Dr.
Cuyahoga Falls, OH 44221

Mountain State ML Supplies
Box 154-1
Williamstown, WV 26187

Mowrey Gun Works
Box 28
Iowa Park, TX 76367

Muzzleloaders Etc., Inc.
9901 Lyndale Ave. S.
Bloomington, MN 55420

Numrich Corp.
W. Hurley, NY 12491

Ox-Yoke Originals
130 Griffin Rd.
West Suffield, CT 06093

Penna. Rifle Works
319 E. Main St.
Ligonier, PA 15658

A.W. Peterson Gun Shop
1693 Old Hwy. 441 N.
Mt. Dora, FL 32757

Richland Arms
321 W. Adrian St.
Blissfield, MI 49228

Rush's Old Colonial Forge
106 Wiltshire Rd.
Baltimore, MD 21221

Salish House, Inc.
P.O. Box 27
Rollins, MT 59931

H.M. Schoeller
569 S. Braddock Ave.
Pittsburgh, PA 15221

Shiloh Products
37 Potter St.
Farmington, NY 11735

C.E. Siler Locks
Rt. 6, Box 5
Chandler, NC 28715

Ken Steggles
17 Bell Lane, Byfield
Nr. Daventry,
Northants NN11 6US
England

Ultra-Hi Products Co.
150 Florence Ave.
Hawthorne, NJ 07506

Upper Missouri Trading Co.
3rd and Harold St.
Crofton, NB 68730

R. Watts
826 Springdale Rd.
Atlanta, GA 30306

Thos. F. White
5801 Westchester Ct.
Worthington, OH 43085

Williamson-Page Gunsmith Serv.
6021 Camp Bowie Blvd.
Ft. Worth, TX 76116

York County Gun Works
R.R. #4
Tottenham, Ont. LOG 1WO
Canada

Reboring and Rerifling

P.O. Ackley
Max B. Graff, Inc.
Rt. 1, Box 24
American Fork, UT

245

J.W. Van Patten
Box 145, Foster Hill
Milford, PA 18837

Robt. G. West
27211 Huey Ave.
Eugene, OR 97402

Atkinson Gun Co.
P.O. Box 512
Prescott, AZ 86301

Bain & Davis Sptg. Gds.
559 W. Las Tunas Dr.
San Gabriel, CA 91776

Fuller Gun Shop
Cooper Landing, AK 99572

Max B. Graff, Inc.
Rt. 1 Box 24
American Fork, UT 84003

Bruce Jones
389 Calla Ave.
Imperial Beach, CA 92032

Les' Gun Shop
Box 511
Kalispell, MT 59901

Morgan's Cust. Reboring
707 Union Ave.
Grants Pass, OR 97526

Nu-Line Guns
3727 Jennings Rd.
St. Louis, MO 63121

Al Petersen
Box 8
Riverhurst, Saskatchewan
Canada SOH3PO

Schuetzen Gun Works (SGW)
624 Old Pacific Hwy.
Olympia, WA 98503

Siegrist Gun Shop
2689 McLean Rd.
Whittemore, MI 48770

Snapp's Gunshop
6911 E. Washington Rd.
Clare, MI 48617

R. Southgate
Rt. 2
Franklin, TN 37064

Rifle Barrel Makers

P.O. Ackley Gun Barrels
Max B. Graff, Inc.
Rt. 1 Box 24
American Fork, UT 84003

Atkinson Gun Co.
P.O. Box 512
Prescott, AZ 86301

Ralph L. Carter
Rt. 1, Box 92
Fountain, CO 80817

Christy Gun Works
875 57th St.
Sacramento, CA 95819

Clerke Prods.
2219 Main St.
Santa Monica, CA 90405

Cuthbert Gun Shop
715 S. 5th
Coos Bay, OR 97420

B.W. Darr
Saeco-Darr Rifle Co.
P.O. Box 778
Carpinteria, CA 93013

Douglas Barrels, Inc.
5504 Big Tyler Rd.
Charleston, WV 25312

Douglas Jackalope Gun &
Sport Shop, Inc.
1048 S. 5th St.
Douglas, WY 82633

Federal Firearms Co., Inc.
Box 145
145 Thomas Run Rd.
Oakdale, PA 15071

C.R. & D.E. Getz
Box 88
Beavertown, PA 17813

A.R. Goode
Rt. 3, Box 139
Catoctin Furnace
Thurmont, MD 21788

Hart Rifle Barrels, Inc.
RD2
Lafayette, NY 13084

Wm. H. Hobaugh
Box M
Philipsburg, MT 59858

David R. Huntington
RFD 1, Box 23
Heber City, UT 83032

Kogot, John Pell
410 College Ave.
Trinidad, CO 81082

Gene Lechner
636 Jane N.E.
Albuquerque, NM 87123

Les' Gun Shop
Box 511
Kalispell, MT 59901

Marquart Precision Co.
Box 1740
Prescott, AZ 86301

Nu-Line Guns, Inc.
3727 Jennings Rd.
St. Louis, MO 63121

Numrich Arms
W. Hurley, NY 12491

Al Petersen
The Rifle Ranch
Box 8
Riverhurst, Sask.
SOH3P0 Canada

Sanders Cust. Gun Serv.
2358 Tyler Lane
Louisville, KY 40205

Ed Shilen Rifles, Inc.
205 Metropark Blvd.
Ennis, TX 75119

W.C. Strutz
Rt. 1
Eagle River, WI 54521

Titus Barrel & Gun Co.
RFD 1 Box 23
Heber City, UT 84032

Wilson Arms
63 Leetes Island Rd.
Branford, CT 06405

Sights, Metallic

B-Square Eng. Co.
Box 11281
Ft. Worth, TX 76110

Behlert Custom Sights, Inc.
725 Lehigh Ave.
Union, NJ 07083

Bo-Mar Tool & Mfg. Co.
Box 168
Carthage, TX 75633

Maynard P. Buehler, Inc.
17 Orinda Hwy.
Orinda, CA 94563

Christy Gun Works
875 57th St.
Sacramento, CA 95819

Jim Day
902 N. Bownen Lane
Florence, SD 29501

E-Z Mount
Ruelle Bros.
P.O. Box 114
Ferndale, MT 48220

Freeland's Scope Stands, Inc.
3734-14th Ave.
Rock Island, IL 61201

Paul T. Haberly
2364 N. Neva
Chicago, IL 60635

Paul Jaeger, Inc.
211 Leedom St.
Jenkintown, PA 19046

Lee's Red Ramps
34220 Cheseboro Rd.
Space 19
Palmdale, CA 93550

Jim Lofland
2275 Larkin Rd.
Boothwyn, PA 19061

Lyman Products Corp.
Rt. 147
Middlefield, CT 06455

Marble Arms Corp.
420 Industrial Park
Gladstone, MI 49837

Merit Gunsight Co.
P.O. Box 995
Sequim, WA 98382

Micro Sight Co.
242 Harbor Blvd.
Belmont, CA 94002

Miniature Machine Co.
210 E. Poplar
Deming, NM 88030

Modern Industries, Inc.
613 W.-11
Erie, PA 16501

C.R. Pedersen & Son
Ludington, MI 49431

Poly Choke Co., Inc.
P.O. Box 296
Hartford, CT 06101

Redfield Gun Sight Co.
5800 E. Jewell St.
Denver, CO 80222

Schwarz's Gun Shop
41 15th St.
Wellsburg, WV 26070

Simmons Gun Specialties, Inc.
700 Rodgers Rd.
Olathe, KS 66061

Slug Site Co.
Whitetail Wilds
Lake Hubert, MN 56469

Sport Service Center
2364 N. Neva
Chicago, IL 60635

Tradewinds, Inc.
Box 1191
Tacoma, WA 98401

Williams Gun Sight Co.
7389 Lapeer Rd.
Davison, MI 48423

Stocks

(Commercial and Custom)

Abe and VanHorn
5124 Huntington Dr.
Los Angeles, CA 90032

Adams Custom Gun Stocks
13461 Quilto Rd.
Saratoga, CA 95070

Ahlman's Inc.
R.R. 1 Box 20
Morristown, MN 55052

Don Allen
Rt. 1, Timberlane
Northfield, MN 55057

Anderson's Guns
Jim Jares
706 S. 23rd St.
Laramie, WY 82070

R.J. Anton
874 Olympic Dr.
Waterloo, IA 50701

Dietrich Apel
See: Paul Jaeger, Inc.

Jim Baiar
490 Halfmoon Rd.
Columbin Falls, MT 59912

Joe J. Balickie
Custom Stocks
Rt. 2 Box 56-G
Apex, NC 27502

Bartas,
Rt. 1, Box 129-A
Cato, WI 54206

John Bianchi
100 Calle Cortez
Temecula, CA 92390

Al Biesen
W. 2039 Sinto Ave.
Spokane, WA 99201

Stephen L. Billeb
Rt. 3 Box 163
Bozeman, MT 59715

E.C. Bishop & Son, Inc.
Box 7
Warsaw, MO 65355

John M. Boltin
P.O. Box 1122
N. Myrtle Beach, SC 29582

Brown Precision Co.
5869 Indian Ave.
San Jose, CA 95123

Lenard M. Brownell
Box 25
Wyarno, WY 82845

E.J. Bryant
3154 Glen St.
Eureka, CA 95501

Jack Burres
10333 San Fernando Rd.
Pacoima, CA 91331

Calico Hardwoods, Inc.
1648 Airport Blvd.
Windsor, CA 95492

Dick Campbell
365 W. Oxford Ave.
Englewood, CO 80110

Winston Churchill
Twenty Mile Stream Rd.
Rt. 1, Box 29B
Proctorsville, VT 05153

Cloward's Gun Shop
Jim Cloward
4023 Aurora Ave.
Seattle, WA 98102

Crane Creek Gun Stock Co.
25 Sherphard Terr.
Madison, WI 53705

Crest Carving Co.
8091 Bolsa Ave.
Midway City, CA 92655

Custom Gunstocks
365 W. Oxford Ave.
Englewood, CO 80110

Dahl's Custom Stocks
Rt. 4 Box 187
Schofield Rd.
Lake Geneva, WI 53147

Jack Dever
8520 N.W. 90
Oklahoma City, OK 73132

Charles De Veto
1087 Irene Rd.
Lyndhurst, OH 44124

Bill Dowtin
P.O. Box 72
Celina, TX 75009

Reinhart Fajen
Box 338
Warsaw, MO 65355

N.B. Fashingbauer
Box 366
Lac Du Flambeau, WI 54538

Ted Fellowes
Beaver Lodge
9245 16th Ave.
Seattle, WA 98106

Clyde E. Fischer
Rt. 1 Box 170-M
Victoria, TX 77901

Jerry Fisher
1244 4th Ave.
Kalispell, MT 59901

Flaig's Lodge
Millvale, PA 15209

Donald E. Folks
205 W. Lincoln St.
Pontiac, IL 61764

Larry L. Forster
Box 212
Gwinner, ND 58040

Horace M. Frantz
Box 128
Farmingdale, NJ 07727

Freeland's Scope Stands, Inc.
3734 14th Ave.
Rock Island, IL 61201

Dale Goens
Box 224
Cedar Crest, NM 87008

Gary Goudy
263 Hedge Rd.
Menlo Park, CA 44025

Gould's Myrtlewood
1692 N. Dogwood
Coquille, OR 97423

Charles E. Grace
10144 Elk Lake Rd.
Williamsburg, MI 49690

Rolf R. Gruning
315 Busby Dr.
San Antonio, TX 78209

Guncraft (Kelowna) Ltd.
1771 Harvey Ave.
Kelowna, B.C. V1Y 6G4
Canada

Half Moon Rifle Shop
490 Halfmoon Rd.
Columbia Falls, MT 59912

Harper's Custom Stocks
928 Lombrano St.
San Antonio, TX 78207

Harris Gun Stocks, Inc.
12 Lake St.
Richfield Springs, NY 13439

Hal Hartley
147 Blairsfork Rd.
Lenoir, NC 28645

Hayes Gunstock Service Co.
914 E. Turner St.
Clearwater, FL 33516

Hubert J. Hecht
55 Rose Meade Circle
Sacramento, CA 95831

Edward O. Hefti
300 Fairview
College Sta., TX 77840

Herter's Inc.
Waseca, MN 56093

Klaus Hiptmayer
1771 Harvey Ave.
Kelowna, B.C. V1Y 6G4
Canada

Richard Hodgson
5589 Arapahoe
Unit 104
Boulder, CO 80301

Hollis Gun Shop
917 Rex St.
Carlsbad, NM 88220

Henry Houser
Ozark Custom Carving
117 Main St.
Warsaw, MO 65355

Jackson's
Box 416
Selman City, TX 75689

Paul Jaeger
211 Leedom St.
Jenkintown, PA 19046

Johnson Wood Prods.
Rt. 1
Strawberry Point, IA 52076

Monte Kennedy
P.O. Box 214
Kalispell, MT 59901

Don Klein
Box 277
Camp Douglas, WI 54618

LeFever Arms Co., Inc.
RD 1
Lee Center Stroke
Lee Center, NY 13363

Lenz Firearms Co.
1480 Elkay Dr.
Eugene, OR 97404

Philip D. Letiecq
Box 251
Story, WY 82842

Al Lind
7821 76th Ave. S.W.
Tacoma, WA 98498

Bill McGuire
1600 N. Eastmont Ave.
East Wenatchee, WA 98801

Gale McMillan
28638 N. 42 St. Box DY72
Cave Creek Stage
Phoenix, AZ 85020

Maurer Arms
2366 Frederick Dr.
Cuyahoga Falls, OH 44221

Leonard Mews
Spring Rd., Box 242
Hortonville, WI 54944

Robt. U. Milhoan & Son
Rt. 3
Elizabeth, WV 26143

C.D. Miller Guns
Purl St.
St. Onge, SD 57779

Mills Custom Stocks
401 N. Ellsworth Ave.
San Mateo, CA 94401

Nelsen's Gun Shop
501 S. Wilson
Olympia, WA 98501

Oakley & Merkley
Box 2446
Sacramento, CA 95811

Maurice Ottmar
Box 657
113 E. Fir
Coulee City, WA 99115

Pachmayr Gun Works
1220 S. Grand Ave.
Los Angeles, CA 90015

Paulsen Gunstocks
Rt. 71 Box 11
Chinook, MT 59523

Peterson Mach. Carving
Box 1065
Sun Valley, CA 91352

Philip Pilkington
P.O. Box 2284
University Station
Enid, OK 73701

R. Neal Rice
Box 12172
Denver, CO 80212

Richards Micro-Fit Stocks
PO Box 1066
Sun Valley, CA 91352

Carl Roth, Jr.
4728 Pineridge Ave.
Cheyenne, WY 82001

Matt Row
19258 Rowland
Covina, CA 91723

Royal Arms, Inc.
10064 Bert Acosta Ct.
Santee, CA 92071

Sanders Cust. Gun Serv.
2358 Tyler Lane
Louisville, KY 40205

Saratoga Arms Co.
RD 3 Box 387
Pottstown, PA 19464

Roy Schaefer
965 W. Hilliard Lane
Eugene, OR 97404

Shaws
Rt. 4 Box 407-L
Escondido, CA 92025

Hank Shows
The Best
1202 N. State
Ukaih, CA 95482

Walter Schultz
RD 3
Pottstown, PA 19464

Sile Dist.
7 Centre Market Pl.
New York, NY 10013

Six Enterprises
6564 Hidden Creek Dr.
San Jose, CA 95120

Ed Sowers
8331 DeCelis Pl.
Sepulveda, CA 91343

Fred D. Speiser
2229 Dearborn
Missoula, MT 59801

Sportsmen's Equip. Co.
915 W. Washington
San Diego, CA 92103

Keith Stegall
Box 696
Gunnison, CO 80230

Stinehour Rifles
Box 84
Cragsmoor, NY 12420

Surf N' Sea., Inc.
62-595 Kam Hwy. Box 268
Haleiwa, HI 96712

Swanson Cust. Firearms
1051 Broadway
Denver, CO 80203

Talmage Enterpr.
43197 E. Whittier
Hemet, CA 92343

Brent L. Umberger
Sportsman's Haven
RR 4
Cambridge, OH 43725

Roy Vail
Rt. 1 Box 8
Warwick, NY 10990

Weatherby's
2781 Firestone
South Gate, CA 90280

Frank R. Wells
350-C E. Prince Rd.
Tucson, AZ 85705

Western Gunstocks Mfg. Co.
550 Valencia School Rd.
Aptos, CA 95003

Duane Wiebe
426 Creekside Rd.
Pleasant Hill, CA 94563

Bob Williams
c/o Hermans-Atlas Custom
Guns
800 E St. NW
Washington, DC 20004

Williamson-Pate Gunsmith
Serv.
6021 Camp Bowie Blvd.
Ft. Worth TX 76116

Robert M. Winter
Box 484
Menno, SD 57045

Mike Yee
4700-46th Ave. S.W.
Seattle, WA 98116

Russell R. Zeeryp
1601 Foard Dr.
Lynn Ross Manor
Morristown, TN 37814

**Triggers,
Related Equipment**

M.H. Canjar Co.
500 E. 45th Ave.
Denver, CO 80216

Custom Products
Neil A. Jones
686 Baldwin St.
Meadville, PA 16335

Dayton-Traister Co.
P.O. Box 593
Oak Harbor, WA 98277

Flaig's
Babcock Blvd. & Thompson
Run Rd.
Millvale, PA 15209

Gager Gage & Tool Co.
27509 Industrial Blvd.
Hayward, CA 94545

Franklin C. Green
Electronic Trigger System
530 W. Oak Grove Rd.
Montrose, CO 81401

Bill Holmes
2405 Pump Sta. Rd.
Springdale, AZ 72764

Paul Jaeger, Inc.
211 Leedom St.
Jenkintown, PA 19046

Michaels of Oregon Co.
P.O. Box 13010
Portland, OR 97213

Miller Single Trigger Mfg. Co.
RD 1 on Rt. 209
Millersburg, PA 17061

Viggo Miller
P.O. Box 4181
Omaha, NB 58104

Ohaus Corp.
29 Hanover Rd.
Florham Park, NJ 07932

Pachmayr Gun Works
1220 S. Grand Ave.
Los Angeles, CA 90015

Pacific Tool Co.
P.O. Drawer 2048
Ordnance Plant Rd.
Grand Island, NB 68801

Richland Arms Co.
321 W. Adrian St.
Blissfield, MI 49228

Sport Service Center
2364 N. Neva
Chicago, IL 60635

Timney Mfg. Co.
2847 E. Siesta Lane
Phoenix, AZ 85024

Melvin Tyler
1326 W. Britton Ave.
Oklahoma City, OK 73114

Williams Gun Sight Co.
7389 Lapeer Rd.
Davison, MI 48423

APPENDIX

Conversion Tables

The tables below will allow you to convert weights and measures into the desired equivalent. Simply find the weight or measure you're working with in the left-hand column and multiply it by the number in the far right-hand column. The correct designation for the resulting figure will be found in the center column.

Conversion Factors

TO CONVERT	INTO	MULTIPLY BY
A		
Abcoulomb	Statcoulombs	2.998×10^{10}
Acre	Sq. chain (Gunters)	10
Acre	Rods	.160
Acre	Square links (Gunters)	1×10^5
Acre	Hectare or sq. hectometer	.4047
acres	sq feet	43,560.0
acres	sq meters	4,047.
acres	sq miles	1.562×10^{-3}
acres	sq yards	4,840.
acre-feet	cu feet	43,560.0
acre-feet	gallons	3.259×10^5
amperes/sq cm	amps/sq in.	6.452
amperes/sq cm	amps/sq meter	10^4
amperes/sq in.	amps/sq cm	0.1550
amperes/sq in.	amps/sq meter	1,550.0
amperes/sq meter	amps/sq cm	10^{-4}
amperes/sq meter	amps/sq in.	6.452×10^{-4}
ampere-hours	coulombs	3,600.0
ampere-hours	faradays	0.03731
ampere-turns	gilberts	1.257
ampere-turns/cm	amp-turns/in.	2.540
ampere-turns/cm	amp-turns/meter	100.0
ampere-turns/cm	gilberts/cm	1.257
ampere-turns/in.	amp-turns/cm	0.3937
ampere-turns/in.	amp-turns/meter	39.37
ampere-turns/in.	gilberts/cm	0.4950
ampere-turns/meter	amp/turns/cm	0.01
ampere-turns/meter	amp-turns/in.	0.0254
ampere-turns/meter	gilberts/cm	0.01257
Angstrom unit	Inch	3937×10^{-9}
Angstrom unit	Meter	1×10^{-10}
Angstrom unit	Micron or (Mu)	1×10^{-4}
Are	Acre (US)	.02471
Ares	sq. yards	119.60
ares	acres	0.02471
ares	sq meters	100.0
Astronomical Unit	Kilometers	1.495×10^3
Atmospheres	Ton/sq. inch	.007348
atmospheres	cms of mercury	76.0
atmospheres	ft of water (at 4°C)	33.90
atmospheres	in. of mercury (at 0°C)	29.92
atmospheres	kgs/sq cm	1.0333
atmospheres	kgs/sq meter	10,332.
atmospheres	pounds/sq. in.	14.70
atmospheres	tons/sq ft	1.058

Conversion Factors

TO CONVERT	INTO	MULTIPLY BY
B		
Barrels (U.S., dry)	cu. inches	7056.
Barrels (U.S., dry)	quarts (dry)	105.0
Barrels (U.S., liquid)	gallons	31.5
barrels (oil)	gallons (oil)	42.0
bars	atmospheres	0.9869
bars	dynes/sq cm	10^6
bars	kgs/sq meter	1.020×10^4
bars	pounds/sq ft	2,089.
bars	pounds/sq in.	14.50
Baryl	Dyne/sq. cm.	1.000
Bolt (US Cloth)	Meters	36.576
Btu	Liter-Atmosphere	10.409
Btu	ergs	1.0550×10^{10}
Btu	foot-lbs	778.3
Btu	gram-calories	252.0
Btu	horsepower-hrs	3.931×10^{-4}
Btu	joules	1,054.8
Btu	kilogram-calories	0.2520
Btu	kilogram-meters	107.5
Btu	kilowatt-hrs	2.928×10^{-4}
Btu/hr	foot-pounds/sec	0.2162
Btu/hr	gram-cal/sec	0.0700
Btu/hr	horsepower-hrs	3.929×10^{-4}
Btu/hr	watts	0.2931
Btu/min	foot-lbs/sec	12.96
Btu/min	horsepower	0.02356
Btu/min	kilowatts	0.01757
Btu/min	watts	17.57
Btu/sq ft/min	watts/sq in.	0.1221
Bucket (Br. dry)	Cubic Cm.	1.818×10^4
bushels	cu ft	1.2445
bushels	cu in.	2,150.4
bushels	cu meters	0.03524
bushels	liters	35.24
bushels	pecks	4.0
bushels	pints (dry)	64.0
bushels	quarts (dry)	32.0
C		
Calories, gram (mean)	Btu (mean)	3.9685×10^{-3}
Candle/sq. cm	Lamberts	3.142
Candle/sq. inch	Lamberts	.4870
centares (centiares)	sq meters	1.0
Celsius	fahrenheit	(C°x9/5) + 32

249

Conversion Factors

TO CONVERT	INTO	MULTIPLY BY
centigrams	grams	0.01
Centiliter	Ounce fluid (US)	.3382
Centiliter	Cubic inch	.6103
Centiliter	drams	2.705
centiliters	liters	0.01
centimeters	feet	3.281×10^{-2}
centimeters	inches	0.3937
centimeters	kilometers	10^{-5}
centimeters	meters	0.01
centimeters	miles	6.214×10^{-6}
centimeters	millimeters	10.0
centimeters	mils	393.7
centimeters	yards	1.094×10^{-2}
centimeter-dynes	cm-grams	1.020×10^{-3}
centimeter-dynes	meter-kgs	1.020×10^{-8}
centimeter-dynes	pound-feet	7.376×10^{-8}
centimeter-grams	cm-dynes	980.7
centimeter-grams	meter-kgs	10^{-5}
centimeter-grams	pound-feet	7.233×10^{-5}
centimeters of mercury	atmospheres	0.01316
centimeters of mercury	feet of water	0.4461
centimeters of mercury	kgs/sq meter	136.0
centimeters of mercury	pounds/sq ft	27.85
centimeters of mercury	pounds/sq in.	0.1934
centimeters/sec	feet/min	1.1969
centimeters/sec	feet/sec	0.03281
centimeters/sec	kilometers/hr	0.036
centimeters-sec	knots	0.1943
centimeters/sec	meters/min	0.6
centimeters/sec	miles/hr	0.02237
centimeters/sec	miles/min	3.728×10^{-4}
centimeters/sec/sec	feet/sec/sec	0.03281
centimeters/sec/sec	kms/hr/sec	0.036
centimeters/sec/sec	meters/sec/sec	0.01
centimeters/sec/sec	miles/hr/sec	0.02237
Chain	Inches	792.00
Chain	meters	20.12
Chain (surveyors' or Gunter's)	yards	22.00
circular mils	sq cms	5.067×10^{-6}
circular mils	sq mils	0.7854
Circumference	Radians	6.283
circular mils	sq inches	7.854×10^{-7}
Cords	cord feet	8
Cord feet	cu. feet	16
Coulomb	Statcoulombs	2.998×10^{9}
coulombs	faradays	1.036×10^{-5}
coulombs/sq cm	coulombs/sq in.	64.52
coulombs/sq cm	coulombs/sq meter	10^{4}
coulombs/sq in.	coulombs/sq cm	0.1550
coulombs/sq in.	coulombs/sq meter	1,550.
coulombs/sq meter	coulombs/sq cm	10^{-4}
coulombs/sq meter	coulombs/sq in.	6.452×10^{-4}
cubic centimeters	cu feet	3.531×10^{-5}
cubic centimeters	cu inches	0.06102
cubic centimeters	cu meters	10^{-6}
cubic centimeters	cu yards	1.308×10^{-6}
cubic centimeters	gallons (U.S. liq.)	2.642×10^{-4}
cubic centimeters	liters	0.001

Conversion Factors

TO CONVERT	INTO	MULTIPLY BY
cubic centimeters	pints (U.S. liq.)	2.113×10^{-3}
cubic centimeters	quarts (U.S. liq.)	1.057×10^{-3}
cubic feet	bushels (dry)	0.8036
cubic feet	cu cms	28,320.0
cubic feet	cu inches	1,728.0
cubic feet	cu meters	0.02832
cubic feet	cu yards	0.03704
cubic feet	gallons (U.S. liq.)	7.48052
cubic feet	liters	28.32
cubic feet	pints (U.S. liq.)	59.84
cubic feet	quarts (U.S. liq.)	29.92
cubic feet/min	cu cms/sec	472.0
cubic feet/min	gallons/sec	0.1247
cubic feet/min	liters/sec	0.4720
cubic feet/min	pounds of water/min.	62.43
cubic feet/sec	million gals/day	0.646317
cubic feet/sec	gallons/min	448.831
cubic inches	cu cms	16.39
cubic inches	cu feet	5.787×10^{-4}
cubic inches	cu meters	1.639×10^{-5}
cubic inches	cu yards	2.143×10^{-5}
cubic inches	gallons	4.329×10^{-3}
cubic inches	liters	0.01639
cubic inches	mil-feet	1.061×10^{5}
cubic inches	pints (U.S. liq.)	0.03463
cubic inches	quarts (U.S. liq.)	0.01732
cubic meters	bushels (dry)	28.38
cubic meters	cu cms	10^{6}
cubic meters	cu feet	35.31
cubic meters	cu inches	61,023.0
cubic meters	cu yards	1.308
cubic meters	gallons (U.S. liq.)	264.2
cubic meters	liters	1,000.0
cubic meters	pints (U.S. liq.)	2,113.0
cubic meters	quarts (U.S. liq.)	1,057.
cubic yards	cu cms	7.646×10^{5}
cubic yards	cu feet	27.0
cubic yards	cu inches	46,656.0
cubic yards	cu meters	0.7646
cubic yards	gallons (U.S. liq.)	202.0
cubic yards	liters	764.6
cubic yards	pints (U.S. liq.)	1,615.9
cubic yards	quarts (U.S. liq.)	807.9
cubic yards/min	cubic ft/sec	0.45
cubic yards/min	gallons/sec	3.367
cubic yards/min	liters/sec	12.74

D

TO CONVERT	INTO	MULTIPLY BY
Dalton	Gram	1.650×10^{-24}
days	seconds	86,400.0
decigrams	grams	0.1
deciliters	liters	0.1
decimeters	meters	0.1
degrees (angle)	quadrants	0.01111
degrees (angle)	radians	0.01745
degrees (angle)	seconds	3,600.0
degrees/sec	radians/sec	0.01745
degrees/sec	revolutions/min	0.1667
degrees/sec	revolutions/sec	2.778×10^{-3}
dekagrams	grams	10.0
dekaliters	liters	10.0
dekameters	meters	10.0
Drams (apothecaries' or troy)	ounces (avoirdupois)	0.1371429

Conversion Factors

TO CONVERT	INTO	MULTIPLY BY
Drams (apothecaries' or troy)	ounces (troy)	0.125
Drams (U.S., fluid or apoth.)	cubic cm.	3.6967
drams	grams	1.7718
drams	grains	27.3437
drams	ounces	0.0625
Dyne/cm	Erg/sq. millimeter	.01
Dyne/sq. cm.	Atmospheres	9.869×10^{-7}
Dyne/sq. cm.	Inch of Mercury at 0°C	2.953×10^{-5}
Dyne/sq. cm.	Inch of Water at 4°C	4.015×10^{-4}
dynes	grame	1.020×10^{-3}
dynes	joules/cm	10^{-7}
dynes	joules/meter (newtons)	10^{-5}
dynes	kilograms	1.020×10^{-6}
dynes	poundals	7.233×10^{-5}
dynes	pounds	2.248×10^{-6}
dynes/sq cm	bars	10^{-6}

E

TO CONVERT	INTO	MULTIPLY BY
Ell	Cm.	114.30
Ell	Inches	45
Em, Pica	Inch	.167
Em, Pica	Cm.	.4233
Erg/sec	Dyne — cm/sec	1.000
ergs	Btu	9.480×10^{-11}
ergs	dyne-centimeters	1.0
ergs	foot-pounds	7.367×10^{-8}
ergs	gram-calories	0.2389×10^{-7}
ergs	gram-cms	1.020×10^{-3}
ergs	horsepower-hrs	3.7250×10^{-14}
ergs	joules	10^{-7}
ergs	kg-calories	2.389×10^{-11}
ergs	kg-meters	1.020×10^{-8}
ergs	kilowatt-hrs	0.2778×10^{-13}
ergs	watt-hours	0.2778×10^{-10}
ergs/sec	Btu/min	$5,688 \times 10^{-9}$
ergs/sec	ft-lbs/min	4.427×10^{-6}
ergs/sec	ft-lbs/sec	7.3756×10^{-8}
ergs/sec	horsepower	1.341×10^{-10}
ergs/sec	kg-calories/min	1.433×10^{-9}
ergs/sec	kilowatts	10^{-10}

F

TO CONVERT	INTO	MULTIPLY BY
farads	microfarads	10^{6}
Faraday/sec	Ampere (absolute)	9.6500×10^{4}
faradays	ampere-hours	26.80
faradays	coulombs	9.649×10^{4}
Fathom	Meter	1.828804
fathoms	feet	6.0
feet	centimeters	30.48
feet	kilometers	3.048×10^{-4}
feet	meters	0.3048
feet	miles (naut.)	1.645×10^{-4}
feet	miles (stat.)	1.894×10^{-4}
feet	millimeters	304.8
feet	mils	1.2×10^{4}
feet of water	atmospheres	0.02950
feet of water	in. of mercury	0.8826
feet of water	kgs/sq cm	0.03048
feet of water	kgs/sq meter	304.8
feet of water	pounds/sq ft	62.43
feet of water	pounds/sq in.	0.4335
feet/min	cms/sec	0.5080
feet/min	feet/sec	0.01667

Conversion Factors

TO CONVERT	INTO	MULTIPLY BY
feet/min	kms/hr	0.01829
feet/min	meters/min	0.3048
feet/min	miles/hr	0.01136
feet/sec	cms/sec	30.48
feet/sec	kms/hr	1.097
feet/sec	knots	0.5921
feet/sec	meters/min	18.29
feet/sec	miles/hr	0.6818
feet/sec	miles/min	0.01136
feet/sec/sec	cms/sec/sec	30.48
feet/sec/sec	kms/hr/sec	1.097
feet/sec/sec	meters/sec/sec	0.3048
feet/sec/sec	miles/hr/sec	0.6818
feet/100 feet	per cent grade	1.0
Foot — candle	Lumen/sq. meter	10.764
foot-pounds	Btu	1.286×10^{-3}
foot-pounds	ergs	1.356×10^{7}
foot-pounds	gram-calories	0.3238
foot-pounds	hp-hrs	5.050×10^{-7}
foot-pounds	joules	1.356
foot-pounds	kg-calories	3.24×10^{-4}
foot-pounds	kg-meters	0.1383
foot-pounds	kilowatt-hrs	3.766×10^{-7}
foot-pounds/min	Btu/min	1.286×10^{-3}
foot-pounds/min	foot-pounds/sec	0.01667
foot-pounds/min	horsepower	3.030×10^{-5}
foot-pounds/min	kg-calories/min	3.24×10^{-4}
foot-pounds/min	kilowatts	2.260×10^{-5}
foot-pounds/sec	Btu/hr	4.6263
foot-pounds/sec	Btu/min	0.07717
foot-pounds/sec	horsepower	1.818×10^{-3}
foot-pounds/sec	kg-calories/min	0.01945
foot-pounds/sec	kilowatts	1.356×10^{-3}
Furlongs	miles (U.S.)	0.125
furlongs	rods	40.0
furlongs	feet	660.0

G

TO CONVERT	INTO	MULTIPLY BY
gallons	cu cms	3,785.0
gallons	cu feet	0.1337
gallons	cu inches	231.0
gallons	cu meters	3.785×10^{-3}
gallons	cu yards	4.951×10^{-3}
gallons	liters	3.785
gallons (liq. Br. Imp.)	gallons (U.S. liq.)	1.20095
gallons (U.S.)	gallons (Imp.)	0.83267
gallons of water	pounds of water	8.3453
gallons/min	cu ft/sec	2.228×10^{-3}
gallons/min	liters/sec	0.06308
gallons/min	cu ft/hr	8.0208
gausses	lines/sw in.	6.452
gausses	webers/sq cm	10^{-8}
gausses	webers/sq in	6.452×10^{-8}
gausses	webers/sq meter	10^{-4}
gilberts	ampere-turns	0.7958
gilberts/cm	amp-turns/cm	0.7958
gilberts/cm	amp-turns/in	2.021
gilberts/cm	amp-turns/meter	79.58
Gills (British)	cubic cm.	142.07
gills	liters	0.1183
gills	pints (liq.)	0.25
Grade	Radian	.01571
Grains	drams (avoirdupois)	0.03657143

251

Conversion Factors

TO CONVERT	INTO	MULTIPLY BY
grains (troy)	grains (avdp)	1.0
grains (troy)	grams	0.06480
grains (troy)	ounces (avdp)	2.0833×10^{-3}
grains (troy)	pennyweight (troy)	0.04167
grains/U.S. gal	parts/million	17.118
grains/U.S. gal	pounds/million gal	142.86
grains/Imp. gal	parts/million	14.286
grams	dynes	980.7
grams	grains	15.43
grams	joules/cm	9.807×10^{-5}
grams	joules/meter (newtons)	9.807×10^{-3}
grams	kilograms	0.001
grams	milligrams	1,000.
grams	ounces (avdp)	0.03527
grams	ounces (troy)	0.03215
grams	poundals	0.07093
grams	pounds	2.205×10^{-3}
grams/cm	pounds/inch	5.600×10^{-3}
grams/cu cm	pounds/cu ft	62.43
grams/cu cm	pounds/cu in	0.03613
grams/cu cm	pounds/mil-foot	3.405×10^{-7}
grams/liter	grains/gal	58.417
grams/liter	pounds/1,000 gal	8.345
grams/liter	pounds/cu ft	0.062427
grams/liter	parts/million	1,000.0
grams/sq cm	pounds/sq ft	2.0481
gram-calories	Btu	3.9683×10^{-3}
gram-calories	ergs	4.1868×10^{7}
gram-calories	foot-pounds	3.0880
gram-calories	horsepower-hrs	1.5596×10^{-6}
gram-calories	kilowatt-hrs	1.1630×10^{-6}
gram-calories	watt-hrs	1.1630×10^{-3}
gram-calories/sec	Btu/hr	14.286
gram-centimeters	Btu	9.297×10^{-8}
gram-centimeters	ergs	980.7
gram-centimeters	joules	9.807×10^{-5}
gram-centimeters	kg-cal	2.343×10^{-8}
gram-centimeters	kg-meters	10^{-5}

H

TO CONVERT	INTO	MULTIPLY BY
Hand	Cm.	10.16
hectares	acres	2.471
hectares	sq feet	1.076×10^{5}
hectograms	grams	100.0
hectoliters	liters	100.0
hectometers	meters	100.0
hectowatts	watts	100.0
henries	millihenries	1,000.0
Hogsheads (British)	cubic feet	10.114
Hogsheads (U.S.)	cubic ft.	8.42184
Hogsheads (U.S.)	gallons (U.S.)	63
horsepower	Btu/min	42.44
horsepower	foot-lbs/min	33,000.
horsepower	foot-lbs/sec	550.0
horsepower (metric) (542.5 ft lb/sec)	horsepower (550 ft lb/sec)	0.9863
horsepower (550 ft lb/sec)	horsepower (metric) (542.5 ft lb/sec)	1.014
horepower	kg-calories/min	10.68
horsepower	kilowatts	0.7457
horsepower	watts	745.7
horsepower (boiler)	Btu/hr	33,479
horsepower (boiler)	kilowatts	9.803
horsepower-hrs	Btu	2,547.

Conversion Factors

TO CONVERT	INTO	MULTIPLY BY
horsepower-hrs	ergs	2.6845×10^{13}
horsepower-hrs	foot-lbs	1.98×10^{6}
horsepower-hrs	gram-calories	641,190.
horsepower-hrs	joules	2.684×10^{6}
horsepower-hrs	kg-calories	641.1
horsepower-hrs	kg-meters	2.737×10^{5}
horsepower-hrs	kilowatt-hrs	0.7457
hours	days	4.167×10^{-2}
hours	weeks	5.952×10^{-3}
Hundredweights (long)	pounds	112
Hundredweights (long)	tons (long)	0.05
Hundredweights (short)	ounces (avoirdupois)	1600
Hundredweights (short)	pounds	100
Hundredweights (short)	tons (metric)	0.0453592
Hundredweights (short)	tons (long)	0.0446429

I

TO CONVERT	INTO	MULTIPLY BY
inches	centimeters	2.540
inches	meters	2.540×10^{-2}
inches	miles	1.578×10^{-5}
inches	millimeters	25.40
inches	mils	1,000.0
inches	yards	2.778×10^{-2}
inches of mercury	atmospheres	0.03342
inches of mercury	feet of water	1.133
inches of mercury	kgs/sq cm	0.03453
inches of mercury	kgs/sq meter	345.3
inches of mercury	pounds/sq ft	70.73
inches of mercury	pounds/sq in.	0.4912
inches of water (at 4° C)	atmospheres	2.458×10^{-3}
inches of water (at 4° C)	inches of mercury	0.07355
inches of water (at 4 ° C)	kgs/sq cm	2.540×10^{-3}
inches of water (at 4° C)	ounces/sq in.	0.5781
inches of water (at 4° C)	pounds/sq ft	5.204
inches of water (at 4° C)	pounds/sq in.	0.03613
International Ampere	Ampere (absolute)	.9998
International Volt	Volts (absolute)	1.0003
International volt	Joules (absolute)	1.593×10^{-19}
International volt	Joules	9.654×10^{4}

J

TO CONVERT	INTO	MULTIPLY BY
joules	Btu	9.480×10^{-4}
joules	ergs	10^{7}
joules	foot-pounds	0.7376
joules	kg-calories	2.389×10^{-4}
joules	kg-meters	0.1020
joules	watt-hrs	2.778×10^{-4}
joules/cm	grams	1.020×10^{4}
joules/cm	dynes	10^{7}
joules/cm	joules/meter (newtons)	100.0
joules/cm	poundals	723.3

Conversion Factors

TO CONVERT	INTO	MULTIPLY BY
joules/cm	pounds	22.48

K

TO CONVERT	INTO	MULTIPLY BY
kelvin	celsius	C° + 273.16
kilograms	dynes	980,665.
kilograms	grams	1,000.0
kilograms	joules/cm	0.09807
kilograms	joules/meter (newtons)	9.807
kilograms	poundals	70.93
kilograms	pounds	2.205
kilograms	tons (long)	9.842×10^{-4}
kilograms	tons (short)	1.102×10^{-3}
kilograms/cu meter	grams/cu cm	0.001
kilograms/cu meter	pounds/cu ft	0.06243
kilograms/cu meter	pounds/cu in.	3.613×10^{-5}
kilograms/cu meter	pounds/mil-foot	3.405×10^{-10}
kilogams/meter	pounds/ft	0.6720
Kilogram/sq. cm.	Dynes	980,665
kilograms/sq cm	atmospheres	0.9678
kilograms/sq cm	feet of water	32.81
kilograms/sq cm	inches of mercury	28.96
kilograms/sq cm	pounds/sq ft	2,048.
kilograms/sq cm	pounds/sq in.	14.22
kilograms/sq meter	atmospheres	9.678×10^{-5}
kilograms/sq meter	bars	98.07×10^{-6}
kilograms/sq meter	feet of water	3.281×10^{-3}
kilograms/sq meter	inches of mercury	2.896×10^{-3}
kilograms/sq meter	pounds/sq ft	0.2048
kilograms/sq meter	pounds/sq in.	1.422×10^{-3}
kilograms/sq mm	kgs/sq meter	10^6
kilogram-calories	Btu	3.968
kilogram-calories	foot-pounds	3,088.
kilogram-calories	hp-hrs	1.560×10^{-3}
kilogram-calories	joules	4,186.
kilogram-calories	kg-meters	426.9
kilogram-calories	kilojoules	4.186
kilogram-calories	kilowatt-hrs	1.163×10^{-3}
kilogram meters	Btu	9.294×10^{-3}
kilogram meters	ergs	9.804×10^7
kilogram meters	foot-pounds	7.233
kilogram meters	joules	9.804
kilogram meters	kg-calories	2.342×10^{-3}
kilogram meters	kilowatt-hrs	2.723×10^{-6}
kilolines	maxwells	1,000.0
kiloliters	liters	1,000.0
kilometers	centimeters	10^5
kilometers	feet	3,281.
kilometers	inches	3.937×10^4
kilometers	meters	1,000.0
kilometers	miles	0.6214
kilometers	millimeters	10^6
kilometers	yards	1,094.
kilometers/hr	cms/sec	27.78
kilometers/hr	feet/min	54.68
kilometers/hr	feet/sec	0.9113
kilometers/hr	knots	0.5396
kilometers/hr	meters/min	16.67
kilometers/hr	miles/hr	0.6214
kilometers/hr/sec	cms/sec/sec	27.78
kilometers/hr/sec	ft/sec/sec	0.9113
kilometers/hr/sec	meters/sec/sec	0.2778
kilometers/hr/sec	miles/hr/sec	0.6214
kilowatts	Btu/min.	56.92

Conversion Factors

TO CONVERT	INTO	MULTIPLY BY
kilowatts	foot-lbs/min	4.426×10^4
kilowatts	foot-lbs/sec	737.6
kilowatts	horsepower	1.341
kilowatts	kg-calories/min	14.34
kilowatts	watts	1,000.0
kilowatt-hrs	Btu	3,413.
kilowatt-hrs	ergs	3.600×10^{13}
kilowatt-hrs	foot-lbs	2.655×10^6
kilowatt-hrs	gram-calories	859,850.
kilowatt-hrs	horsepower-hrs	1.341
kilowatt-hrs	joules	3.6×10^6
kilowatt-hrs	kg-calories	860.5
kilowatt-hrs	kg-meters	3.671×10^5
kilowatt-hrs	pounds of water evaporated from and at 212° F.	3.53
kilowatt-hrs	pounds of water raised from 62° to 212° F.	22.75
knots	feet/hr	6,080.
knots	kilometers/hr	1.8532
knots	nautical miles/hr	1.0
knots	statute miles/hr	1.151
knots	yards/hr	2,027.
knots	feet/sec	1.689
league	miles (approx.)	3.0
Light year	Miles	5.9×10^{12}
Light year	Kilometers	9.46091×10^{12}
lines/sq cm	gausses	1.0
lines/sq in.	gausses	0.1550
lines/sq in.	webers/sq cm	1.550×10^{-9}
lines/sq in.	webers/sq in.	10^{-8}
lines/sq in.	webers/sq meter	1.550×10^{-5}
links (engineer's)	inches	12.0
links (surveyor's)	inches	7.92
liters	bushels (U.S. dry)	0.02838
liters	cu cm	1,000.0
liters	cu feet	0.03531
liters	cu inches	61.02
liters	cu meters	0.001
liters	cu yards	1.308×10^{-3}
liters	gallons (U.S. liq.)	0.2642
liters	pints (U.S. liq.)	2.113
liters	quarts (U.S. liq.)	1.057
liters/min	cu ft/sec	5.886×10^{-4}
liters/min	gals/sec	4.403×10^{-3}
lumens/sq ft	foot-candles	1.0
Lumen	Spherical candle power	.07958
Lumen	Watt	.001496
Lumen/sq. ft.	Lumen/sq. meter	10.76
lux	foot-candles	0.0929

M

TO CONVERT	INTO	MULTIPLY BY
maxwells	kilolines	0.001
maxwells	webers	10^{-8}
megalines	maxwells	10^6
megohms	microhms	10^{12}
megohms	ohms	10^6
meters	centimeters	100.0
meters	feet	3.281
meters	inches	39.37

253

Conversion Factors

TO CONVERT	INTO	MULTIPLY BY
meters	kilometers	0.001
meters	miles (naut.)	5.396 x 10^{-4}
meters	miles (stat.)	6.214 x 10^{-4}
meters	millimeters	1,000.0
meters	yards	1.094
meters	varas	1.179
meters/min	cms/sec	1.667
meters/min	feet/min	3.281
meters/min	feet/sec	0.05468
meters/min	kms/hr	0.06
meters/min	knots	0.03238
meters/min	miles/hr	0.03728
meters/sec	feet/min	196.8
meters/sec	feet/sec	3.281
meters/sec	kilometers/hr	3.6
meters/sec	kilometers/min	0.06
meters/sec	miles/hr	2.237
meters/sec	miles/min	0.03728
meters/sec/sec	cms/sec/sec	100.0
meters/sec/sec	ft/sec/sec	3.281
meters/sec/sec	kms/hr/sec	3.6
meters/sec/sec	miles/hr/sec	2.237
meter-kilograms	cm-dynes	9.807 x 10^7
meter-kilograms	cm-grams	10^5
meter-kilograms	pound-feet	7.233
microfarad	farads	10^{-6}
micrograms	grams	10^{-6}
microhms	megohms	10^{-12}
microhms	ohms	10^{-6}
microliters	liters	10^{-6}
Microns	meters	1 x 10^{-6}
miles (naut.)	feet	6,080.27
miles (naut.)	kilometers	1.853
miles (naut.)	meters	1,853.
miles (naut.)	miles (statute)	1.1516
miles (naut.)	yards	2,027.
miles (statute)	centimeters	1.609 x 10^5
miles (statute)	feet	5,280.
miles (statute)	inches	6.336 x 10^4
miles (statute)	kilometers	1.609
miles (statute)	meters	1,609.
miles (statute)	miles (naut.)	0.8684
miles (statute)	yards	1,760.
miles/hr	cms/sec	44.70
miles/hr	feet/min	88.
miles/hr	feet/sec	1.467
miles/hr	kms/hr	1.609
miles/hr	kms/min	0.02682
miles/hr	knots	0.8684
miles/hr	meters/min	26.82
miles/hr	miles/min	0.1667
miles/hr/sec	cms/sec/sec	44.70
miles/hr/sec	feet/sec/sec	1.467
miles/hr/sec	kms/hr/sec	1.609
miles/hr/sec	meters/sec/sec	0.4470
miles/min	cms/sec	2,682.
miles/min	feet/sec	88.
miles/min	kms/min	1.609
miles/min	knots/min	0.8684
miles/min	miles/hr	60.0
mil-feet	cu inches	9.425 x 10^{-6}
milliers	kilograms	1,000.
Millimicrons	meters	1 x 10^{-9}
Milligrams	grains	0.01543236

Conversion Factors

TO CONVERT	INTO	MULTIPLY BY
milligrams	grams	0.001
milligrams/liter	parts/million	1.0
millihenries	henries	0.001
milliliters	liters	0.001
millimeters	centimeters	0.1
millimeters	feet	3.281 x 10^{-3}
millimeters	inches	0.03937
millimeters	kilometers	10^{-6}
millimeters	meters	0.001
millimeters	miles	6.214 x 10^{-7}
millimeters	mils	39.37
millimeters	yards	1.094 x 10^{-3}
million gals/day	cu ft/sec	1.54723
mils	centimeters	2.540 x 10^{-3}
mils	feet	8.333 x 10^{-5}
mils	inches	0.001
mils	kilometers	2.540 x 10^{-8}
mils	yards	2.778 x 10^{-5}
miner's inches	cu ft/min	1.5
Minims (British)	cubic cm.	0.059192
Minims (U.S., fluid)	cubic cm.	0.061612
minutes (angles)	degrees	0.01667
minutes (angles)	quadrants	1.852 x 10^{-4}
minutes (angles)	radians	2.909 x 10^{-4}
minutes (angles)	seconds	60.0
myriagrams	kilograms	10.0
myriameters	kilometers	10.0
myriawatts	kilowatts	10.0

N

TO CONVERT	INTO	MULTIPLY BY
nepers	decibels	8.686
Newton	Dynes	1 x 10^5

O

TO CONVERT	INTO	MULTIPLY BY
OHM (International)	OHM (absolute)	1.0005
ohms	megohms	10^{-6}
ohms	microhms	10^6
ounces	drams	16.0
ounces	grains	437.5
ounces	grams	28.349527
ounces	pounds	0.0625
ounces	ounces (troy)	0.9115
ounces	tons (long)	2.790 x 10^{-5}
ounces	tons (metric)	2.835 x 10^{-5}
ounces (fluid)	cu inches	1.805
ounces (fluid)	liters	0.02957
ounces (troy)	grains	480.0
ounces (troy)	grams	31.103481
ounces (troy)	ounces (avdp.)	1.09714
ounces (troy)	pennyweights (troy)	20.0
ounces (troy)	pounds (troy)	0.08333
Ounce/sq. inch	Dynes/sq. cm.	4309
ounces/sq in.	pounds/sq in.	0.0625

P

TO CONVERT	INTO	MULTIPLY BY
Parsec	Miles	19 x 10^{12}
Parsec	Kilometers	3.084 x 10^{13}
parts/million	grains/U.S. gal	0.0584
parts/million	grains/Imp. gal	0.07016
parts/million	pounds/million gal	8.345
Pecks (British)	cubic inches	554.6
Pecks (British)	liters	9.091901
Pecks (U.S.)	bushels	0.25
Pecks (U.S.)	cubic inches	537.605

Conversion Factors

TO CONVERT	INTO	MULTIPLY BY
Pecks (U.S.)	liters	8.809582
Pecks (U.S.)	quarts (dry)	8
pennyweights (troy)	grains	24.0
pennyweights (troy)	ounces (troy)	0.05
pennyweights (troy)	grams	1.55517
pennyweights (troy)	pounds (troy)	4.1667×10^{-3}
pints (dry)	cu inches	33.60
pints (liq.)	cu cms.	473.2
pints (liq.)	cu feet	0.01671
pints (liq.)	cu inches	28.87
pints (liq.)	cu meters	4.732×10^{-4}
pints (liq.)	cu yards	6.189×10^{-4}
pints (liq.)	gallons	0.125
pints (liq.)	liters	0.4732
pints (liq.)	quarts (liq.)	0.5
Planck's quantum	Erg — second	6.624×10^{-27}
Poise	Gram/cm. sec.	1.00
Pounds (avoirdupois)	ounces (troy)	14.5833
poundals	dynes	13,826.
poundals	grams	14.10
poundals	joules/cm	1.383×10^{-3}
poundals	joules/meter (newtons)	0.1383
poundals	kilograms	0.01410
poundals	pounds	0.03108
pounds	drams	256.
pounds	dynes	44.4823×10^{4}
pounds	grains	7,000.
pounds	grams	453.5924
pounds	joules/cm	0.04448
pounds	joules/meter (newtons)	4.448
pounds	kilograms	0.4536
pounds	ounces	16.0
pounds	ounces (troy)	14.5833
pounds	poundals	32.17
pounds	pounds (troy)	1.21528
pounds	tons (short)	0.0005
pounds (troy)	grains	5,760.
pounds (troy)	grams	373.24177
pounds (troy)	ounces (avdp.)	13.1657
pounds (troy)	ounces (troy)	12.0
pounds (troy)	pennyweights (troy)	240.0
pounds (troy)	pounds (avdp.)	0.822857
pounds (troy)	tons (long)	3.6735×10^{-4}
pounds (troy)	tons (metric)	3.7324×10^{-4}
pounds (troy)	tons (short)	4.1143×10^{-4}
pounds of water	cu feet	0.01602
pounds of water	cu inches	27.68
pounds of water	gallons	0.1198
pounds of water/min	cu ft/sec	2.670×10^{-4}
pound-feet	cm-dynes	1.356×10^{7}
pound-feet	cm-grams	13,825.
pound-feet	meter-kgs	0.1383
pounds/cu ft	grams/cu cm	0.01602
pounds/cu ft	kgs/cu meter	16.02
pounds/cu ft	pounds/cu in.	5.787×10^{-4}
pounds/cu ft	pounds/mil-foot	5.456×10^{-9}
pounds/cu in.	gms/cu cm	27.68
pounds/cu in.	kgs/cu meter	2.768×10^{4}
pounds/cu in.	pounds/cu ft	1,728.
pounds/cu in.	pounds/mil-foot	9.425×10^{-6}
pounds/ft	kgs/meter	1.488
pounds/in.	gms/cm	178.6

Conversion Factors

TO CONVERT	INTO	MULTIPLY BY
pounds/mil-foot	gms/cu cm	2.306×10^{6}
pounds/sq ft	atmospheres	4.725×10^{-4}
pounds/sq ft	feet of water	0.01602
pounds/sq ft	inches of mercury	0.01414
pounds/sq ft	kgs/sq meter	4.882
pounds/sq ft	pounds/sq in.	6.944×10^{-3}
pounds/sq in.	atmospheres	0.06804
pounds/sq in.	feet of water	2.307
pounds/sq in.	inches of mercury	2.036
pounds/sq in.	kgs/sq meter	703.1
pounds/sq in.	pounds/sq ft	144.0

Q

TO CONVERT	INTO	MULTIPLY BY
quadrants (angle)	degrees	90.0
quadrants (angle)	minutes	5,400.0
quadrants (angle)	radians	1.571
quadrants (angle)	seconds	3.24×10^{5}
quarts (dry)	cu inches	67.20
quarts (liq.)	cu cms	946.4
quarts (liq.)	cu feet	0.03342
quarts (liq.)	cu inches	57.75
quarts (liq.)	cu meters	9.464×10^{-4}
quarts (liq.)	cu yards	1.238×10^{-3}
quarts (liq.)	gallons	0.25
quarts (liq.)	liters	0.9463

R

TO CONVERT	INTO	MULTIPLY BY
radians	degrees	57.30
radians	minutes	3,438.
radians	quadrants	0.6366
radians	seconds	2.063×10^{5}
radians/sec	degrees/sec	57.30
radians/sec	revolutions/min	9.549
radians/sec	revolutions/sec	0.1592
radians/sec/sec	revs/min/min	573.0
radians/sec/sec	revs/min/sec	9.549
radians/sec/sec	revs/sec/sec	0.1592
rankin	fahrenheit	F° + 459.69
revolutions	degrees	360.0
revolutions	quadrants	4.0
revolutions	radians	6.283
revolutions/min	degrees/sec	6.0
revolutions/min	radians/sec	0.1047
revolutions/min	revs/sec	0.01667
revolutions/min/min	radians/sec/sec	1.745×10^{-3}
revolutions/min/min	revs/min/sec	0.01667
revolutions/min/min	revs/sec/sec	2.778×10^{-4}
revolutions/sec	degrees/sec	360.0
revolutions/sec	radians/sec	6.283
revolutions/sec	revs/min	60.0
revolutions/sec/sec	radians/sec/sec	6.283
revolutions/sec/sec	revs/min/min	3,600.0
revolutions/sec/sec	revs/min/sec	60.0
Rod	Chain (Gunters)	.25
Rod	Meters	5.029
Rods (Surveyors' meas.)	yards	5.5
rods	feet	16.5

S

TO CONVERT	INTO	MULTIPLY BY
Scruples	grains	20
seconds (angle)	degrees	2.778×10^{-4}
seconds (angle)	minutes	0.01667
seconds (angle)	quadrants	3.087×10^{-6}

Conversion Factors

TO CONVERT	INTO	MULTIPLY BY
seconds (angle)	radians	4.848×10^{-6}
Slug	Kilogram	14.59
Slug	Pounds	32.17
Sphere	Steradians	12.57
square centimeters	circular mils	1.973×10^{5}
square centimeters	sq feet	1.076×10^{-3}
square centimeters	sq inches	0.1550
square centimeters	sq meters	0.0001
square centimeters	sq miles	3.861×10^{-11}
square centimeters	sq millimeters	100.0
square centimeters	sq yards	1.196×10^{-4}
square feet	acres	2.296×10^{-5}
square feet	circular mils	1.833×10^{8}
square feet	sq cms	929.0
square feet	sq inches	144.0
square feet	sq meters	0.09290
square feet	sq miles	3.587×10^{-8}
square feet	sq millimeters	9.290×10^{4}
square feet	sq yards	0.1111
square inches	circular mils	1.273×10^{6}
square inches	sq cms	6.452
square inches	sq feet	6.944×10^{-3}
square inches	sq millimeters	645.2
square inches	sq mils	10^{6}
square inches	sq yards	7.716×10^{-4}
square kilometers	acres	247.1
square kilometers	sq cms	10^{10}
square kilometers	sq ft	10.76×10^{6}
square kilometers	sq inches	1.550×10^{9}
square kilometers	sq meters	10^{6}
square kilometers	sq miles	0.3861
square kilometers	sq yards	1.196×10^{6}
square meters	acres	2.471×10^{-4}
square meters	sq cms	10^{4}
square meters	sq feet	10.76
square meters	sq inches	1,550.
square meters	sq miles	3.861×10^{-7}
square meters	sq millimeters	10^{6}
square meters	sq yards	1.196
square miles	acres	640.0
square miles	sq feet	27.88×10^{6}
square miles	sq kms	2.590
square miles	sq meters	2.590×10^{6}
square miles	sq yards	3.098×10^{6}
square millimeters	circular mils	1,973.
square millimeters	sq cms	0.01
square millimeters	sq feet	1.076×10^{-5}
square millimeters	sq inches	1.550×10^{-3}
square mils	circular mils	1.273
square mils	sq cms	6.452×10^{-6}
square mils	sq inches	10^{-6}
square yards	acres	2.066×10^{-4}
square yards	sq cms	8,361.
square yards	sq feet	9.0
square yards	sq inches	1,296.
square yards	sq meters	0.8361
square yards	sq miles	3.228×10^{-7}
square yards	sq millimeters	8.361×10^{5}

T

TO CONVERT	INTO	MULTIPLY BY
temperature (°C) + 273	absolute temperature (°C)	1.0
temperature (°C) + 17.78	temperature (°F)	1.8

Conversion Factors

TO CONVERT	INTO	MULTIPLY BY
temperature (°F) + 460	absolute temperature (°F)	1.0
temperature (°F) −32	temperature (°C)	5/9
tons (long)	kilograms	1,016.
tons (long)	pounds	2,240.
tons (long)	tons (short)	1.120
tons (metric)	kilograms	1,000.
tons (metric)	pounds	2,205.
tons (short)	kilograms	907.1848
tons (short)	ounces	32,000.
tons (short)	ounces (troy)	29,166.66
tons (short)	pounds	2,000
tons (short)	pounds (troy)	2,430.56
tons (short)	tons (long)	0.89287
tons (short)	tons (metric)	0.9078
tons (short)/sq ft	kgs/sq meter	9,765.
tons (short)/sq ft	pounds/sq in.	2,000.
tons of water/24 hrs	pounds of water/hr	83.333
tons of water/24 hrs	gallons/min	0.16643
tons of water/24 hrs	cu ft/hr	1.3349

V

TO CONVERT	INTO	MULTIPLY BY
Volt/inch	Volt/cm.	.39370
Volt (absolute)	Statvolts	.003336

W

TO CONVERT	INTO	MULTIPLY BY
watts	Btu/hr	3.4129
watts	Btu/min	0.05688
watts	ergs/sec	107.
watts	foot-lbs/min	44.27
watts	foot-lbs/sec	0.7378
watts	horsepower	1.341×10^{-3}
watts	horsepower (metric)	1.360×10^{-3}
watts	kg-calories/min	0.01433
watts	kilowatts	0.001
Watts (Abs.)	B.T.U. (mean)/min.	0.056884
Watts (Abs.)	joules/sec.	1
watt-hours	Btu	3.413
watt-hours	ergs	3.60×10^{10}
watt-hours	foot-pounds	2,656.
watt-hours	gram-calories	859.85
watt-hours	horsepower-hrs	1.341×10^{-3}
watt-hours	kilogram-calories	0.8605
watt-hours	kilogram-meters	367.2
watt-hours	kilowatt-hrs	0.001
Watt (International)	Watt (absolute)	1.0002
webers	maxwells	10^{8}
webers	kilolines	10^{5}
webers/sq in.	gausses	1.550×10^{7}
webers/sq in.	lines/sq in.	10^{8}
webers/sq in.	webers/sq cm	0.1550
webers/sq in.	webers/sq meter	1,550.
webers/sq meter	gausses	10^{4}
webers/sq meter	lines/sq in.	6.452×10^{4}
webers/sq meter	webers/sq cm	10^{-4}
webers/sq meter	webers/sq in.	6.452×10^{-4}

Y

TO CONVERT	INTO	MULTIPLY BY
yards	centimeters	91.44
yards	kilometers	9.144×10^{-4}
yards	meters	0.9144
yards	miles (naut.)	4.934×10^{-4}
yards	miles (stat.)	5.682×10^{-4}
yards	millimeters	914.4